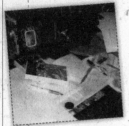

Time passes by very fast in this series, but please read it as if it were all occurring in the present. I have no clue what the manga business will be like in the future.

—Tsugumi Ohba

The cover illustration underneath the book cover is the line art before it was colored. I think the use of unfinished work like that is a unique part of this manga.

—Takeshi Obata

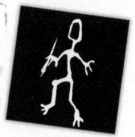

Tsugumi Ohba
Born in Tokyo, Tsugumi Ohba is the author of the hit series *Death Note*. His current series *Bakuman.* is serialized in *Weekly Shonen Jump*.

Takeshi Obata
Takeshi Obata was born in 1969 in Niigata, Japan, and is the artist of the wildly popular SHONEN JUMP title *Hikaru no Go*, which won the 2003 Tezuka Osamu Cultural Prize: Shinsei "New Hope" award and the 2000 Shogakukan Manga award. Obata is also the artist of *Arabian Majin Bokentan Lamp Lamp*, *Ayatsuri Sakon*, *Cyborg Jichan G.*, and the smash hit manga *Death Note*. His current series *Bakuman.* is serialized in *Weekly Shonen Jump*.

BAKUMAN。

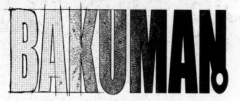

Volume 4

SHONEN JUMP Manga Edition

Story by **TSUGUMI OHBA**
Art by **TAKESHI OBATA**

Translation | **Tetsuichiro Miyaki**
English Adaptation | **Hope Donovan**
Touch-up Art & Lettering | **James Gaubatz**
Design | **Fawn Lau**
Editor | **Alexis Kirsch**

Printed in the U.S.A.

Published by VIZ Media, LLC
P.O. Box 77010
San Francisco, CA 94107

10 9 8 7 6 5 4 3 2 1
First printing, April 2011

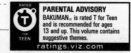

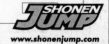

BAKUMAN.

4

PHONE CALL and THE NIGHT BEFORE

STORY BY

ART BY

TSUGUMI OHBA

TAKESHI OBATA

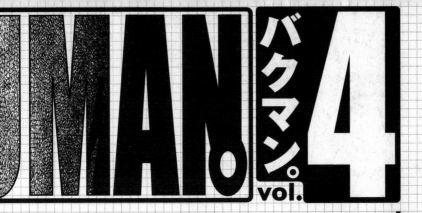

JMAN。 バクマン。 vol. 4

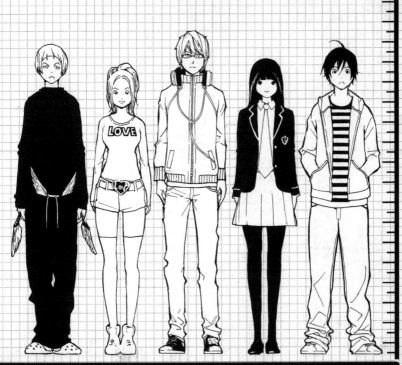

EIJI
Nizuma

A manga prodigy and Tezuka Award winner at the age of 15. He's in high school and already has a series running in *Jump*.

Age: 16

KAYA
Miyoshi

Miho's friend and Akito's girlfriend. A nice girl who actively works as the interceder between Moritaka and Azuki.

Age: 16

AKITO
Takagi

Aspiring manga writer. An extremely smart guy who gets the best grades in his class. A cool guy who becomes very passionate when it comes to manga.

Age: 15

MIHO
Azuki

A girl who dreams of becoming a voice actress. She promised to marry Moritaka under the condition that they not see each other until their dreams come true.

Age: 15

MORITAKA
Mashiro

Aspiring manga artist. An extreme romantic who believes that he will marry Miho Azuki once their dreams come true.

Age: 15

*These ages are from August 2009.

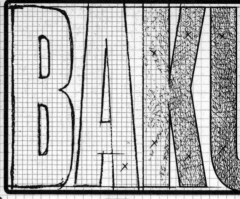

STORY In order to attain the glory that only a handful of people can, two young men decide to walk the rough "path of manga" and become professional manga creators. This is the story of a great artist, Moritaka Mashiro, a talented writer, Akito Takagi, and their quest to become manga legends!

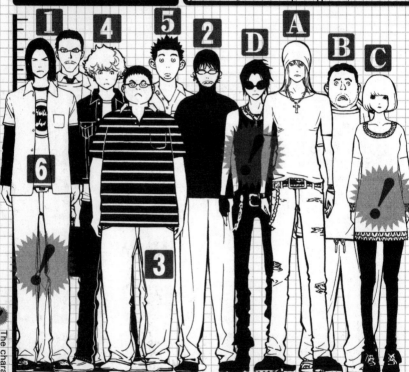

The characters with this mark appear for the first time in volume 4.

WEEKLY SHONEN JUMP
Editorial Office

1 Editor in Chief Sasaki	Age: 46
2 Deputy Editor in Chief Heishi	Age: 41
3 Soichi Aida	Age: 34
4 Yujiro Hattori	Age: 27
5 Akira Hattori	Age: 29
6 Koji Yoshida	Age: 31

UP AND COMING MANGA ARTISTS

A	**SHINTA Fukuda** Age: 19	Nizuma's assistant, and a manga artist the editorial office has high hopes for.
B	**TAKURO Nakai** Age: 33	A veteran assistant. He still has dreams of becoming a manga artist.
C	**KO Aoki** Age: 20	Storyboard Creator.
D	**KOJI Makaino** Age: 29	A mysterious person who is trying to get his own series.

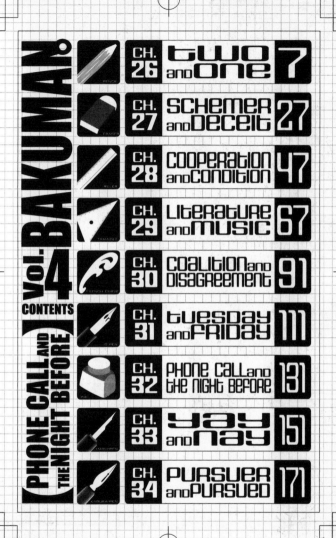

BAKUMAN。 Vol. 4

(PHONE CALL AND THE NIGHT BEFORE)

CONTENTS

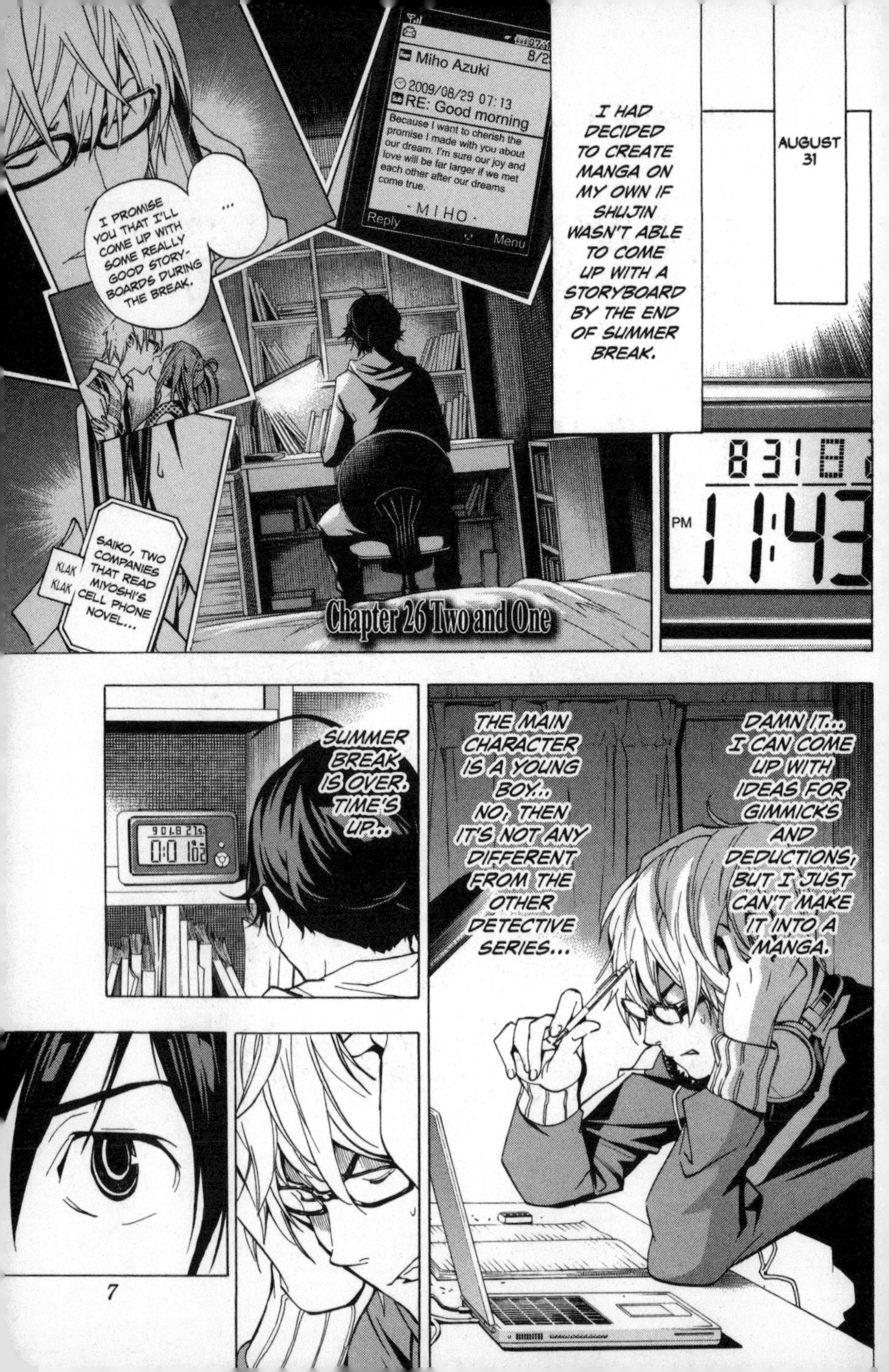
AUGUST 31
I HAD DECIDED TO CREATE MANGA ON MY OWN IF SHUJIN WASN'T ABLE TO COME UP WITH A STORYBOARD BY THE END OF SUMMER BREAK.
PM 11:43
Miho Azuki
2009/08/29 07:13
RE: Good morning
Because I want to cherish the promise I made with you about our dream. I'm sure our joy and love will be far larger if we met each other after our dreams come true.
-MIHO-
Reply
Menu
...
I PROMISE YOU THAT I'LL COME UP WITH SOME REALLY GOOD STORY-BOARDS DURING THE BREAK.
SAIKO, TWO COMPANIES THAT READ MIYOSHI'S CELL PHONE NOVEL...
KLAK KLAK
Chapter 26 Two and One
DAMN IT... I CAN COME UP WITH IDEAS FOR GIMMICKS AND DEDUCTIONS, BUT I JUST CAN'T MAKE IT INTO A MANGA.
THE MAIN CHARACTER IS A YOUNG BOY... NO, THEN IT'S NOT ANY DIFFERENT FROM THE OTHER DETECTIVE SERIES...
SUMMER BREAK IS OVER. TIME'S UP...

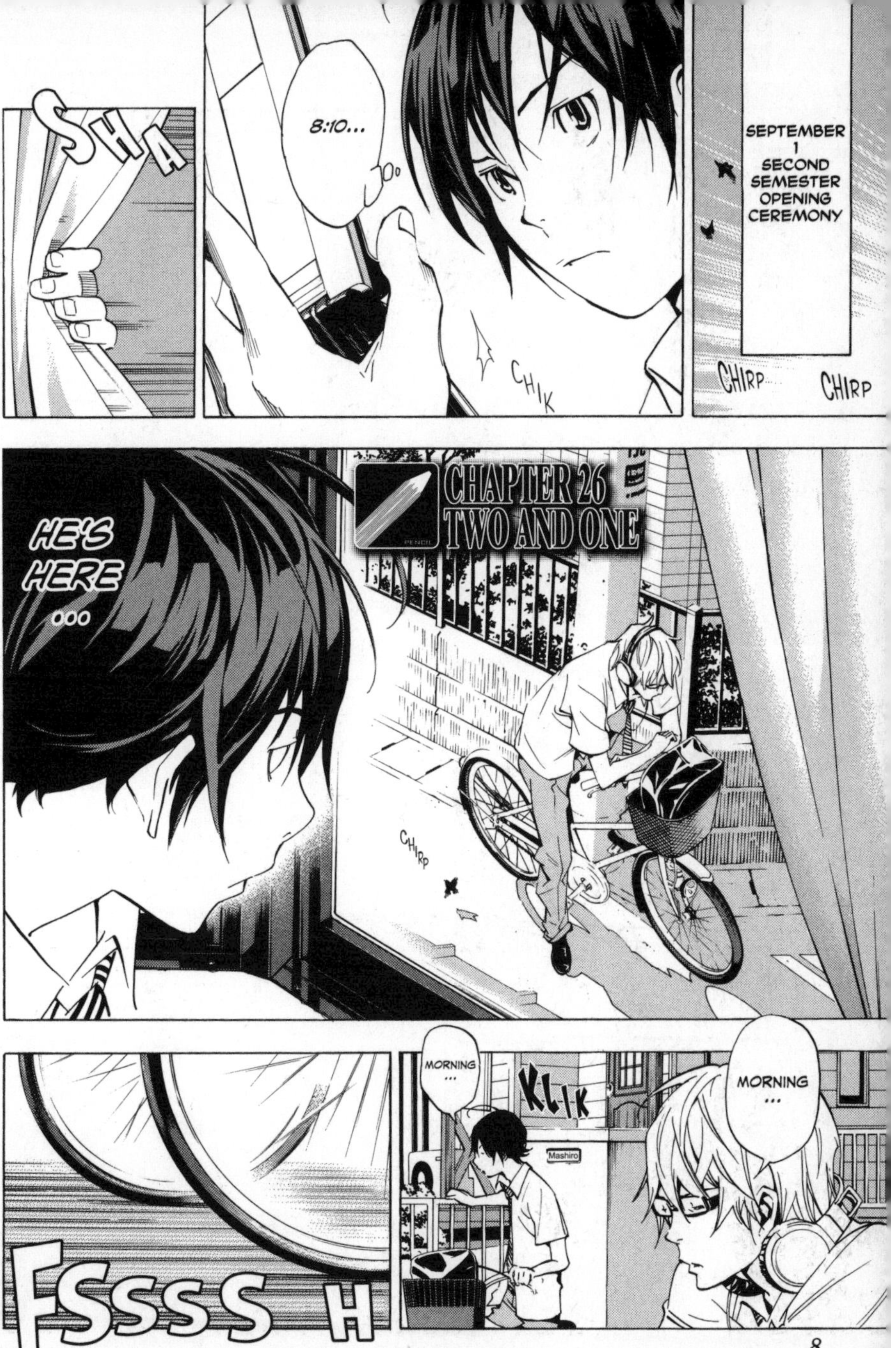
SEPTEMBER 1 SECOND SEMESTER OPENING CEREMONY
CHIRP
CHIRP
8:10...
CHIK
SHA
CHAPTER 26 TWO AND ONE
PENCIL
HE'S HERE ...
CHIRP
MORNING ...
KLIK
MORNING ...
Mashiro
FSSSSH

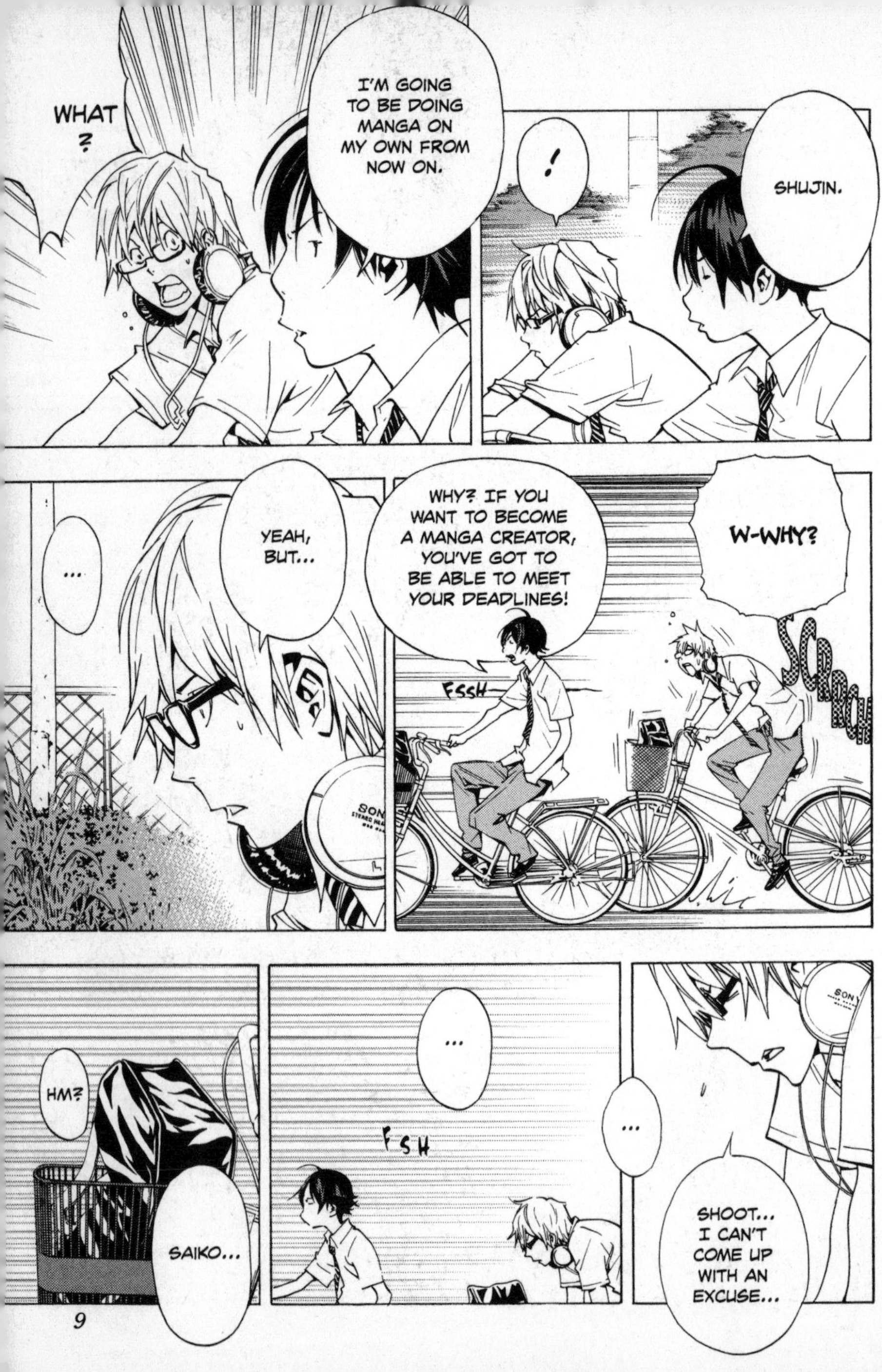
SHUJIN.
!
I'M GOING TO BE DOING MANGA ON MY OWN FROM NOW ON.
WHAT?
W-WHY?
WHY? IF YOU WANT TO BECOME A MANGA CREATOR, YOU'VE GOT TO BE ABLE TO MEET YOUR DEADLINES!
FSSH
YEAH, BUT...
...
...
SHOOT... I CAN'T COME UP WITH AN EXCUSE...
...
FSH
HM?
SAIKO...

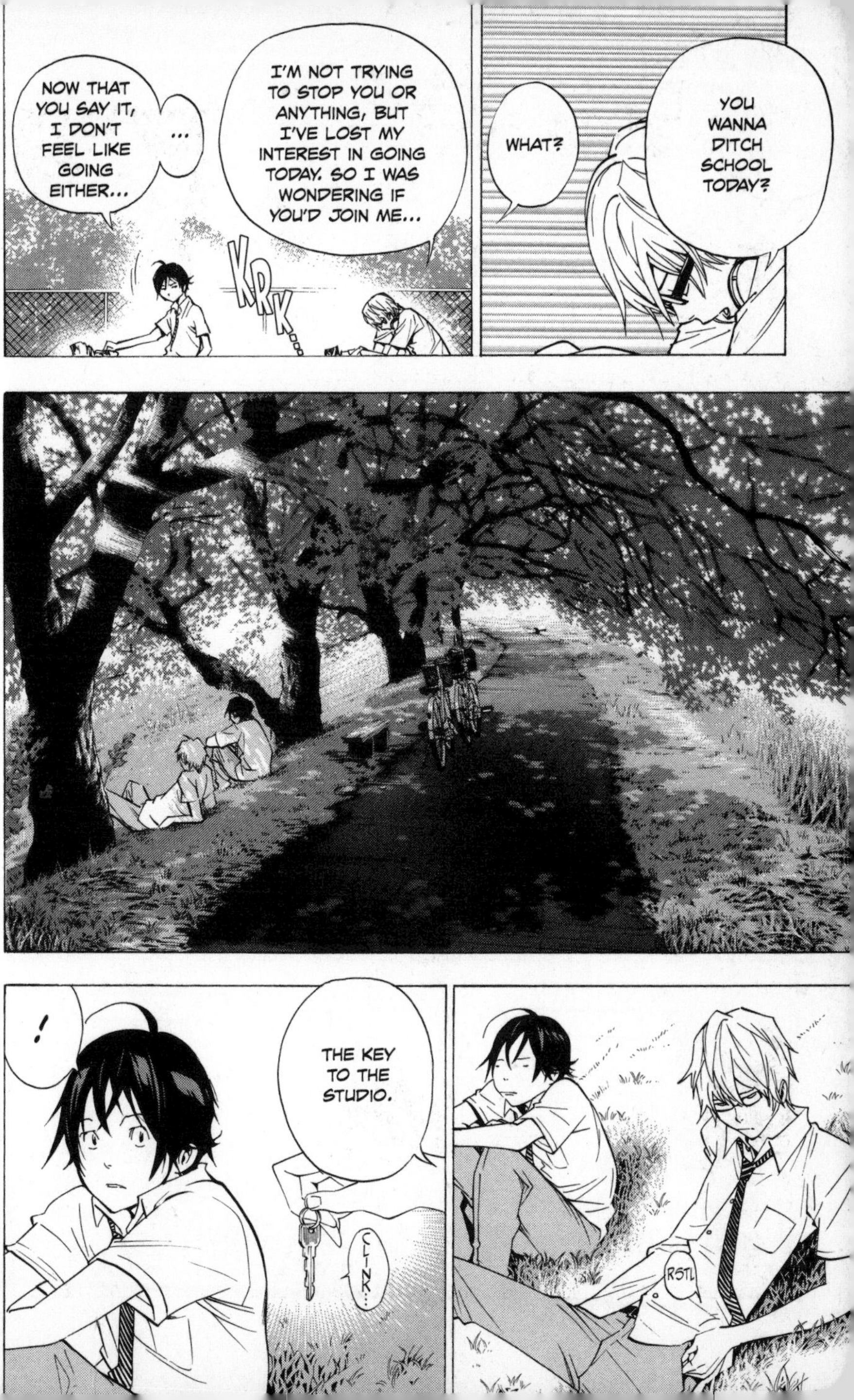
YOU WANNA DITCH SCHOOL TODAY?
WHAT?
I'M NOT TRYING TO STOP YOU OR ANYTHING, BUT I'VE LOST MY INTEREST IN GOING TODAY. SO I WAS WONDERING IF YOU'D JOIN ME...
...
NOW THAT YOU SAY IT, I DON'T FEEL LIKE GOING EITHER...
KRK...
RSTL
THE KEY TO THE STUDIO.
!
CLINK...

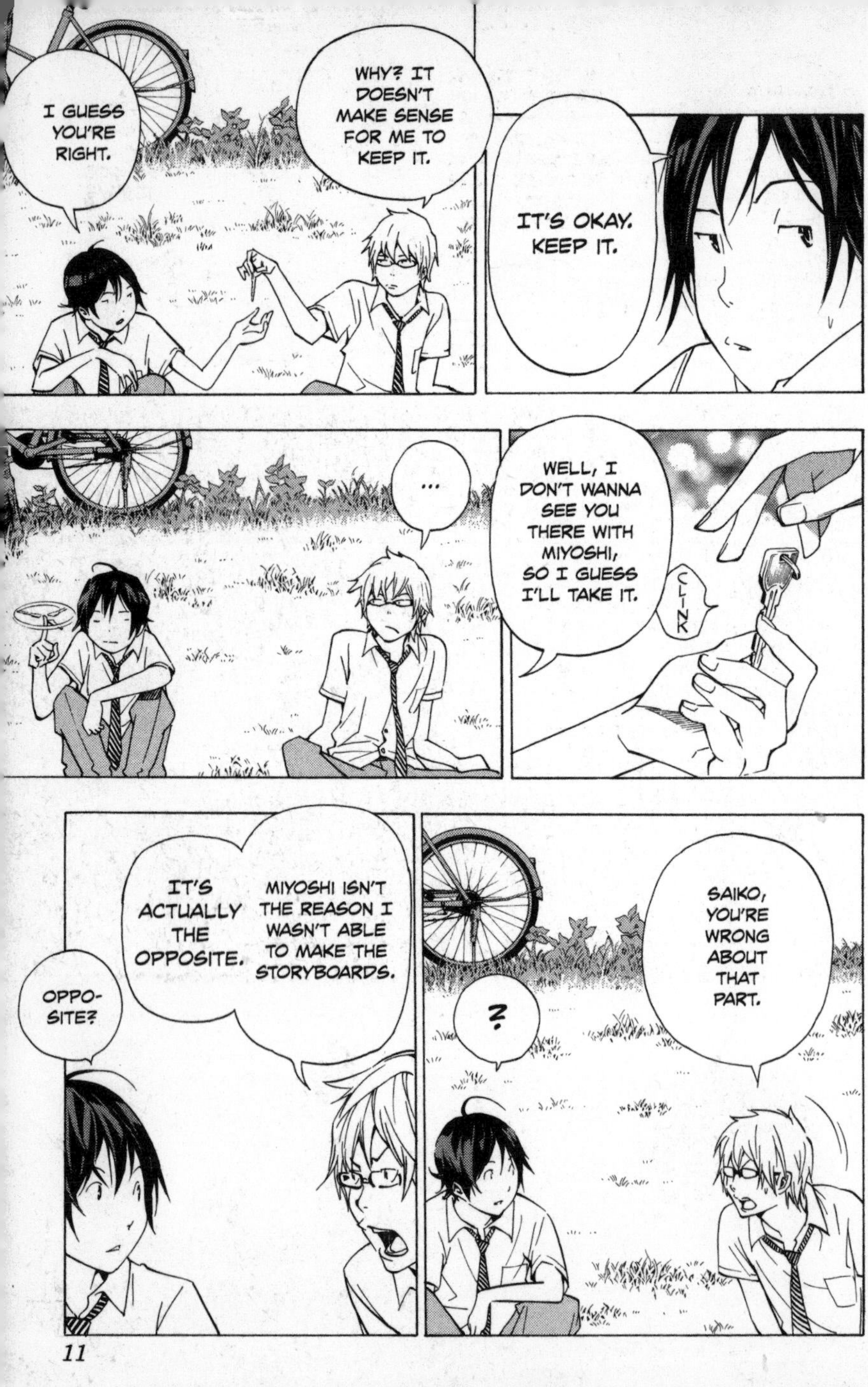
IT'S OKAY. KEEP IT.
WHY? IT DOESN'T MAKE SENSE FOR ME TO KEEP IT.
I GUESS YOU'RE RIGHT.
WELL, I DON'T WANNA SEE YOU THERE WITH MIYOSHI, SO I GUESS I'LL TAKE IT.
CLINK
...
SAIKO, YOU'RE WRONG ABOUT THAT PART.
?
MIYOSHI ISN'T THE REASON I WASN'T ABLE TO MAKE THE STORYBOARDS.
IT'S ACTUALLY THE OPPOSITE.
OPPO-SITE?

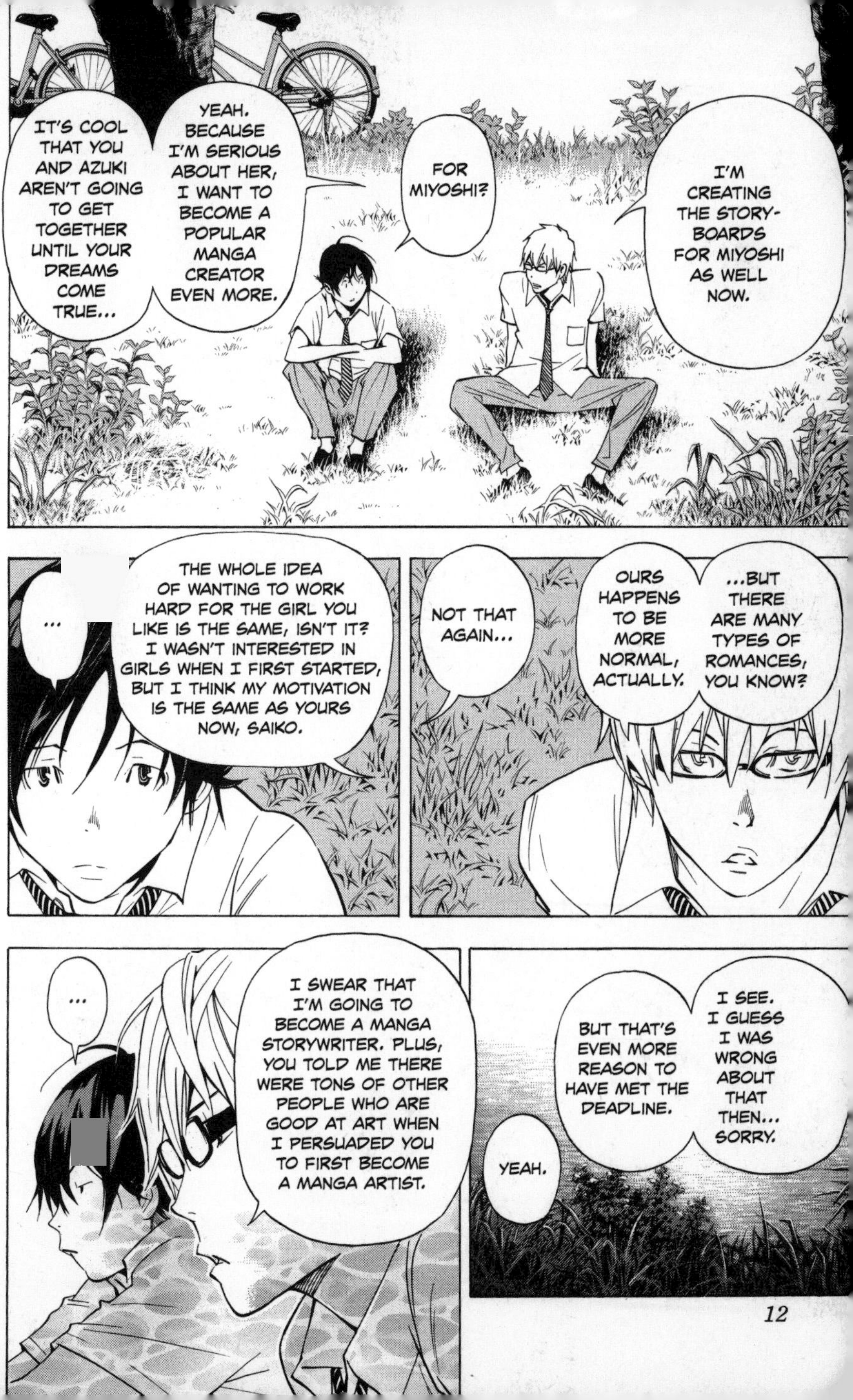
I'M CREATING THE STORYBOARDS FOR MIYOSHI AS WELL NOW.
FOR MIYOSHI?
YEAH. BECAUSE I'M SERIOUS ABOUT HER, I WANT TO BECOME A POPULAR MANGA CREATOR EVEN MORE.
IT'S COOL THAT YOU AND AZUKI AREN'T GOING TO GET TOGETHER UNTIL YOUR DREAMS COME TRUE...
...BUT THERE ARE MANY TYPES OF ROMANCES, YOU KNOW?
OURS HAPPENS TO BE MORE NORMAL, ACTUALLY.
NOT THAT AGAIN...
THE WHOLE IDEA OF WANTING TO WORK HARD FOR THE GIRL YOU LIKE IS THE SAME, ISN'T IT? I WASN'T INTERESTED IN GIRLS WHEN I FIRST STARTED, BUT I THINK MY MOTIVATION IS THE SAME AS YOURS NOW, SAIKO.
...
I SEE. I GUESS I WAS WRONG ABOUT THAT THEN... SORRY.
BUT THAT'S EVEN MORE REASON TO HAVE MET THE DEADLINE.
YEAH.
I SWEAR THAT I'M GOING TO BECOME A MANGA STORYWRITER. PLUS, YOU TOLD ME THERE WERE TONS OF OTHER PEOPLE WHO ARE GOOD AT ART WHEN I PERSUADED YOU TO FIRST BECOME A MANGA ARTIST.
...

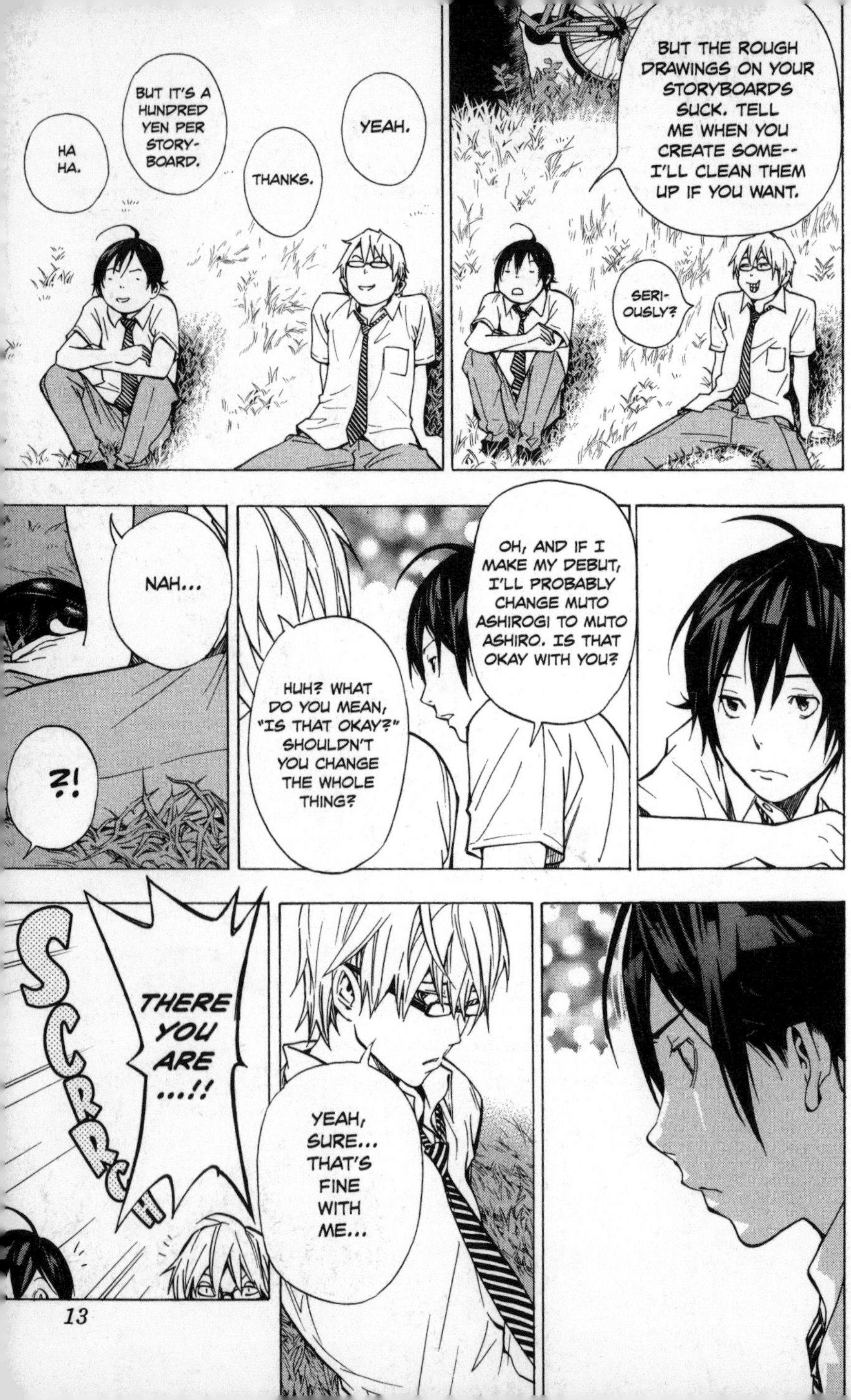

BUT THE ROUGH DRAWINGS ON YOUR STORYBOARDS SUCK. TELL ME WHEN YOU CREATE SOME-- I'LL CLEAN THEM UP IF YOU WANT.
SERIOUSLY?
YEAH.
THANKS.
BUT IT'S A HUNDRED YEN PER STORYBOARD.
HA HA.
OH, AND IF I MAKE MY DEBUT, I'LL PROBABLY CHANGE MUTO ASHIROGI TO MUTO ASHIRO. IS THAT OKAY WITH YOU?
HUH? WHAT DO YOU MEAN, "IS THAT OKAY?" SHOULDN'T YOU CHANGE THE WHOLE THING?
NAH...
?!
YEAH, SURE... THAT'S FINE WITH ME...
THERE YOU ARE...!!
SCRRCH

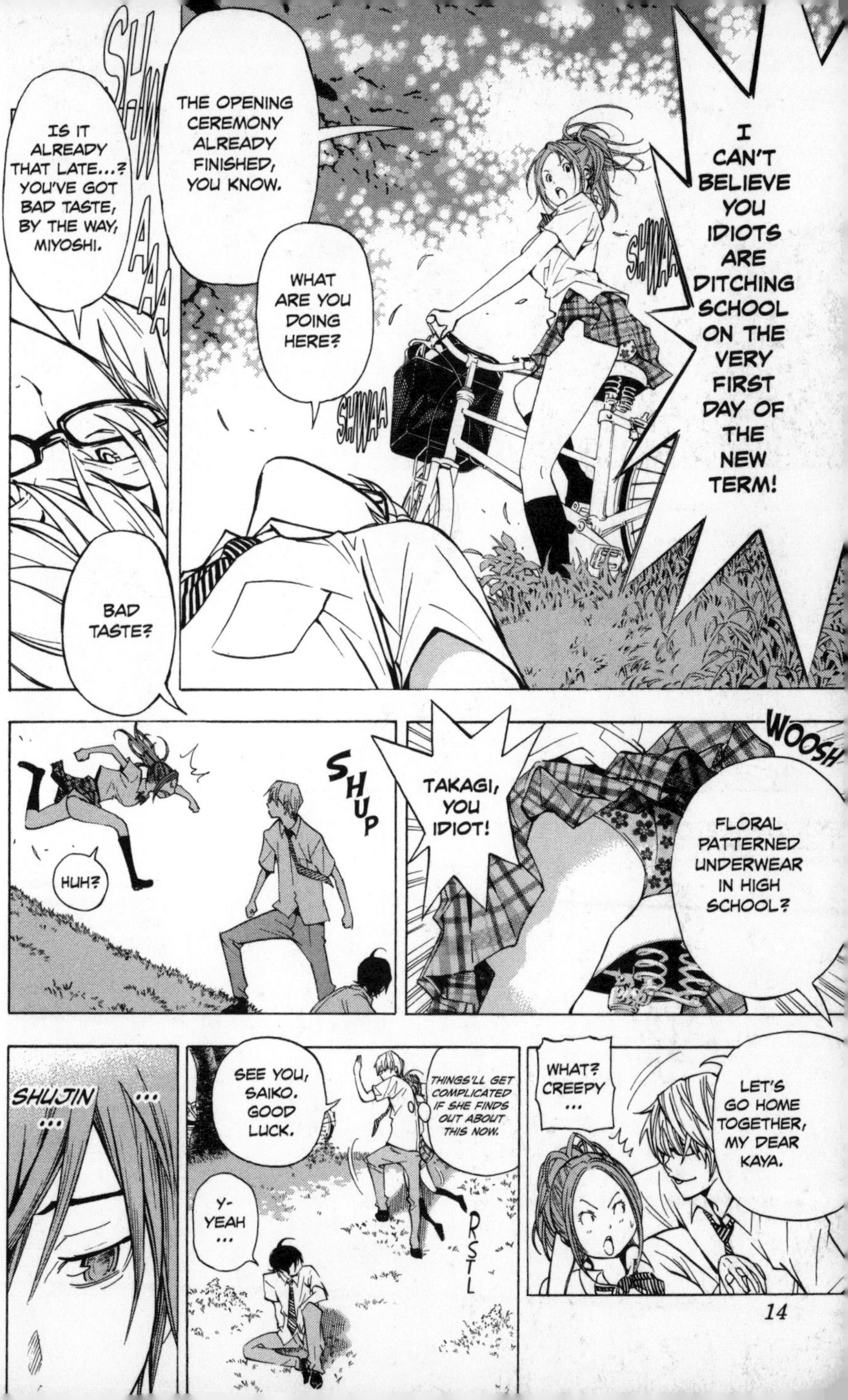
I CAN'T BELIEVE YOU IDIOTS ARE DITCHING SCHOOL ON THE VERY FIRST DAY OF THE NEW TERM!
SHWAA
THE OPENING CEREMONY ALREADY FINISHED, YOU KNOW.
WHAT ARE YOU DOING HERE?
SHWAA
SHWAAAA
IS IT ALREADY THAT LATE...? YOU'VE GOT BAD TASTE, BY THE WAY, MIYOSHI.
BAD TASTE?
WOOSH
FLORAL PATTERNED UNDERWEAR IN HIGH SCHOOL?
TAKAGI, YOU IDIOT!
SHUP
HUH?
LET'S GO HOME TOGETHER, MY DEAR KAYA.
WHAT? CREEPY ...
THINGS'LL GET COMPLICATED IF SHE FINDS OUT ABOUT THIS NOW.
SEE YOU, SAIKO. GOOD LUCK.
Y-YEAH ...
RSTL
SHUJIN ...
...

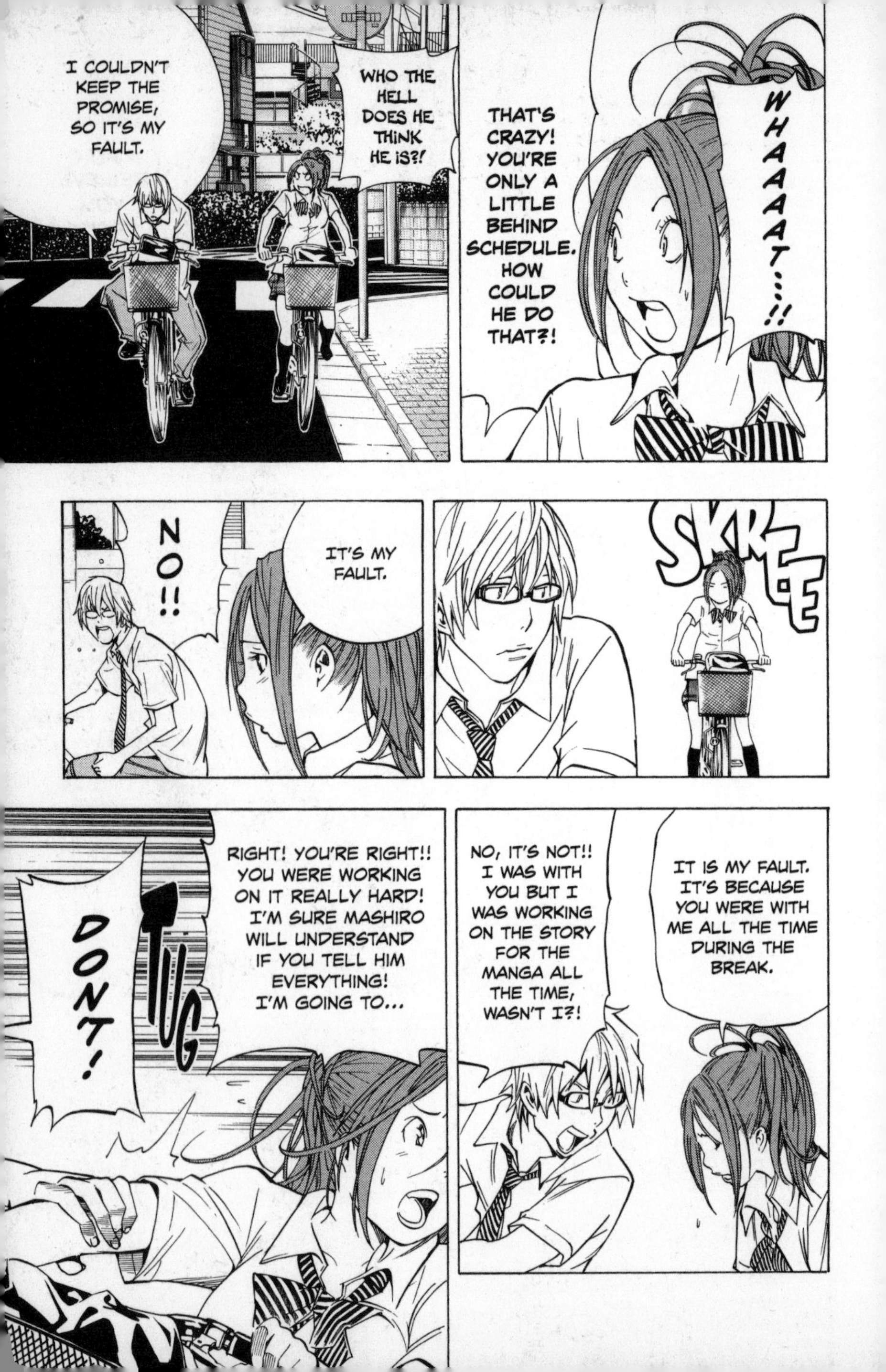
WHAAAAT...!!
THAT'S CRAZY! YOU'RE ONLY A LITTLE BEHIND SCHEDULE. HOW COULD HE DO THAT?!
WHO THE HELL DOES HE THINK HE IS?!
I COULDN'T KEEP THE PROMISE, SO IT'S MY FAULT.
SKREE
IT'S MY FAULT.
NO!!
IT IS MY FAULT. IT'S BECAUSE YOU WERE WITH ME ALL THE TIME DURING THE BREAK.
NO, IT'S NOT!! I WAS WITH YOU BUT I WAS WORKING ON THE STORY FOR THE MANGA ALL THE TIME, WASN'T I?!
RIGHT! YOU'RE RIGHT!! YOU WERE WORKING ON IT REALLY HARD! I'M SURE MASHIRO WILL UNDERSTAND IF YOU TELL HIM EVERYTHING! I'M GOING TO...
TUG
DON'T!

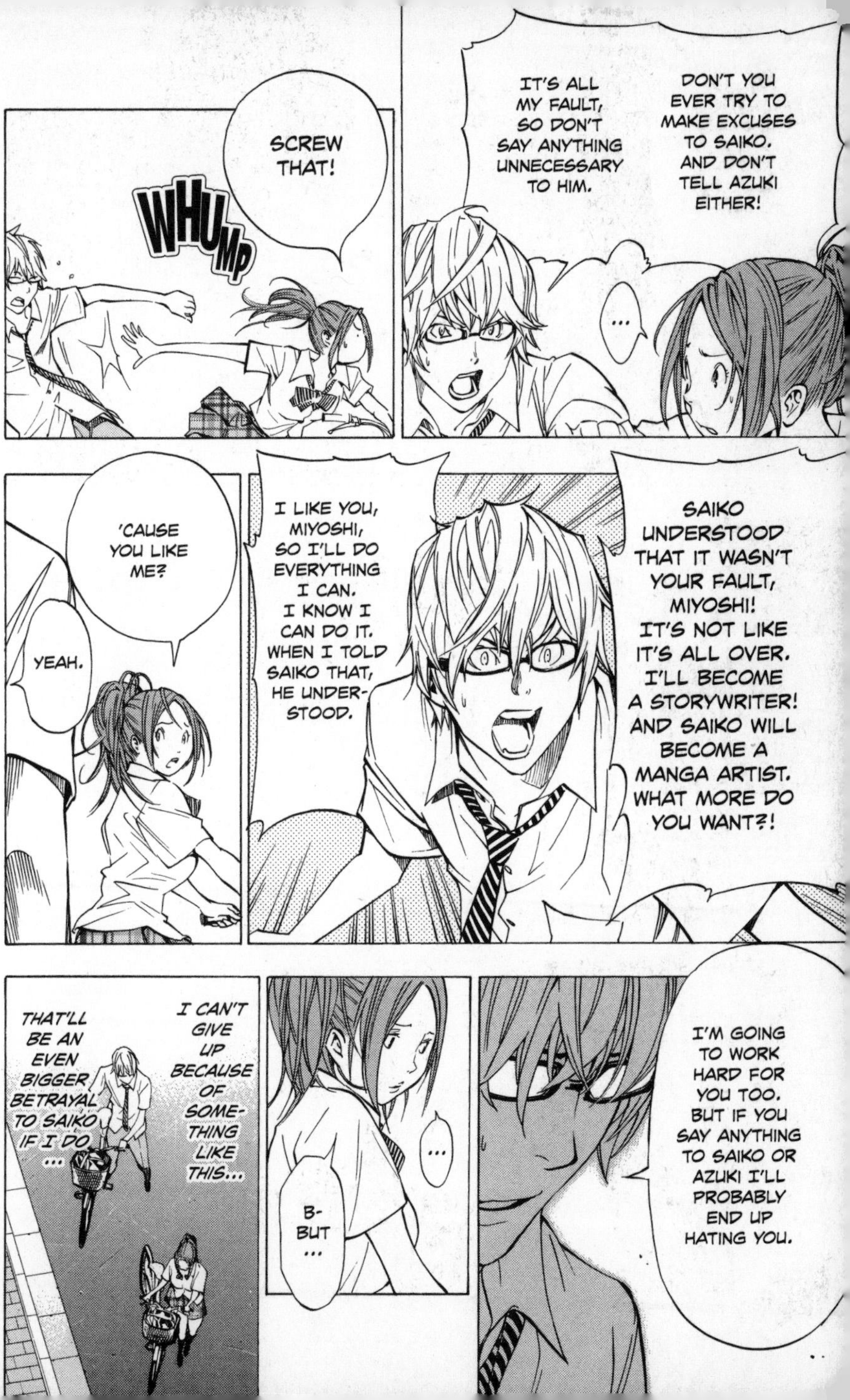

DON'T YOU EVER TRY TO MAKE EXCUSES TO SAIKO. AND DON'T TELL AZUKI EITHER!
IT'S ALL MY FAULT, SO DON'T SAY ANYTHING UNNECESSARY TO HIM.
...
SCREW THAT!
WHUMP
SAIKO UNDERSTOOD THAT IT WASN'T YOUR FAULT, MIYOSHI! IT'S NOT LIKE IT'S ALL OVER. I'LL BECOME A STORYWRITER! AND SAIKO WILL BECOME A MANGA ARTIST. WHAT MORE DO YOU WANT?!
I LIKE YOU, MIYOSHI, SO I'LL DO EVERYTHING I CAN. I KNOW I CAN DO IT. WHEN I TOLD SAIKO THAT, HE UNDER-STOOD.
'CAUSE YOU LIKE ME?
YEAH.
I'M GOING TO WORK HARD FOR YOU TOO. BUT IF YOU SAY ANYTHING TO SAIKO OR AZUKI I'LL PROBABLY END UP HATING YOU.
...
B-BUT ...
I CAN'T GIVE UP BECAUSE OF SOME-THING LIKE THIS...
THAT'LL BE AN EVEN BIGGER BETRAYAL TO SAIKO IF I DO ...

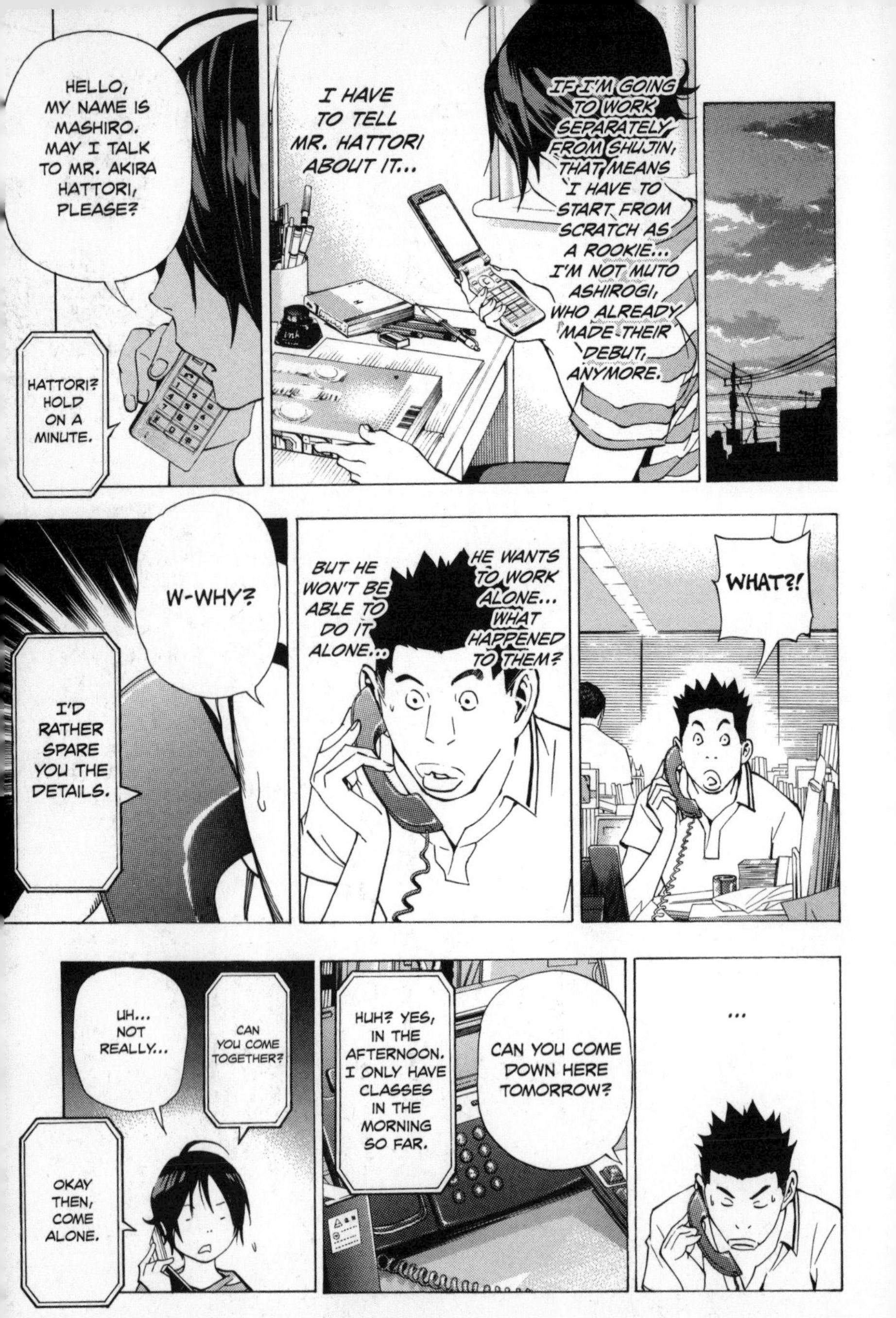

IF I'M GOING TO WORK SEPARATELY FROM SHUJIN, THAT MEANS I HAVE TO START FROM SCRATCH AS A ROOKIE... I'M NOT MUTO ASHIROGI, WHO ALREADY MADE THEIR DEBUT, ANYMORE.
I HAVE TO TELL MR. HATTORI ABOUT IT...
HELLO, MY NAME IS MASHIRO. MAY I TALK TO MR. AKIRA HATTORI, PLEASE?
HATTORI? HOLD ON A MINUTE.
WHAT?!
HE WANTS TO WORK ALONE... WHAT HAPPENED TO THEM?
BUT HE WON'T BE ABLE TO DO IT ALONE...
W-WHY?
I'D RATHER SPARE YOU THE DETAILS.
...
CAN YOU COME DOWN HERE TOMORROW?
HUH? YES, IN THE AFTERNOON. I ONLY HAVE CLASSES IN THE MORNING SO FAR.
CAN YOU COME TOGETHER?
UH... NOT REALLY...
OKAY THEN, COME ALONE.

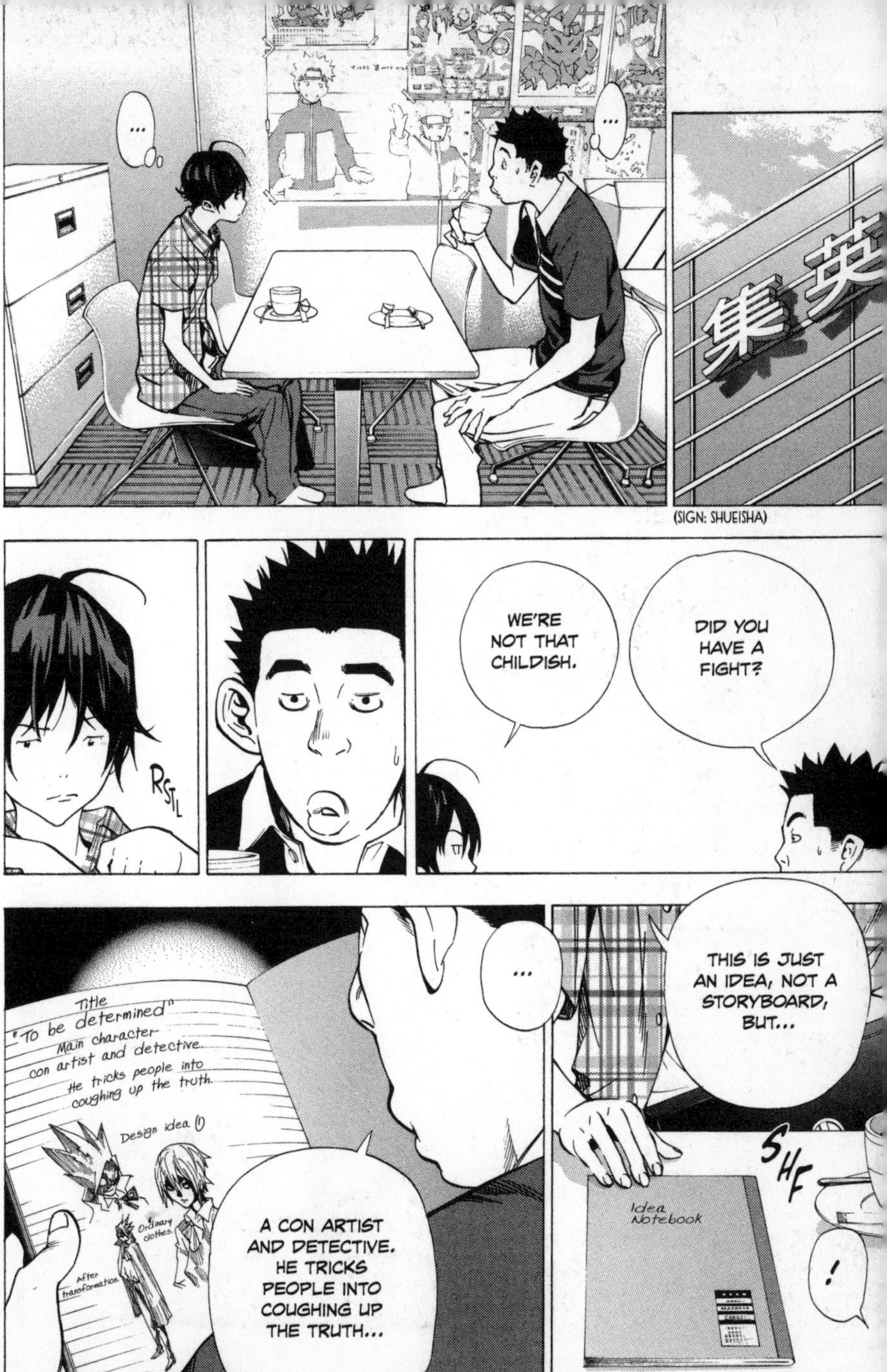
集英
(SIGN: SHUEISHA)
...
...
DID YOU HAVE A FIGHT?
WE'RE NOT THAT CHILDISH.
RSTL
THIS IS JUST AN IDEA, NOT A STORYBOARD, BUT...
SHF
!
Idea Notebook
...
Title "To be determined"
Main character- con artist and detective.
He tricks people into coughing up the truth.
Design idea (!)
Ordinary clothes.
After transformation.
A CON ARTIST AND DETECTIVE. HE TRICKS PEOPLE INTO COUGHING UP THE TRUTH...

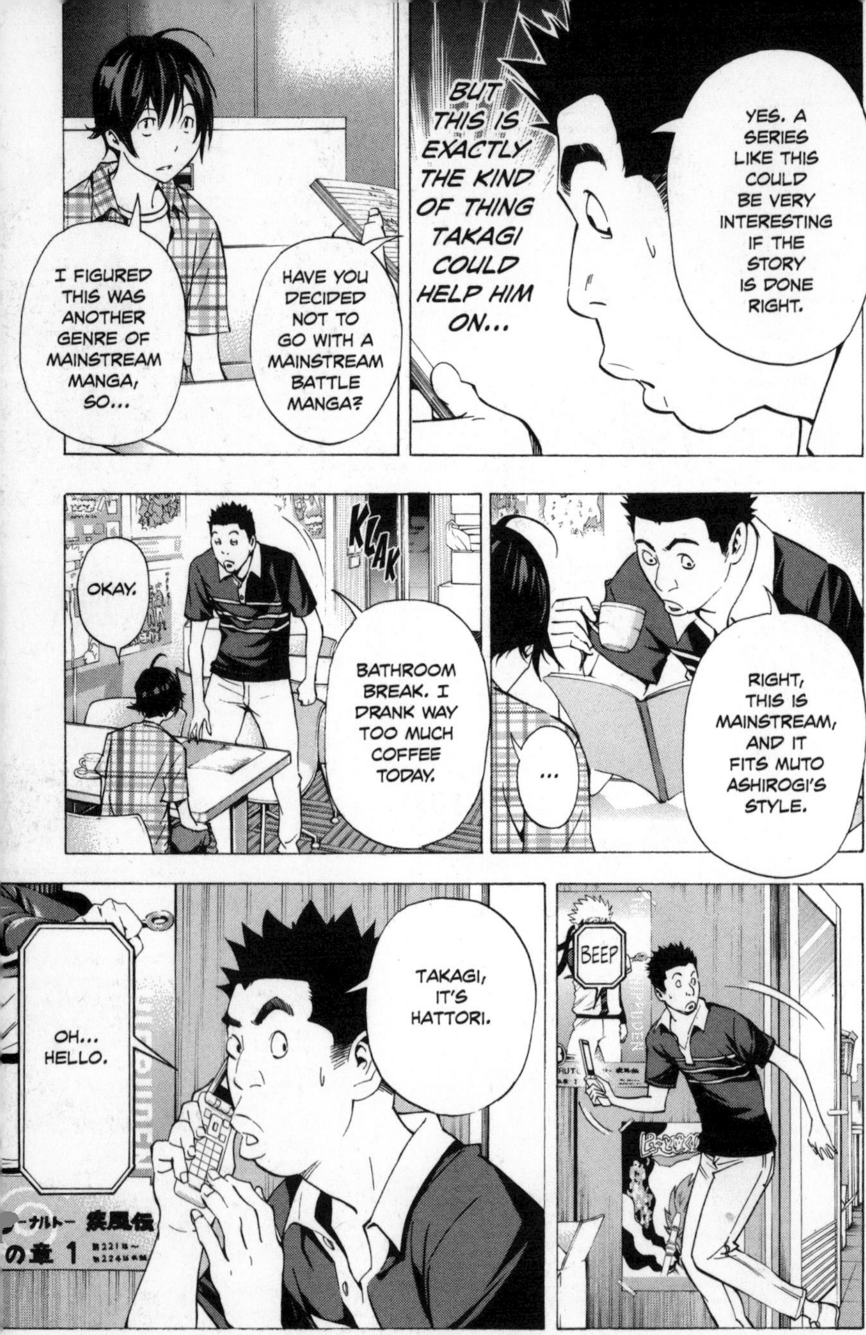
YES. A SERIES LIKE THIS COULD BE VERY INTERESTING IF THE STORY IS DONE RIGHT.
BUT THIS IS EXACTLY THE KIND OF THING TAKAGI COULD HELP HIM ON...
HAVE YOU DECIDED NOT TO GO WITH A MAINSTREAM BATTLE MANGA?
I FIGURED THIS WAS ANOTHER GENRE OF MAINSTREAM MANGA, SO...
RIGHT, THIS IS MAINSTREAM, AND IT FITS MUTO ASHIROGI'S STYLE.
...
KLAK
BATHROOM BREAK. I DRANK WAY TOO MUCH COFFEE TODAY.
OKAY.
BEEP
TAKAGI, IT'S HATTORI.
OH... HELLO.

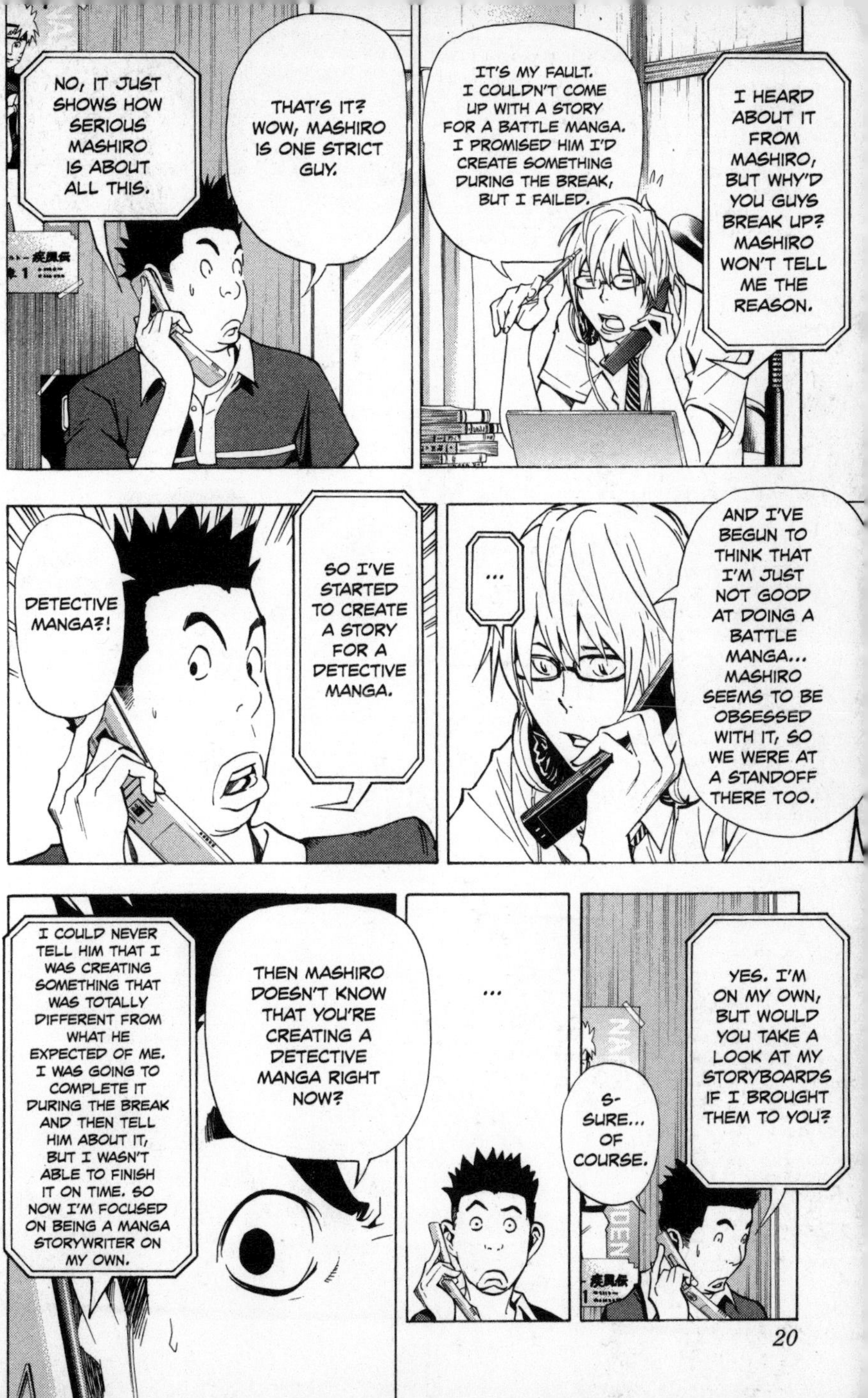
I HEARD ABOUT IT FROM MASHIRO, BUT WHY'D YOU GUYS BREAK UP? MASHIRO WON'T TELL ME THE REASON.
IT'S MY FAULT. I COULDN'T COME UP WITH A STORY FOR A BATTLE MANGA. I PROMISED HIM I'D CREATE SOMETHING DURING THE BREAK, BUT I FAILED.
THAT'S IT? WOW, MASHIRO IS ONE STRICT GUY.
NO, IT JUST SHOWS HOW SERIOUS MASHIRO IS ABOUT ALL THIS.
AND I'VE BEGUN TO THINK THAT I'M JUST NOT GOOD AT DOING A BATTLE MANGA... MASHIRO SEEMS TO BE OBSESSED WITH IT, SO WE WERE AT A STANDOFF THERE TOO.
...
SO I'VE STARTED TO CREATE A STORY FOR A DETECTIVE MANGA.
DETECTIVE MANGA?!
YES. I'M ON MY OWN, BUT WOULD YOU TAKE A LOOK AT MY STORYBOARDS IF I BROUGHT THEM TO YOU?
S-SURE... OF COURSE.
...
THEN MASHIRO DOESN'T KNOW THAT YOU'RE CREATING A DETECTIVE MANGA RIGHT NOW?
I COULD NEVER TELL HIM THAT I WAS CREATING SOMETHING THAT WAS TOTALLY DIFFERENT FROM WHAT HE EXPECTED OF ME. I WAS GOING TO COMPLETE IT DURING THE BREAK AND THEN TELL HIM ABOUT IT, BUT I WASN'T ABLE TO FINISH IT ON TIME. SO NOW I'M FOCUSED ON BEING A MANGA STORYWRITER ON MY OWN.

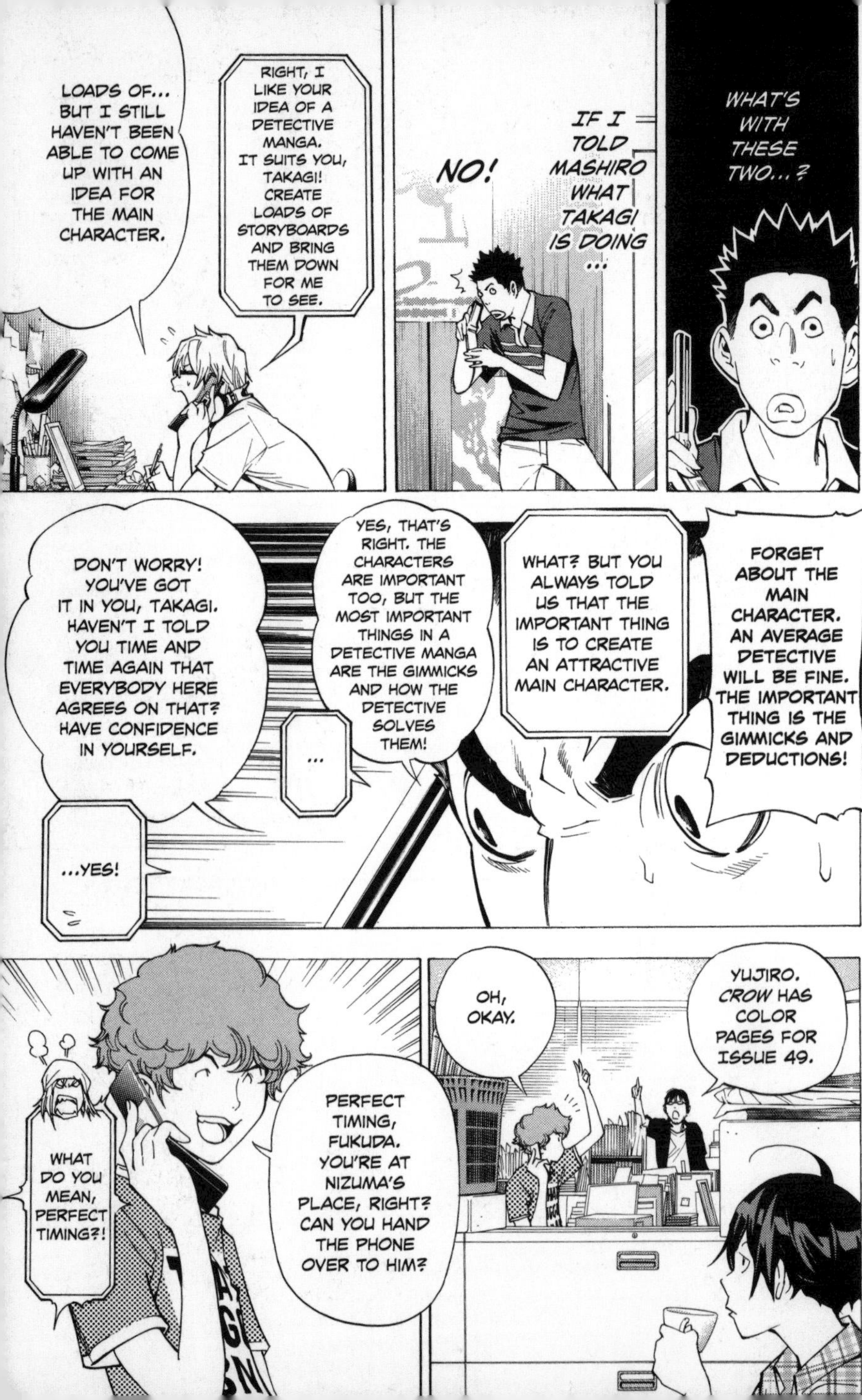
WHAT'S WITH THESE TWO...?
IF I TOLD MASHIRO WHAT TAKAGI IS DOING...
NO!
RIGHT, I LIKE YOUR IDEA OF A DETECTIVE MANGA. IT SUITS YOU, TAKAGI! CREATE LOADS OF STORYBOARDS AND BRING THEM DOWN FOR ME TO SEE.
LOADS OF... BUT I STILL HAVEN'T BEEN ABLE TO COME UP WITH AN IDEA FOR THE MAIN CHARACTER.
FORGET ABOUT THE MAIN CHARACTER. AN AVERAGE DETECTIVE WILL BE FINE. THE IMPORTANT THING IS THE GIMMICKS AND DEDUCTIONS!
WHAT? BUT YOU ALWAYS TOLD US THAT THE IMPORTANT THING IS TO CREATE AN ATTRACTIVE MAIN CHARACTER.
YES, THAT'S RIGHT. THE CHARACTERS ARE IMPORTANT TOO, BUT THE MOST IMPORTANT THINGS IN A DETECTIVE MANGA ARE THE GIMMICKS AND HOW THE DETECTIVE SOLVES THEM!
...
DON'T WORRY! YOU'VE GOT IT IN YOU, TAKAGI. HAVEN'T I TOLD YOU TIME AND TIME AGAIN THAT EVERYBODY HERE AGREES ON THAT? HAVE CONFIDENCE IN YOURSELF.
...YES!
YUJIRO. CROW HAS COLOR PAGES FOR ISSUE 49.
OH, OKAY.
PERFECT TIMING, FUKUDA. YOU'RE AT NIZUMA'S PLACE, RIGHT? CAN YOU HAND THE PHONE OVER TO HIM?
WHAT DO YOU MEAN, PERFECT TIMING?!

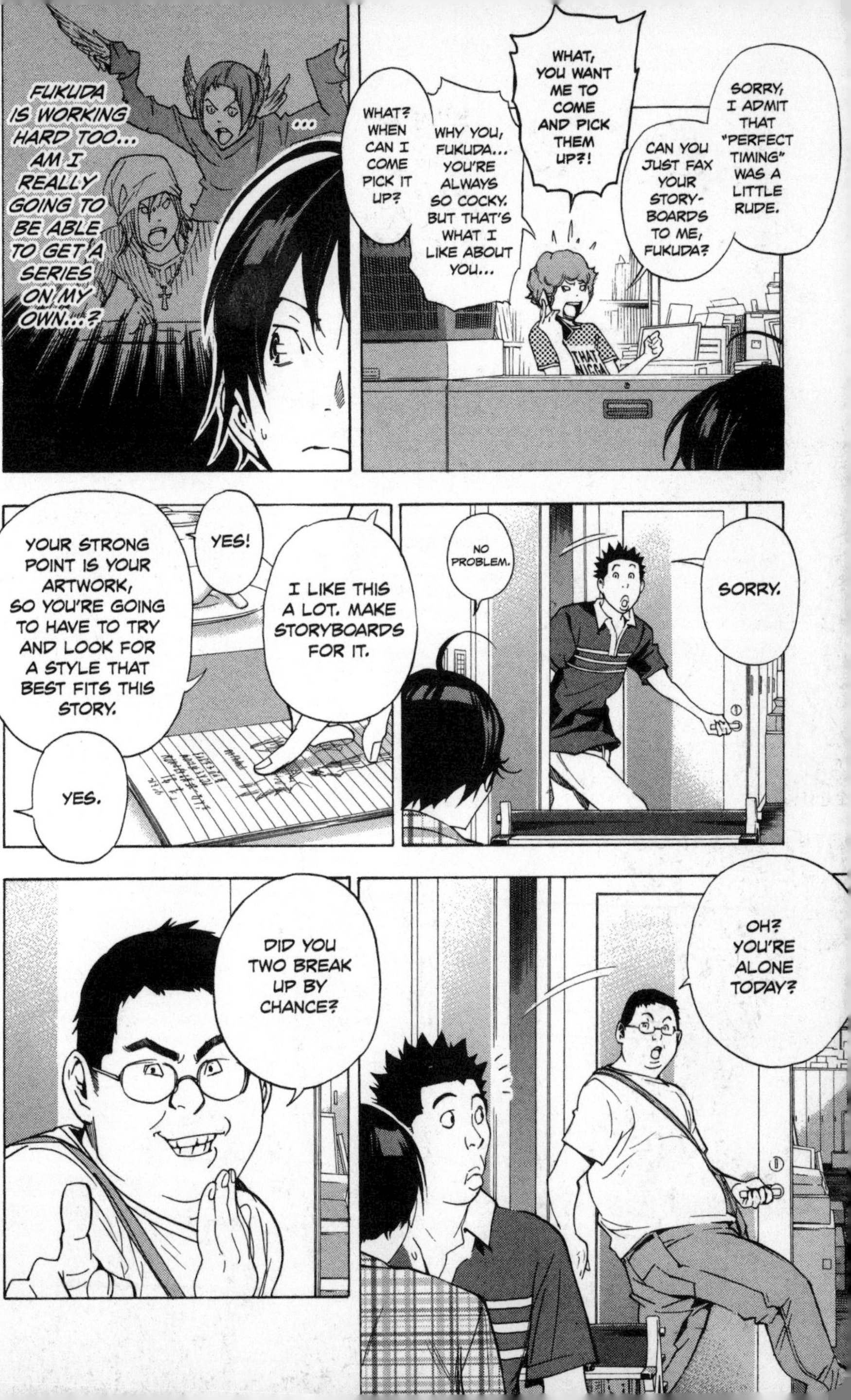
SORRY, I ADMIT THAT "PERFECT TIMING" WAS A LITTLE RUDE.
CAN YOU JUST FAX YOUR STORY-BOARDS TO ME, FUKUDA?
WHAT, YOU WANT ME TO COME AND PICK THEM UP?!
WHY YOU, FUKUDA... YOU'RE ALWAYS SO COCKY. BUT THAT'S WHAT I LIKE ABOUT YOU...
WHAT? WHEN CAN I COME PICK IT UP?
...
FUKUDA IS WORKING HARD TOO... AM I REALLY GOING TO BE ABLE TO GET A SERIES ON MY OWN...?
SORRY.
NO PROBLEM.
I LIKE THIS A LOT. MAKE STORYBOARDS FOR IT.
YES!
YOUR STRONG POINT IS YOUR ARTWORK, SO YOU'RE GOING TO HAVE TO TRY AND LOOK FOR A STYLE THAT BEST FITS THIS STORY.
YES.
OH? YOU'RE ALONE TODAY?
DID YOU TWO BREAK UP BY CHANCE?

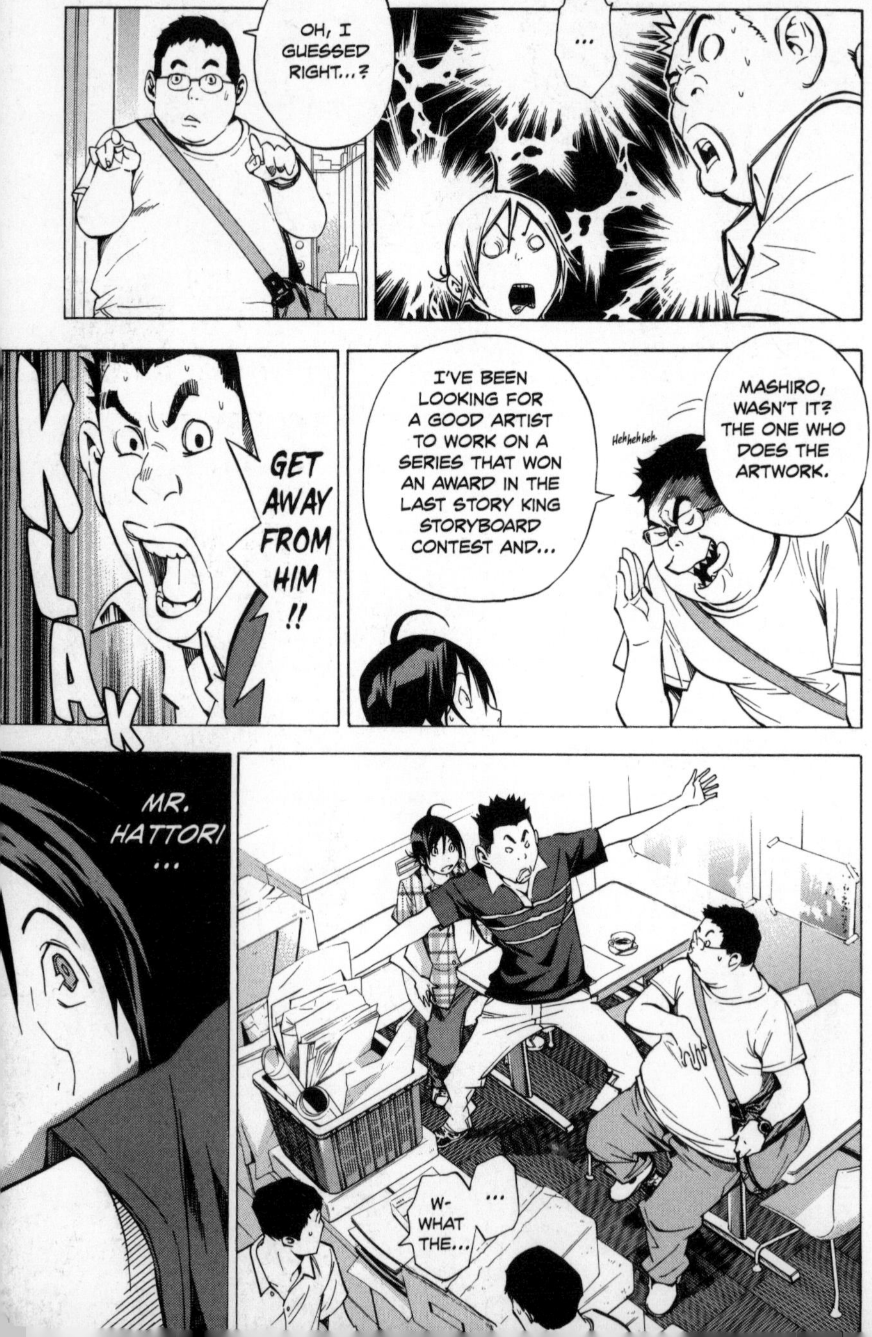
...
OH, I GUESSED RIGHT...?
MASHIRO, WASN'T IT? THE ONE WHO DOES THE ARTWORK.
Hehhehheh.
I'VE BEEN LOOKING FOR A GOOD ARTIST TO WORK ON A SERIES THAT WON AN AWARD IN THE LAST STORY KING STORYBOARD CONTEST AND...
KLAK
GET AWAY FROM HIM!!
W- WHAT THE...
...
MR. HATTORI ...

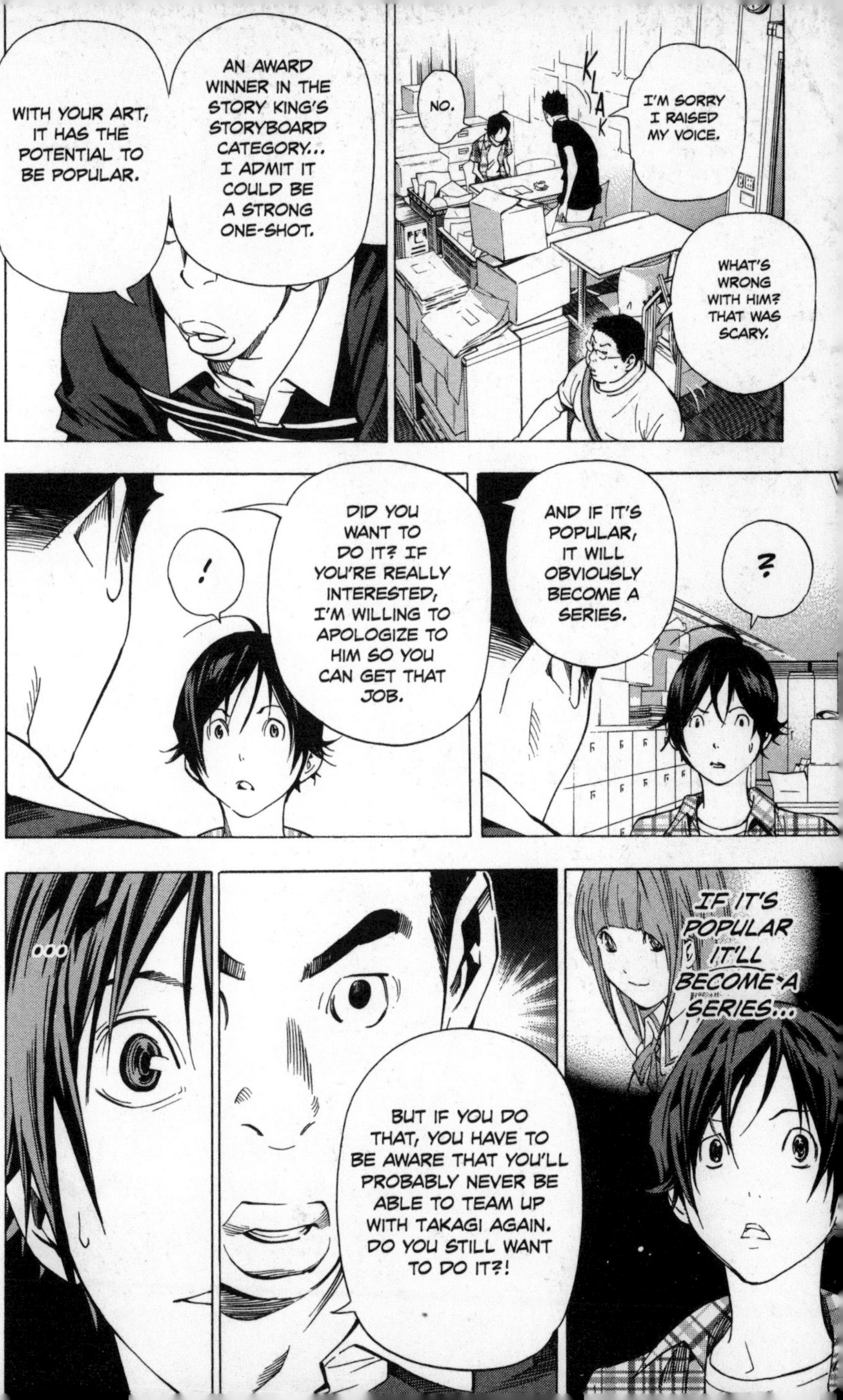

I'M SORRY I RAISED MY VOICE.
KLAK
NO.
WHAT'S WRONG WITH HIM? THAT WAS SCARY.
AN AWARD WINNER IN THE STORY KING'S STORYBOARD CATEGORY... I ADMIT IT COULD BE A STRONG ONE-SHOT.
WITH YOUR ART, IT HAS THE POTENTIAL TO BE POPULAR.
AND IF IT'S POPULAR, IT WILL OBVIOUSLY BECOME A SERIES.
?
DID YOU WANT TO DO IT? IF YOU'RE REALLY INTERESTED, I'M WILLING TO APOLOGIZE TO HIM SO YOU CAN GET THAT JOB.
!
IF IT'S POPULAR IT'LL BECOME A SERIES...
BUT IF YOU DO THAT, YOU HAVE TO BE AWARE THAT YOU'LL PROBABLY NEVER BE ABLE TO TEAM UP WITH TAKAGI AGAIN. DO YOU STILL WANT TO DO IT?!
...

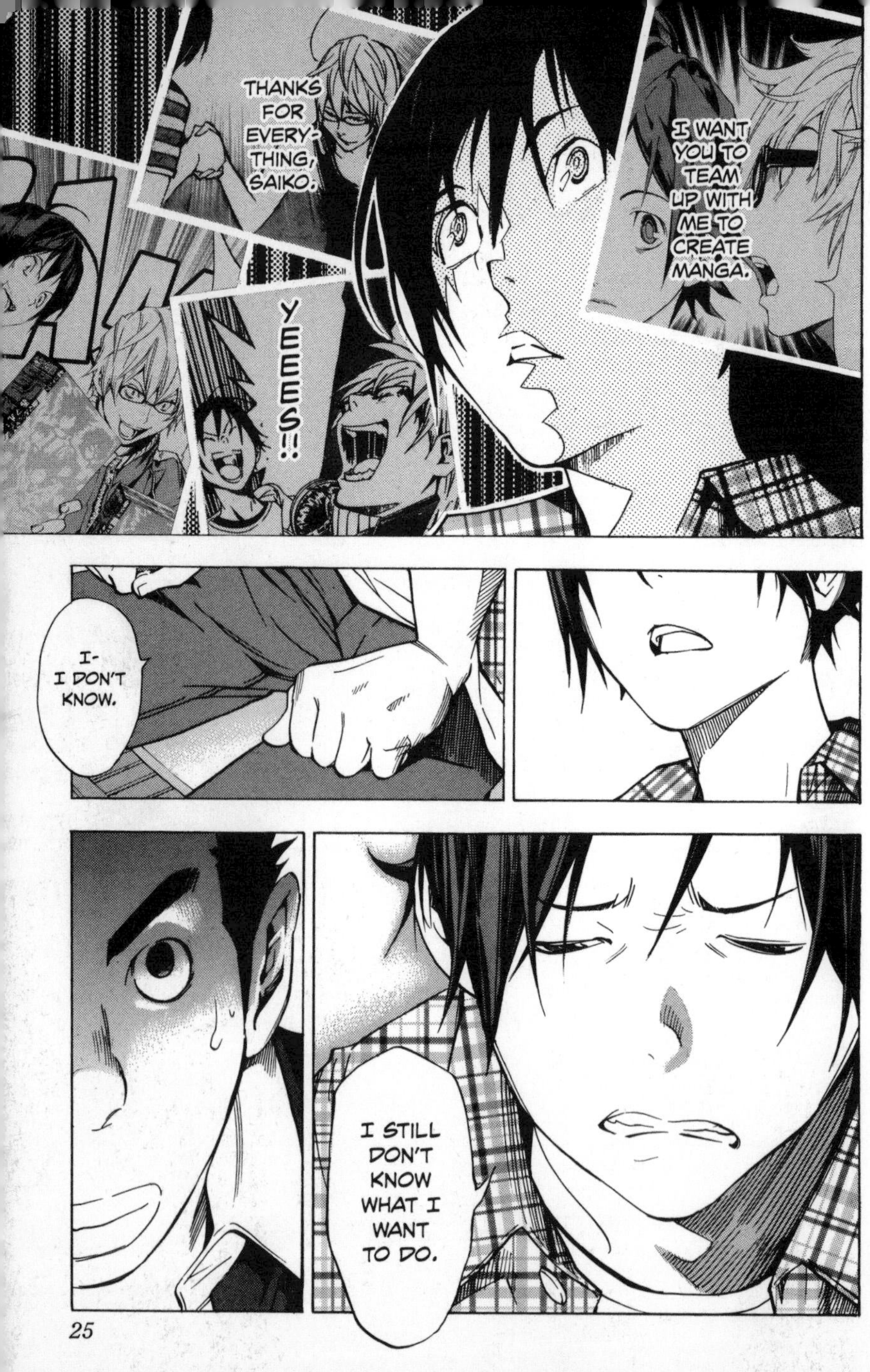
I WANT YOU TO TEAM UP WITH ME TO CREATE MANGA.
THANKS FOR EVERYTHING, SAIKO.
YEEEES!!
I- I DON'T KNOW.
I STILL DON'T KNOW WHAT I WANT TO DO.

OHBA'S STORYBOARD

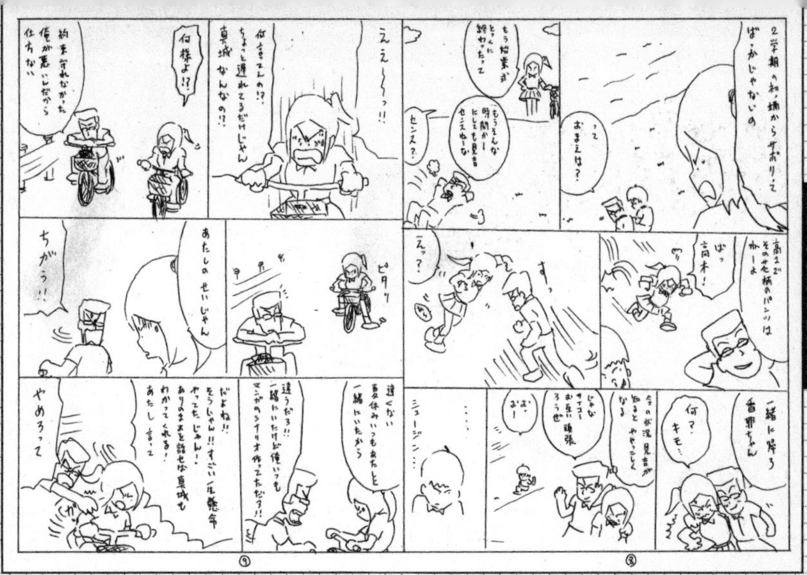

2学期の初っ端からサボりって ばっかじゃないの
って おまえは？
もう始業式とっくに終わったって
もうそんな時間か～ にしても見吉センスねーな
センス？
高1でその花柄のパンツはねーよ
ばっ 高木！
えっ？
すっ
一緒に帰ろ 香耶ちゃん
何？ キモ…
今の状況見吉が知るとややこしくなる
じゃな サイコー お互い頑張ろうぜ
はっ おー！
ニュージン…
⑧
ええ～～っ!!
何言ってんの!? ちょっと遅れてるだけじゃん 真城なんなの!?
何様よ!?
約束守れなかった俺が悪いんだから仕方ない
ピタッ
あたしのせいじゃん
ちがう!!
違くない 夏休みいつもあたしと一緒にいたから
違うだろ!! 一緒にいたけど俺いつもマンガのシナリオ作ってただろ!!
だよね!! そうじゃん!! すごい一生懸命やってたじゃん! ありのままを話せば真城もわかってくれる! あたし言って
やめろって
⑨

OBATA'S STORYBOARD

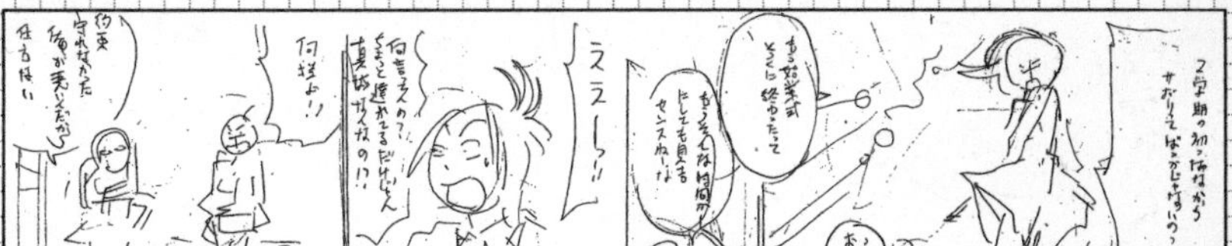

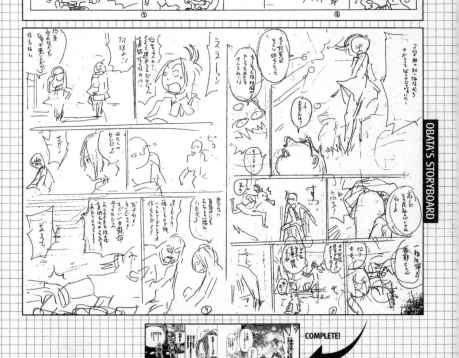

COMPLETE!

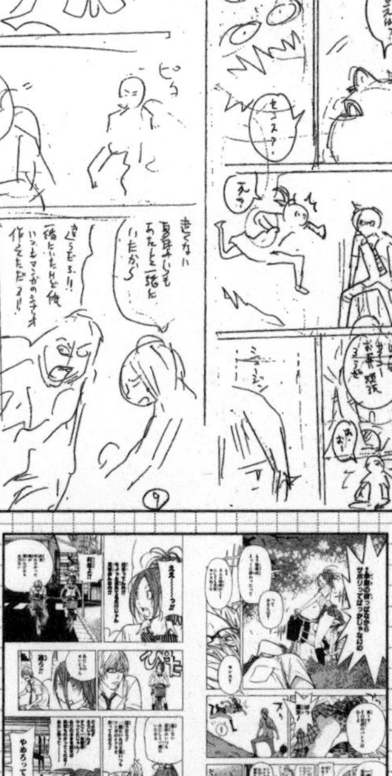

*CREATOR STORYBOARDS AND FINISHED PAGES IN JAPANESE

BAKUMAN。 vol.4

"Until the Final Draft Is Complete"

Chapter 26, pp. 14-15

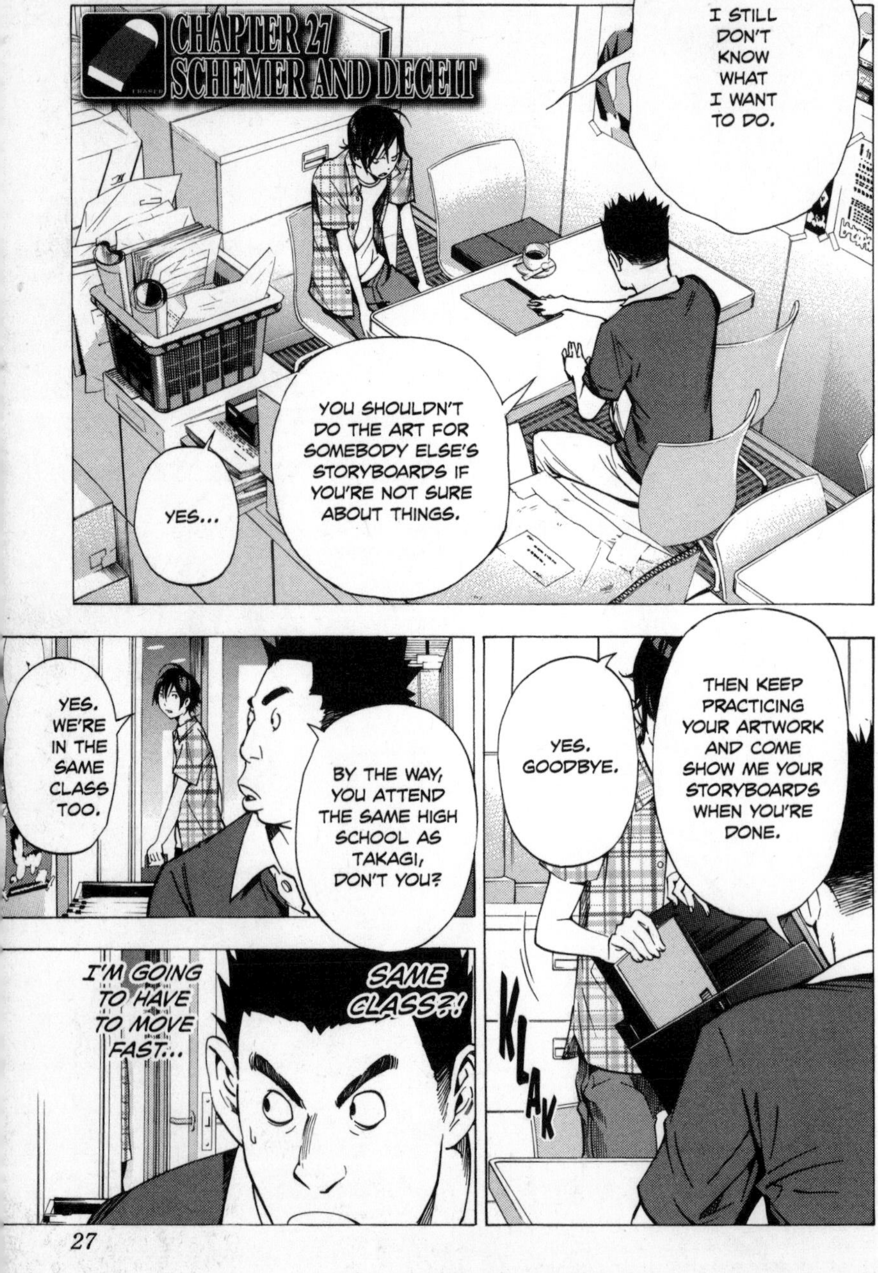
CHAPTER 27
SCHEMER AND DECEIT
I STILL DON'T KNOW WHAT I WANT TO DO.
YOU SHOULDN'T DO THE ART FOR SOMEBODY ELSE'S STORYBOARDS IF YOU'RE NOT SURE ABOUT THINGS.
YES...
THEN KEEP PRACTICING YOUR ARTWORK AND COME SHOW ME YOUR STORYBOARDS WHEN YOU'RE DONE.
YES. GOODBYE.
KLAK
BY THE WAY, YOU ATTEND THE SAME HIGH SCHOOL AS TAKAGI, DON'T YOU?
YES. WE'RE IN THE SAME CLASS TOO.
SAME CLASS?!
I'M GOING TO HAVE TO MOVE FAST...

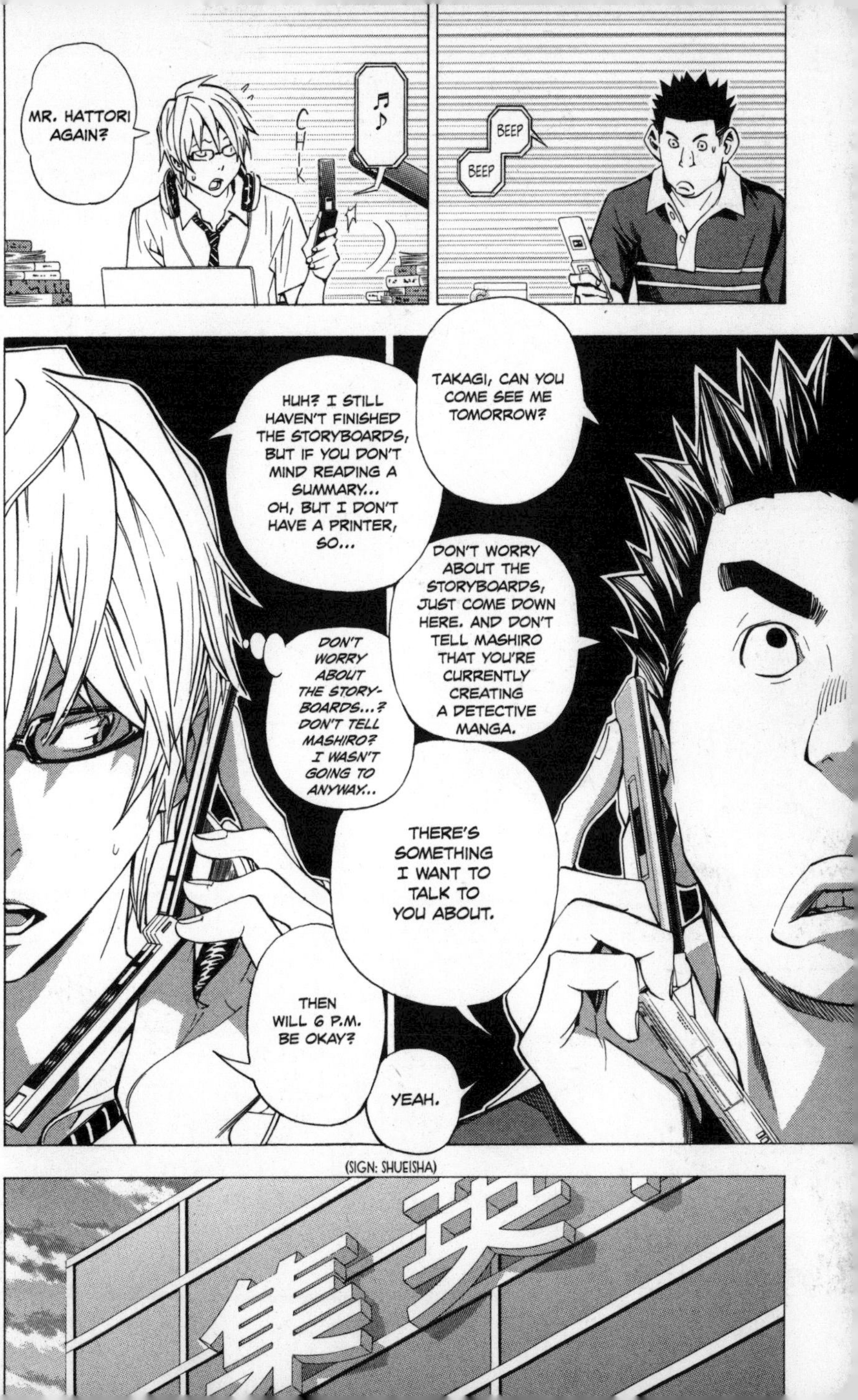
BEEP
BEEP
MR. HATTORI AGAIN?
CHIK
TAKAGI, CAN YOU COME SEE ME TOMORROW?
HUH? I STILL HAVEN'T FINISHED THE STORYBOARDS, BUT IF YOU DON'T MIND READING A SUMMARY... OH, BUT I DON'T HAVE A PRINTER, SO...
DON'T WORRY ABOUT THE STORYBOARDS, JUST COME DOWN HERE. AND DON'T TELL MASHIRO THAT YOU'RE CURRENTLY CREATING A DETECTIVE MANGA.
DON'T WORRY ABOUT THE STORY-BOARDS...? DON'T TELL MASHIRO? I WASN'T GOING TO ANYWAY...
THERE'S SOMETHING I WANT TO TALK TO YOU ABOUT.
THEN WILL 6 P.M. BE OKAY?
YEAH.
(SIGN: SHUEISHA)

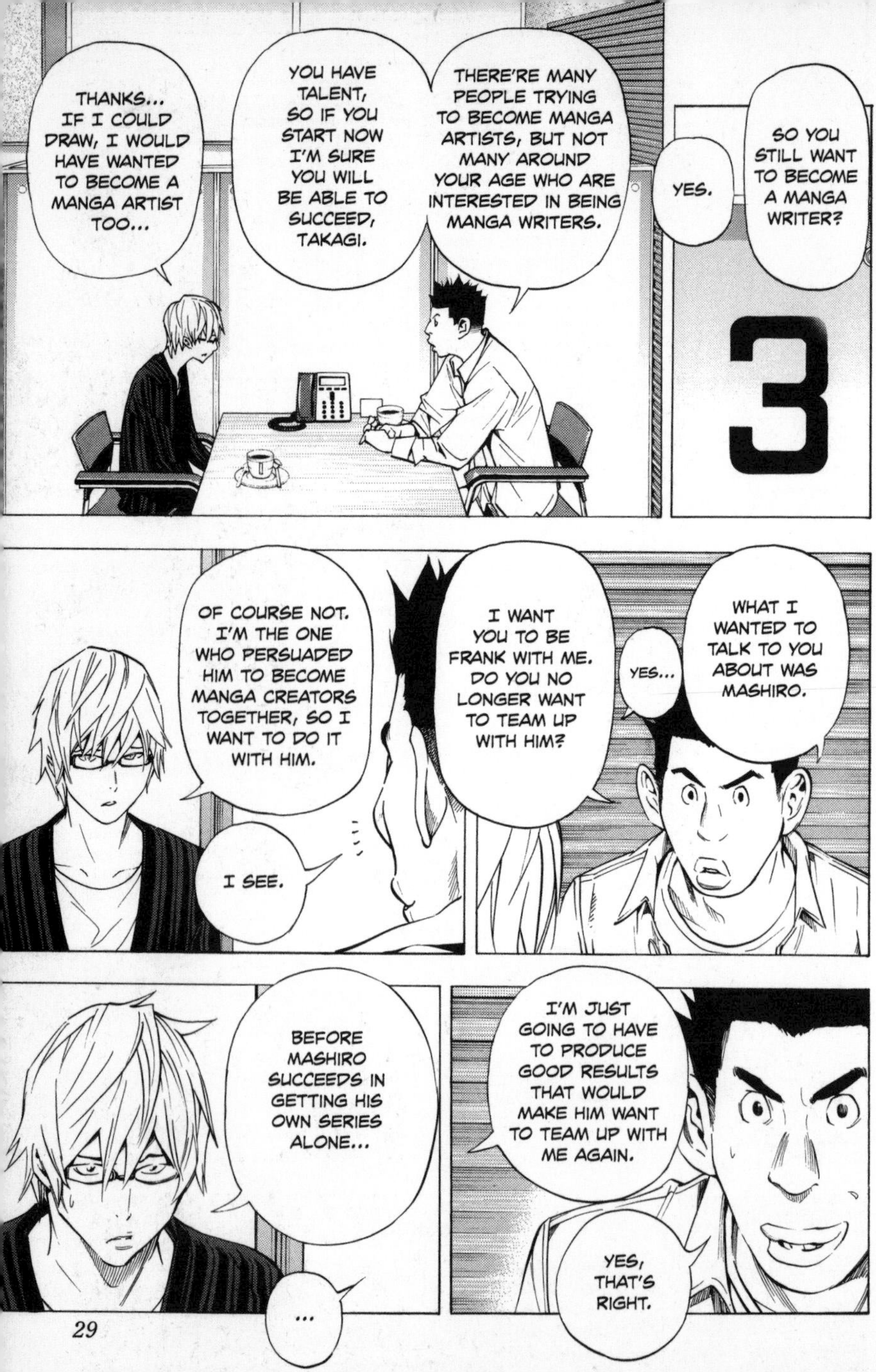
SO YOU STILL WANT TO BECOME A MANGA WRITER?
YES.
3
THERE'RE MANY PEOPLE TRYING TO BECOME MANGA ARTISTS, BUT NOT MANY AROUND YOUR AGE WHO ARE INTERESTED IN BEING MANGA WRITERS.
YOU HAVE TALENT, SO IF YOU START NOW I'M SURE YOU WILL BE ABLE TO SUCCEED, TAKAGI.
THANKS... IF I COULD DRAW, I WOULD HAVE WANTED TO BECOME A MANGA ARTIST TOO...
WHAT I WANTED TO TALK TO YOU ABOUT WAS MASHIRO.
YES...
I WANT YOU TO BE FRANK WITH ME. DO YOU NO LONGER WANT TO TEAM UP WITH HIM?
OF COURSE NOT. I'M THE ONE WHO PERSUADED HIM TO BECOME MANGA CREATORS TOGETHER, SO I WANT TO DO IT WITH HIM.
I SEE.
I'M JUST GOING TO HAVE TO PRODUCE GOOD RESULTS THAT WOULD MAKE HIM WANT TO TEAM UP WITH ME AGAIN.
YES, THAT'S RIGHT.
BEFORE MASHIRO SUCCEEDS IN GETTING HIS OWN SERIES ALONE...
...

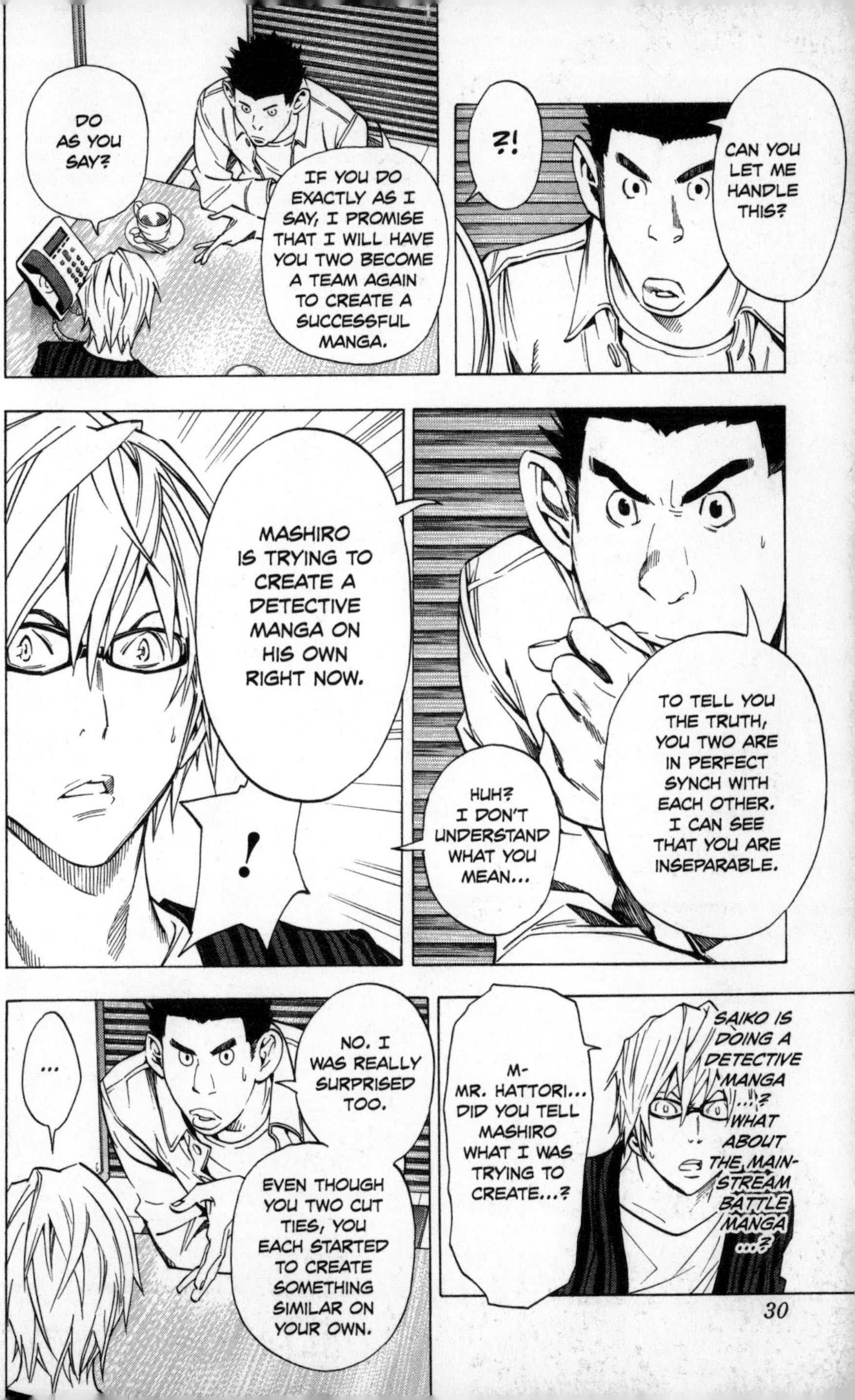
CAN YOU LET ME HANDLE THIS?
?!
IF YOU DO EXACTLY AS I SAY, I PROMISE THAT I WILL HAVE YOU TWO BECOME A TEAM AGAIN TO CREATE A SUCCESSFUL MANGA.
DO AS YOU SAY?
TO TELL YOU THE TRUTH, YOU TWO ARE IN PERFECT SYNCH WITH EACH OTHER. I CAN SEE THAT YOU ARE INSEPARABLE.
HUH? I DON'T UNDERSTAND WHAT YOU MEAN...
MASHIRO IS TRYING TO CREATE A DETECTIVE MANGA ON HIS OWN RIGHT NOW.
!
SAIKO IS DOING A DETECTIVE MANGA ...!? WHAT ABOUT THE MAIN-STREAM BATTLE MANGA ...?
M- MR. HATTORI... DID YOU TELL MASHIRO WHAT I WAS TRYING TO CREATE...?
NO. I WAS REALLY SURPRISED TOO.
EVEN THOUGH YOU TWO CUT TIES, YOU EACH STARTED TO CREATE SOMETHING SIMILAR ON YOUR OWN.
...

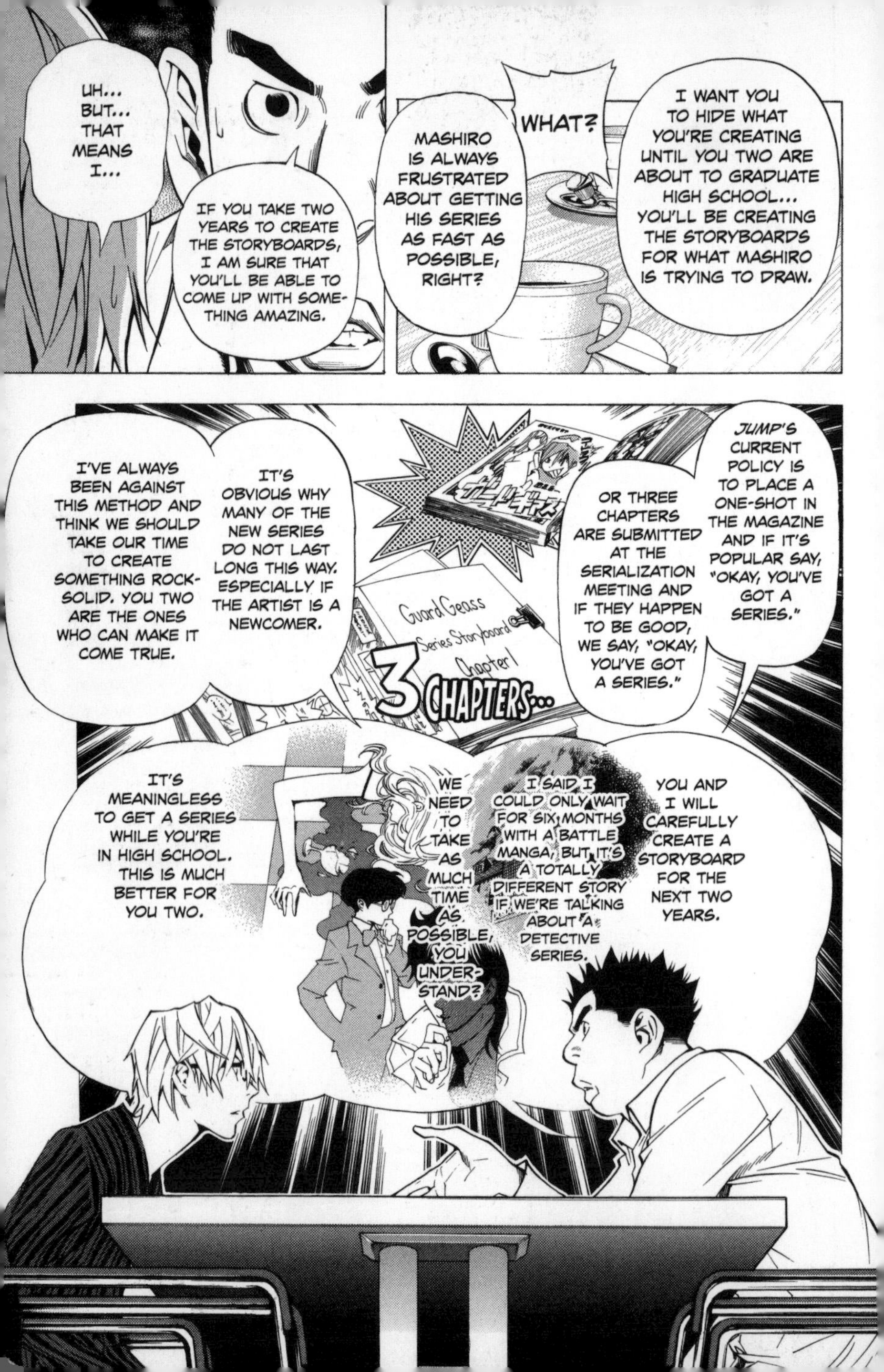
I WANT YOU TO HIDE WHAT YOU'RE CREATING UNTIL YOU TWO ARE ABOUT TO GRADUATE HIGH SCHOOL... YOU'LL BE CREATING THE STORYBOARDS FOR WHAT MASHIRO IS TRYING TO DRAW.
WHAT?
MASHIRO IS ALWAYS FRUSTRATED ABOUT GETTING HIS SERIES AS FAST AS POSSIBLE, RIGHT?
IF YOU TAKE TWO YEARS TO CREATE THE STORYBOARDS, I AM SURE THAT YOU'LL BE ABLE TO COME UP WITH SOMETHING AMAZING.
UH... BUT... THAT MEANS I...
JUMP'S CURRENT POLICY IS TO PLACE A ONE-SHOT IN THE MAGAZINE AND IF IT'S POPULAR SAY, "OKAY, YOU'VE GOT A SERIES."
OR THREE CHAPTERS ARE SUBMITTED AT THE SERIALIZATION MEETING AND IF THEY HAPPEN TO BE GOOD, WE SAY, "OKAY, YOU'VE GOT A SERIES."
Guard Geass
Series Storyboard
Chapter 1
3 CHAPTERS...
IT'S OBVIOUS WHY MANY OF THE NEW SERIES DO NOT LAST LONG THIS WAY. ESPECIALLY IF THE ARTIST IS A NEWCOMER.
I'VE ALWAYS BEEN AGAINST THIS METHOD AND THINK WE SHOULD TAKE OUR TIME TO CREATE SOMETHING ROCK-SOLID. YOU TWO ARE THE ONES WHO CAN MAKE IT COME TRUE.
YOU AND I WILL CAREFULLY CREATE A STORYBOARD FOR THE NEXT TWO YEARS.
I SAID I COULD ONLY WAIT FOR SIX MONTHS WITH A BATTLE MANGA, BUT IT'S A TOTALLY DIFFERENT STORY IF WE'RE TALKING ABOUT A DETECTIVE SERIES.
WE NEED TO TAKE AS MUCH TIME AS POSSIBLE, YOU UNDERSTAND?
IT'S MEANINGLESS TO GET A SERIES WHILE YOU'RE IN HIGH SCHOOL. THIS IS MUCH BETTER FOR YOU TWO.

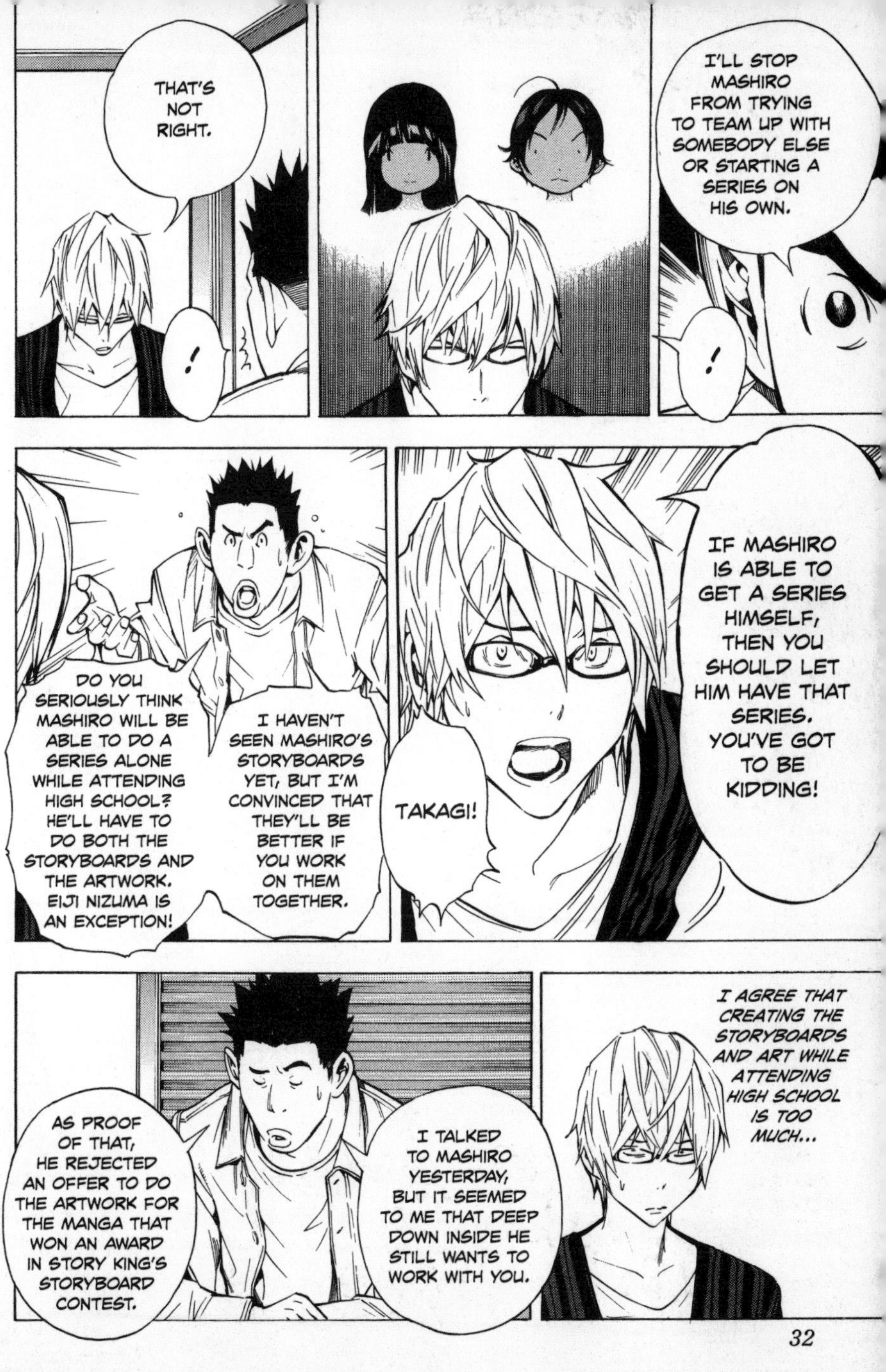
I'LL STOP MASHIRO FROM TRYING TO TEAM UP WITH SOMEBODY ELSE OR STARTING A SERIES ON HIS OWN.
!
THAT'S NOT RIGHT.
!
IF MASHIRO IS ABLE TO GET A SERIES HIMSELF, THEN YOU SHOULD LET HIM HAVE THAT SERIES. YOU'VE GOT TO BE KIDDING!
TAKAGI!
I HAVEN'T SEEN MASHIRO'S STORYBOARDS YET, BUT I'M CONVINCED THAT THEY'LL BE BETTER IF YOU WORK ON THEM TOGETHER.
DO YOU SERIOUSLY THINK MASHIRO WILL BE ABLE TO DO A SERIES ALONE WHILE ATTENDING HIGH SCHOOL? HE'LL HAVE TO DO BOTH THE STORYBOARDS AND THE ARTWORK. EIJI NIZUMA IS AN EXCEPTION!
I AGREE THAT CREATING THE STORYBOARDS AND ART WHILE ATTENDING HIGH SCHOOL IS TOO MUCH...
I TALKED TO MASHIRO YESTERDAY, BUT IT SEEMED TO ME THAT DEEP DOWN INSIDE HE STILL WANTS TO WORK WITH YOU.
AS PROOF OF THAT, HE REJECTED AN OFFER TO DO THE ARTWORK FOR THE MANGA THAT WON AN AWARD IN STORY KING'S STORYBOARD CONTEST.

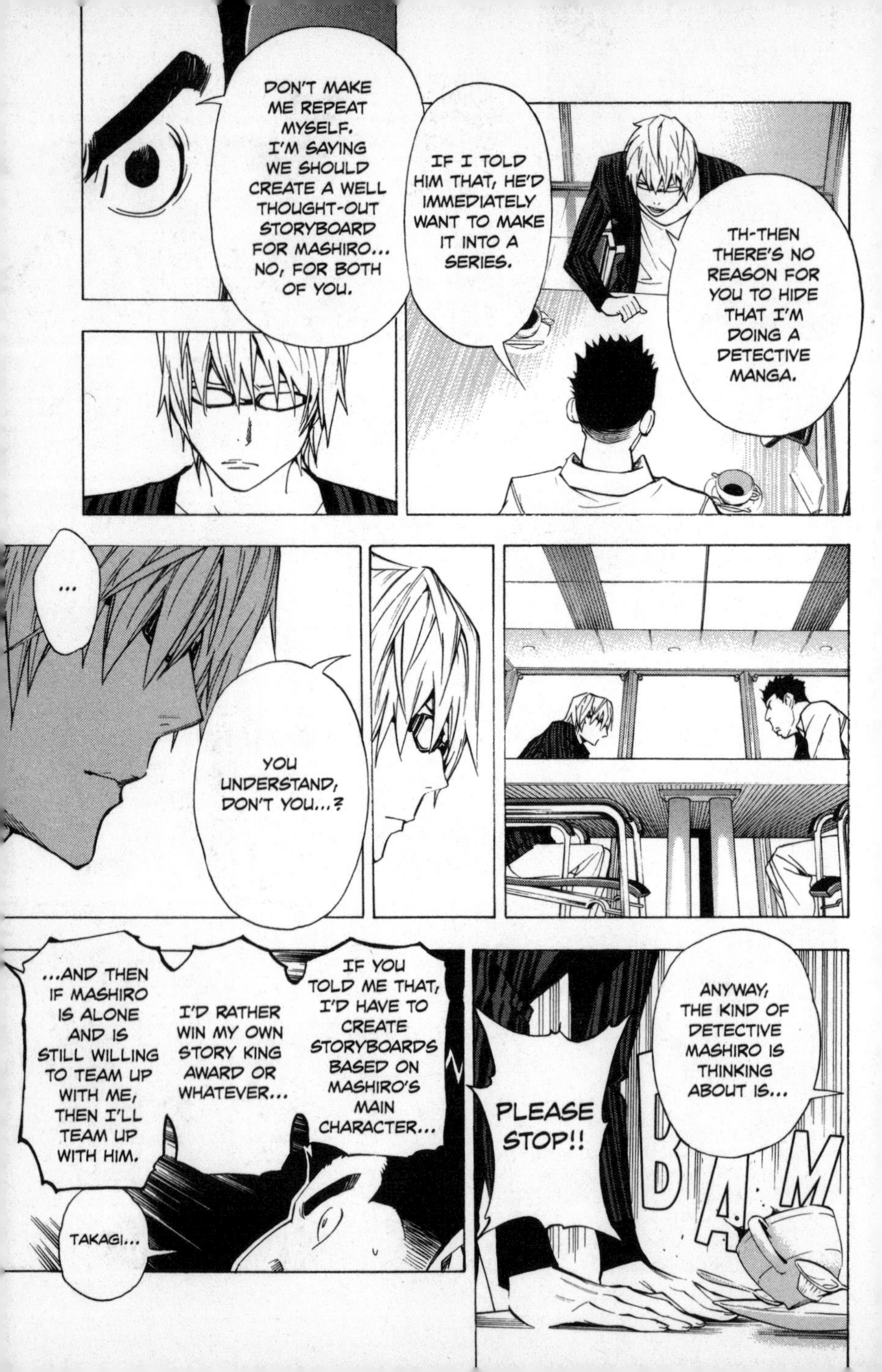
TH-THEN THERE'S NO REASON FOR YOU TO HIDE THAT I'M DOING A DETECTIVE MANGA.
IF I TOLD HIM THAT, HE'D IMMEDIATELY WANT TO MAKE IT INTO A SERIES.
DON'T MAKE ME REPEAT MYSELF. I'M SAYING WE SHOULD CREATE A WELL THOUGHT-OUT STORYBOARD FOR MASHIRO... NO, FOR BOTH OF YOU.
YOU UNDERSTAND, DON'T YOU...?
...
ANYWAY, THE KIND OF DETECTIVE MASHIRO IS THINKING ABOUT IS...
PLEASE STOP!!
BAM
IF YOU TOLD ME THAT, I'D HAVE TO CREATE STORYBOARDS BASED ON MASHIRO'S MAIN CHARACTER...
I'D RATHER WIN MY OWN STORY KING AWARD OR WHATEVER...
...AND THEN IF MASHIRO IS ALONE AND IS STILL WILLING TO TEAM UP WITH ME, THEN I'LL TEAM UP WITH HIM.
TAKAGI...

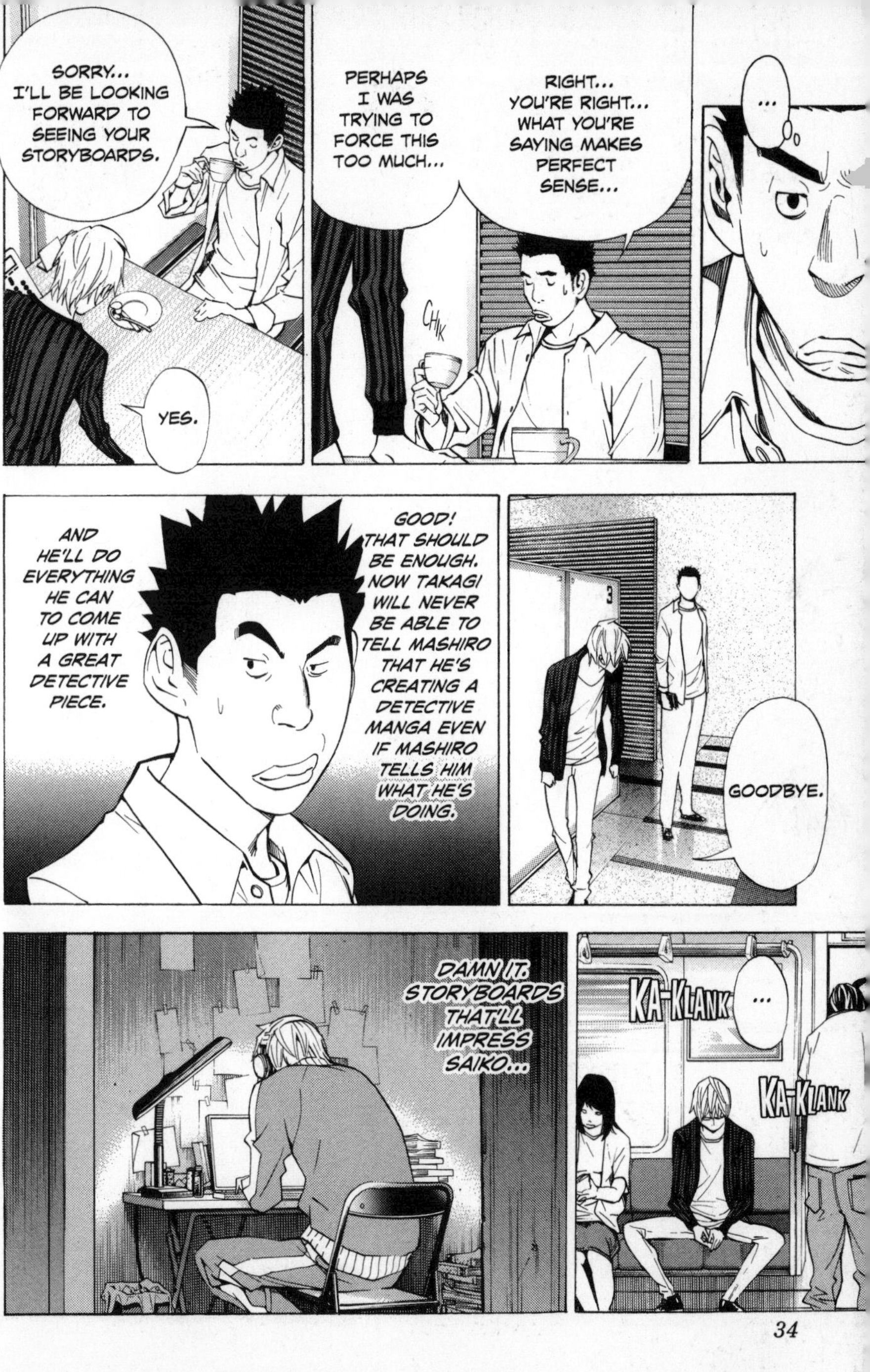
...
RIGHT... YOU'RE RIGHT... WHAT YOU'RE SAYING MAKES PERFECT SENSE...
PERHAPS I WAS TRYING TO FORCE THIS TOO MUCH...
CHIK
SORRY... I'LL BE LOOKING FORWARD TO SEEING YOUR STORYBOARDS.
YES.
GOODBYE.
GOOD! THAT SHOULD BE ENOUGH. NOW TAKAGI WILL NEVER BE ABLE TO TELL MASHIRO THAT HE'S CREATING A DETECTIVE MANGA EVEN IF MASHIRO TELLS HIM WHAT HE'S DOING.
AND HE'LL DO EVERYTHING HE CAN TO COME UP WITH A GREAT DETECTIVE PIECE.
KA-KLANK
...
KA-KLANK
DAMN IT. STORYBOARDS THAT'LL IMPRESS SAIKO...

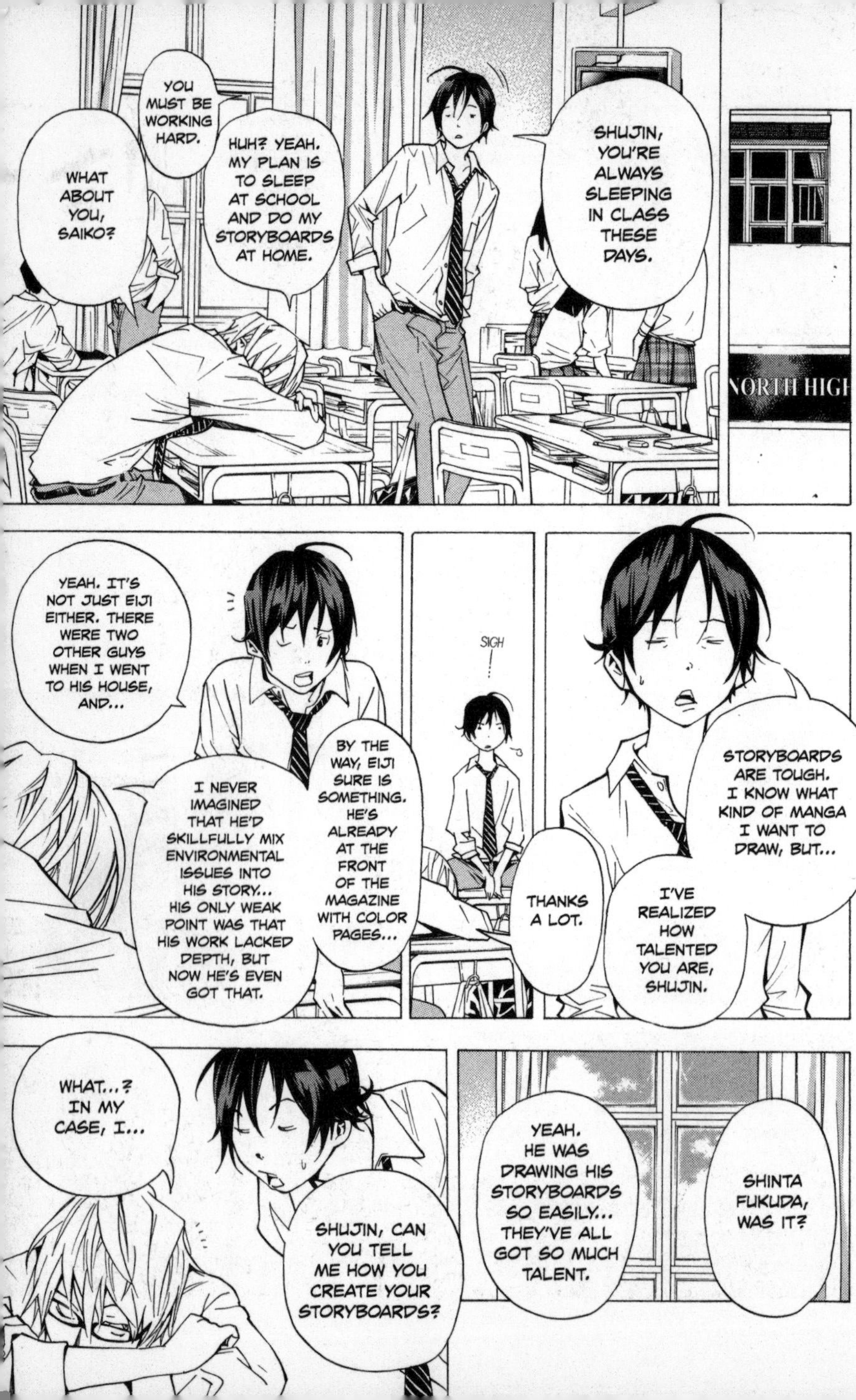
NORTH HIGH
SHUJIN, YOU'RE ALWAYS SLEEPING IN CLASS THESE DAYS.
HUH? YEAH. MY PLAN IS TO SLEEP AT SCHOOL AND DO MY STORYBOARDS AT HOME.
YOU MUST BE WORKING HARD.
WHAT ABOUT YOU, SAIKO?
STORYBOARDS ARE TOUGH. I KNOW WHAT KIND OF MANGA I WANT TO DRAW, BUT...
I'VE REALIZED HOW TALENTED YOU ARE, SHUJIN.
THANKS A LOT.
SIGH
BY THE WAY, EIJI SURE IS SOMETHING. HE'S ALREADY AT THE FRONT OF THE MAGAZINE WITH COLOR PAGES...
I NEVER IMAGINED THAT HE'D SKILLFULLY MIX ENVIRONMENTAL ISSUES INTO HIS STORY... HIS ONLY WEAK POINT WAS THAT HIS WORK LACKED DEPTH, BUT NOW HE'S EVEN GOT THAT.
YEAH. IT'S NOT JUST EIJI EITHER. THERE WERE TWO OTHER GUYS WHEN I WENT TO HIS HOUSE, AND...
SHINTA FUKUDA, WAS IT?
YEAH. HE WAS DRAWING HIS STORYBOARDS SO EASILY... THEY'VE ALL GOT SO MUCH TALENT.
SHUJIN, CAN YOU TELL ME HOW YOU CREATE YOUR STORYBOARDS?
WHAT...? IN MY CASE, I...

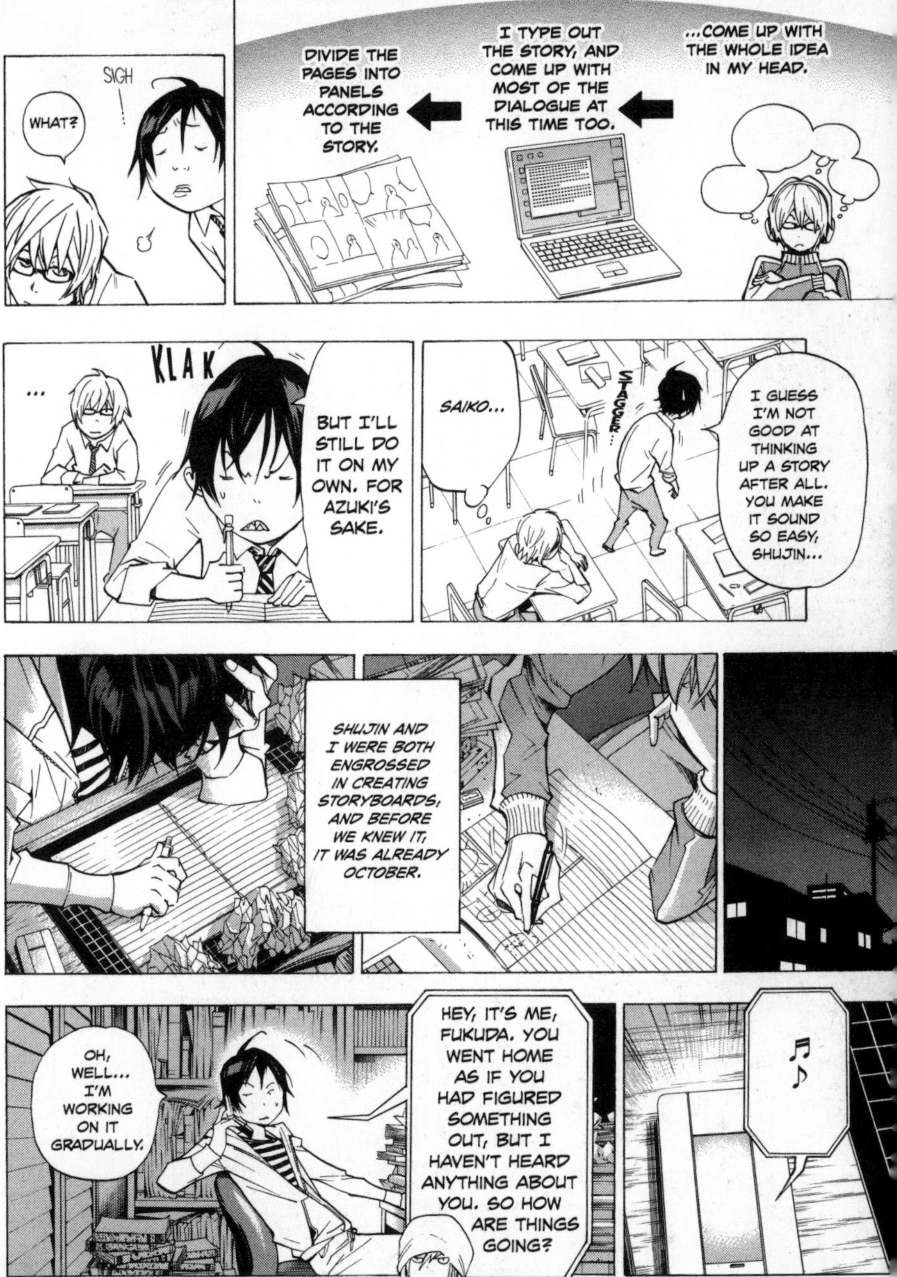

...COME UP WITH THE WHOLE IDEA IN MY HEAD.
I TYPE OUT THE STORY, AND COME UP WITH MOST OF THE DIALOGUE AT THIS TIME TOO.
DIVIDE THE PAGES INTO PANELS ACCORDING TO THE STORY.
SIGH
WHAT?
I GUESS I'M NOT GOOD AT THINKING UP A STORY AFTER ALL. YOU MAKE IT SOUND SO EASY, SHUJIN...
STAGGER...
SAIKO...
BUT I'LL STILL DO IT ON MY OWN. FOR AZUKI'S SAKE.
KLAK
...
SHUJIN AND I WERE BOTH ENGROSSED IN CREATING STORYBOARDS, AND BEFORE WE KNEW IT, IT WAS ALREADY OCTOBER.
♪ ♪
HEY, IT'S ME, FUKUDA. YOU WENT HOME AS IF YOU HAD FIGURED SOMETHING OUT, BUT I HAVEN'T HEARD ANYTHING ABOUT YOU. SO HOW ARE THINGS GOING?
OH, WELL... I'M WORKING ON IT GRADUALLY.

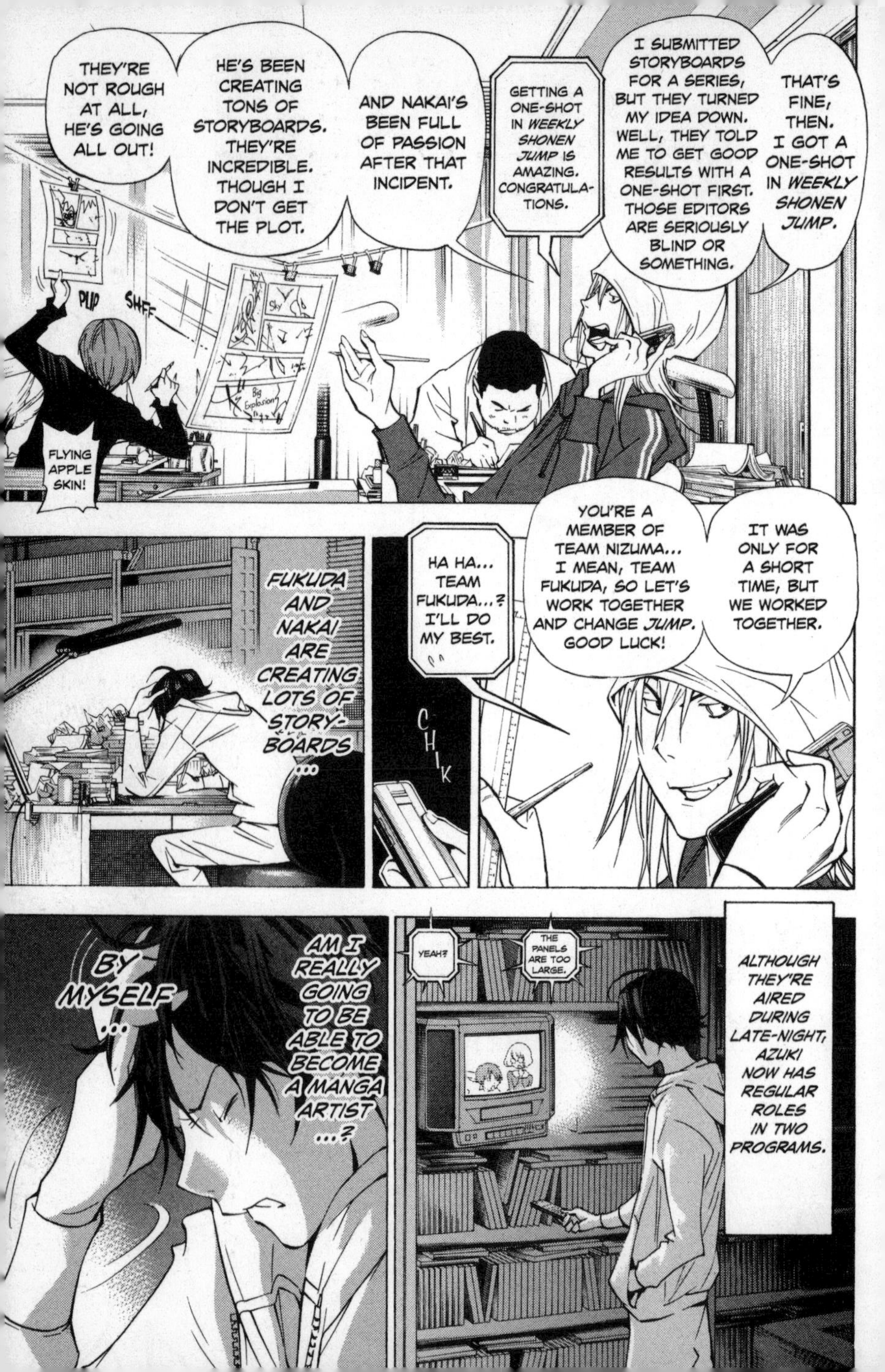
THAT'S FINE, THEN. I GOT A ONE-SHOT IN *WEEKLY SHONEN JUMP*.
I SUBMITTED STORYBOARDS FOR A SERIES, BUT THEY TURNED MY IDEA DOWN. WELL, THEY TOLD ME TO GET GOOD RESULTS WITH A ONE-SHOT FIRST. THOSE EDITORS ARE SERIOUSLY BLIND OR SOMETHING.
GETTING A ONE-SHOT IN *WEEKLY SHONEN JUMP* IS AMAZING. CONGRATULATIONS.
AND NAKAI'S BEEN FULL OF PASSION AFTER THAT INCIDENT.
HE'S BEEN CREATING TONS OF STORYBOARDS. THEY'RE INCREDIBLE. THOUGH I DON'T GET THE PLOT.
THEY'RE NOT ROUGH AT ALL, HE'S GOING ALL OUT!
Sky
Big Explosion
SHFF
PLIP
FLYING APPLE SKIN!
IT WAS ONLY FOR A SHORT TIME, BUT WE WORKED TOGETHER.
YOU'RE A MEMBER OF TEAM NIZUMA... I MEAN, TEAM FUKUDA, SO LET'S WORK TOGETHER AND CHANGE *JUMP*. GOOD LUCK!
HA HA... TEAM FUKUDA...? I'LL DO MY BEST.
CHIK
FUKUDA AND NAKAI ARE CREATING LOTS OF STORYBOARDS...
ALTHOUGH THEY'RE AIRED DURING LATE-NIGHT, AZUKI NOW HAS REGULAR ROLES IN TWO PROGRAMS.
THE PANELS ARE TOO LARGE.
YEAH?
AM I REALLY GOING TO BE ABLE TO BECOME A MANGA ARTIST...?
BY MYSELF...

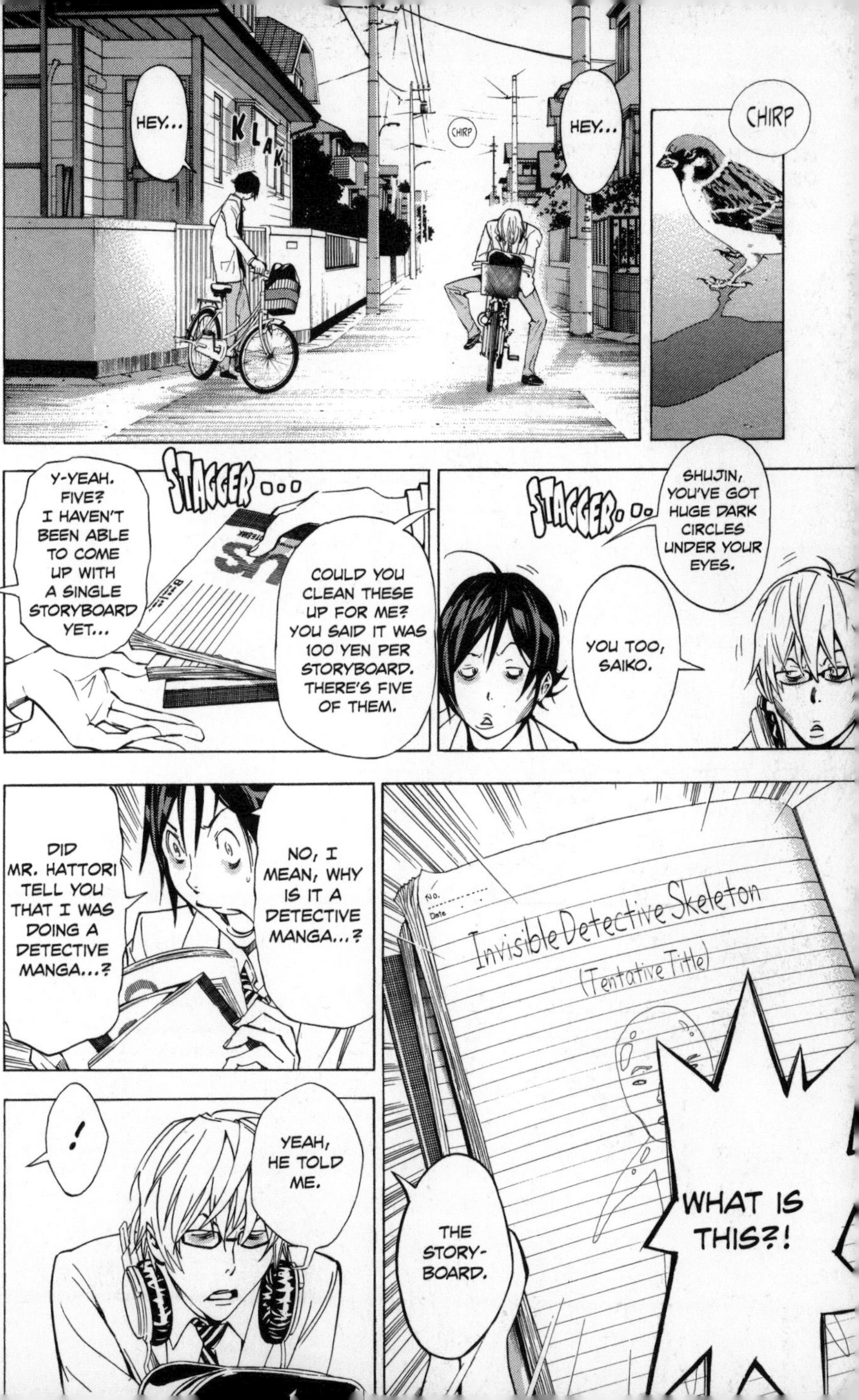
CHIRP
HEY...
CHIRP
KLAK
HEY...
SHUJIN, YOU'VE GOT HUGE DARK CIRCLES UNDER YOUR EYES.
STAGGER
YOU TOO, SAIKO.
COULD YOU CLEAN THESE UP FOR ME? YOU SAID IT WAS 100 YEN PER STORYBOARD. THERE'S FIVE OF THEM.
STAGGER
Y-YEAH. FIVE? I HAVEN'T BEEN ABLE TO COME UP WITH A SINGLE STORYBOARD YET...
Invisible Detective Skeleton
(Tentative Title)
WHAT IS THIS?!
THE STORY-BOARD.
NO, I MEAN, WHY IS IT A DETECTIVE MANGA...?
DID MR. HATTORI TELL YOU THAT I WAS DOING A DETECTIVE MANGA...?
YEAH, HE TOLD ME.
!

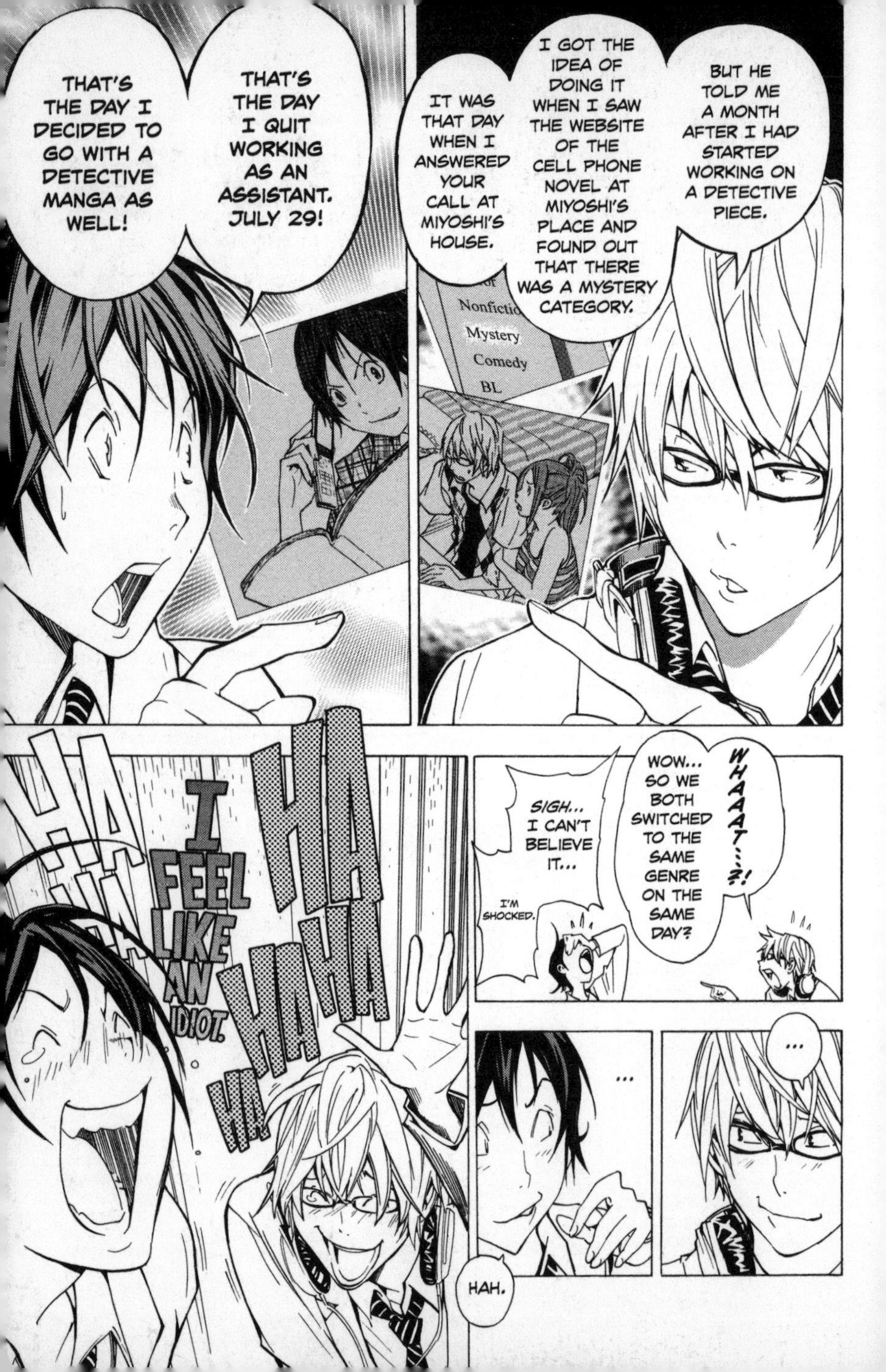
BUT HE TOLD ME A MONTH AFTER I HAD STARTED WORKING ON A DETECTIVE PIECE.
I GOT THE IDEA OF DOING IT WHEN I SAW THE WEBSITE OF THE CELL PHONE NOVEL AT MIYOSHI'S PLACE AND FOUND OUT THAT THERE WAS A MYSTERY CATEGORY.
IT WAS THAT DAY WHEN I ANSWERED YOUR CALL AT MIYOSHI'S HOUSE.
Nonfictio
Mystery
Comedy
BL
THAT'S THE DAY I QUIT WORKING AS AN ASSISTANT. JULY 29!
THAT'S THE DAY I DECIDED TO GO WITH A DETECTIVE MANGA AS WELL!
WHAAAAT...?!
WOW... SO WE BOTH SWITCHED TO THE SAME GENRE ON THE SAME DAY?
SIGH... I CAN'T BELIEVE IT...
I'M SHOCKED.
...
...
HA
HAHA
I FEEL LIKE AN IDIOT.
HAH.

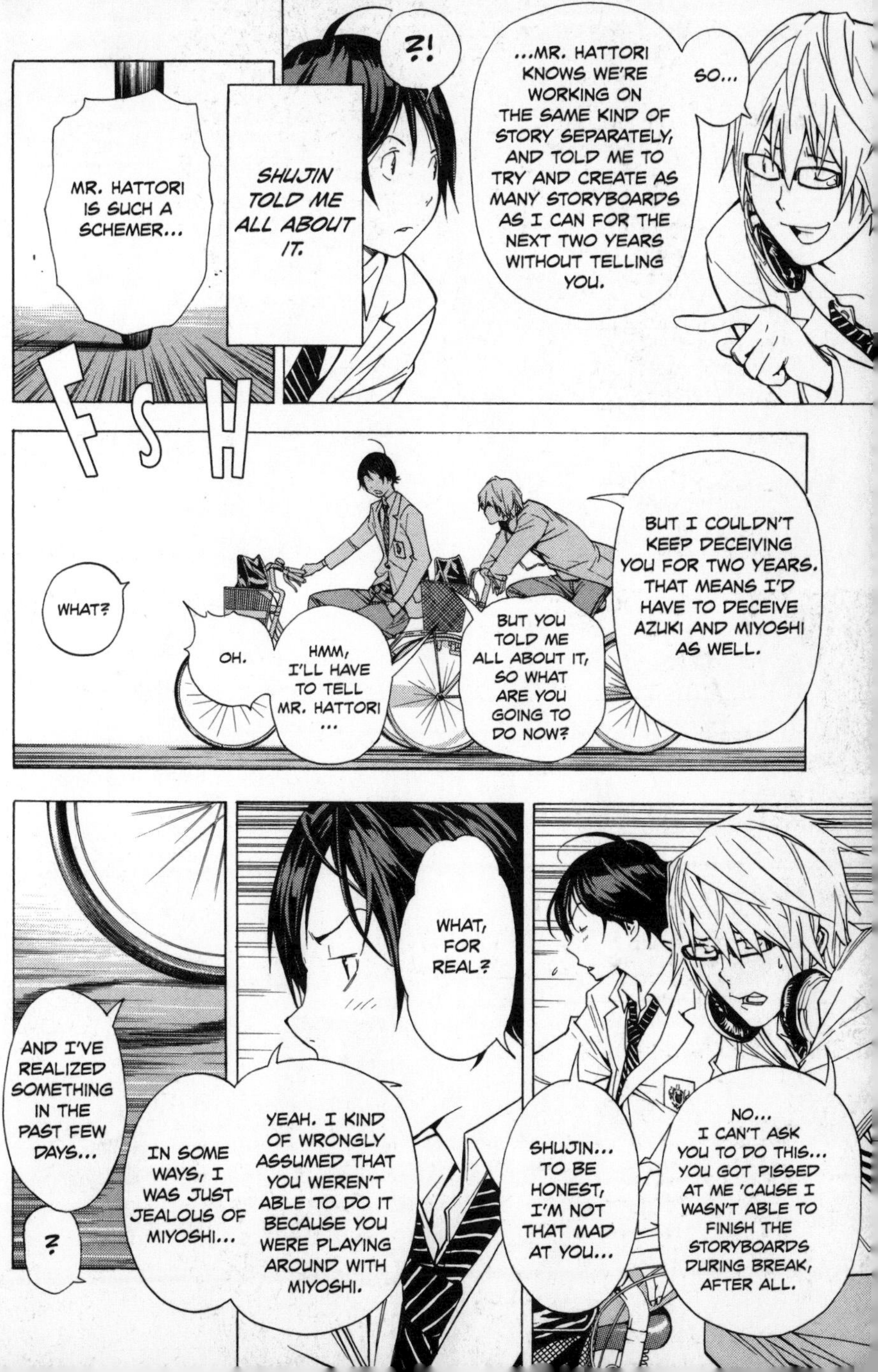
SO...
...MR. HATTORI KNOWS WE'RE WORKING ON THE SAME KIND OF STORY SEPARATELY, AND TOLD ME TO TRY AND CREATE AS MANY STORYBOARDS AS I CAN FOR THE NEXT TWO YEARS WITHOUT TELLING YOU.
?!
SHUJIN TOLD ME ALL ABOUT IT.
MR. HATTORI IS SUCH A SCHEMER...
FSH
BUT I COULDN'T KEEP DECEIVING YOU FOR TWO YEARS. THAT MEANS I'D HAVE TO DECEIVE AZUKI AND MIYOSHI AS WELL.
BUT YOU TOLD ME ALL ABOUT IT, SO WHAT ARE YOU GOING TO DO NOW?
HMM, I'LL HAVE TO TELL MR. HATTORI...
OH.
WHAT?
NO... I CAN'T ASK YOU TO DO THIS... YOU GOT PISSED AT ME 'CAUSE I WASN'T ABLE TO FINISH THE STORYBOARDS DURING BREAK, AFTER ALL.
SHUJIN... TO BE HONEST, I'M NOT THAT MAD AT YOU...
WHAT, FOR REAL?
YEAH. I KIND OF WRONGLY ASSUMED THAT YOU WEREN'T ABLE TO DO IT BECAUSE YOU WERE PLAYING AROUND WITH MIYOSHI.
IN SOME WAYS, I WAS JUST JEALOUS OF MIYOSHI...
AND I'VE REALIZED SOMETHING IN THE PAST FEW DAYS...
?

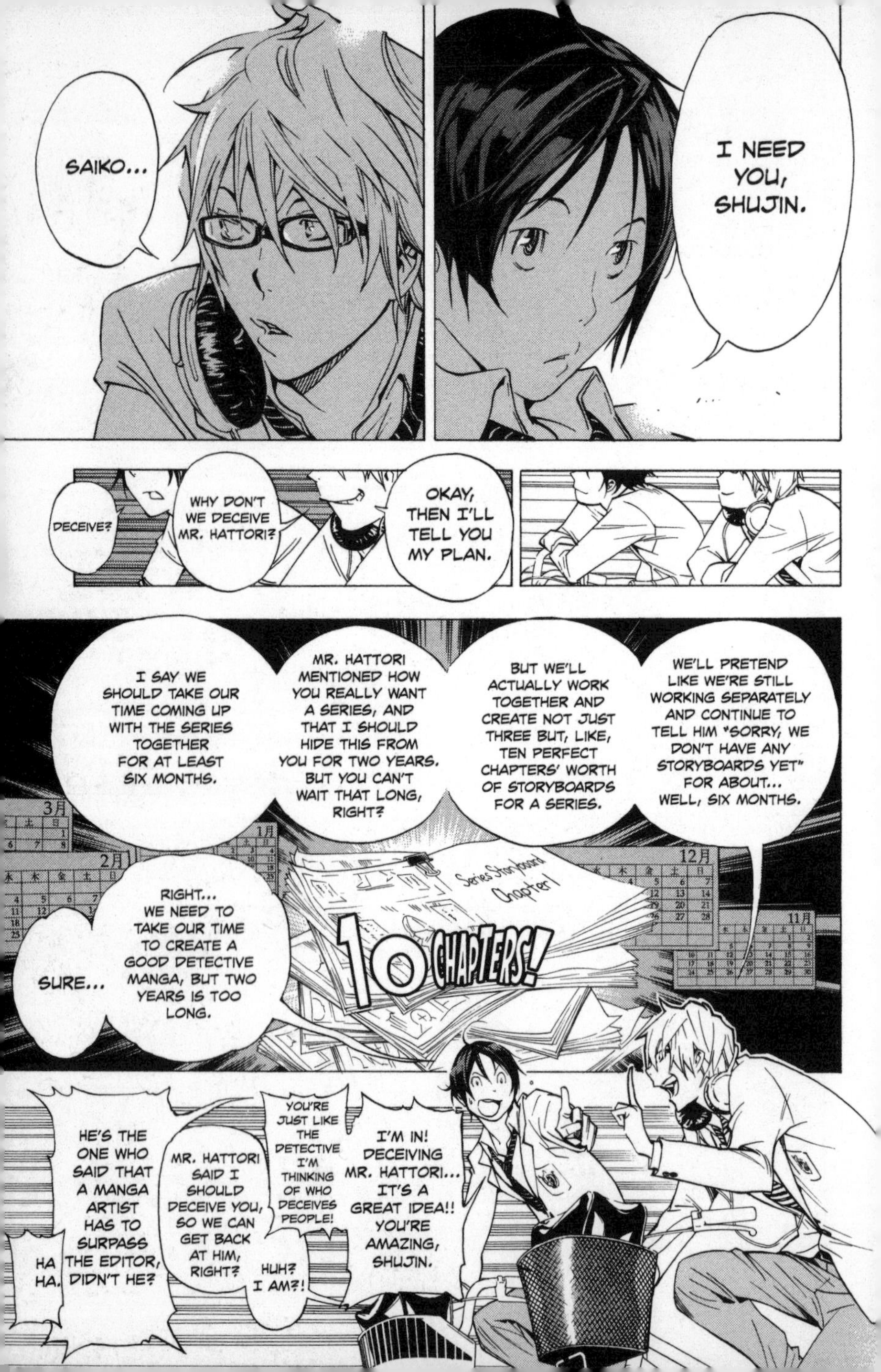
I NEED YOU, SHUJIN.
...
SAIKO...
OKAY, THEN I'LL TELL YOU MY PLAN.
WHY DON'T WE DECEIVE MR. HATTORI?
DECEIVE?
WE'LL PRETEND LIKE WE'RE STILL WORKING SEPARATELY AND CONTINUE TO TELL HIM "SORRY, WE DON'T HAVE ANY STORYBOARDS YET" FOR ABOUT... WELL, SIX MONTHS.
BUT WE'LL ACTUALLY WORK TOGETHER AND CREATE NOT JUST THREE BUT, LIKE, TEN PERFECT CHAPTERS' WORTH OF STORYBOARDS FOR A SERIES.
MR. HATTORI MENTIONED HOW YOU REALLY WANT A SERIES, AND THAT I SHOULD HIDE THIS FROM YOU FOR TWO YEARS. BUT YOU CAN'T WAIT THAT LONG, RIGHT?
I SAY WE SHOULD TAKE OUR TIME COMING UP WITH THE SERIES TOGETHER FOR AT LEAST SIX MONTHS.
Series Storyboard Chapter 1
10 CHAPTERS!
RIGHT... WE NEED TO TAKE OUR TIME TO CREATE A GOOD DETECTIVE MANGA, BUT TWO YEARS IS TOO LONG.
SURE...
I'M IN! DECEIVING MR. HATTORI... IT'S A GREAT IDEA!! YOU'RE AMAZING, SHUJIN.
YOU'RE JUST LIKE THE DETECTIVE I'M THINKING OF WHO DECEIVES PEOPLE!
HUH? I AM?!
MR. HATTORI SAID I SHOULD DECEIVE YOU, SO WE CAN GET BACK AT HIM, RIGHT?
HE'S THE ONE WHO SAID THAT A MANGA ARTIST HAS TO SURPASS THE EDITOR, DIDN'T HE?
HA HA.

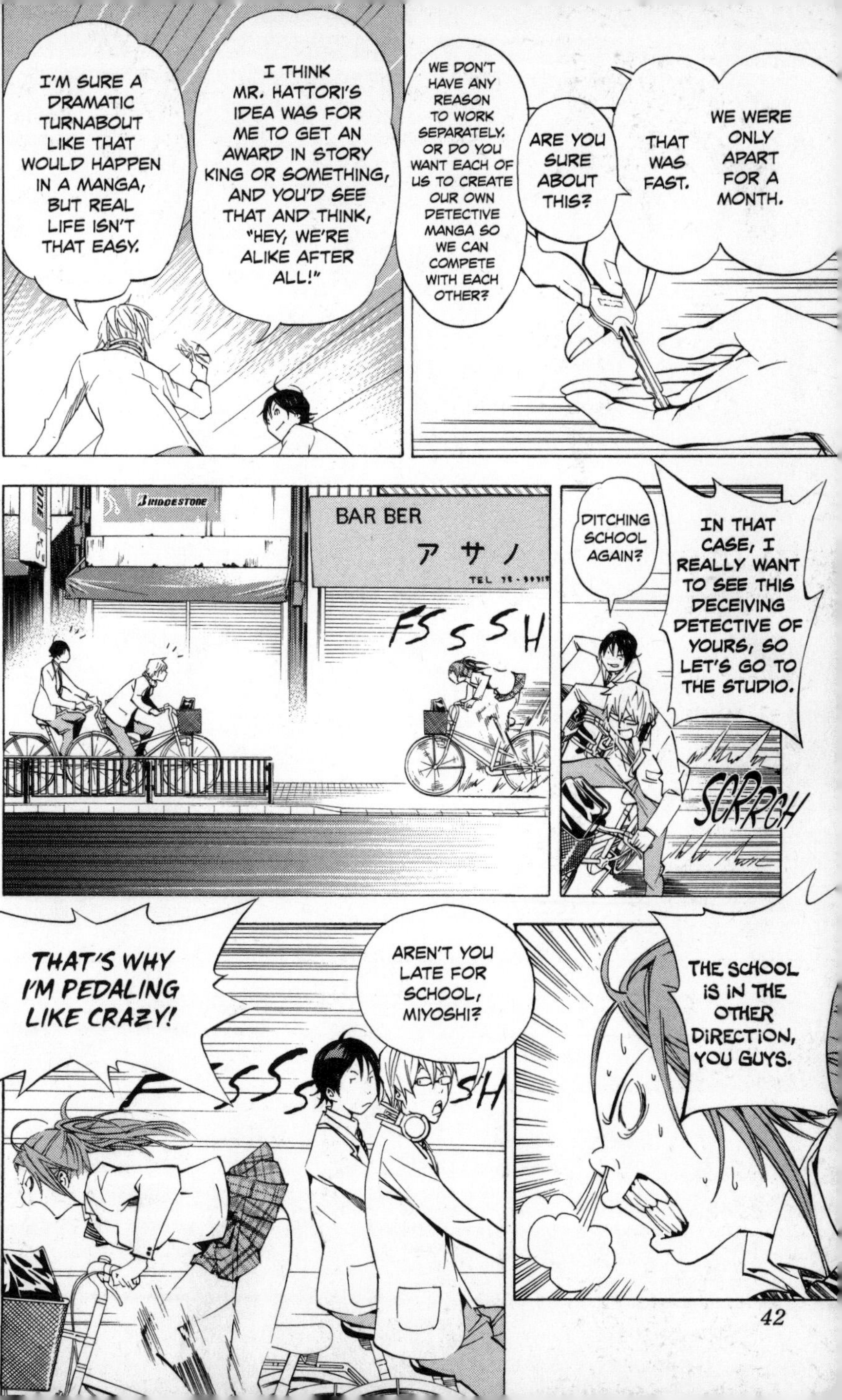
WE WERE ONLY APART FOR A MONTH.
THAT WAS FAST.
ARE YOU SURE ABOUT THIS?
WE DON'T HAVE ANY REASON TO WORK SEPARATELY. OR DO YOU WANT EACH OF US TO CREATE OUR OWN DETECTIVE MANGA SO WE CAN COMPETE WITH EACH OTHER?
I THINK MR. HATTORI'S IDEA WAS FOR ME TO GET AN AWARD IN STORY KING OR SOMETHING, AND YOU'D SEE THAT AND THINK, "HEY, WE'RE ALIKE AFTER ALL!"
I'M SURE A DRAMATIC TURNABOUT LIKE THAT WOULD HAPPEN IN A MANGA, BUT REAL LIFE ISN'T THAT EASY.
IN THAT CASE, I REALLY WANT TO SEE THIS DECEIVING DETECTIVE OF YOURS, SO LET'S GO TO THE STUDIO.
DITCHING SCHOOL AGAIN?
SCRRGH
BAR BER
アサノ
FSSSH
THE SCHOOL IS IN THE OTHER DIRECTION, YOU GUYS.
AREN'T YOU LATE FOR SCHOOL, MIYOSHI?
THAT'S WHY I'M PEDALING LIKE CRAZY!
FSSSSSH

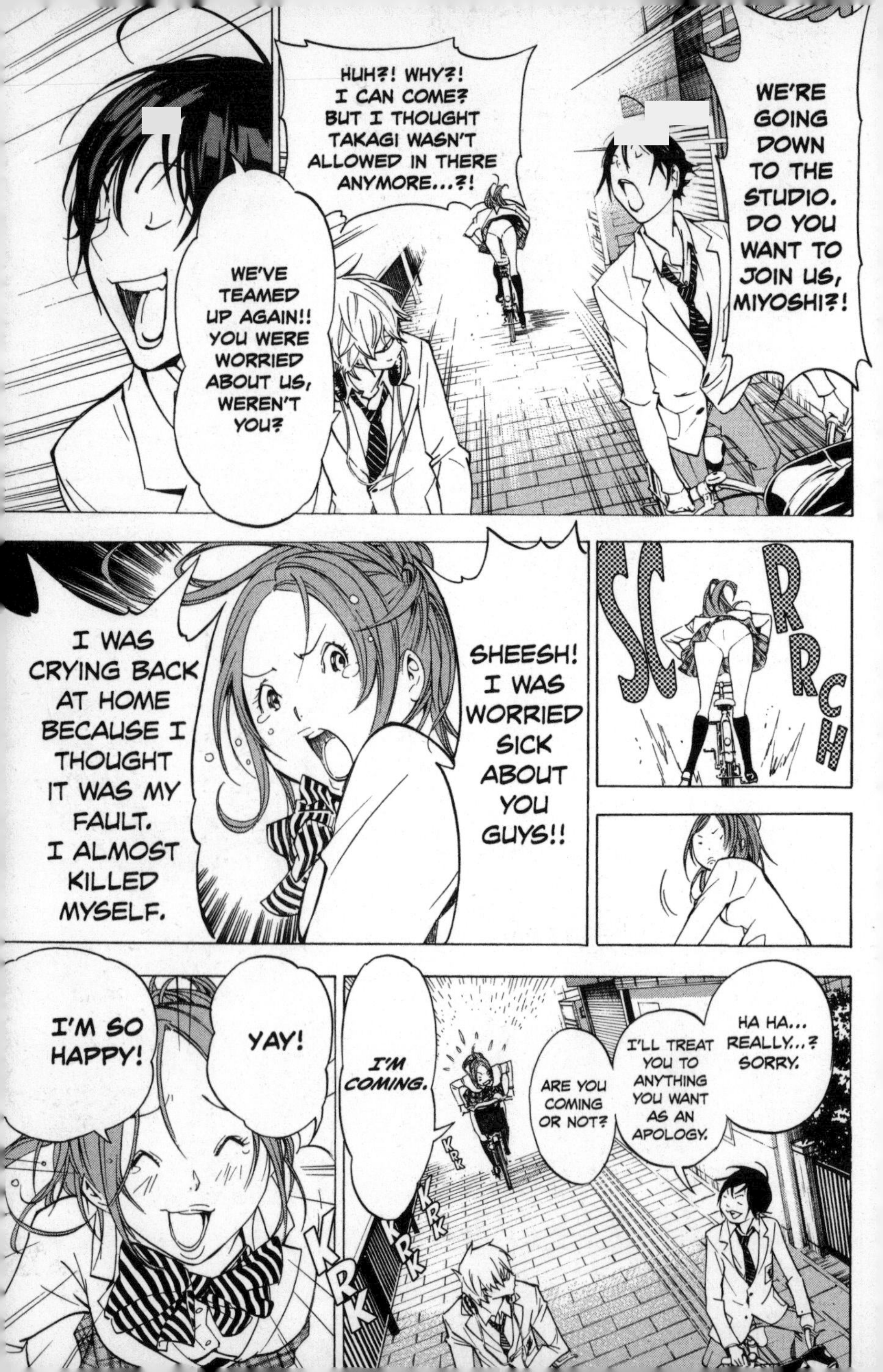
WE'RE GOING DOWN TO THE STUDIO. DO YOU WANT TO JOIN US, MIYOSHI?!
HUH?! WHY?! I CAN COME? BUT I THOUGHT TAKAGI WASN'T ALLOWED IN THERE ANYMORE...?!
WE'VE TEAMED UP AGAIN!! YOU WERE WORRIED ABOUT US, WEREN'T YOU?
SCRRCH
SHEESH! I WAS WORRIED SICK ABOUT YOU GUYS!!
I WAS CRYING BACK AT HOME BECAUSE I THOUGHT IT WAS MY FAULT. I ALMOST KILLED MYSELF.
HA HA... REALLY...? SORRY.
I'LL TREAT YOU TO ANYTHING YOU WANT AS AN APOLOGY.
ARE YOU COMING OR NOT?
I'M COMING.
KRK
KRK KRK
KRK
YAY!
I'M SO HAPPY!

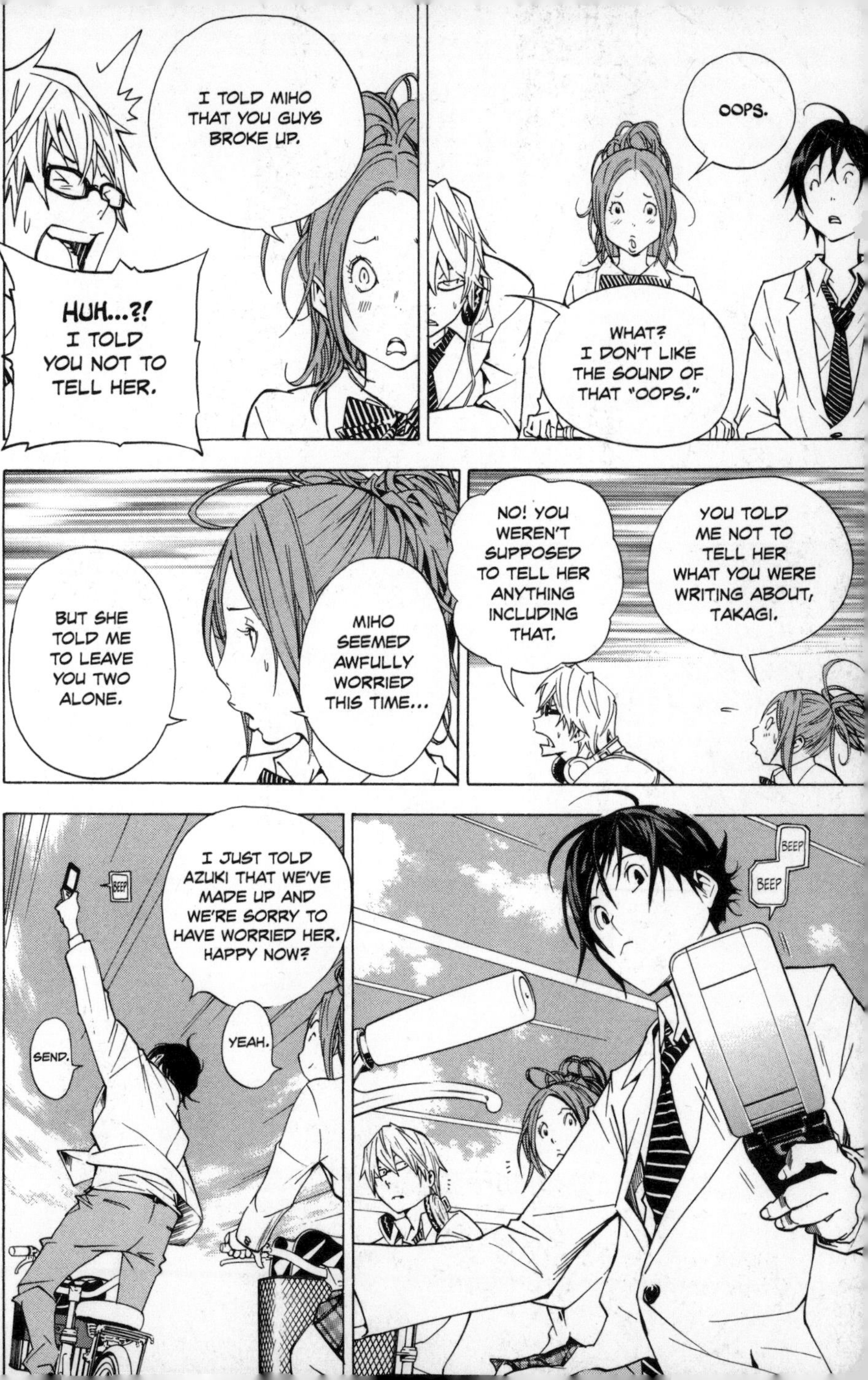
OOPS.
WHAT? I DON'T LIKE THE SOUND OF THAT "OOPS."
I TOLD MIHO THAT YOU GUYS BROKE UP.
HUH...?! I TOLD YOU NOT TO TELL HER.
YOU TOLD ME NOT TO TELL HER WHAT YOU WERE WRITING ABOUT, TAKAGI.
NO! YOU WEREN'T SUPPOSED TO TELL HER ANYTHING INCLUDING THAT.
MIHO SEEMED AWFULLY WORRIED THIS TIME...
BUT SHE TOLD ME TO LEAVE YOU TWO ALONE.
BEEP
BEEP
I JUST TOLD AZUKI THAT WE'VE MADE UP AND WE'RE SORRY TO HAVE WORRIED HER. HAPPY NOW?
YEAH.
SEND.
BEEP

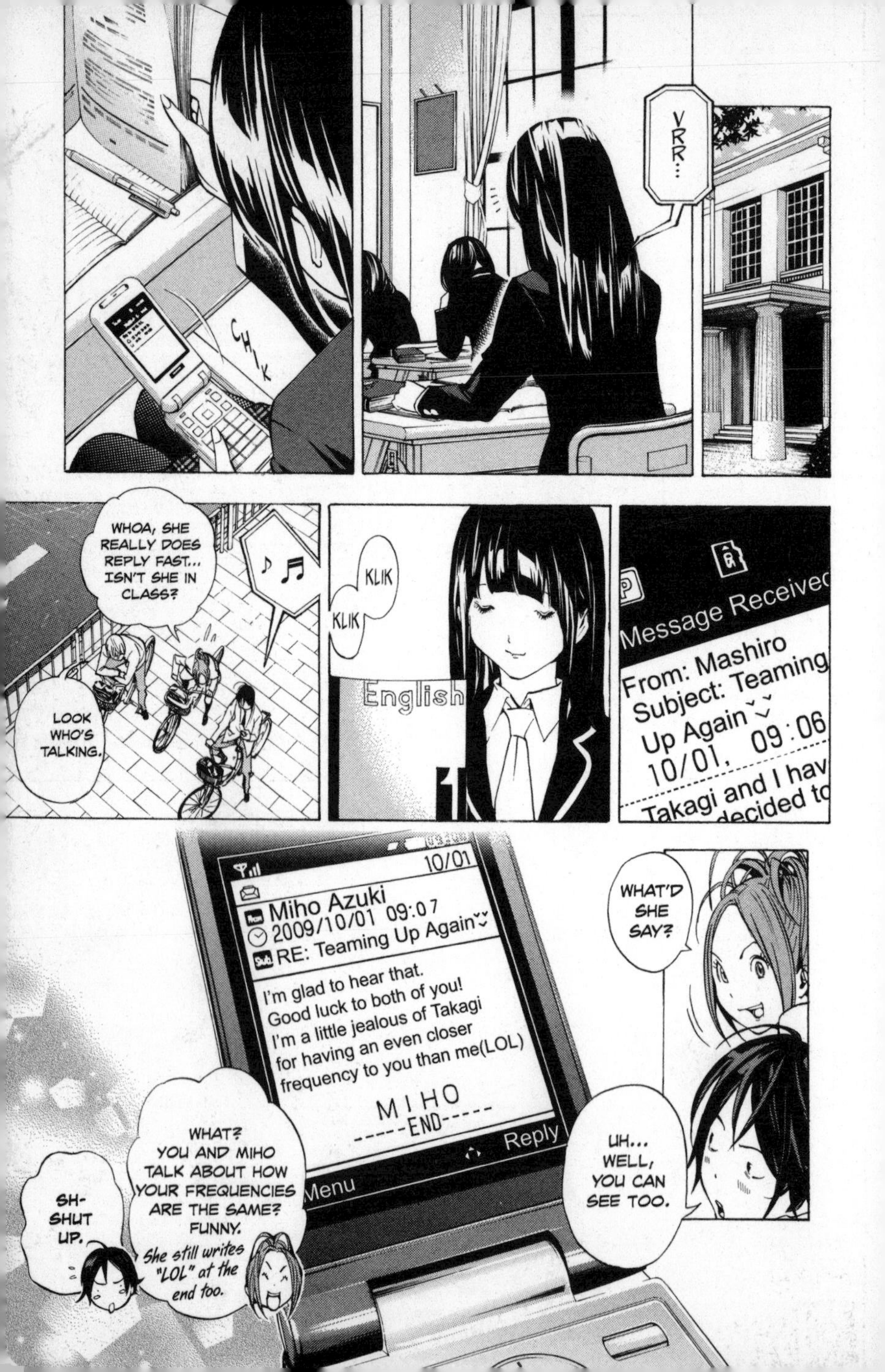
VRR...
CHIK
Message Received
From: Mashiro
Subject: Teaming Up Again
10/01, 09:06
Takagi and I hav
decided to
KLIK
KLIK
English
♪ ♬
WHOA, SHE REALLY DOES REPLY FAST... ISN'T SHE IN CLASS?
LOOK WHO'S TALKING.
WHAT'D SHE SAY?
10/01
Miho Azuki
2009/10/01 09:07
RE: Teaming Up Again
I'm glad to hear that.
Good luck to both of you!
I'm a little jealous of Takagi
for having an even closer
frequency to you than me(LOL)
MIHO
-----END-----
Reply
Menu
UH... WELL, YOU CAN SEE TOO.
WHAT? YOU AND MIHO TALK ABOUT HOW YOUR FREQUENCIES ARE THE SAME? FUNNY.
She still writes "LOL" at the end too.
SH-SHUT UP.

OHBA'S STORYBOARD

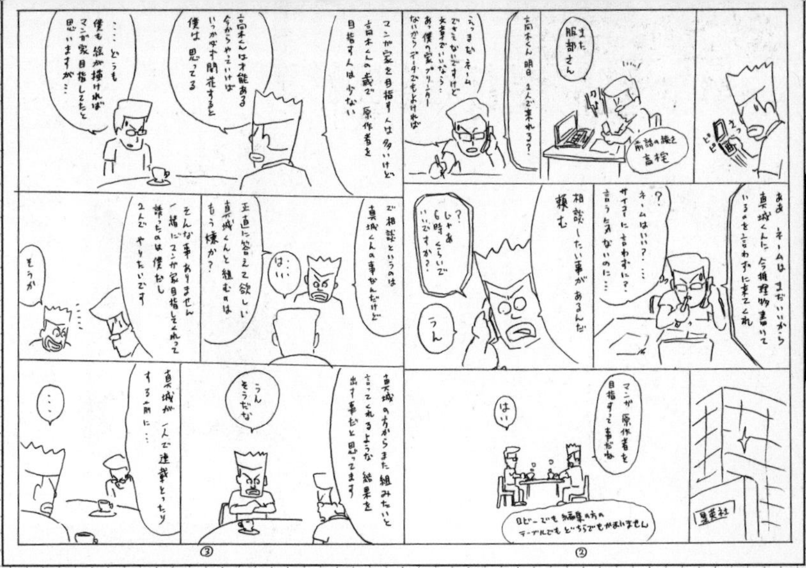
ピピ
また服部さん
前話の続き 高校
高木くん明日1人で来れる?
えっまだネームできてないですけど文章でいいなら…あっ僕の家プリンターないからデータでもよければ
ああ ネームはまだいいから真城くんに今推理物書いているのを言わずに来てくれ
?ネームはいい?…サイコーに言わずに? 言う気ないのに…
相談したい事があるんだ 頼む
?じゃあ6時くらいでいいですか?
うん
集英社
マンガ原作者を目指すって事だな
はい
ロビーででも編集の方のテーブルでもどっちでもかまいません
②
マンガ家を目指す人は多いけど高木くんの歳で原作者を目指す人は少ない
高木くんは才能ある今からやっていけばいつか必ず開花すると僕は思ってる
…どうも僕も絵が描ければマンガ家目指してたと思いますが…
で相談というのは真城くんの事なんだけど
はい
正直に答えて欲しい 真城くんと組むのはもう嫌か?
そんな事ありません 一緒にマンガ家目指そうと誘ったのは僕だし 2人でやりたいです
……
そうか
真城の方からまた組みたいと言ってくれるような結果を出す事だと思ってます
うん そうだな
真城が一人で連載とったりする前に…
…
③

OBATA'S STORYBOARD

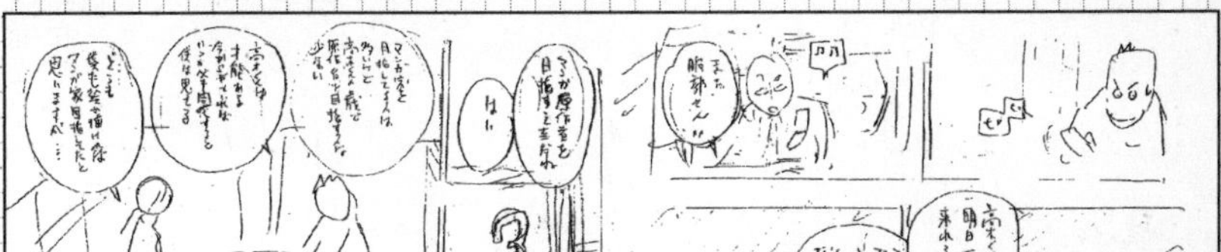

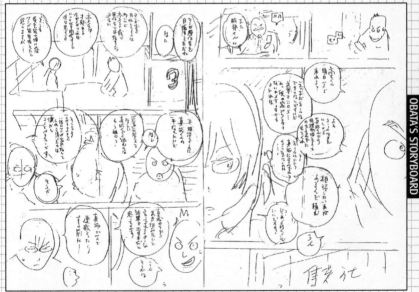

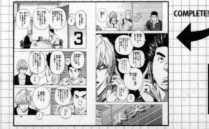

COMPLETE!

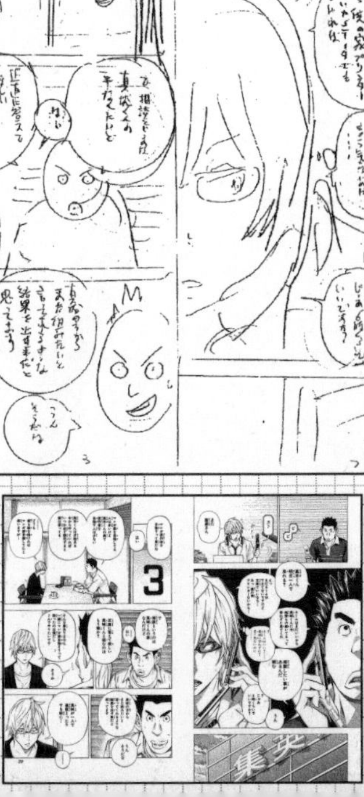

*CREATOR STORYBOARDS AND FINISHED PAGES IN JAPANESE

BAKUMAN。 vol.4

"Until the Final Draft Is Complete"

Chapter 27, pp. 28-29

CHAPTER 28
COOPERATION AND CONDITION

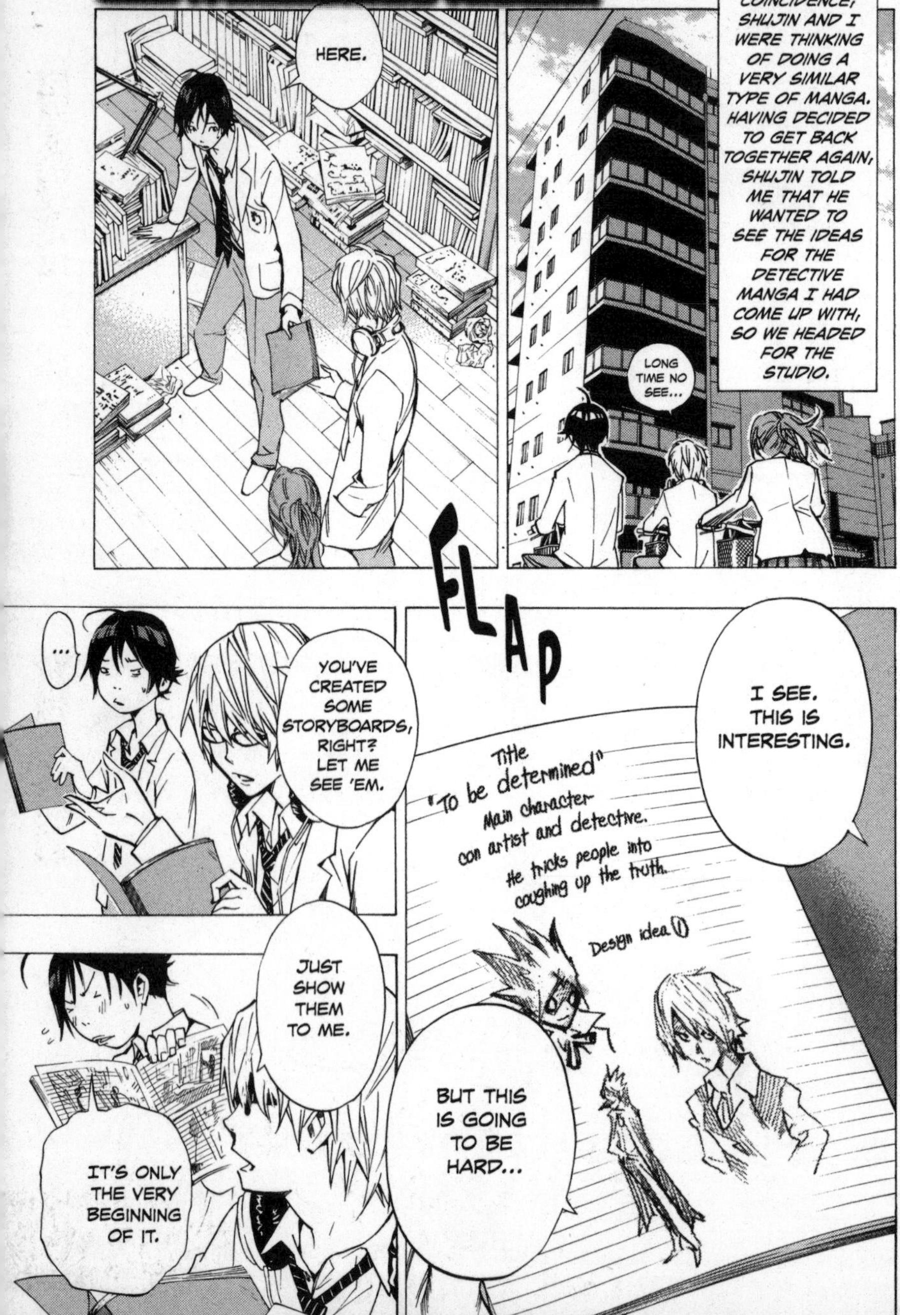
BY PURE COINCIDENCE, SHUJIN AND I WERE THINKING OF DOING A VERY SIMILAR TYPE OF MANGA. HAVING DECIDED TO GET BACK TOGETHER AGAIN, SHUJIN TOLD ME THAT HE WANTED TO SEE THE IDEAS FOR THE DETECTIVE MANGA I HAD COME UP WITH, SO WE HEADED FOR THE STUDIO.
LONG TIME NO SEE...
HERE.
FLAP
I SEE. THIS IS INTERESTING.
Title "To be determined"
Main character con artist and detective.
He tricks people into coughing up the truth.
Design idea ①
BUT THIS IS GOING TO BE HARD...
...
YOU'VE CREATED SOME STORYBOARDS, RIGHT? LET ME SEE 'EM.
JUST SHOW THEM TO ME.
IT'S ONLY THE VERY BEGINNING OF IT.

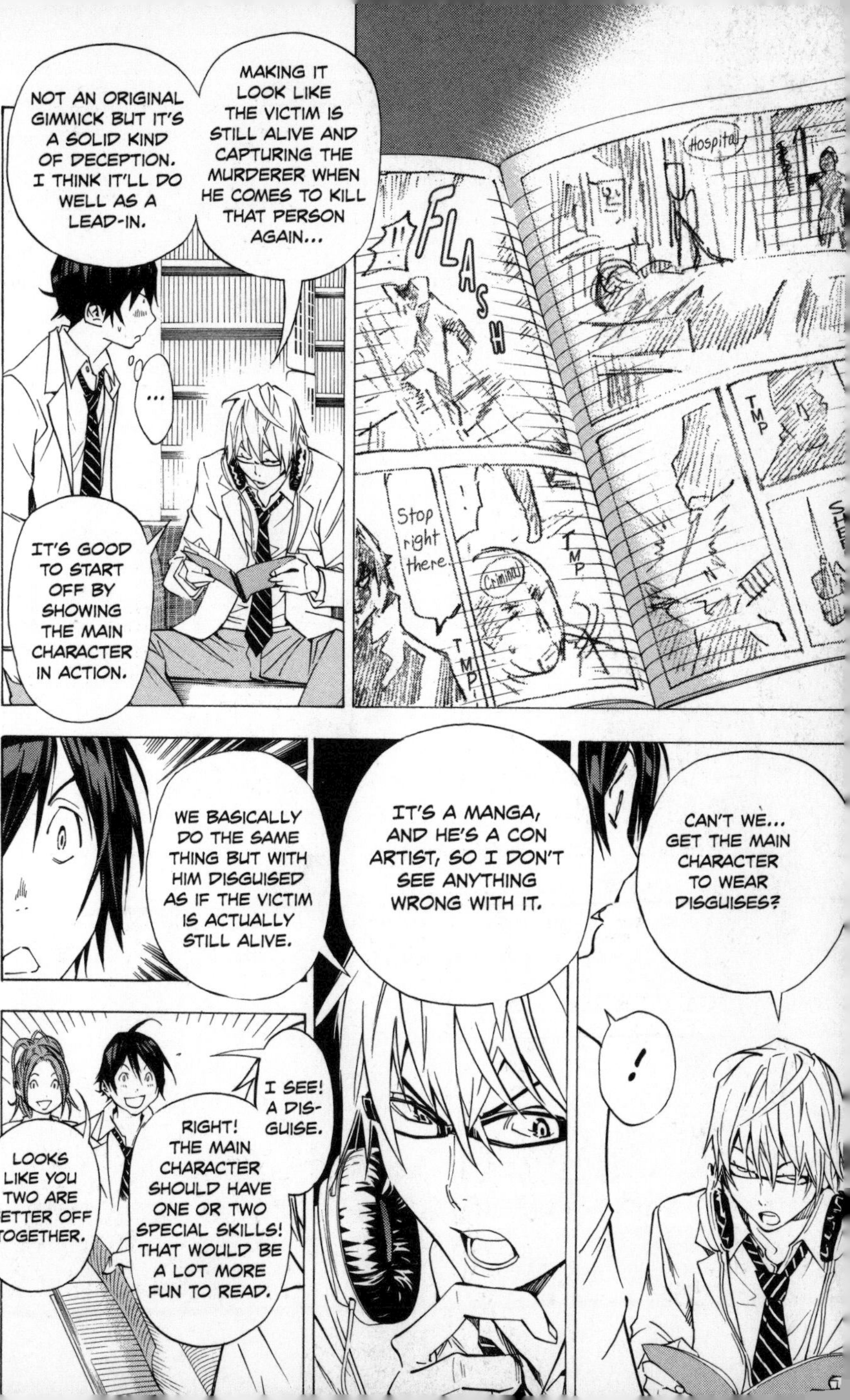
Hospital
FLASH
TMP
Stop right there.
TMP
TMP
MAKING IT LOOK LIKE THE VICTIM IS STILL ALIVE AND CAPTURING THE MURDERER WHEN HE COMES TO KILL THAT PERSON AGAIN...
NOT AN ORIGINAL GIMMICK BUT IT'S A SOLID KIND OF DECEPTION. I THINK IT'LL DO WELL AS A LEAD-IN.
...
IT'S GOOD TO START OFF BY SHOWING THE MAIN CHARACTER IN ACTION.
CAN'T WE... GET THE MAIN CHARACTER TO WEAR DISGUISES?
!
IT'S A MANGA, AND HE'S A CON ARTIST, SO I DON'T SEE ANYTHING WRONG WITH IT.
WE BASICALLY DO THE SAME THING BUT WITH HIM DISGUISED AS IF THE VICTIM IS ACTUALLY STILL ALIVE.
I SEE! A DIS-GUISE.
RIGHT! THE MAIN CHARACTER SHOULD HAVE ONE OR TWO SPECIAL SKILLS! THAT WOULD BE A LOT MORE FUN TO READ.
LOOKS LIKE YOU TWO ARE BETTER OFF TOGETHER.

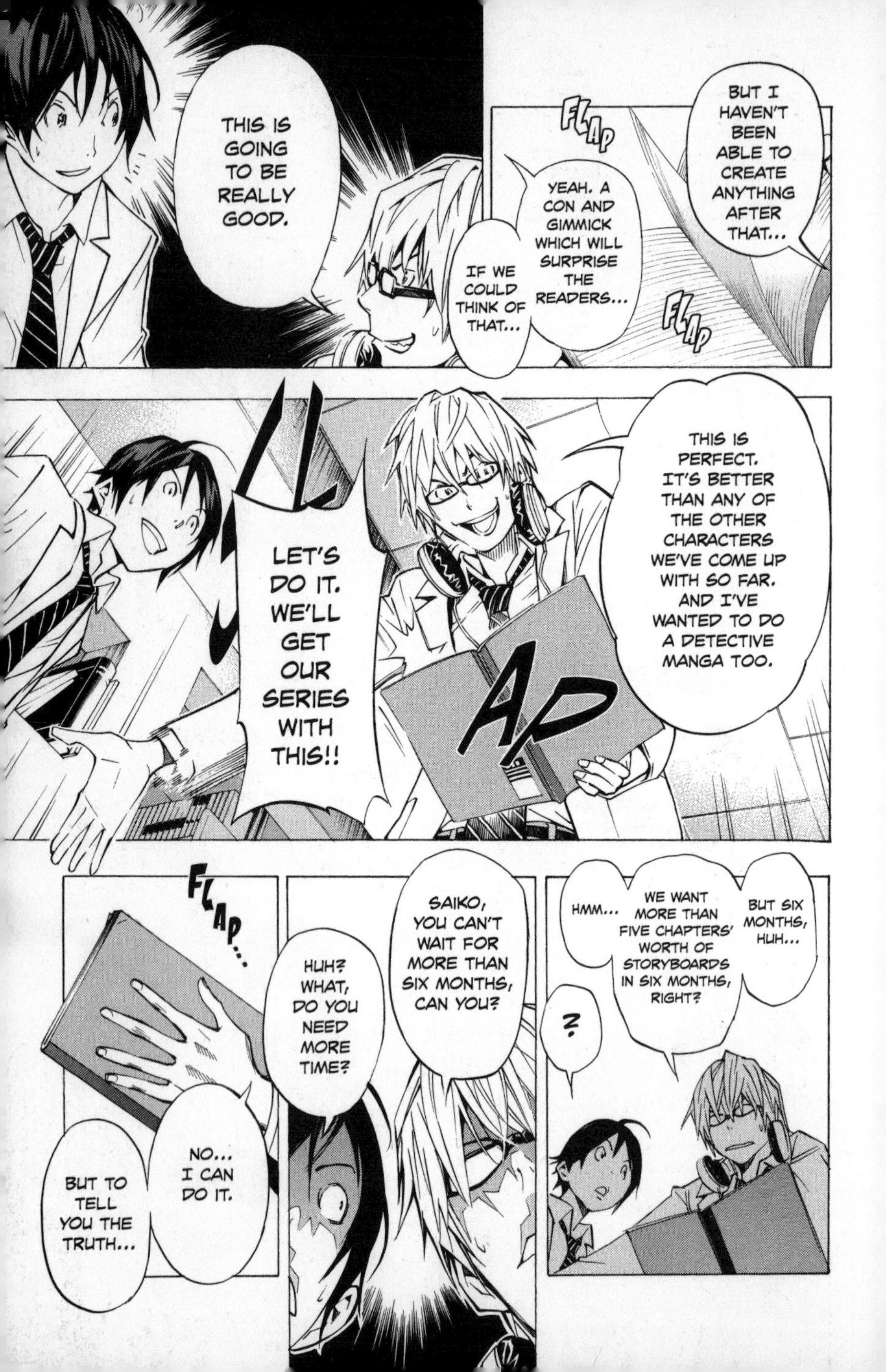
FLAP
BUT I HAVEN'T BEEN ABLE TO CREATE ANYTHING AFTER THAT...
FLAP
YEAH. A CON AND GIMMICK WHICH WILL SURPRISE THE READERS...
IF WE COULD THINK OF THAT...
THIS IS GOING TO BE REALLY GOOD.
THIS IS PERFECT. IT'S BETTER THAN ANY OF THE OTHER CHARACTERS WE'VE COME UP WITH SO FAR. AND I'VE WANTED TO DO A DETECTIVE MANGA TOO.
AP
LET'S DO IT. WE'LL GET OUR SERIES WITH THIS!!
BUT SIX MONTHS, HUH...
WE WANT MORE THAN FIVE CHAPTERS' WORTH OF STORYBOARDS IN SIX MONTHS, RIGHT?
HMM...
?
SAIKO, YOU CAN'T WAIT FOR MORE THAN SIX MONTHS, CAN YOU?
HUH? WHAT, DO YOU NEED MORE TIME?
NO... I CAN DO IT.
FLAP...
BUT TO TELL YOU THE TRUTH...

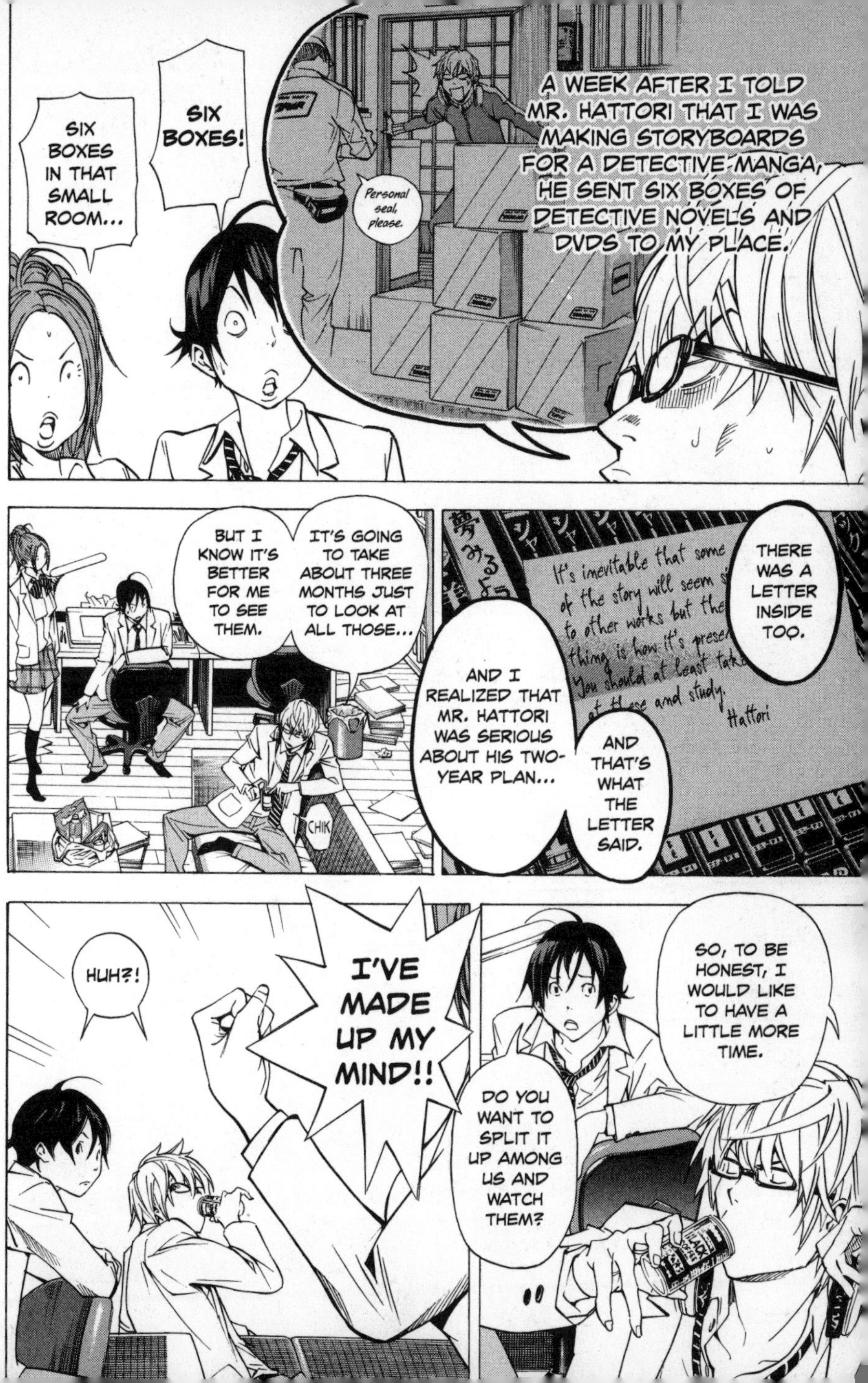
A WEEK AFTER I TOLD MR. HATTORI THAT I WAS MAKING STORYBOARDS FOR A DETECTIVE MANGA, HE SENT SIX BOXES OF DETECTIVE NOVELS AND DVDS TO MY PLACE.
Personal seal, please.
SIX BOXES!
SIX BOXES IN THAT SMALL ROOM...
THERE WAS A LETTER INSIDE TOO.
It's inevitable that some
of the story will seem si
to other works but the
thing is how it's prese
You should at least take
at these and study.
Hattori
AND THAT'S WHAT THE LETTER SAID.
AND I REALIZED THAT MR. HATTORI WAS SERIOUS ABOUT HIS TWO-YEAR PLAN...
IT'S GOING TO TAKE ABOUT THREE MONTHS JUST TO LOOK AT ALL THOSE...
BUT I KNOW IT'S BETTER FOR ME TO SEE THEM.
CHIK
SO, TO BE HONEST, I WOULD LIKE TO HAVE A LITTLE MORE TIME.
DO YOU WANT TO SPLIT IT UP AMONG US AND WATCH THEM?
I'VE MADE UP MY MIND!!
HUH?!

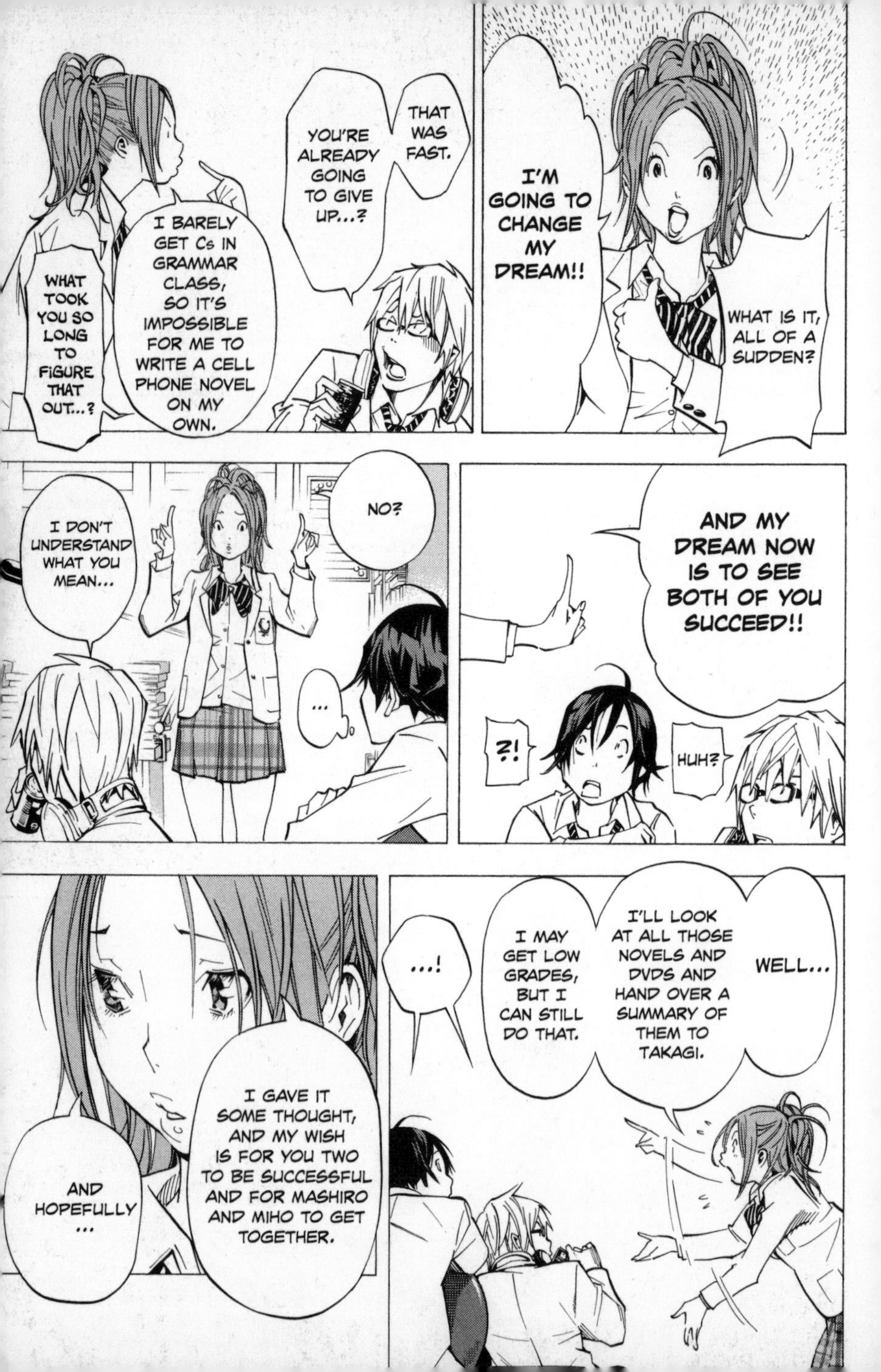
I'M GOING TO CHANGE MY DREAM!!
WHAT IS IT, ALL OF A SUDDEN?
THAT WAS FAST.
YOU'RE ALREADY GOING TO GIVE UP...?
I BARELY GET Cs IN GRAMMAR CLASS, SO IT'S IMPOSSIBLE FOR ME TO WRITE A CELL PHONE NOVEL ON MY OWN.
WHAT TOOK YOU SO LONG TO FIGURE THAT OUT...?
AND MY DREAM NOW IS TO SEE BOTH OF YOU SUCCEED!!
HUH?
?!
NO?
I DON'T UNDERSTAND WHAT YOU MEAN...
...
WELL...
I'LL LOOK AT ALL THOSE NOVELS AND DVDS AND HAND OVER A SUMMARY OF THEM TO TAKAGI.
I MAY GET LOW GRADES, BUT I CAN STILL DO THAT.
...!
I GAVE IT SOME THOUGHT, AND MY WISH IS FOR YOU TWO TO BE SUCCESSFUL AND FOR MASHIRO AND MIHO TO GET TOGETHER.
AND HOPEFULLY ...

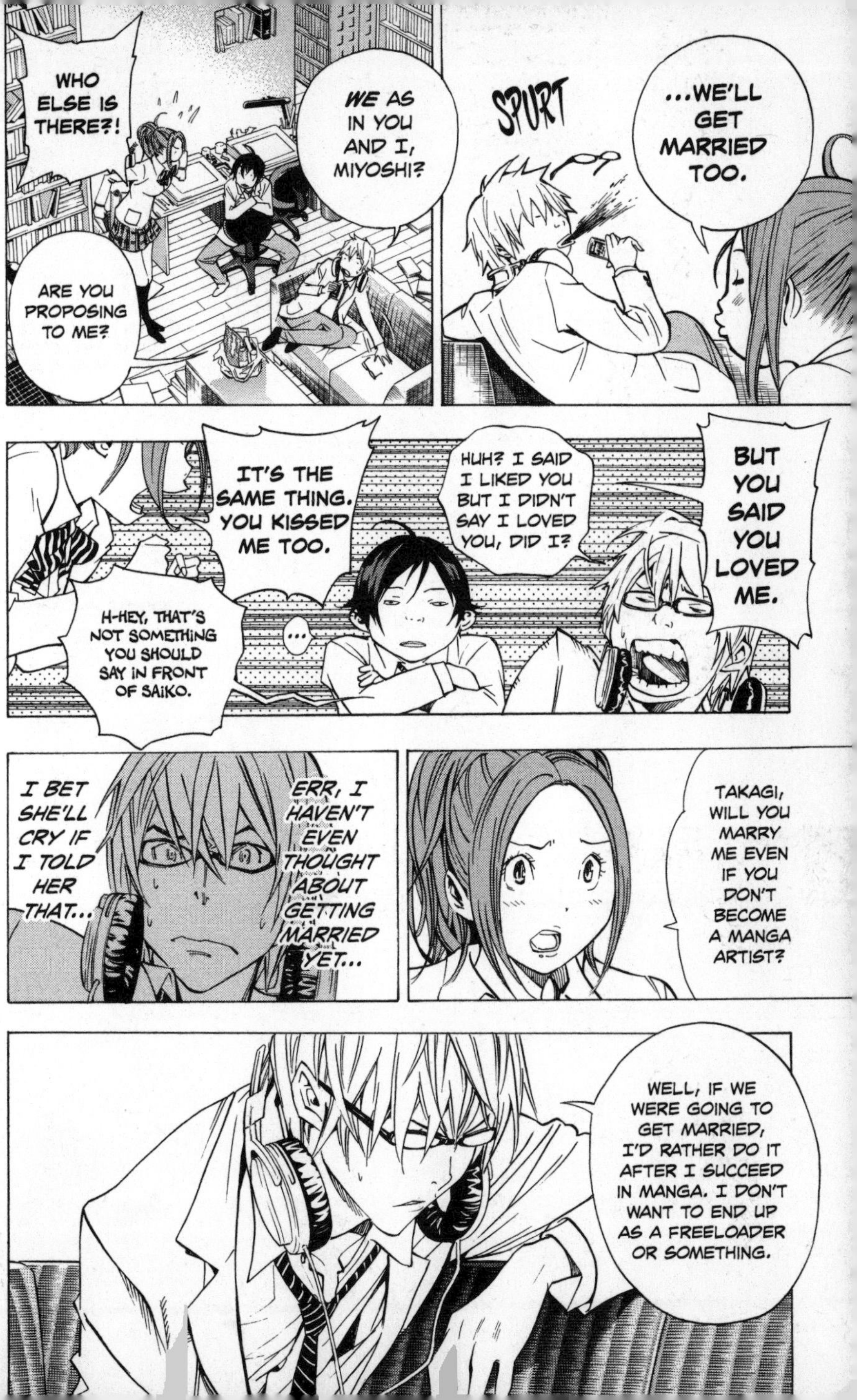
...WE'LL GET MARRIED TOO.
SPURT
WE AS IN YOU AND I, MIYOSHI?
WHO ELSE IS THERE?!
ARE YOU PROPOSING TO ME?
BUT YOU SAID YOU LOVED ME.
HUH? I SAID I LIKED YOU BUT I DIDN'T SAY I LOVED YOU, DID I?
IT'S THE SAME THING. YOU KISSED ME TOO.
...
H-HEY, THAT'S NOT SOMETHING YOU SHOULD SAY IN FRONT OF SAIKO.
TAKAGI, WILL YOU MARRY ME EVEN IF YOU DON'T BECOME A MANGA ARTIST?
ERR, I HAVEN'T EVEN THOUGHT ABOUT GETTING MARRIED YET...
I BET SHE'LL CRY IF I TOLD HER THAT...
WELL, IF WE WERE GOING TO GET MARRIED, I'D RATHER DO IT AFTER I SUCCEED IN MANGA. I DON'T WANT TO END UP AS A FREELOADER OR SOMETHING.

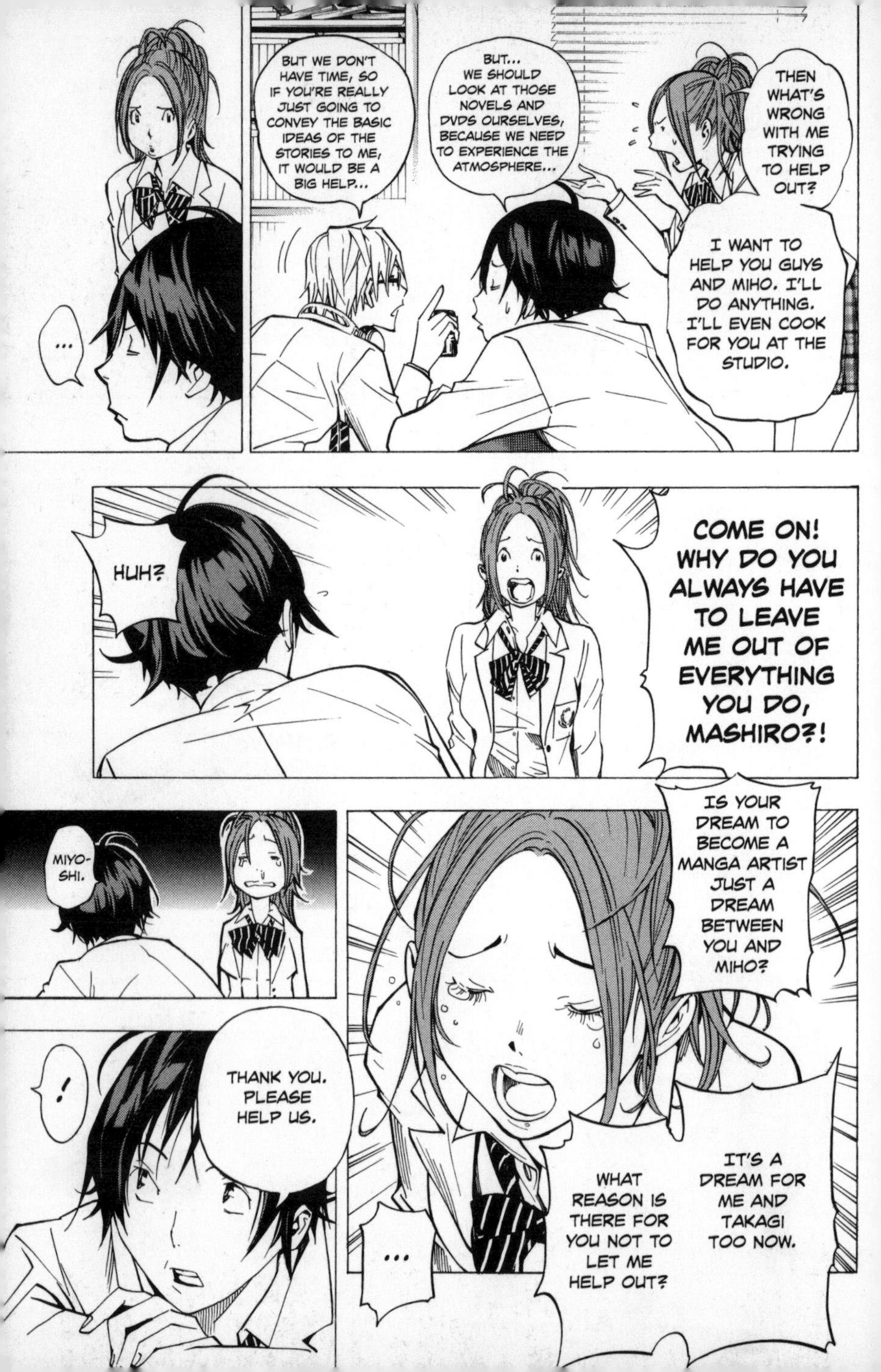

BUT... WE SHOULD LOOK AT THOSE NOVELS AND DVDS OURSELVES, BECAUSE WE NEED TO EXPERIENCE THE ATMOSPHERE...
BUT WE DON'T HAVE TIME, SO IF YOU'RE REALLY JUST GOING TO CONVEY THE BASIC IDEAS OF THE STORIES TO ME, IT WOULD BE A BIG HELP...
THEN WHAT'S WRONG WITH ME TRYING TO HELP OUT?
I WANT TO HELP YOU GUYS AND MIHO. I'LL DO ANYTHING. I'LL EVEN COOK FOR YOU AT THE STUDIO.
...
COME ON! WHY DO YOU ALWAYS HAVE TO LEAVE ME OUT OF EVERYTHING YOU DO, MASHIRO?!
HUH?
IS YOUR DREAM TO BECOME A MANGA ARTIST JUST A DREAM BETWEEN YOU AND MIHO?
IT'S A DREAM FOR ME AND TAKAGI TOO NOW.
WHAT REASON IS THERE FOR YOU NOT TO LET ME HELP OUT?
...
MIYO-SHI.
!
THANK YOU. PLEASE HELP US.

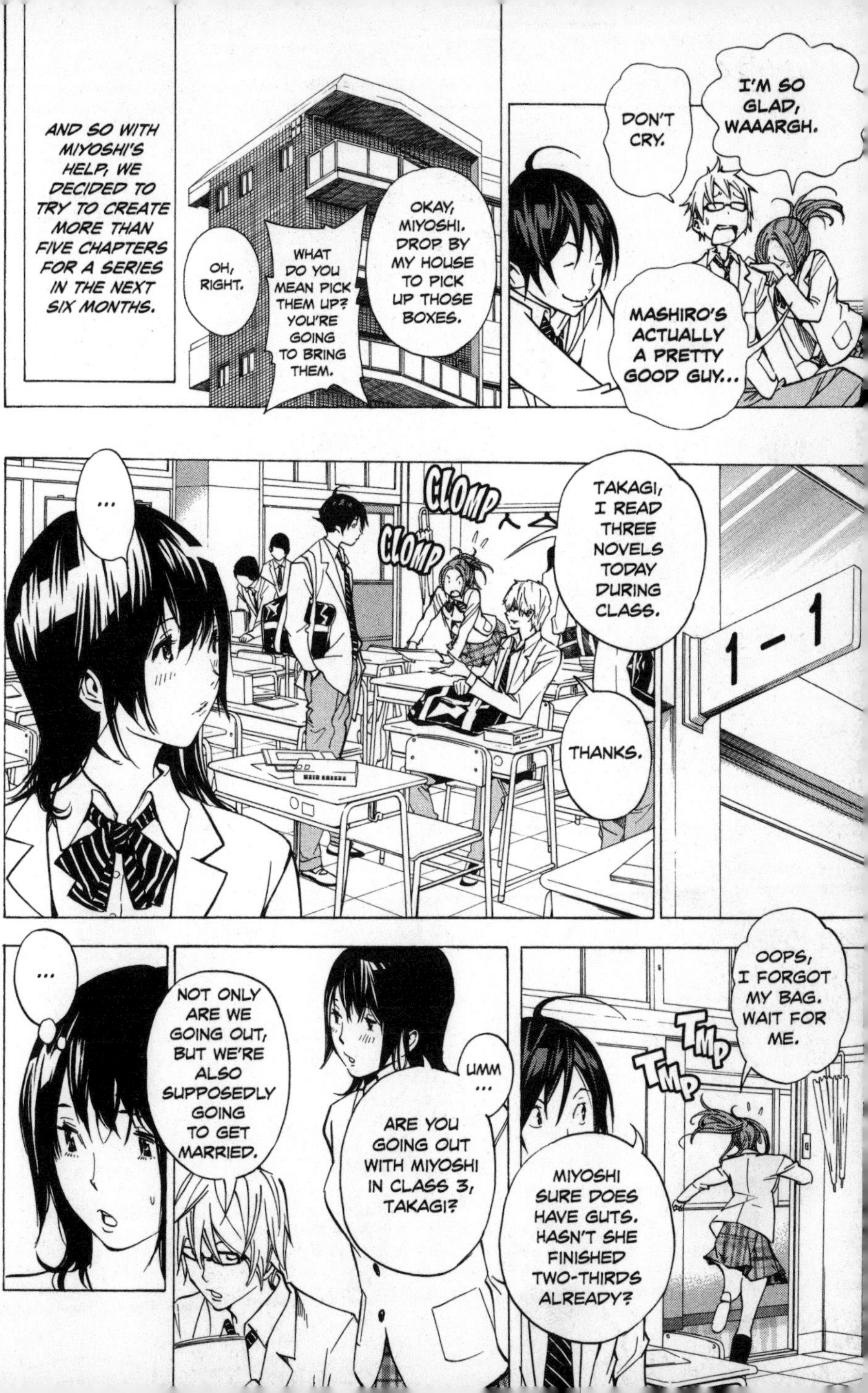
I'M SO GLAD, WAAARGH.
DON'T CRY.
MASHIRO'S ACTUALLY A PRETTY GOOD GUY...
OKAY, MIYOSHI. DROP BY MY HOUSE TO PICK UP THOSE BOXES.
WHAT DO YOU MEAN PICK THEM UP? YOU'RE GOING TO BRING THEM.
OH, RIGHT.
AND SO WITH MIYOSHI'S HELP, WE DECIDED TO TRY TO CREATE MORE THAN FIVE CHAPTERS FOR A SERIES IN THE NEXT SIX MONTHS.
TAKAGI, I READ THREE NOVELS TODAY DURING CLASS.
CLOMP
CLOMP
1-1
THANKS.
...
OOPS, I FORGOT MY BAG. WAIT FOR ME.
TMP
TMP
MIYOSHI SURE DOES HAVE GUTS. HASN'T SHE FINISHED TWO-THIRDS ALREADY?
UMM ...
ARE YOU GOING OUT WITH MIYOSHI IN CLASS 3, TAKAGI?
NOT ONLY ARE WE GOING OUT, BUT WE'RE ALSO SUPPOSEDLY GOING TO GET MARRIED.
...

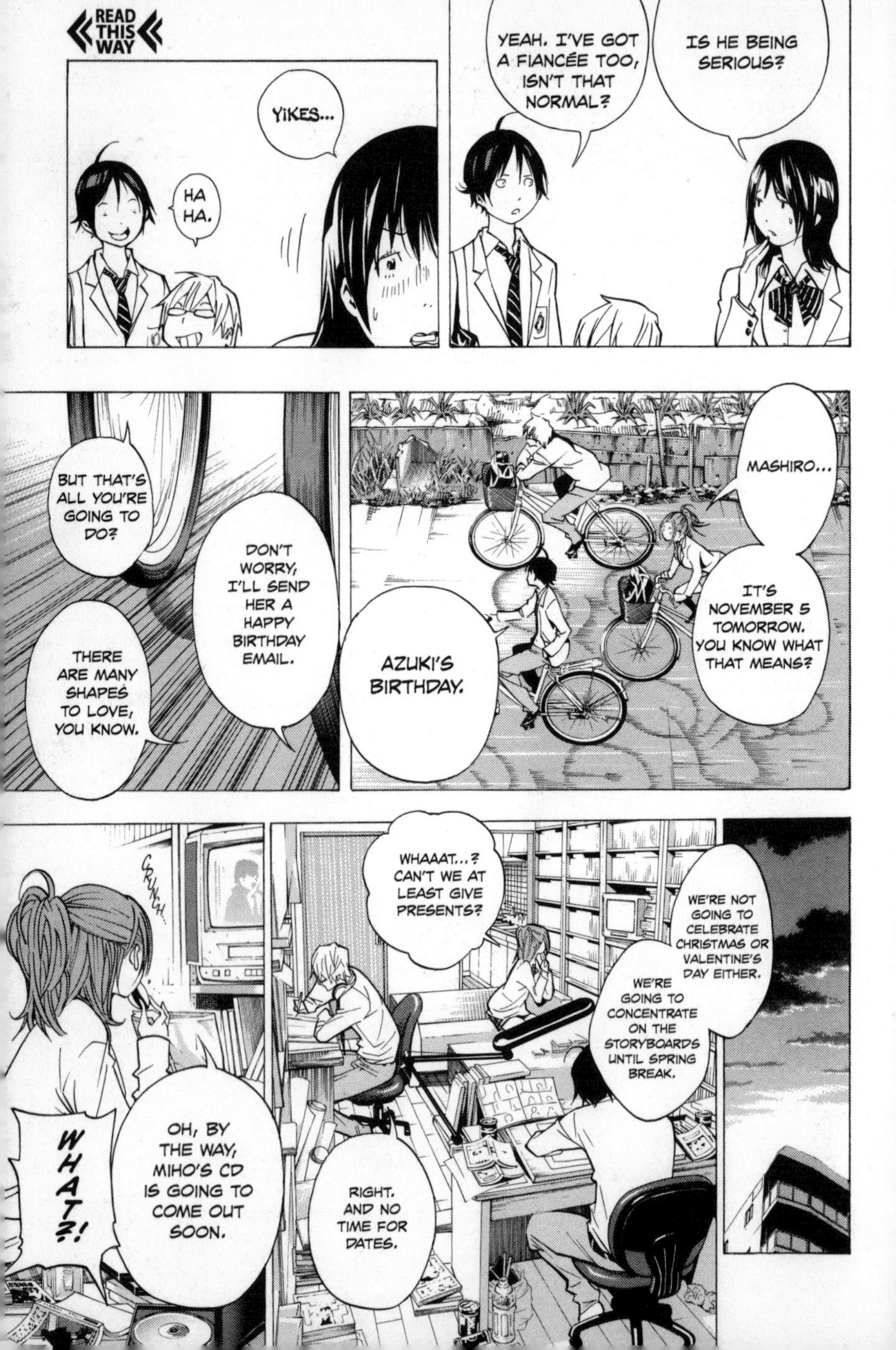
READ THIS WAY
IS HE BEING SERIOUS?
YEAH. I'VE GOT A FIANCÉE TOO, ISN'T THAT NORMAL?
YIKES...
HA HA.
MASHIRO...
IT'S NOVEMBER 5 TOMORROW. YOU KNOW WHAT THAT MEANS?
AZUKI'S BIRTHDAY.
DON'T WORRY, I'LL SEND HER A HAPPY BIRTHDAY EMAIL.
BUT THAT'S ALL YOU'RE GOING TO DO?
THERE ARE MANY SHAPES TO LOVE, YOU KNOW.
WE'RE NOT GOING TO CELEBRATE CHRISTMAS OR VALENTINE'S DAY EITHER.
WHAAAT...? CAN'T WE AT LEAST GIVE PRESENTS?
WE'RE GOING TO CONCENTRATE ON THE STORYBOARDS UNTIL SPRING BREAK.
RIGHT. AND NO TIME FOR DATES.
CRUNCH...
OH, BY THE WAY, MIHO'S CD IS GOING TO COME OUT SOON.
WHAT?!

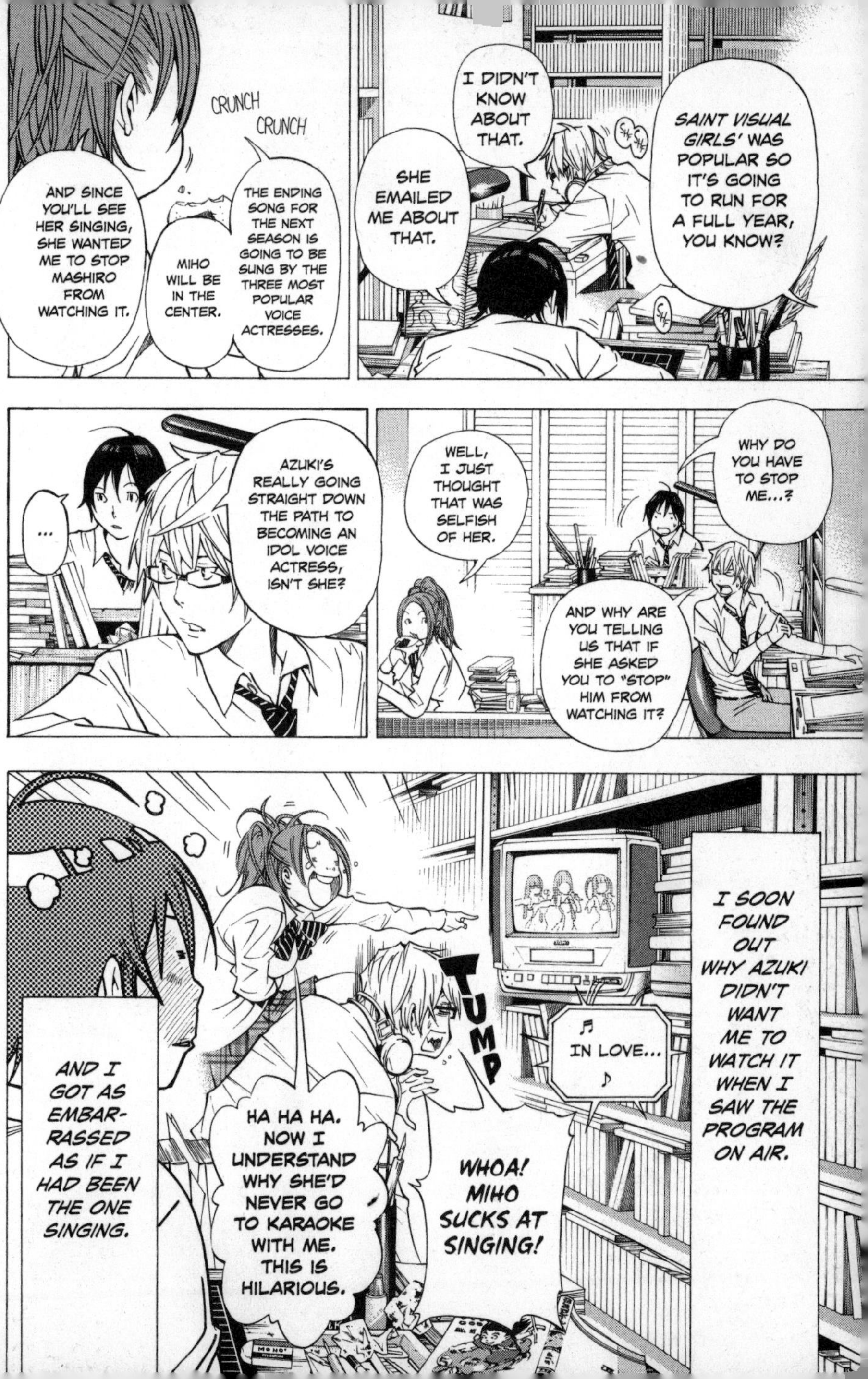
SAINT VISUAL GIRLS' WAS POPULAR SO IT'S GOING TO RUN FOR A FULL YEAR, YOU KNOW?
SHF SHF
I DIDN'T KNOW ABOUT THAT.
SHE EMAILED ME ABOUT THAT.
SHF
CRUNCH
CRUNCH
THE ENDING SONG FOR THE NEXT SEASON IS GOING TO BE SUNG BY THE THREE MOST POPULAR VOICE ACTRESSES.
MIHO WILL BE IN THE CENTER.
AND SINCE YOU'LL SEE HER SINGING, SHE WANTED ME TO STOP MASHIRO FROM WATCHING IT.
WHY DO YOU HAVE TO STOP ME...?
AND WHY ARE YOU TELLING US THAT IF SHE ASKED YOU TO "STOP" HIM FROM WATCHING IT?
WELL, I JUST THOUGHT THAT WAS SELFISH OF HER.
AZUKI'S REALLY GOING STRAIGHT DOWN THE PATH TO BECOMING AN IDOL VOICE ACTRESS, ISN'T SHE?
...
I SOON FOUND OUT WHY AZUKI DIDN'T WANT ME TO WATCH IT WHEN I SAW THE PROGRAM ON AIR.
♪ IN LOVE... ♪
TUMP
WHOA! MIHO SUCKS AT SINGING!
HA HA HA. NOW I UNDERSTAND WHY SHE'D NEVER GO TO KARAOKE WITH ME. THIS IS HILARIOUS.
AND I GOT AS EMBARRASSED AS IF I HAD BEEN THE ONE SINGING.

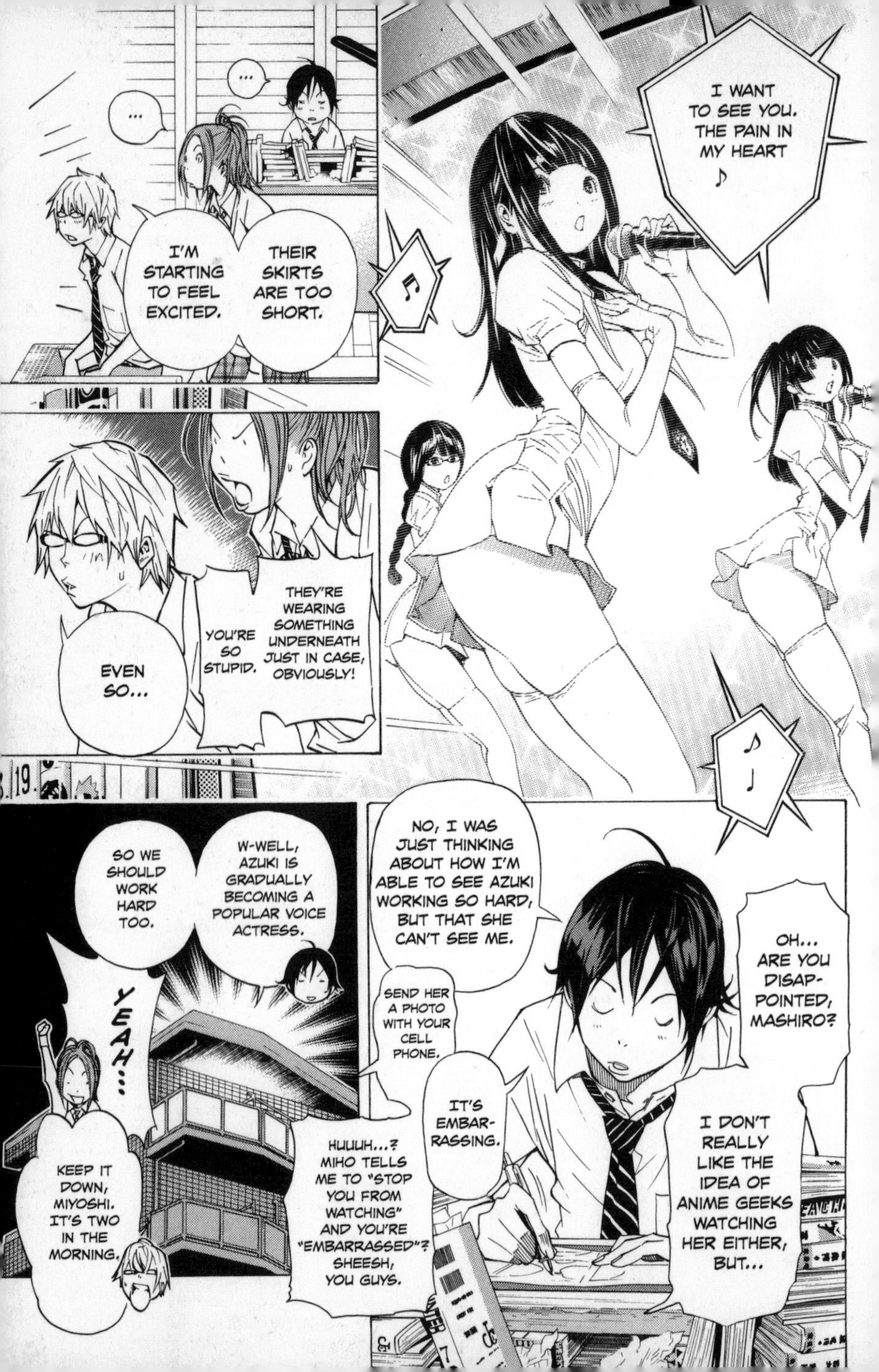
I WANT TO SEE YOU. THE PAIN IN MY HEART ♪
♪
♪ ♩
...
...
THEIR SKIRTS ARE TOO SHORT.
I'M STARTING TO FEEL EXCITED.
THEY'RE WEARING SOMETHING UNDERNEATH JUST IN CASE, OBVIOUSLY!
YOU'RE SO STUPID.
EVEN SO...
OH... ARE YOU DISAP-POINTED, MASHIRO?
NO, I WAS JUST THINKING ABOUT HOW I'M ABLE TO SEE AZUKI WORKING SO HARD, BUT THAT SHE CAN'T SEE ME.
I DON'T REALLY LIKE THE IDEA OF ANIME GEEKS WATCHING HER EITHER, BUT...
SEND HER A PHOTO WITH YOUR CELL PHONE.
IT'S EMBAR-RASSING.
HUUUH...? MIHO TELLS ME TO "STOP YOU FROM WATCHING" AND YOU'RE "EMBARRASSED"? SHEESH, YOU GUYS.
W-WELL, AZUKI IS GRADUALLY BECOMING A POPULAR VOICE ACTRESS.
SO WE SHOULD WORK HARD TOO.
YEAH...
KEEP IT DOWN, MIYOSHI. IT'S TWO IN THE MORNING.

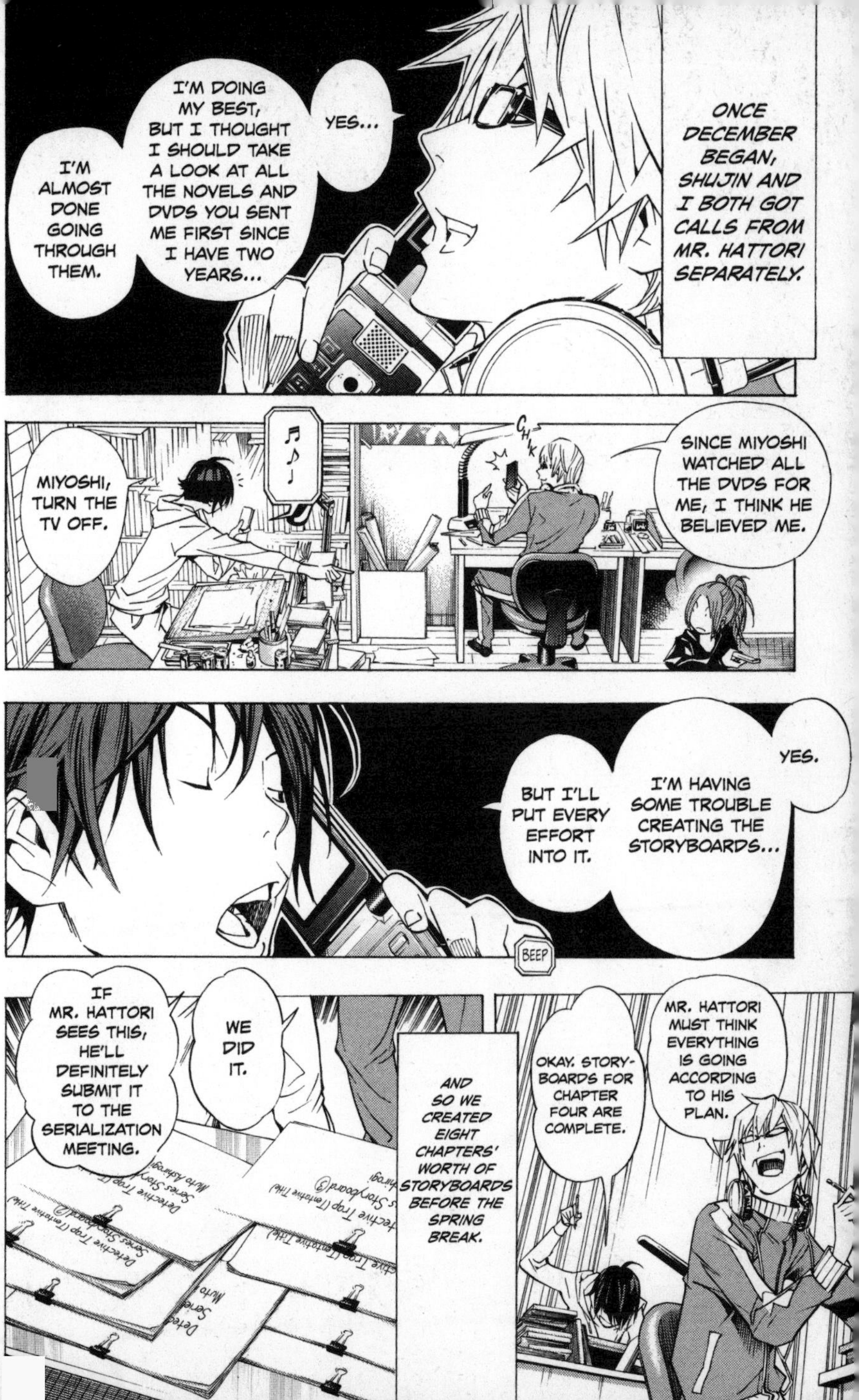
ONCE DECEMBER BEGAN, SHUJIN AND I BOTH GOT CALLS FROM MR. HATTORI SEPARATELY.
YES...
I'M DOING MY BEST, BUT I THOUGHT I SHOULD TAKE A LOOK AT ALL THE NOVELS AND DVDS YOU SENT ME FIRST SINCE I HAVE TWO YEARS...
I'M ALMOST DONE GOING THROUGH THEM.
SINCE MIYOSHI WATCHED ALL THE DVDS FOR ME, I THINK HE BELIEVED ME.
CHIK
♪ ♪
MIYOSHI, TURN THE TV OFF.
YES.
I'M HAVING SOME TROUBLE CREATING THE STORYBOARDS...
BUT I'LL PUT EVERY EFFORT INTO IT.
BEEP
MR. HATTORI MUST THINK EVERYTHING IS GOING ACCORDING TO HIS PLAN.
OKAY. STORYBOARDS FOR CHAPTER FOUR ARE COMPLETE.
AND SO WE CREATED EIGHT CHAPTERS' WORTH OF STORYBOARDS BEFORE THE SPRING BREAK.
WE DID IT.
IF MR. HATTORI SEES THIS, HE'LL DEFINITELY SUBMIT IT TO THE SERIALIZATION MEETING.

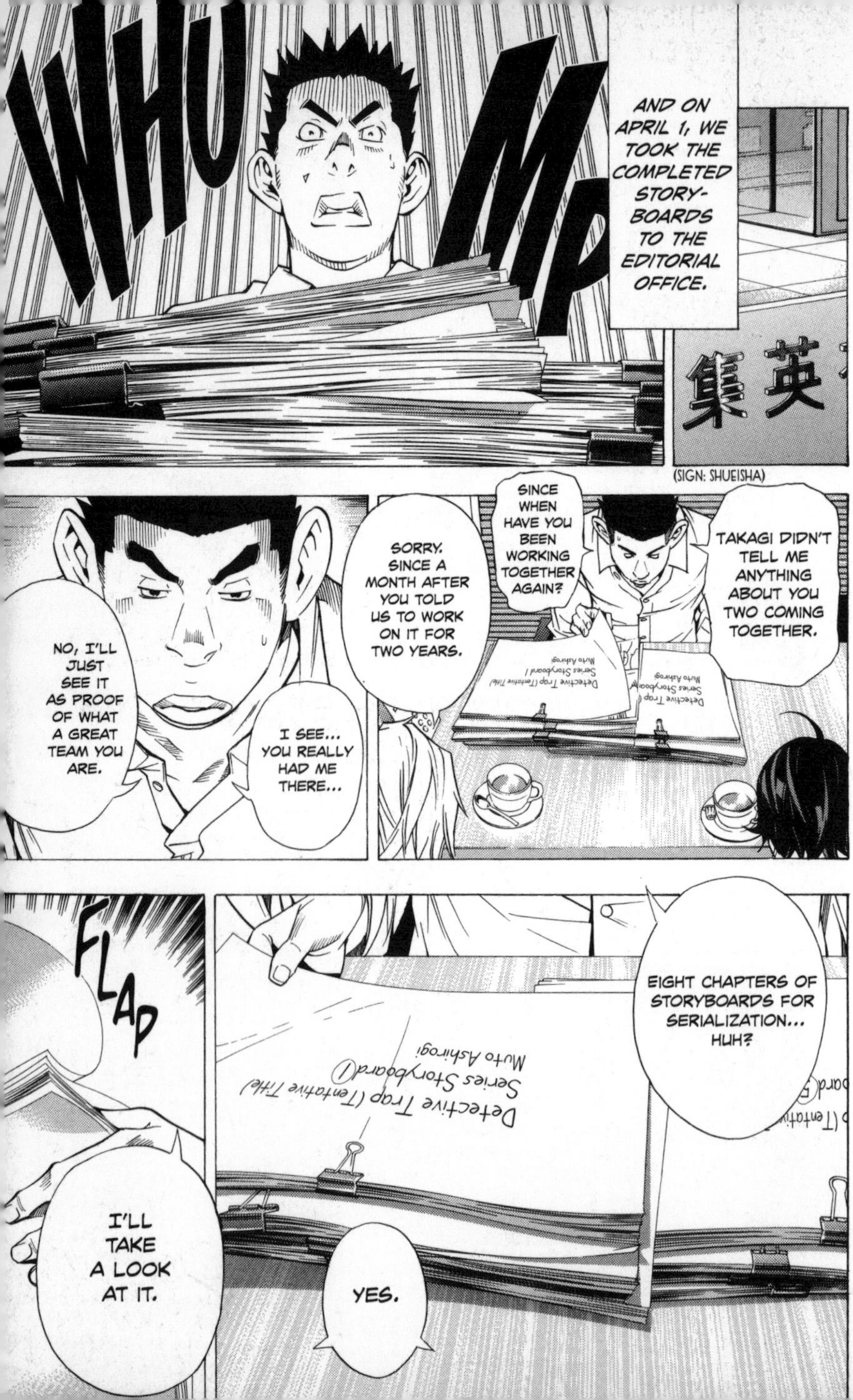
AND ON APRIL 1, WE TOOK THE COMPLETED STORY-BOARDS TO THE EDITORIAL OFFICE.
集英
(SIGN: SHUEISHA)
WHUMP
TAKAGI DIDN'T TELL ME ANYTHING ABOUT YOU TWO COMING TOGETHER.
SINCE WHEN HAVE YOU BEEN WORKING TOGETHER AGAIN?
SORRY. SINCE A MONTH AFTER YOU TOLD US TO WORK ON IT FOR TWO YEARS.
I SEE... YOU REALLY HAD ME THERE...
NO, I'LL JUST SEE IT AS PROOF OF WHAT A GREAT TEAM YOU ARE.
EIGHT CHAPTERS OF STORYBOARDS FOR SERIALIZATION... HUH?
YES.
FLAP
I'LL TAKE A LOOK AT IT.

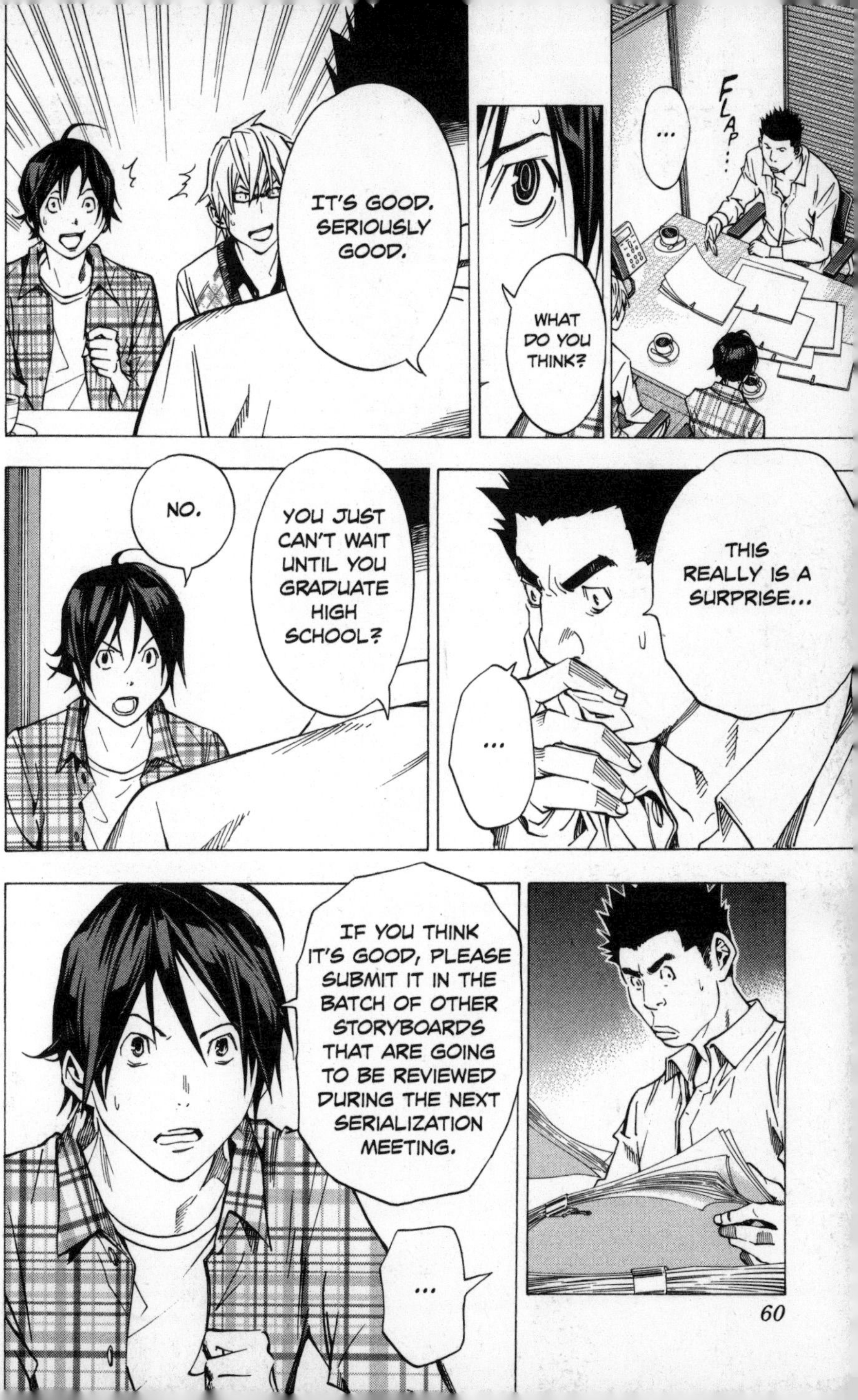
FLAP...
...
WHAT DO YOU THINK?
IT'S GOOD. SERIOUSLY GOOD.
THIS REALLY IS A SURPRISE...
...
YOU JUST CAN'T WAIT UNTIL YOU GRADUATE HIGH SCHOOL?
NO.
IF YOU THINK IT'S GOOD, PLEASE SUBMIT IT IN THE BATCH OF OTHER STORYBOARDS THAT ARE GOING TO BE REVIEWED DURING THE NEXT SERIALIZATION MEETING.
...

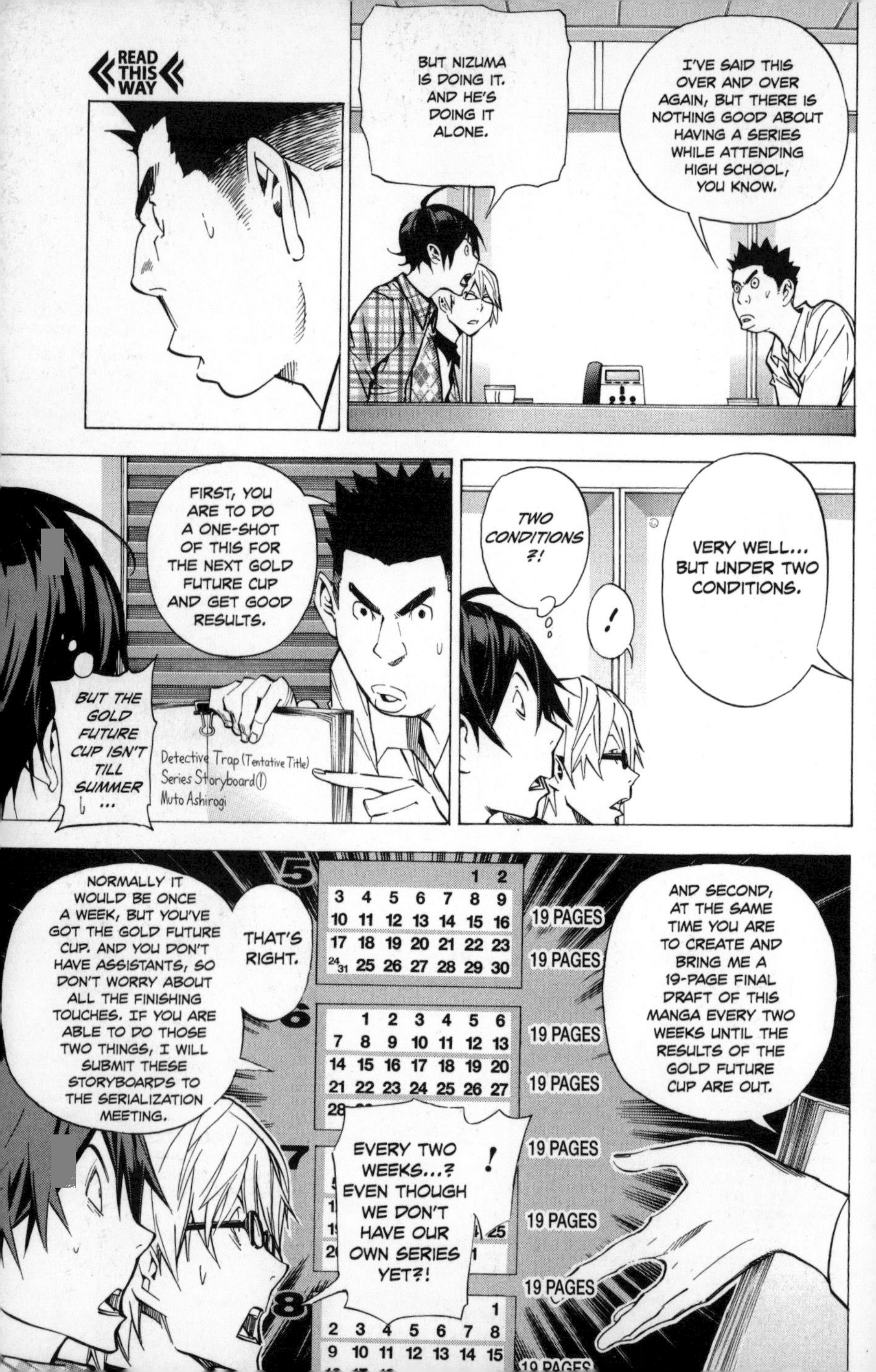
READ THIS WAY
I'VE SAID THIS OVER AND OVER AGAIN, BUT THERE IS NOTHING GOOD ABOUT HAVING A SERIES WHILE ATTENDING HIGH SCHOOL, YOU KNOW.
BUT NIZUMA IS DOING IT. AND HE'S DOING IT ALONE.
VERY WELL... BUT UNDER TWO CONDITIONS.
TWO CONDITIONS?!
!
FIRST, YOU ARE TO DO A ONE-SHOT OF THIS FOR THE NEXT GOLD FUTURE CUP AND GET GOOD RESULTS.
BUT THE GOLD FUTURE CUP ISN'T TILL SUMMER...
Detective Trap (Tentative Title)
Series Storyboard (1)
Muto Ashirogi
AND SECOND, AT THE SAME TIME YOU ARE TO CREATE AND BRING ME A 19-PAGE FINAL DRAFT OF THIS MANGA EVERY TWO WEEKS UNTIL THE RESULTS OF THE GOLD FUTURE CUP ARE OUT.
5
6
7
8
19 PAGES
19 PAGES
19 PAGES
19 PAGES
19 PAGES
19 PAGES
19 PAGES
NORMALLY IT WOULD BE ONCE A WEEK, BUT YOU'VE GOT THE GOLD FUTURE CUP. AND YOU DON'T HAVE ASSISTANTS, SO DON'T WORRY ABOUT ALL THE FINISHING TOUCHES. IF YOU ARE ABLE TO DO THOSE TWO THINGS, I WILL SUBMIT THESE STORYBOARDS TO THE SERIALIZATION MEETING.
THAT'S RIGHT.
EVERY TWO WEEKS...? EVEN THOUGH WE DON'T HAVE OUR OWN SERIES YET?!
!

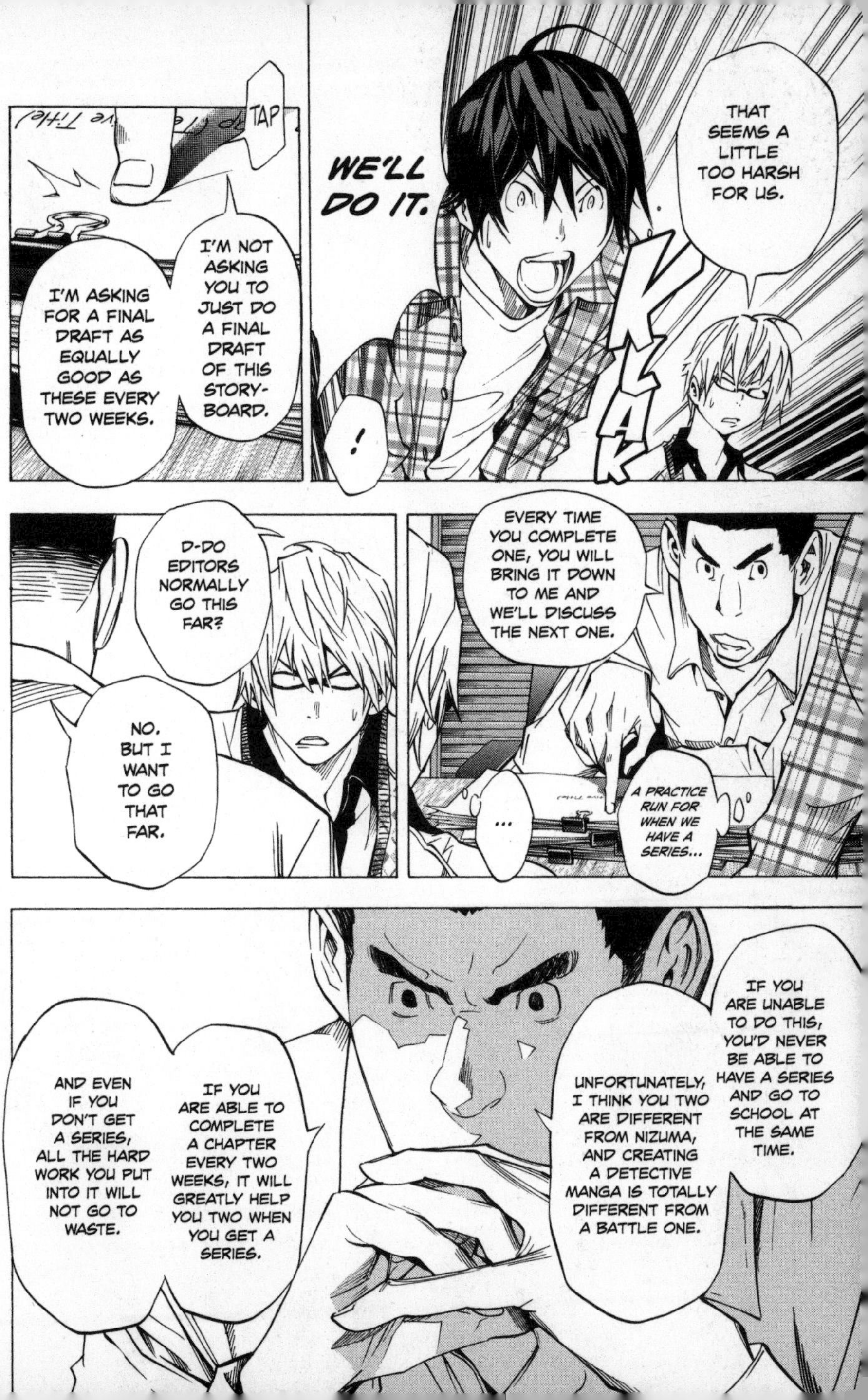
THAT SEEMS A LITTLE TOO HARSH FOR US.
KLAK
WE'LL DO IT.
!
TAP
I'M NOT ASKING YOU TO JUST DO A FINAL DRAFT OF THIS STORY-BOARD.
I'M ASKING FOR A FINAL DRAFT AS EQUALLY GOOD AS THESE EVERY TWO WEEKS.
EVERY TIME YOU COMPLETE ONE, YOU WILL BRING IT DOWN TO ME AND WE'LL DISCUSS THE NEXT ONE.
A PRACTICE RUN FOR WHEN WE HAVE A SERIES...
...
D-DO EDITORS NORMALLY GO THIS FAR?
NO. BUT I WANT TO GO THAT FAR.
IF YOU ARE UNABLE TO DO THIS, YOU'D NEVER BE ABLE TO HAVE A SERIES AND GO TO SCHOOL AT THE SAME TIME.
UNFORTUNATELY, I THINK YOU TWO ARE DIFFERENT FROM NIZUMA, AND CREATING A DETECTIVE MANGA IS TOTALLY DIFFERENT FROM A BATTLE ONE.
IF YOU ARE ABLE TO COMPLETE A CHAPTER EVERY TWO WEEKS, IT WILL GREATLY HELP YOU TWO WHEN YOU GET A SERIES.
AND EVEN IF YOU DON'T GET A SERIES, ALL THE HARD WORK YOU PUT INTO IT WILL NOT GO TO WASTE.

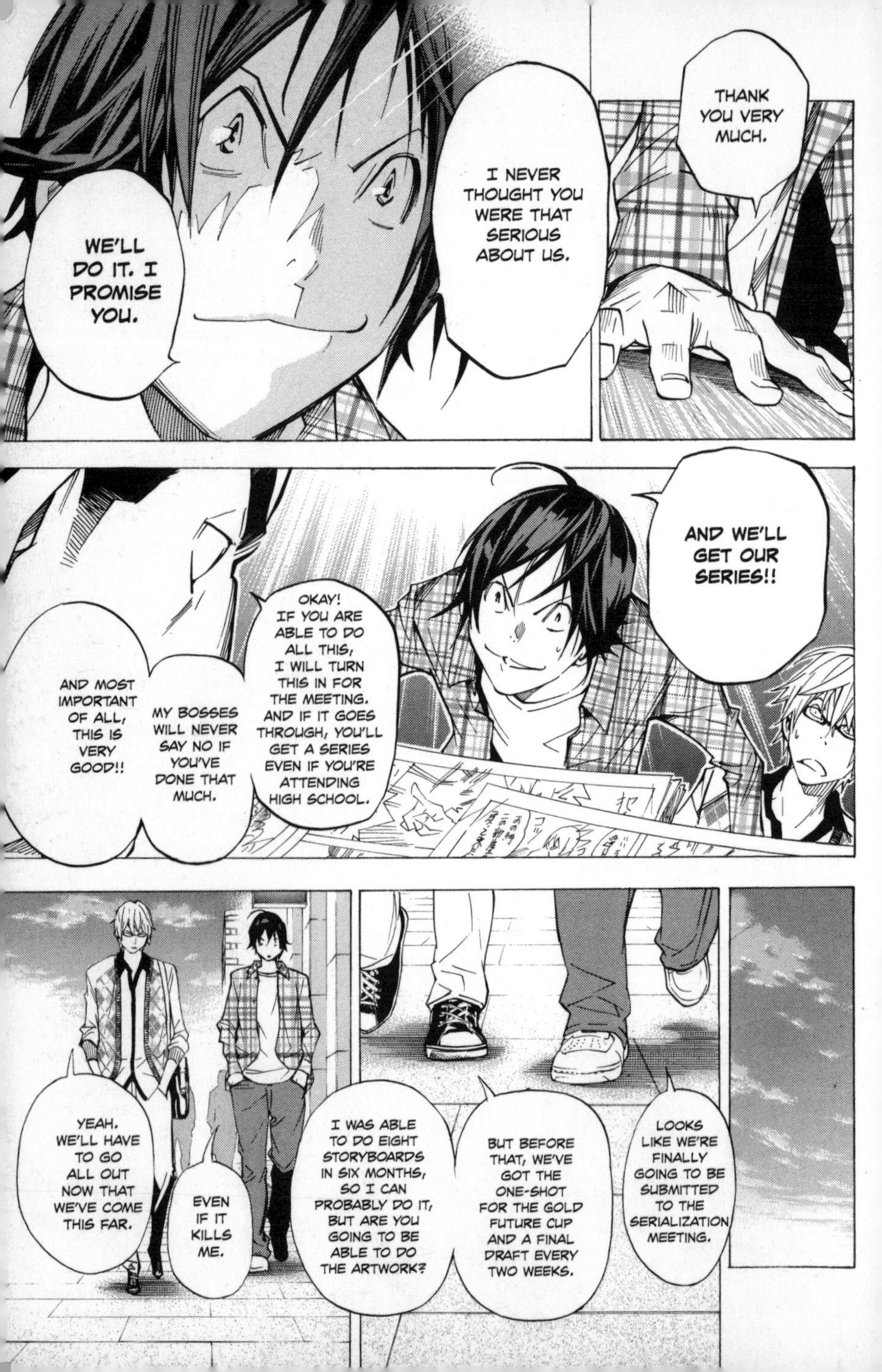
THANK YOU VERY MUCH.
I NEVER THOUGHT YOU WERE THAT SERIOUS ABOUT US.
WE'LL DO IT. I PROMISE YOU.
AND WE'LL GET OUR SERIES!!
OKAY! IF YOU ARE ABLE TO DO ALL THIS, I WILL TURN THIS IN FOR THE MEETING. AND IF IT GOES THROUGH, YOU'LL GET A SERIES EVEN IF YOU'RE ATTENDING HIGH SCHOOL.
MY BOSSES WILL NEVER SAY NO IF YOU'VE DONE THAT MUCH.
AND MOST IMPORTANT OF ALL, THIS IS VERY GOOD!!
LOOKS LIKE WE'RE FINALLY GOING TO BE SUBMITTED TO THE SERIALIZATION MEETING.
BUT BEFORE THAT, WE'VE GOT THE ONE-SHOT FOR THE GOLD FUTURE CUP AND A FINAL DRAFT EVERY TWO WEEKS.
I WAS ABLE TO DO EIGHT STORYBOARDS IN SIX MONTHS, SO I CAN PROBABLY DO IT, BUT ARE YOU GOING TO BE ABLE TO DO THE ARTWORK?
YEAH. WE'LL HAVE TO GO ALL OUT NOW THAT WE'VE COME THIS FAR.
EVEN IF IT KILLS ME.

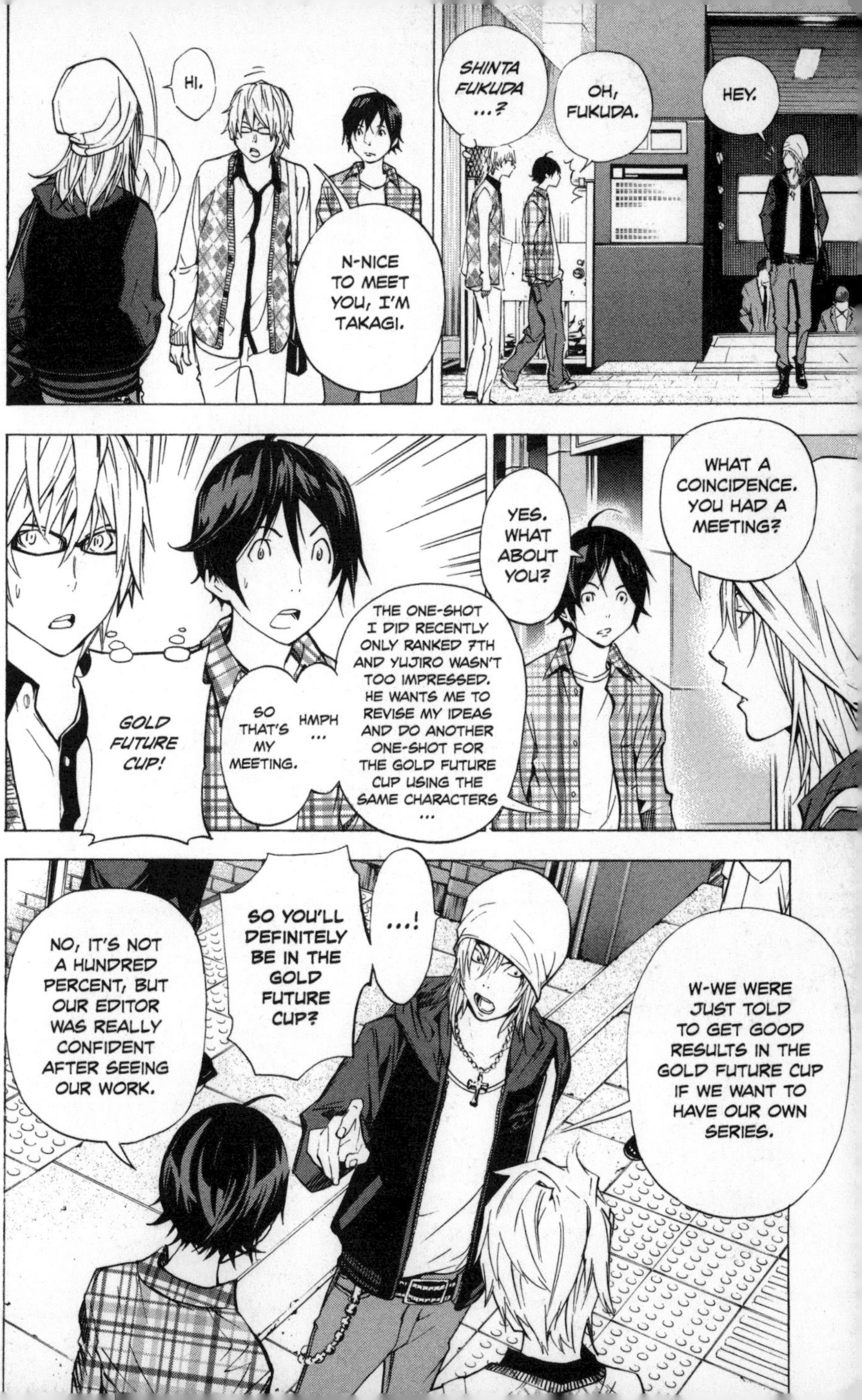
HEY.
OH, FUKUDA.
SHINTA FUKUDA ...?
HI.
N-NICE TO MEET YOU, I'M TAKAGI.
WHAT A COINCIDENCE. YOU HAD A MEETING?
YES. WHAT ABOUT YOU?
THE ONE-SHOT I DID RECENTLY ONLY RANKED 7TH AND YUJIRO WASN'T TOO IMPRESSED. HE WANTS ME TO REVISE MY IDEAS AND DO ANOTHER ONE-SHOT FOR THE GOLD FUTURE CUP USING THE SAME CHARACTERS ...
HMPH ...
SO THAT'S MY MEETING.
GOLD FUTURE CUP!
W-WE WERE JUST TOLD TO GET GOOD RESULTS IN THE GOLD FUTURE CUP IF WE WANT TO HAVE OUR OWN SERIES.
...!
SO YOU'LL DEFINITELY BE IN THE GOLD FUTURE CUP?
NO, IT'S NOT A HUNDRED PERCENT, BUT OUR EDITOR WAS REALLY CONFIDENT AFTER SEEING OUR WORK.

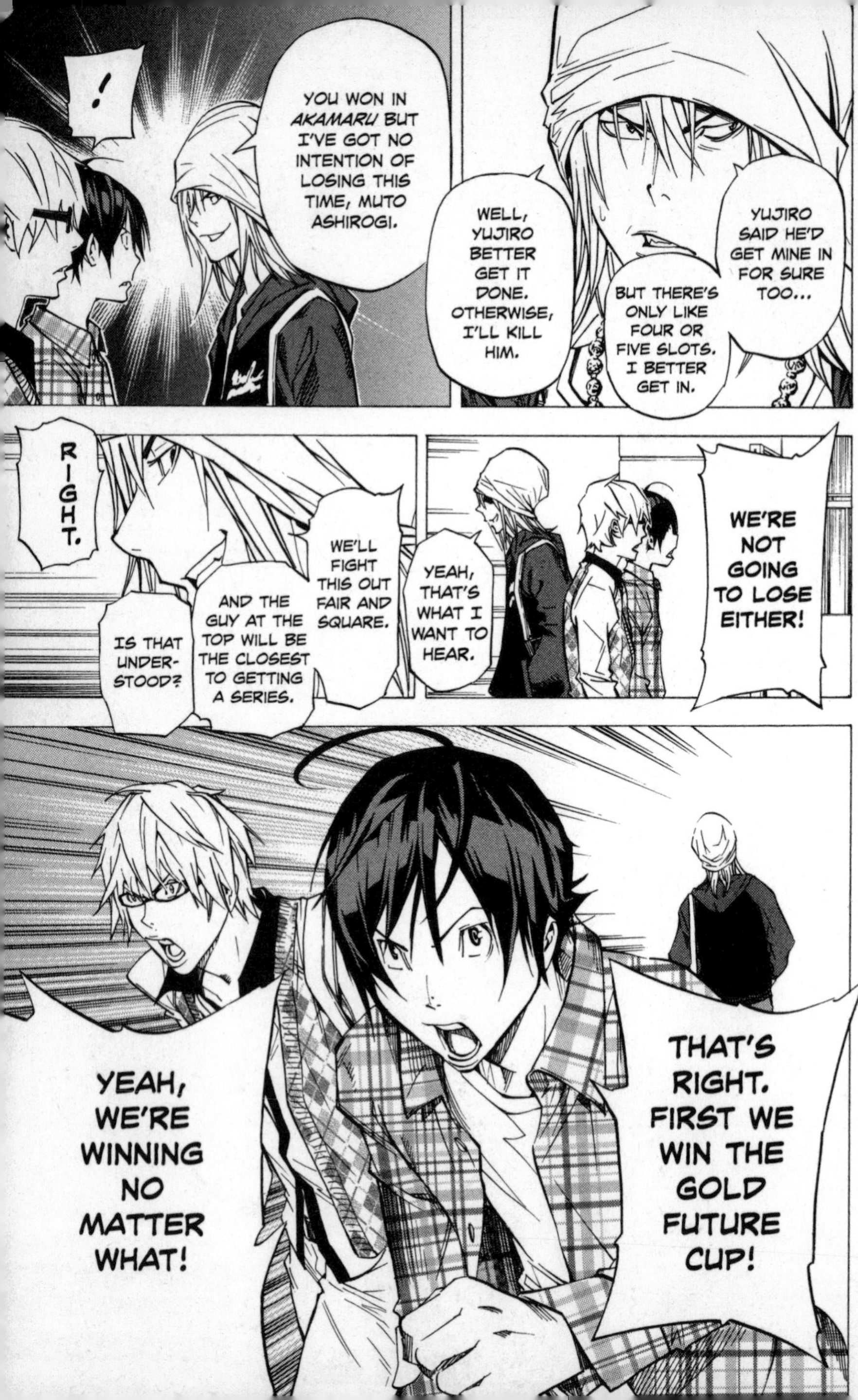
YUJIRO SAID HE'D GET MINE IN FOR SURE TOO...
BUT THERE'S ONLY LIKE FOUR OR FIVE SLOTS. I BETTER GET IN.
WELL, YUJIRO BETTER GET IT DONE. OTHERWISE, I'LL KILL HIM.
YOU WON IN *AKAMARU* BUT I'VE GOT NO INTENTION OF LOSING THIS TIME, MUTO ASHIROGI.
!
WE'RE NOT GOING TO LOSE EITHER!
YEAH, THAT'S WHAT I WANT TO HEAR.
WE'LL FIGHT THIS OUT FAIR AND SQUARE.
AND THE GUY AT THE TOP WILL BE THE CLOSEST TO GETTING A SERIES.
IS THAT UNDER-STOOD?
RIGHT.
THAT'S RIGHT. FIRST WE WIN THE GOLD FUTURE CUP!
YEAH, WE'RE WINNING NO MATTER WHAT!

OHBA'S STORYBOARD

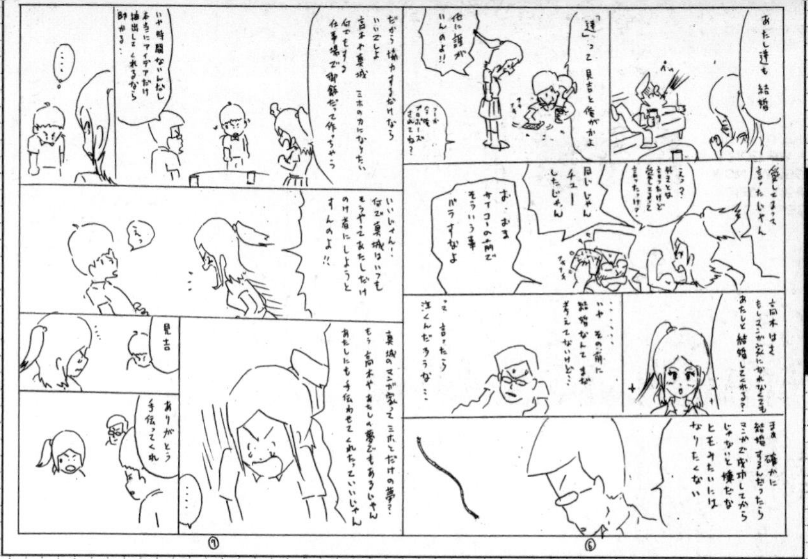
あたし達も結婚
「蓮」って見吉と俺がかよ
他に誰がいんのよ!!
つーか今俺プロポーズされてね?
愛してるって言ったじゃん
えっ? 好きとは言ったけど愛してるって言ったっけ?
同じじゃん チューしたじゃん
お、おまサイコーの前でそういう事バラすなよ
高木はさ もしマンガ家になれなくても あたしと結婚してくれる?
いや その前に結婚なんてまだ考えてないけど…
って言ったら泣くんだろうな…
まぁ確かに結婚するんだったらマンガで成功してからじゃないと嫌だな ヒモみたいにはなりたくない
だから協力するだけなら いいでしょ 高木や真城 ミホの力になりたい 何でもする 仕事場で御飯だって作っちゃう
いや時間ないんだし 本当にアイデアだけ抽出しまくれるなら助かる…
…
いいじゃん! 何で真城はいつもそうやってあたしだけのけ者にしようとすんのよ!!
えっ
見吉
真城のマンガ家って ミホとだけの夢? もう高木やあたしの夢でもあるじゃん あたしにも手伝わせてくれたっていいじゃん
ありがとう 手伝ってくれ
…

OBATA'S STORYBOARD

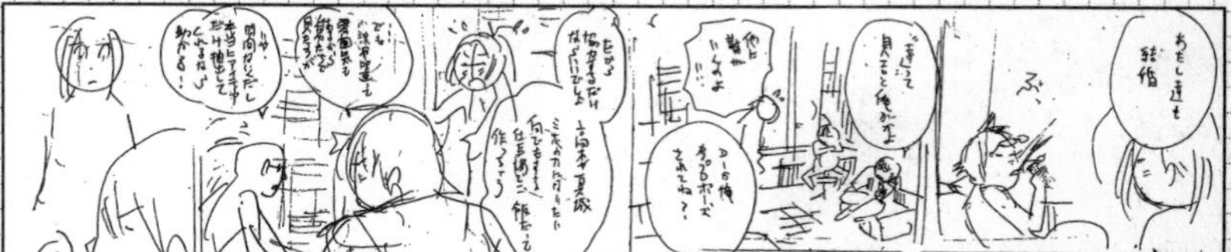
あたし達も結婚
ぶっ
愛してるって言ったじゃん
見吉!

COMPLETE!

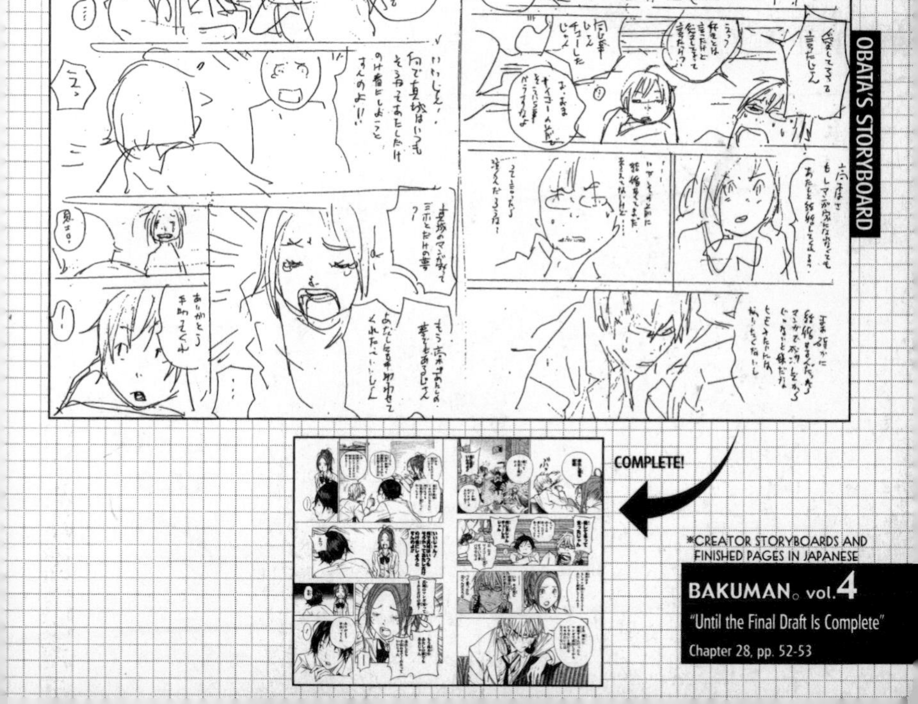

*CREATOR STORYBOARDS AND FINISHED PAGES IN JAPANESE

BAKUMAN。 vol.4

"Until the Final Draft Is Complete"

Chapter 28, pp. 52-53

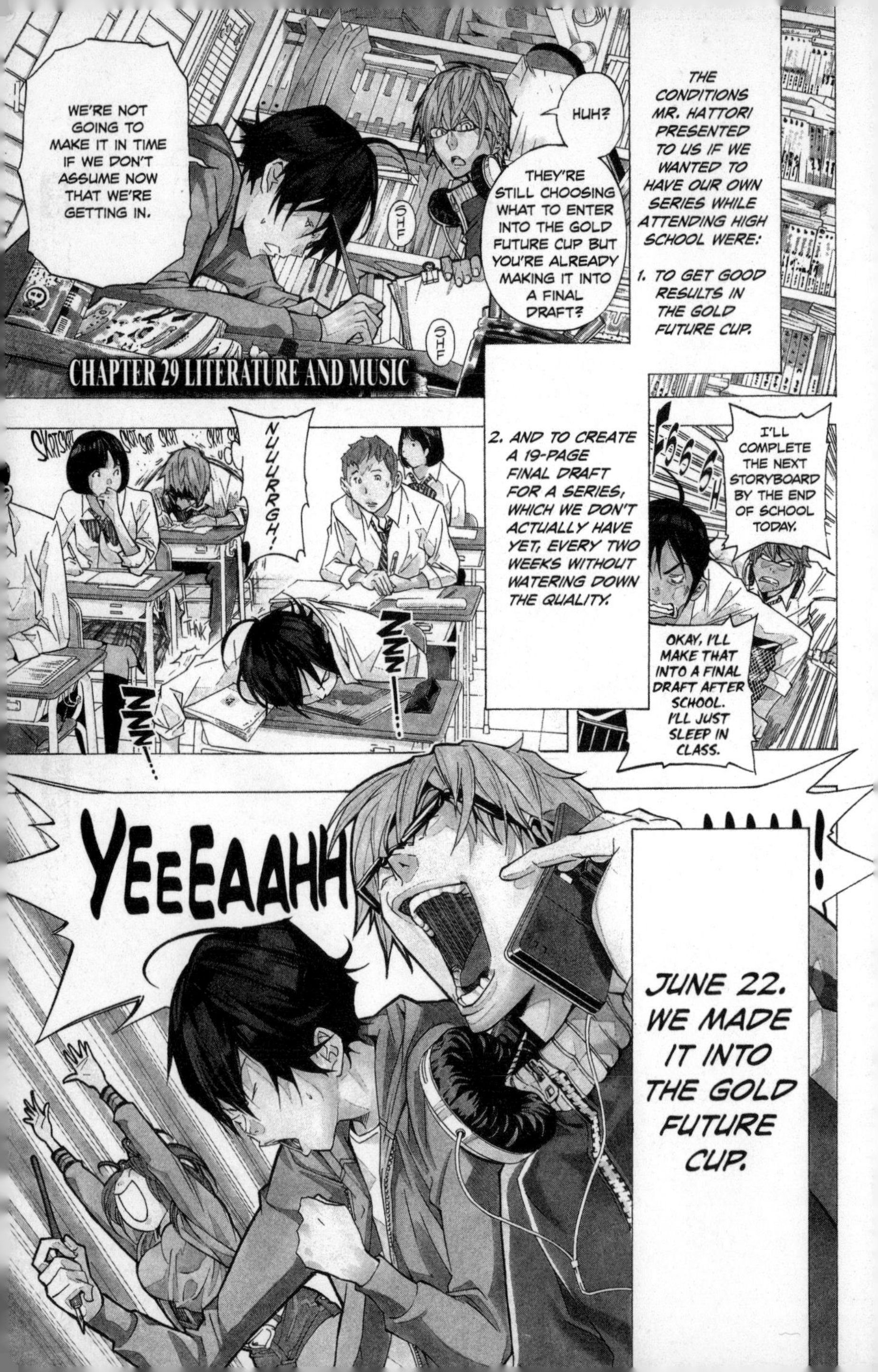
THE CONDITIONS MR. HATTORI PRESENTED TO US IF WE WANTED TO HAVE OUR OWN SERIES WHILE ATTENDING HIGH SCHOOL WERE:
1. TO GET GOOD RESULTS IN THE GOLD FUTURE CUP.
HUH?
THEY'RE STILL CHOOSING WHAT TO ENTER INTO THE GOLD FUTURE CUP BUT YOU'RE ALREADY MAKING IT INTO A FINAL DRAFT?
SHF
SHF
WE'RE NOT GOING TO MAKE IT IN TIME IF WE DON'T ASSUME NOW THAT WE'RE GETTING IN.
CHAPTER 29 LITERATURE AND MUSIC
I'LL COMPLETE THE NEXT STORYBOARD BY THE END OF SCHOOL TODAY.
OKAY, I'LL MAKE THAT INTO A FINAL DRAFT AFTER SCHOOL. I'LL JUST SLEEP IN CLASS.
2. AND TO CREATE A 19-PAGE FINAL DRAFT FOR A SERIES, WHICH WE DON'T ACTUALLY HAVE YET, EVERY TWO WEEKS WITHOUT WATERING DOWN THE QUALITY.
NUUURRGH!
ZZZ...
ZZZ...
JUNE 22. WE MADE IT INTO THE GOLD FUTURE CUP.
YEEEAAHH!

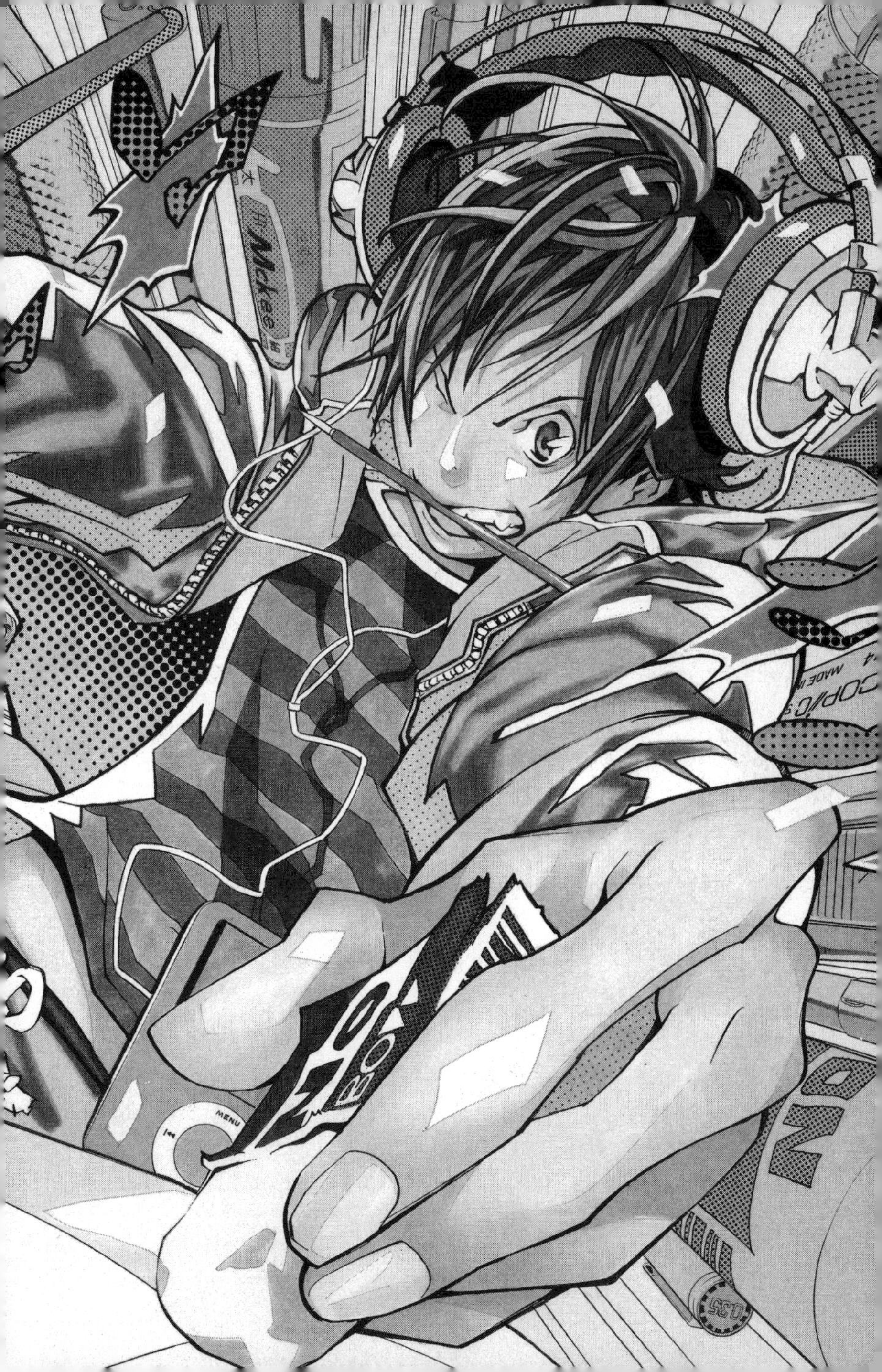
MENU

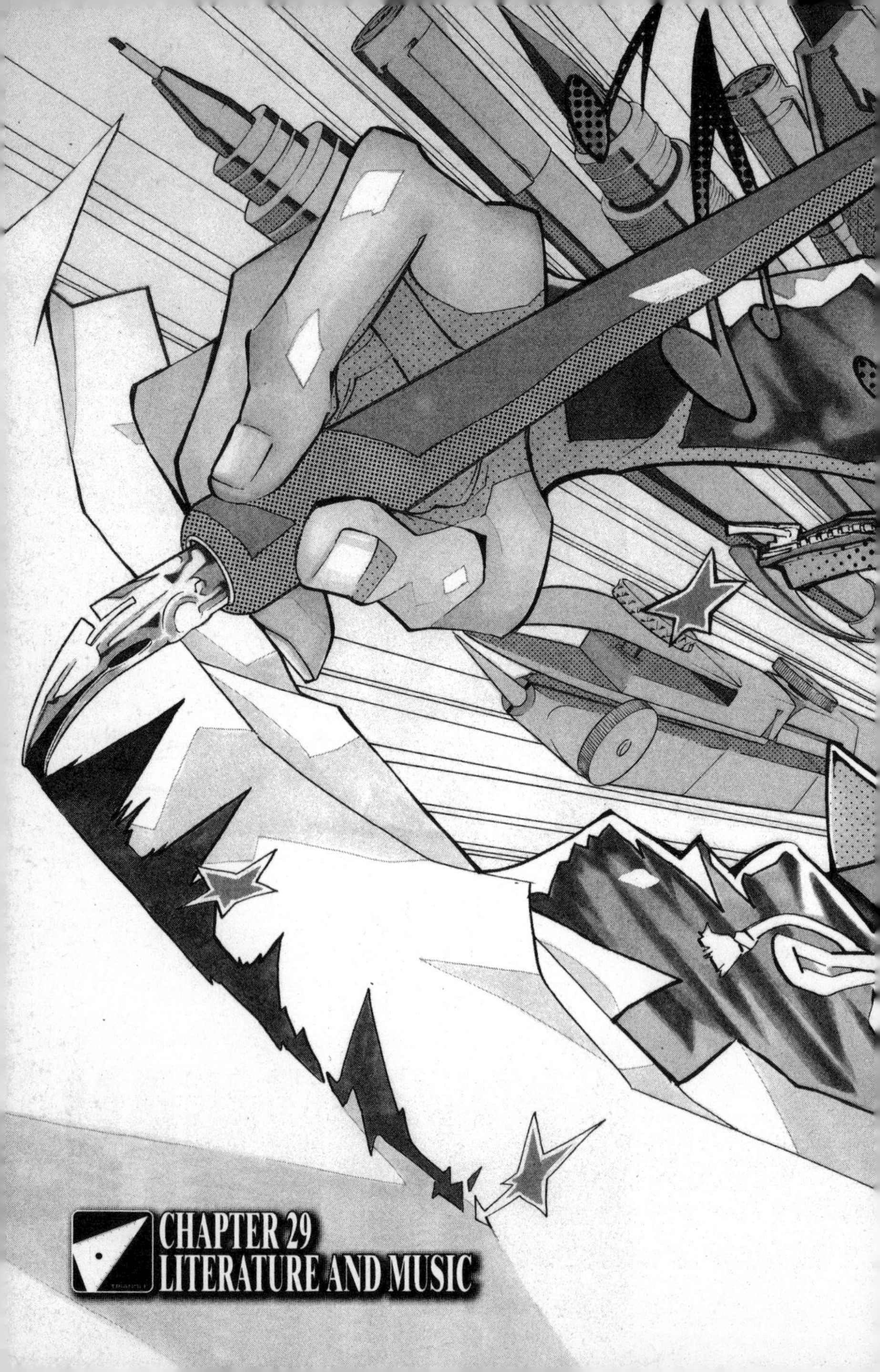

CHAPTER 29
LITERATURE AND MUSIC

BAKUMAN。

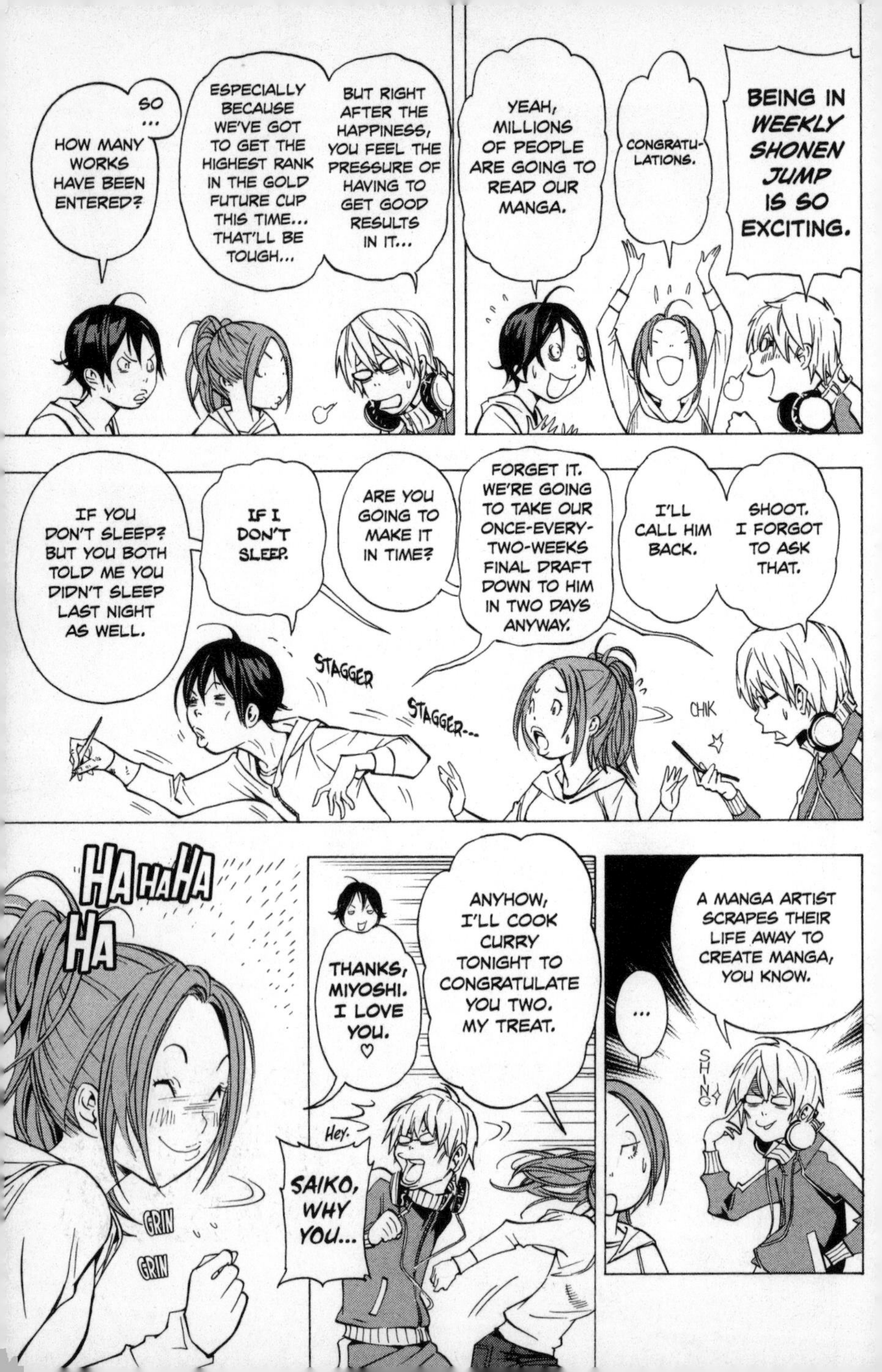

BEING IN WEEKLY SHONEN JUMP IS SO EXCITING.
CONGRATULATIONS.
YEAH, MILLIONS OF PEOPLE ARE GOING TO READ OUR MANGA.
BUT RIGHT AFTER THE HAPPINESS, YOU FEEL THE PRESSURE OF HAVING TO GET GOOD RESULTS IN IT...
ESPECIALLY BECAUSE WE'VE GOT TO GET THE HIGHEST RANK IN THE GOLD FUTURE CUP THIS TIME... THAT'LL BE TOUGH...
SO... HOW MANY WORKS HAVE BEEN ENTERED?
SHOOT. I FORGOT TO ASK THAT.
I'LL CALL HIM BACK.
CHIK
FORGET IT. WE'RE GOING TO TAKE OUR ONCE-EVERY-TWO-WEEKS FINAL DRAFT DOWN TO HIM IN TWO DAYS ANYWAY.
ARE YOU GOING TO MAKE IT IN TIME?
STAGGER...
STAGGER
IF I DON'T SLEEP.
IF YOU DON'T SLEEP? BUT YOU BOTH TOLD ME YOU DIDN'T SLEEP LAST NIGHT AS WELL.
A MANGA ARTIST SCRAPES THEIR LIFE AWAY TO CREATE MANGA, YOU KNOW.
SHING
...
ANYHOW, I'LL COOK CURRY TONIGHT TO CONGRATULATE YOU TWO. MY TREAT.
THANKS, MIYOSHI. I LOVE YOU. ♡
Hey.
SAIKO, WHY YOU...
HA HAHA HA HA
GRIN
GRIN

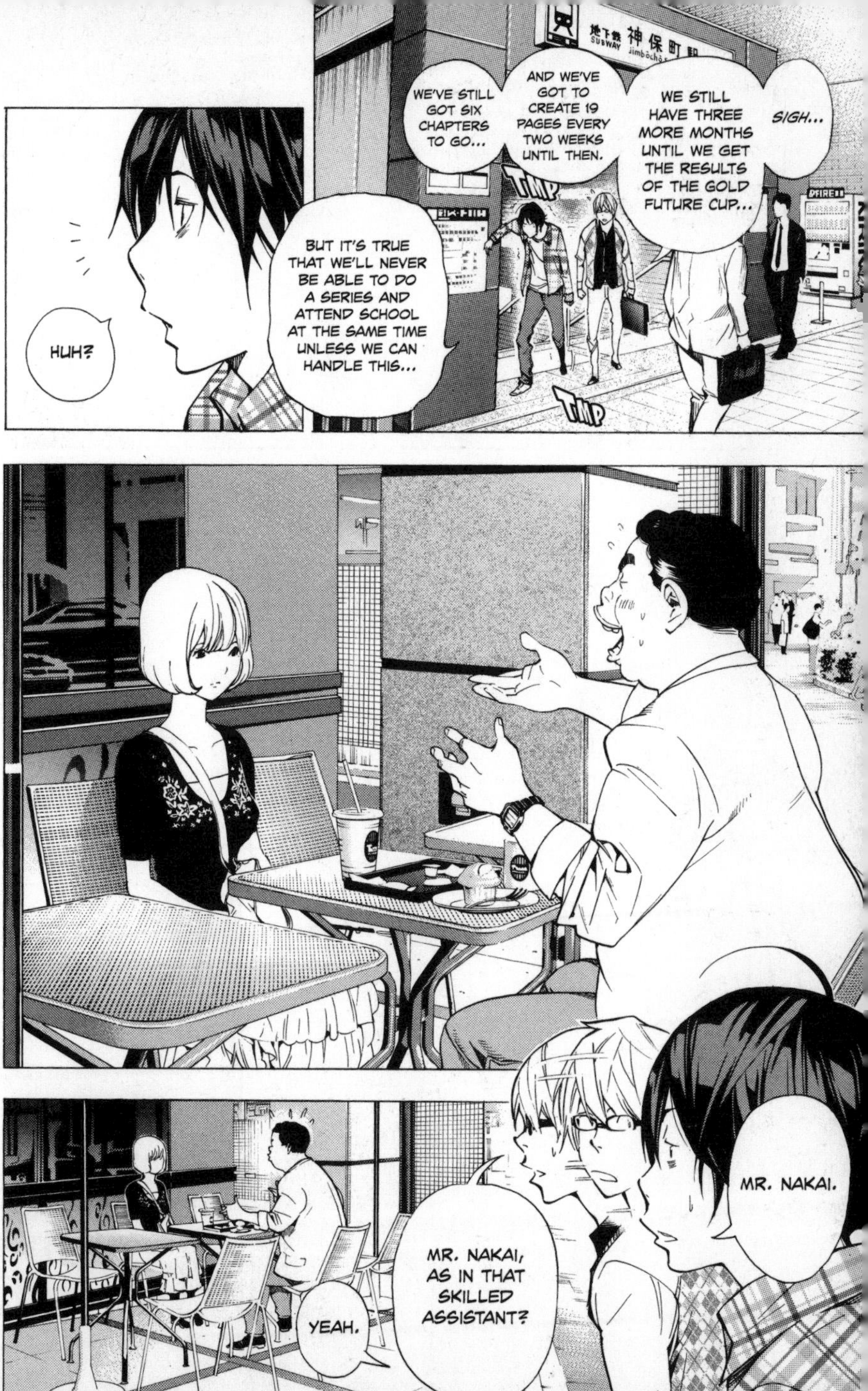
SIGH...
WE STILL HAVE THREE MORE MONTHS UNTIL WE GET THE RESULTS OF THE GOLD FUTURE CUP...
AND WE'VE GOT TO CREATE 19 PAGES EVERY TWO WEEKS UNTIL THEN.
WE'VE STILL GOT SIX CHAPTERS TO GO...
TMP
BUT IT'S TRUE THAT WE'LL NEVER BE ABLE TO DO A SERIES AND ATTEND SCHOOL AT THE SAME TIME UNLESS WE CAN HANDLE THIS...
TMP
HUH?
MR. NAKAI.
MR. NAKAI, AS IN THAT SKILLED ASSISTANT?
YEAH.

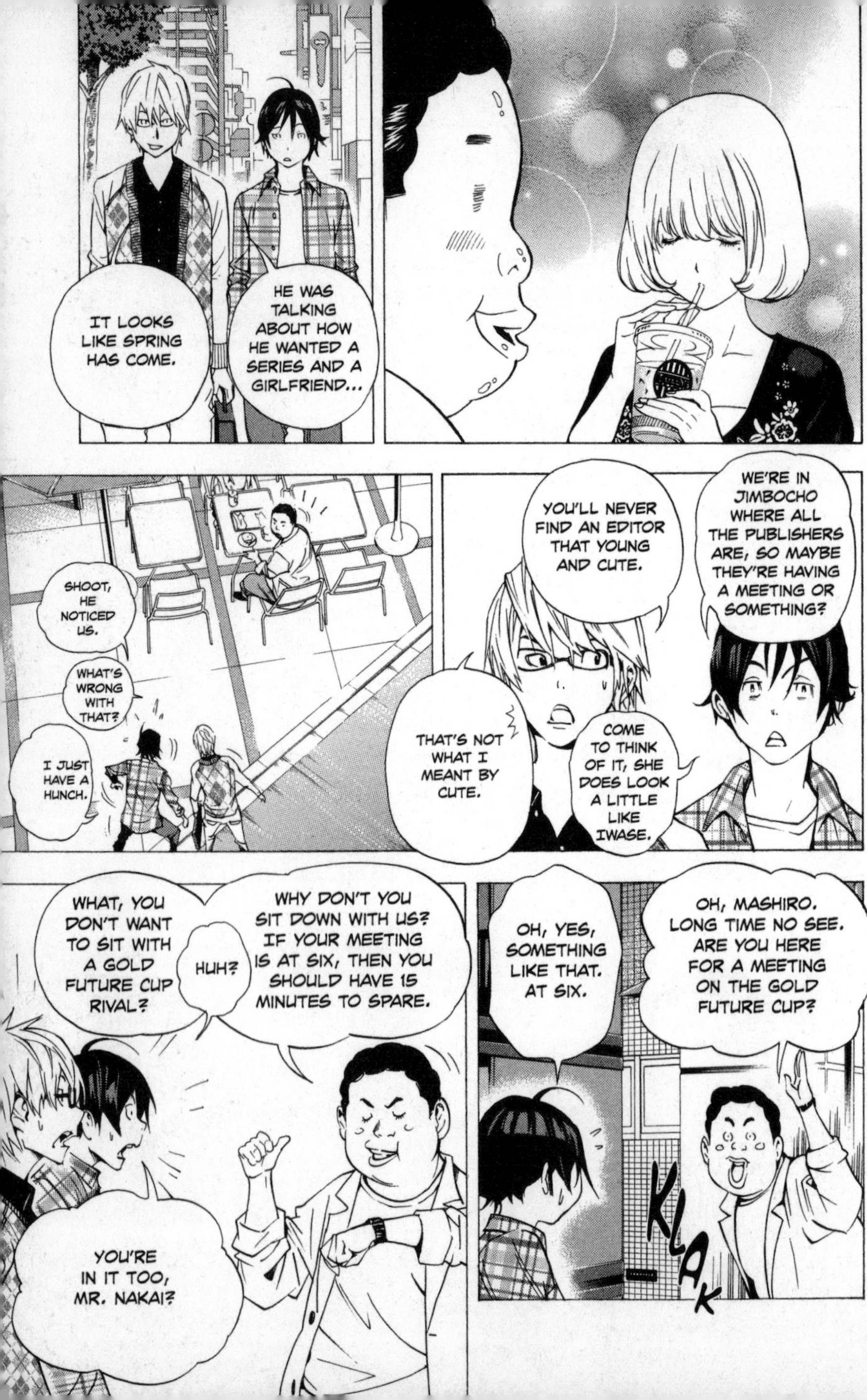
HE WAS TALKING ABOUT HOW HE WANTED A SERIES AND A GIRLFRIEND...
IT LOOKS LIKE SPRING HAS COME.
WE'RE IN JIMBOCHO WHERE ALL THE PUBLISHERS ARE, SO MAYBE THEY'RE HAVING A MEETING OR SOMETHING?
YOU'LL NEVER FIND AN EDITOR THAT YOUNG AND CUTE.
COME TO THINK OF IT, SHE DOES LOOK A LITTLE LIKE IWASE.
THAT'S NOT WHAT I MEANT BY CUTE.
SHOOT, HE NOTICED US.
WHAT'S WRONG WITH THAT?
I JUST HAVE A HUNCH.
OH, MASHIRO. LONG TIME NO SEE. ARE YOU HERE FOR A MEETING ON THE GOLD FUTURE CUP?
OH, YES, SOMETHING LIKE THAT. AT SIX.
KLAK
WHY DON'T YOU SIT DOWN WITH US? IF YOUR MEETING IS AT SIX, THEN YOU SHOULD HAVE 15 MINUTES TO SPARE.
HUH?
WHAT, YOU DON'T WANT TO SIT WITH A GOLD FUTURE CUP RIVAL?
YOU'RE IN IT TOO, MR. NAKAI?

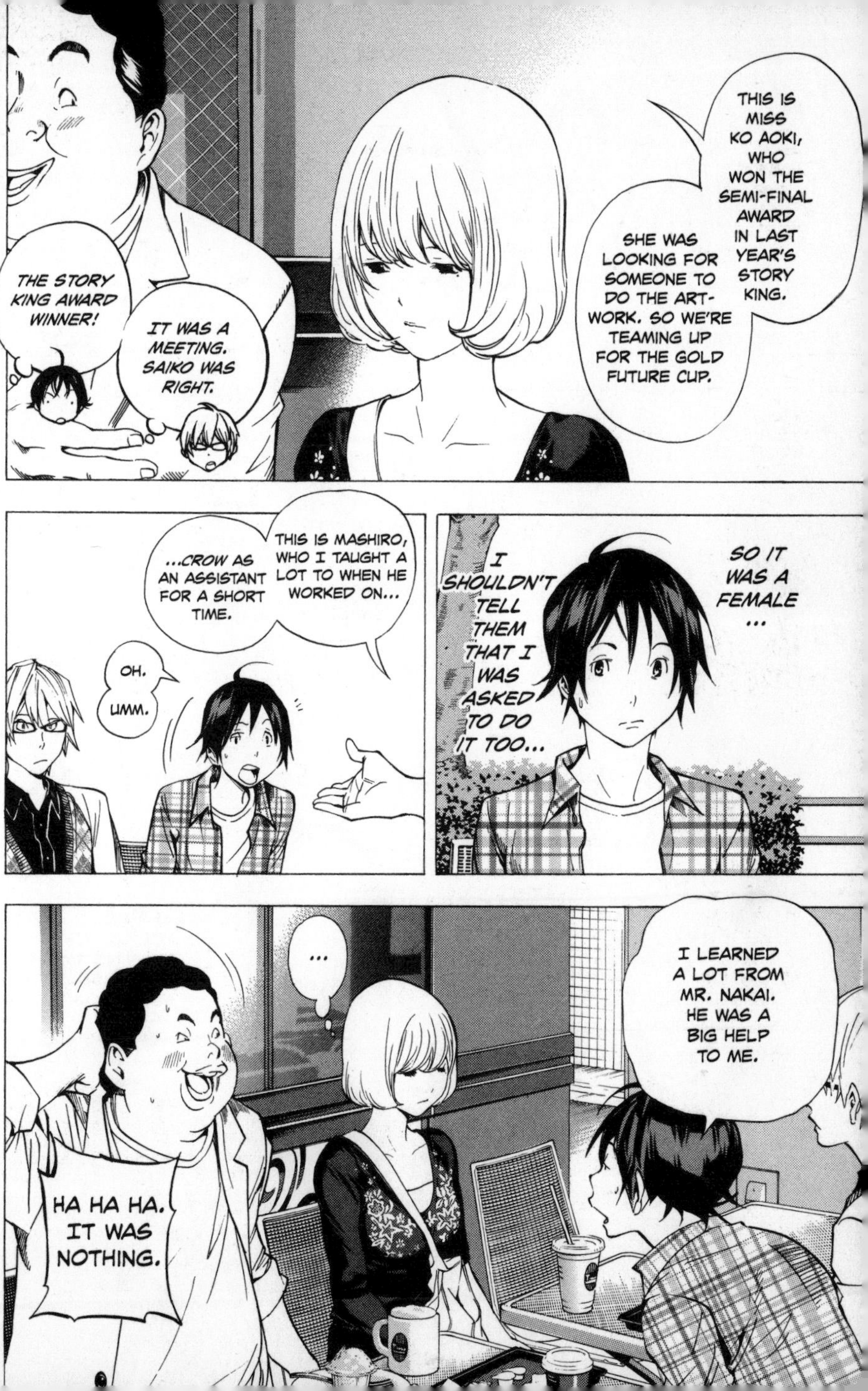
THIS IS MISS KO AOKI, WHO WON THE SEMI-FINAL AWARD IN LAST YEAR'S STORY KING.
SHE WAS LOOKING FOR SOMEONE TO DO THE ART-WORK. SO WE'RE TEAMING UP FOR THE GOLD FUTURE CUP.
IT WAS A MEETING. SAIKO WAS RIGHT.
THE STORY KING AWARD WINNER!
SO IT WAS A FEMALE...
I SHOULDN'T TELL THEM THAT I WAS ASKED TO DO IT TOO...
THIS IS MASHIRO, WHO I TAUGHT A LOT TO WHEN HE WORKED ON...
...CROW AS AN ASSISTANT FOR A SHORT TIME.
OH.
UMM.
I LEARNED A LOT FROM MR. NAKAI. HE WAS A BIG HELP TO ME.
...
HA HA HA. IT WAS NOTHING.

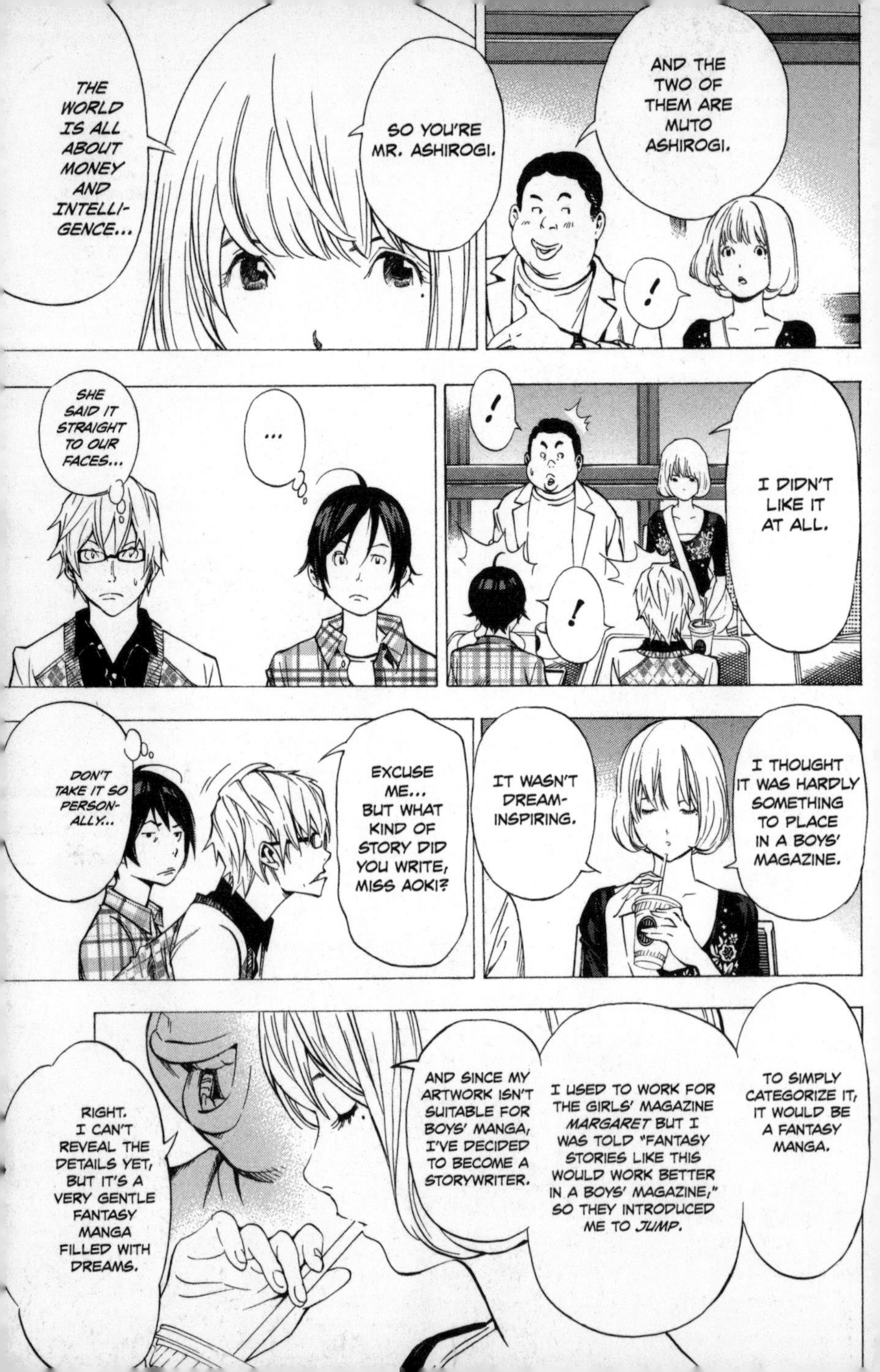
AND THE TWO OF THEM ARE MUTO ASHIROGI.
!
SO YOU'RE MR. ASHIROGI.
THE WORLD IS ALL ABOUT MONEY AND INTELLI-GENCE...
I DIDN'T LIKE IT AT ALL.
!
!
...
SHE SAID IT STRAIGHT TO OUR FACES...
I THOUGHT IT WAS HARDLY SOMETHING TO PLACE IN A BOYS' MAGAZINE.
IT WASN'T DREAM-INSPIRING.
EXCUSE ME... BUT WHAT KIND OF STORY DID YOU WRITE, MISS AOKI?
DON'T TAKE IT SO PERSON-ALLY...
TO SIMPLY CATEGORIZE IT, IT WOULD BE A FANTASY MANGA.
I USED TO WORK FOR THE GIRLS' MAGAZINE *MARGARET* BUT I WAS TOLD "FANTASY STORIES LIKE THIS WOULD WORK BETTER IN A BOYS' MAGAZINE," SO THEY INTRODUCED ME TO *JUMP*.
AND SINCE MY ARTWORK ISN'T SUITABLE FOR BOYS' MANGA, I'VE DECIDED TO BECOME A STORYWRITER.
RIGHT. I CAN'T REVEAL THE DETAILS YET, BUT IT'S A VERY GENTLE FANTASY MANGA FILLED WITH DREAMS.

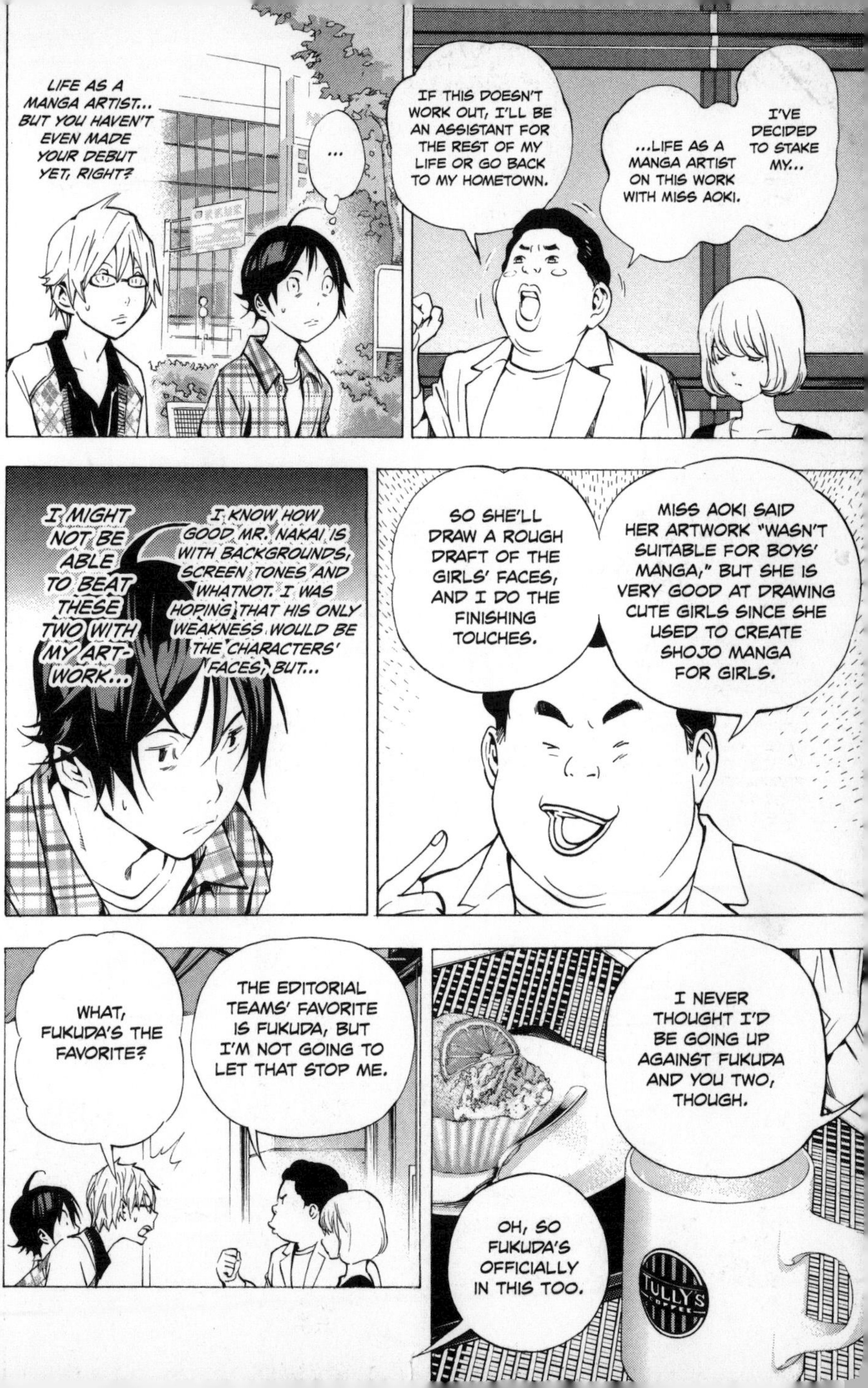
I'VE DECIDED TO STAKE MY...
...LIFE AS A MANGA ARTIST ON THIS WORK WITH MISS AOKI.
IF THIS DOESN'T WORK OUT, I'LL BE AN ASSISTANT FOR THE REST OF MY LIFE OR GO BACK TO MY HOMETOWN.
LIFE AS A MANGA ARTIST... BUT YOU HAVEN'T EVEN MADE YOUR DEBUT YET, RIGHT?
...
MISS AOKI SAID HER ARTWORK "WASN'T SUITABLE FOR BOYS' MANGA," BUT SHE IS VERY GOOD AT DRAWING CUTE GIRLS SINCE SHE USED TO CREATE SHOJO MANGA FOR GIRLS.
SO SHE'LL DRAW A ROUGH DRAFT OF THE GIRLS' FACES, AND I DO THE FINISHING TOUCHES.
I KNOW HOW GOOD MR. NAKAI IS WITH BACKGROUNDS, SCREEN TONES AND WHATNOT. I WAS HOPING THAT HIS ONLY WEAKNESS WOULD BE THE CHARACTERS' FACES, BUT...
I MIGHT NOT BE ABLE TO BEAT THESE TWO WITH MY ART-WORK...
I NEVER THOUGHT I'D BE GOING UP AGAINST FUKUDA AND YOU TWO, THOUGH.
OH, SO FUKUDA'S OFFICIALLY IN THIS TOO.
TULLY'S
THE EDITORIAL TEAMS' FAVORITE IS FUKUDA, BUT I'M NOT GOING TO LET THAT STOP ME.
WHAT, FUKUDA'S THE FAVORITE?

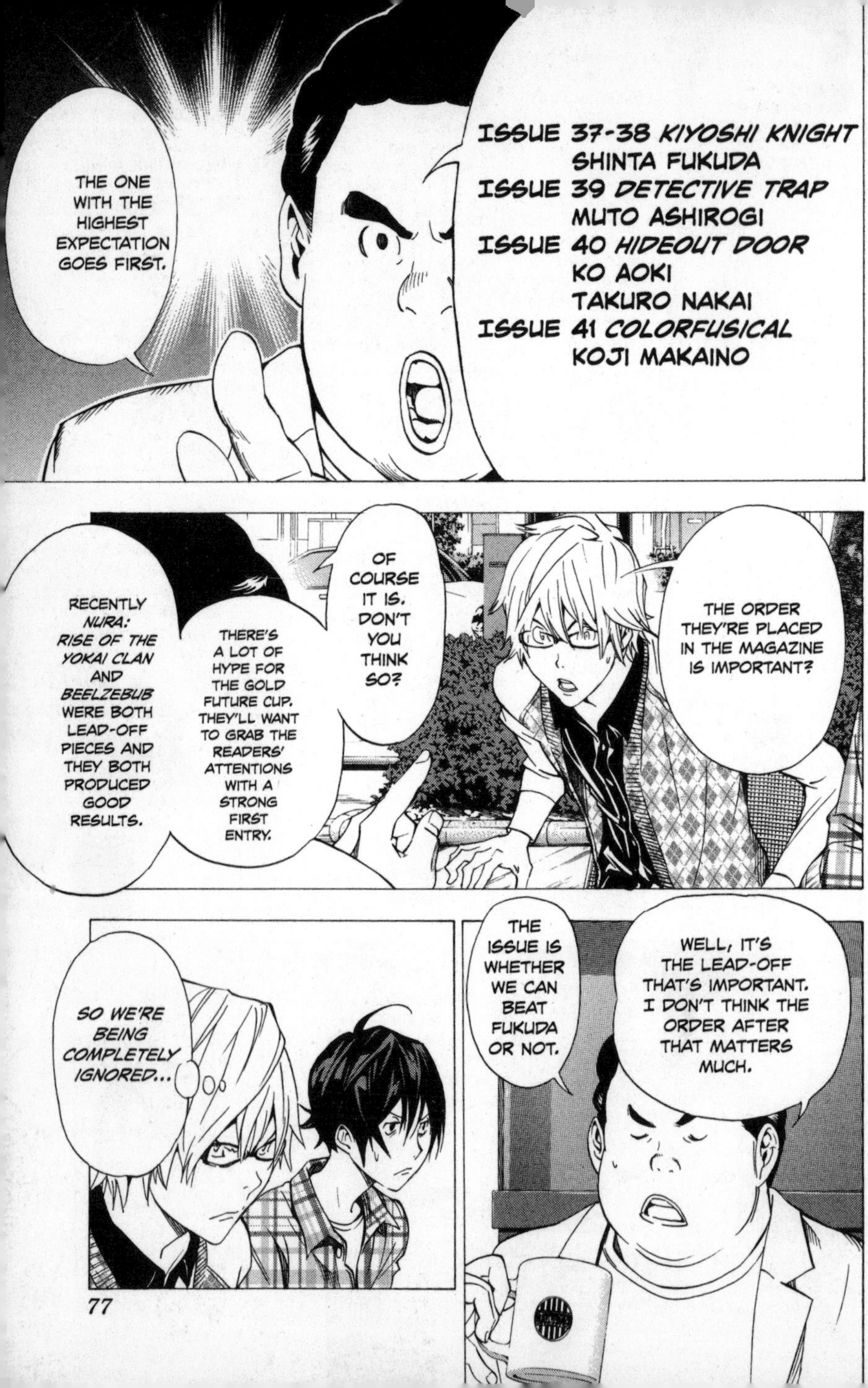
ISSUE 37-38 KIYOSHI KNIGHT SHINTA FUKUDA ISSUE 39 DETECTIVE TRAP MUTO ASHIROGI ISSUE 40 HIDEOUT DOOR KO AOKI TAKURO NAKAI ISSUE 41 COLORFUSICAL KOJI MAKAINO
THE ONE WITH THE HIGHEST EXPECTATION GOES FIRST.
THE ORDER THEY'RE PLACED IN THE MAGAZINE IS IMPORTANT?
OF COURSE IT IS. DON'T YOU THINK SO?
THERE'S A LOT OF HYPE FOR THE GOLD FUTURE CUP. THEY'LL WANT TO GRAB THE READERS' ATTENTIONS WITH A STRONG FIRST ENTRY.
RECENTLY NURA: RISE OF THE YOKAI CLAN AND BEELZEBUB WERE BOTH LEAD-OFF PIECES AND THEY BOTH PRODUCED GOOD RESULTS.
WELL, IT'S THE LEAD-OFF THAT'S IMPORTANT. I DON'T THINK THE ORDER AFTER THAT MATTERS MUCH.
THE ISSUE IS WHETHER WE CAN BEAT FUKUDA OR NOT.
SO WE'RE BEING COMPLETELY IGNORED...

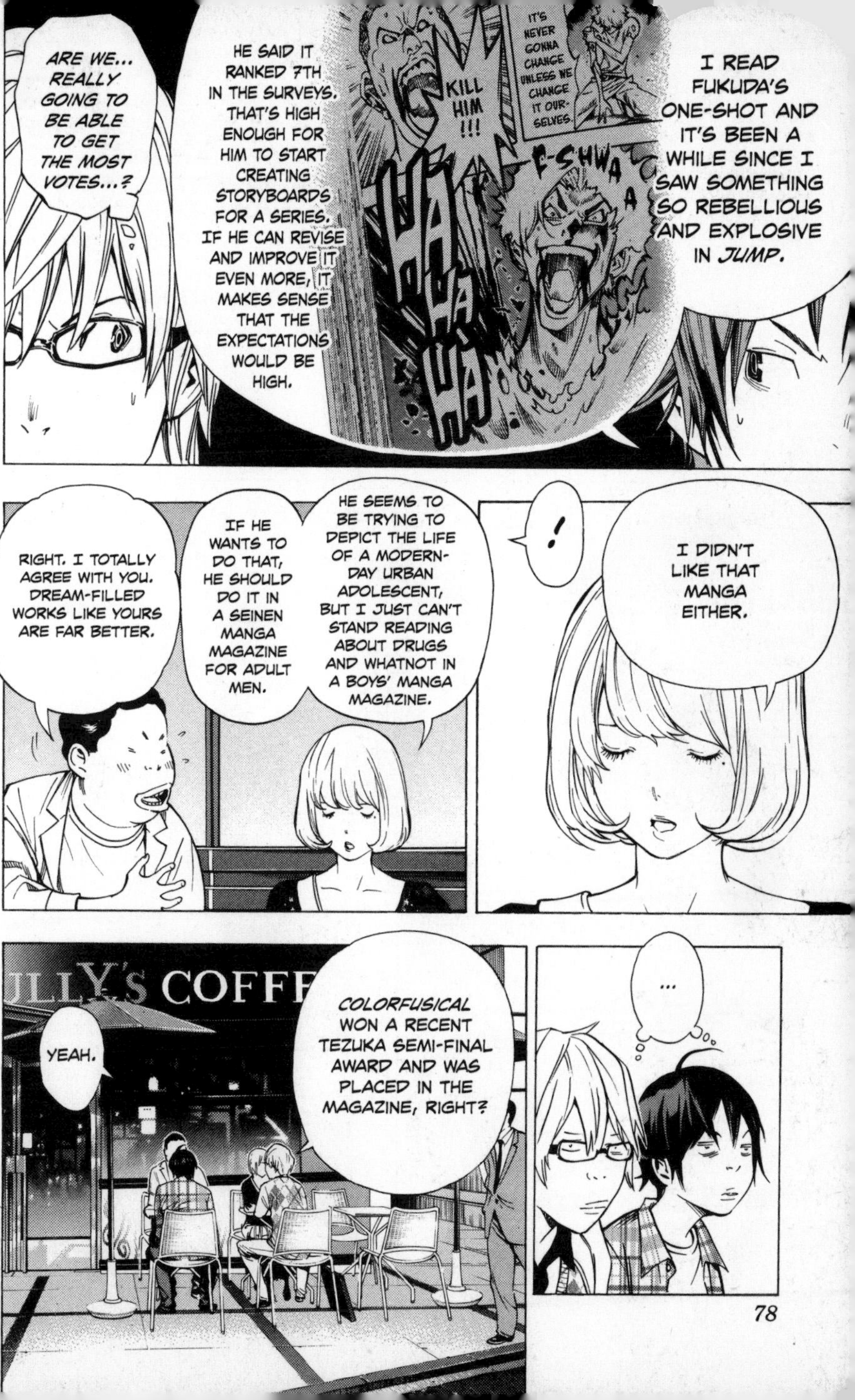
I READ FUKUDA'S ONE-SHOT AND IT'S BEEN A WHILE SINCE I SAW SOMETHING SO REBELLIOUS AND EXPLOSIVE IN *JUMP*.
IT'S NEVER GONNA CHANGE UNLESS WE CHANGE IT OUR-SELVES.
KILL HIM !!!
E-SHWA A
HA HA HA HA
HE SAID IT RANKED 7TH IN THE SURVEYS. THAT'S HIGH ENOUGH FOR HIM TO START CREATING STORYBOARDS FOR A SERIES. IF HE CAN REVISE AND IMPROVE IT EVEN MORE, IT MAKES SENSE THAT THE EXPECTATIONS WOULD BE HIGH.
ARE WE... REALLY GOING TO BE ABLE TO GET THE MOST VOTES...?
I DIDN'T LIKE THAT MANGA EITHER.
!
HE SEEMS TO BE TRYING TO DEPICT THE LIFE OF A MODERN-DAY URBAN ADOLESCENT, BUT I JUST CAN'T STAND READING ABOUT DRUGS AND WHATNOT IN A BOYS' MANGA MAGAZINE.
IF HE WANTS TO DO THAT, HE SHOULD DO IT IN A SEINEN MANGA MAGAZINE FOR ADULT MEN.
RIGHT. I TOTALLY AGREE WITH YOU. DREAM-FILLED WORKS LIKE YOURS ARE FAR BETTER.
...
ULLY'S COFFE
COLORFUSICAL WON A RECENT TEZUKA SEMI-FINAL AWARD AND WAS PLACED IN THE MAGAZINE, RIGHT?
YEAH.

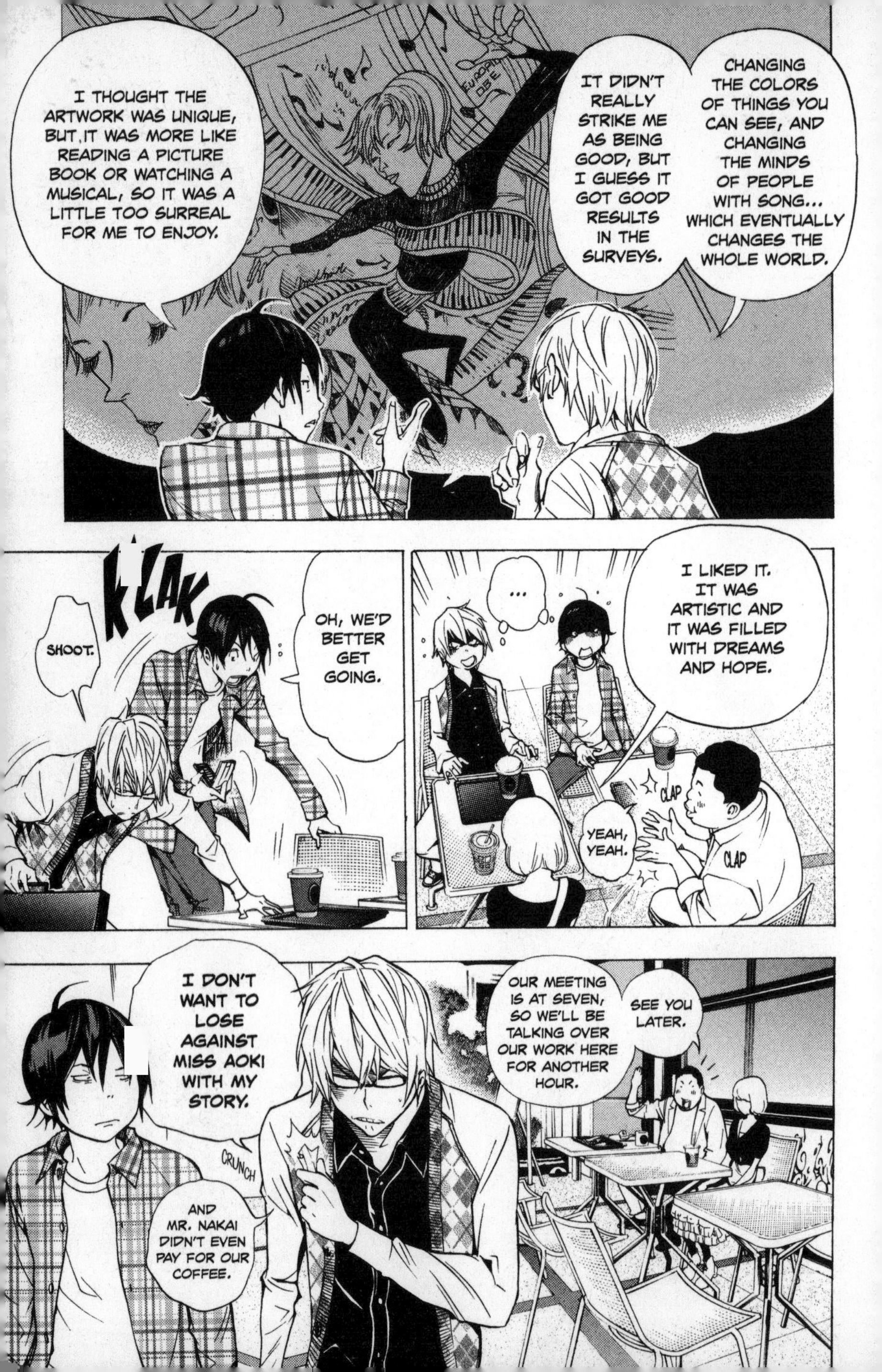
CHANGING THE COLORS OF THINGS YOU CAN SEE, AND CHANGING THE MINDS OF PEOPLE WITH SONG... WHICH EVENTUALLY CHANGES THE WHOLE WORLD.
IT DIDN'T REALLY STRIKE ME AS BEING GOOD, BUT I GUESS IT GOT GOOD RESULTS IN THE SURVEYS.
I THOUGHT THE ARTWORK WAS UNIQUE, BUT IT WAS MORE LIKE READING A PICTURE BOOK OR WATCHING A MUSICAL, SO IT WAS A LITTLE TOO SURREAL FOR ME TO ENJOY.
...
I LIKED IT. IT WAS ARTISTIC AND IT WAS FILLED WITH DREAMS AND HOPE.
CLAP
YEAH, YEAH.
CLAP
OH, WE'D BETTER GET GOING.
KLAK
SHOOT.
SEE YOU LATER.
OUR MEETING IS AT SEVEN, SO WE'LL BE TALKING OVER OUR WORK HERE FOR ANOTHER HOUR.
I DON'T WANT TO LOSE AGAINST MISS AOKI WITH MY STORY.
CRUNCH
AND MR. NAKAI DIDN'T EVEN PAY FOR OUR COFFEE.

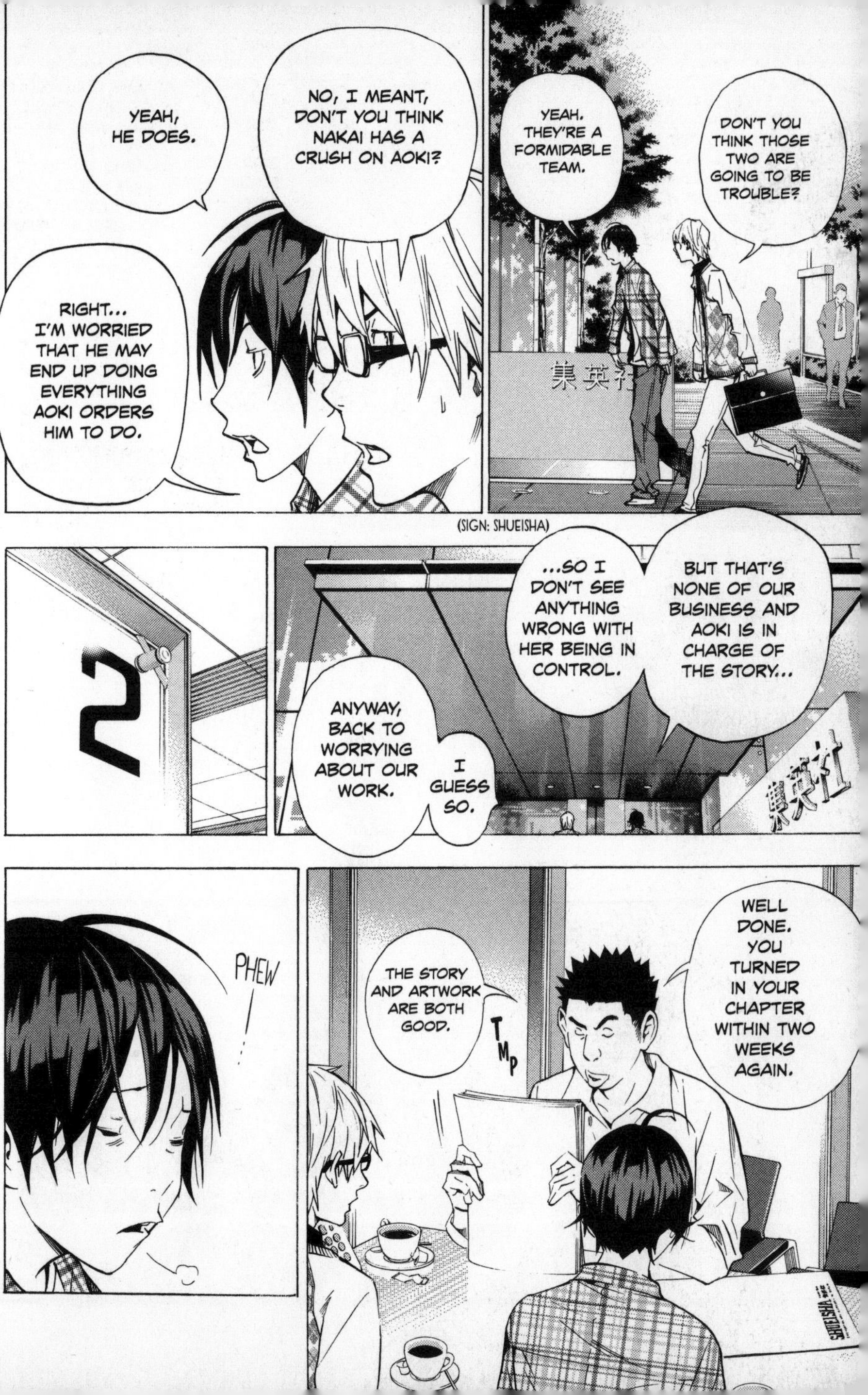
DON'T YOU THINK THOSE TWO ARE GOING TO BE TROUBLE?
YEAH. THEY'RE A FORMIDABLE TEAM.
(SIGN: SHUEISHA)
NO, I MEANT, DON'T YOU THINK NAKAI HAS A CRUSH ON AOKI?
YEAH, HE DOES.
RIGHT... I'M WORRIED THAT HE MAY END UP DOING EVERYTHING AOKI ORDERS HIM TO DO.
BUT THAT'S NONE OF OUR BUSINESS AND AOKI IS IN CHARGE OF THE STORY...
...SO I DON'T SEE ANYTHING WRONG WITH HER BEING IN CONTROL.
ANYWAY, BACK TO WORRYING ABOUT OUR WORK.
I GUESS SO.
2
WELL DONE. YOU TURNED IN YOUR CHAPTER WITHIN TWO WEEKS AGAIN.
THE STORY AND ARTWORK ARE BOTH GOOD.
TMP
PHEW

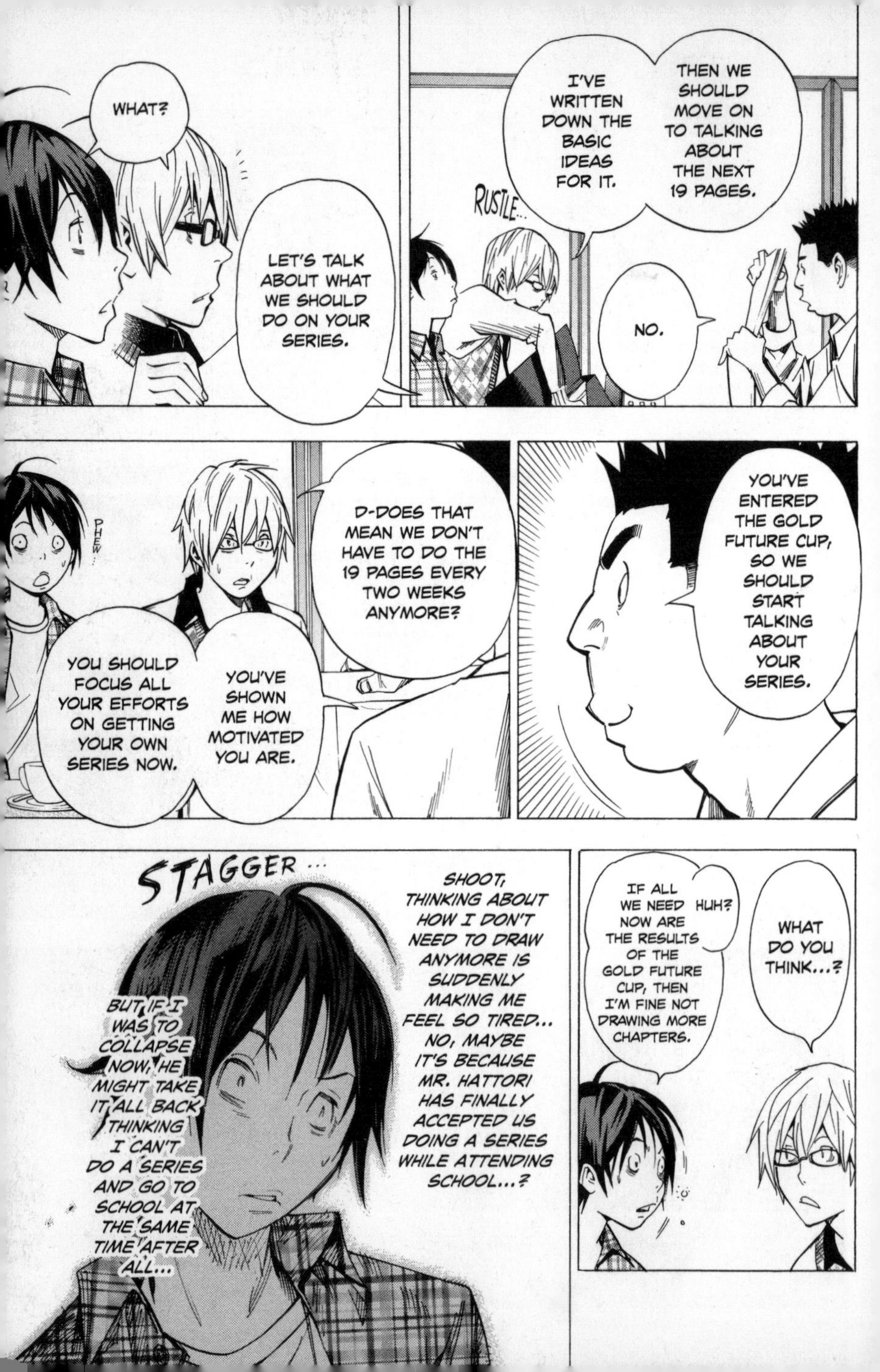
THEN WE SHOULD MOVE ON TO TALKING ABOUT THE NEXT 19 PAGES.
I'VE WRITTEN DOWN THE BASIC IDEAS FOR IT.
RUSTLE...
NO.
LET'S TALK ABOUT WHAT WE SHOULD DO ON YOUR SERIES.
WHAT?
YOU'VE ENTERED THE GOLD FUTURE CUP, SO WE SHOULD START TALKING ABOUT YOUR SERIES.
D-DOES THAT MEAN WE DON'T HAVE TO DO THE 19 PAGES EVERY TWO WEEKS ANYMORE?
PHEW...
YOU'VE SHOWN ME HOW MOTIVATED YOU ARE.
YOU SHOULD FOCUS ALL YOUR EFFORTS ON GETTING YOUR OWN SERIES NOW.
WHAT DO YOU THINK...?
HUH?
IF ALL WE NEED NOW ARE THE RESULTS OF THE GOLD FUTURE CUP, THEN I'M FINE NOT DRAWING MORE CHAPTERS.
STAGGER...
SHOOT, THINKING ABOUT HOW I DON'T NEED TO DRAW ANYMORE IS SUDDENLY MAKING ME FEEL SO TIRED... NO, MAYBE IT'S BECAUSE MR. HATTORI HAS FINALLY ACCEPTED US DOING A SERIES WHILE ATTENDING SCHOOL...?
BUT IF I WAS TO COLLAPSE NOW, HE MIGHT TAKE IT ALL BACK THINKING I CAN'T DO A SERIES AND GO TO SCHOOL AT THE SAME TIME AFTER ALL...

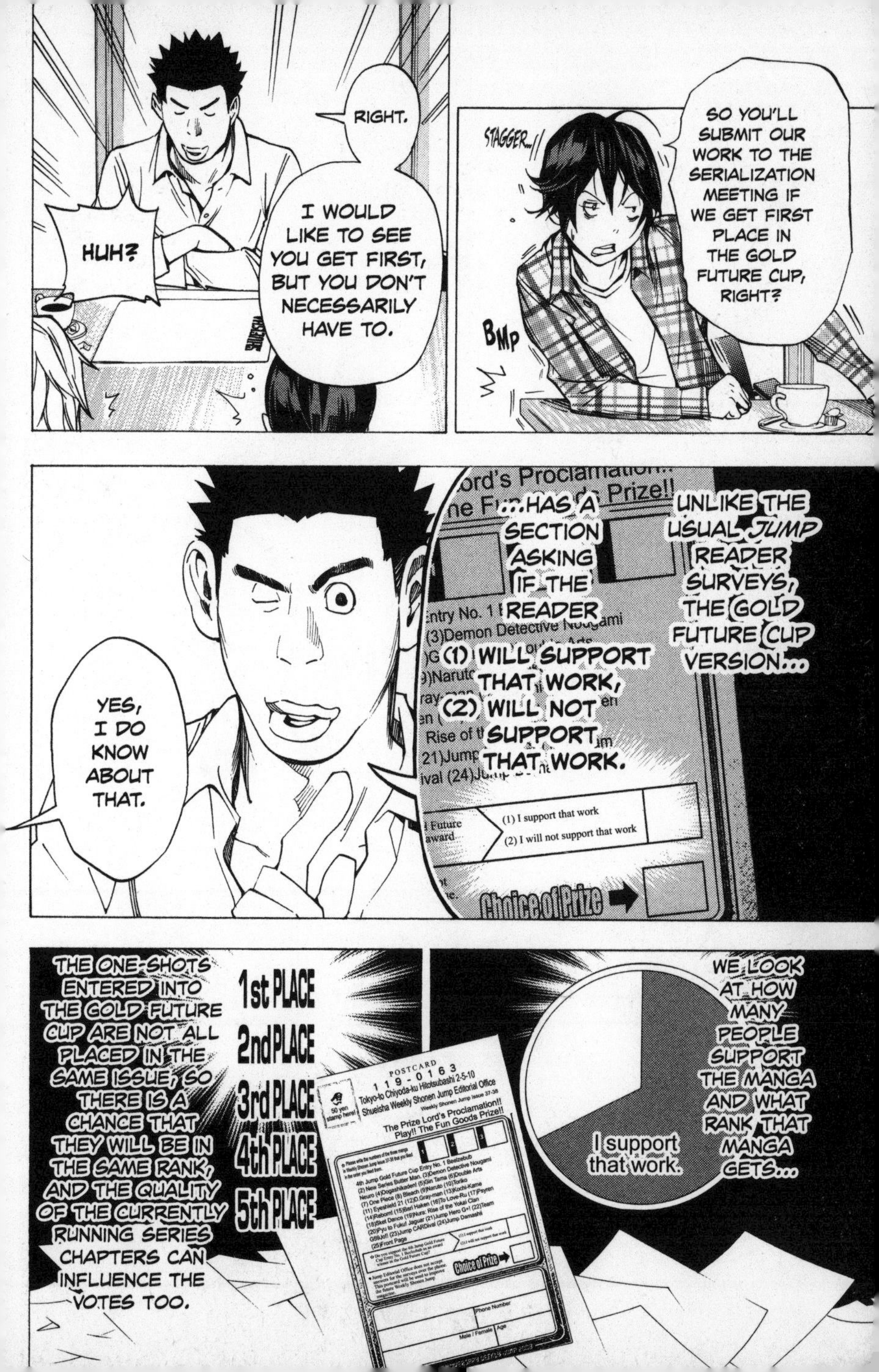
STAGGER...
SO YOU'LL SUBMIT OUR WORK TO THE SERIALIZATION MEETING IF WE GET FIRST PLACE IN THE GOLD FUTURE CUP, RIGHT?
BMP
RIGHT.
I WOULD LIKE TO SEE YOU GET FIRST, BUT YOU DON'T NECESSARILY HAVE TO.
HUH?
UNLIKE THE USUAL JUMP READER SURVEYS, THE GOLD FUTURE CUP VERSION...
...HAS A SECTION ASKING IF THE READER (1) WILL SUPPORT THAT WORK, (2) WILL NOT SUPPORT THAT WORK.
(1) I support that work
(2) I will not support that work
Choice of Prize
YES, I DO KNOW ABOUT THAT.
WE LOOK AT HOW MANY PEOPLE SUPPORT THE MANGA AND WHAT RANK THAT MANGA GETS...
I support that work.
THE ONE-SHOTS ENTERED INTO THE GOLD FUTURE CUP ARE NOT ALL PLACED IN THE SAME ISSUE, SO THERE IS A CHANCE THAT THEY WILL BE IN THE SAME RANK, AND THE QUALITY OF THE CURRENTLY RUNNING SERIES CHAPTERS CAN INFLUENCE THE VOTES TOO.
1st PLACE
2nd PLACE
3rd PLACE
4th PLACE
5th PLACE
POSTCARD
119-0163
Tokyo-to Chiyoda-ku Hitotsubashi 2-5-10
Shueisha Weekly Shonen Jump Editorial Office
The Prize Lord's Proclamation!!
Play!! The Fun Goods Prize!!
Choice of Prize

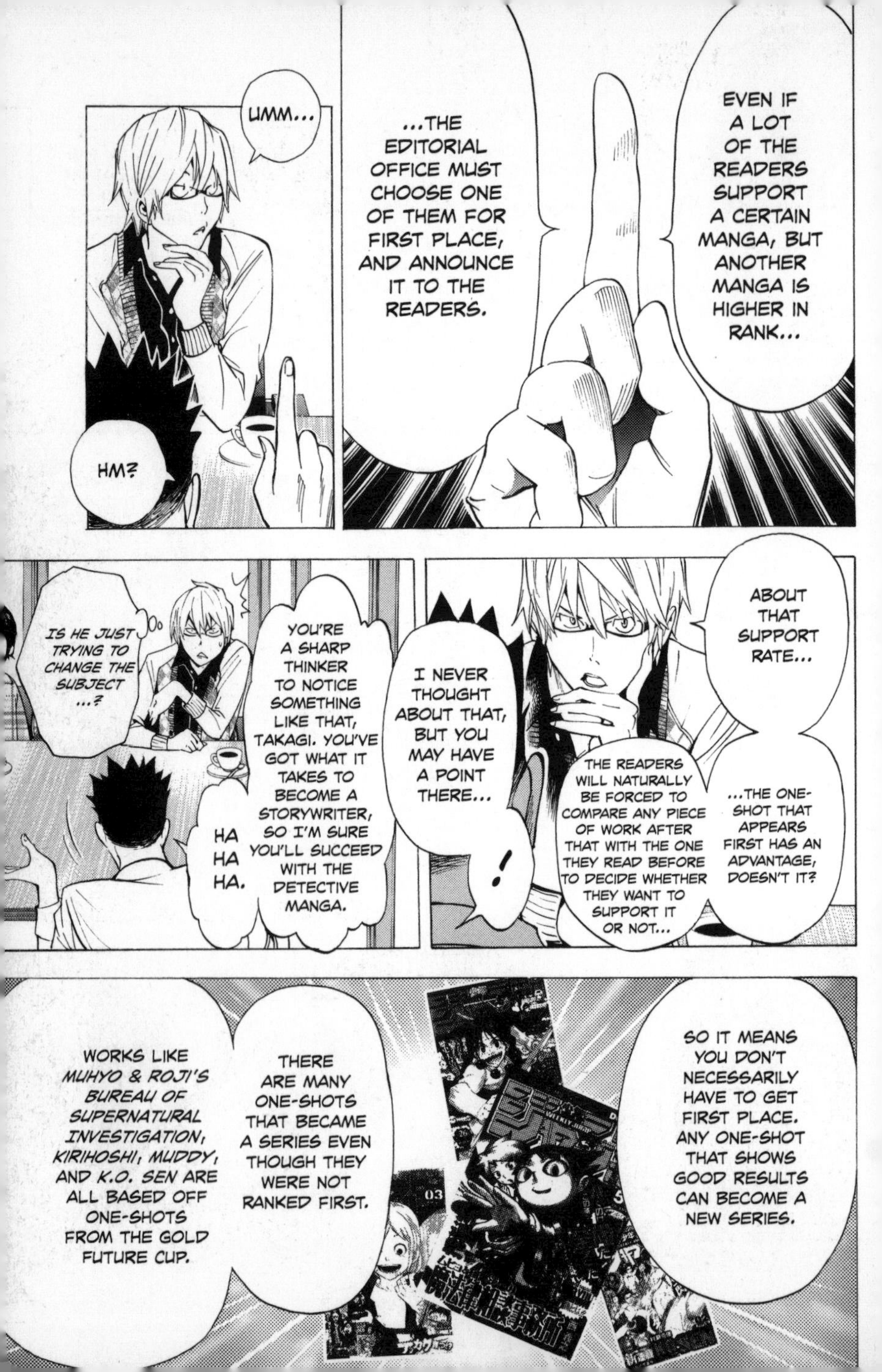
EVEN IF A LOT OF THE READERS SUPPORT A CERTAIN MANGA, BUT ANOTHER MANGA IS HIGHER IN RANK...
...THE EDITORIAL OFFICE MUST CHOOSE ONE OF THEM FOR FIRST PLACE, AND ANNOUNCE IT TO THE READERS.
UMM...
HM?
ABOUT THAT SUPPORT RATE...
...THE ONE-SHOT THAT APPEARS FIRST HAS AN ADVANTAGE, DOESN'T IT?
THE READERS WILL NATURALLY BE FORCED TO COMPARE ANY PIECE OF WORK AFTER THAT WITH THE ONE THEY READ BEFORE TO DECIDE WHETHER THEY WANT TO SUPPORT IT OR NOT...
!
I NEVER THOUGHT ABOUT THAT, BUT YOU MAY HAVE A POINT THERE...
YOU'RE A SHARP THINKER TO NOTICE SOMETHING LIKE THAT, TAKAGI. YOU'VE GOT WHAT IT TAKES TO BECOME A STORYWRITER, SO I'M SURE YOU'LL SUCCEED WITH THE DETECTIVE MANGA.
HA HA HA.
IS HE JUST TRYING TO CHANGE THE SUBJECT ...?
SO IT MEANS YOU DON'T NECESSARILY HAVE TO GET FIRST PLACE. ANY ONE-SHOT THAT SHOWS GOOD RESULTS CAN BECOME A NEW SERIES.
THERE ARE MANY ONE-SHOTS THAT BECAME A SERIES EVEN THOUGH THEY WERE NOT RANKED FIRST.
WORKS LIKE *MUHYO & ROJI'S BUREAU OF SUPERNATURAL INVESTIGATION*, *KIRIHOSHI*, *MUDDY*, AND *K.O. SEN* ARE ALL BASED OFF ONE-SHOTS FROM THE GOLD FUTURE CUP.

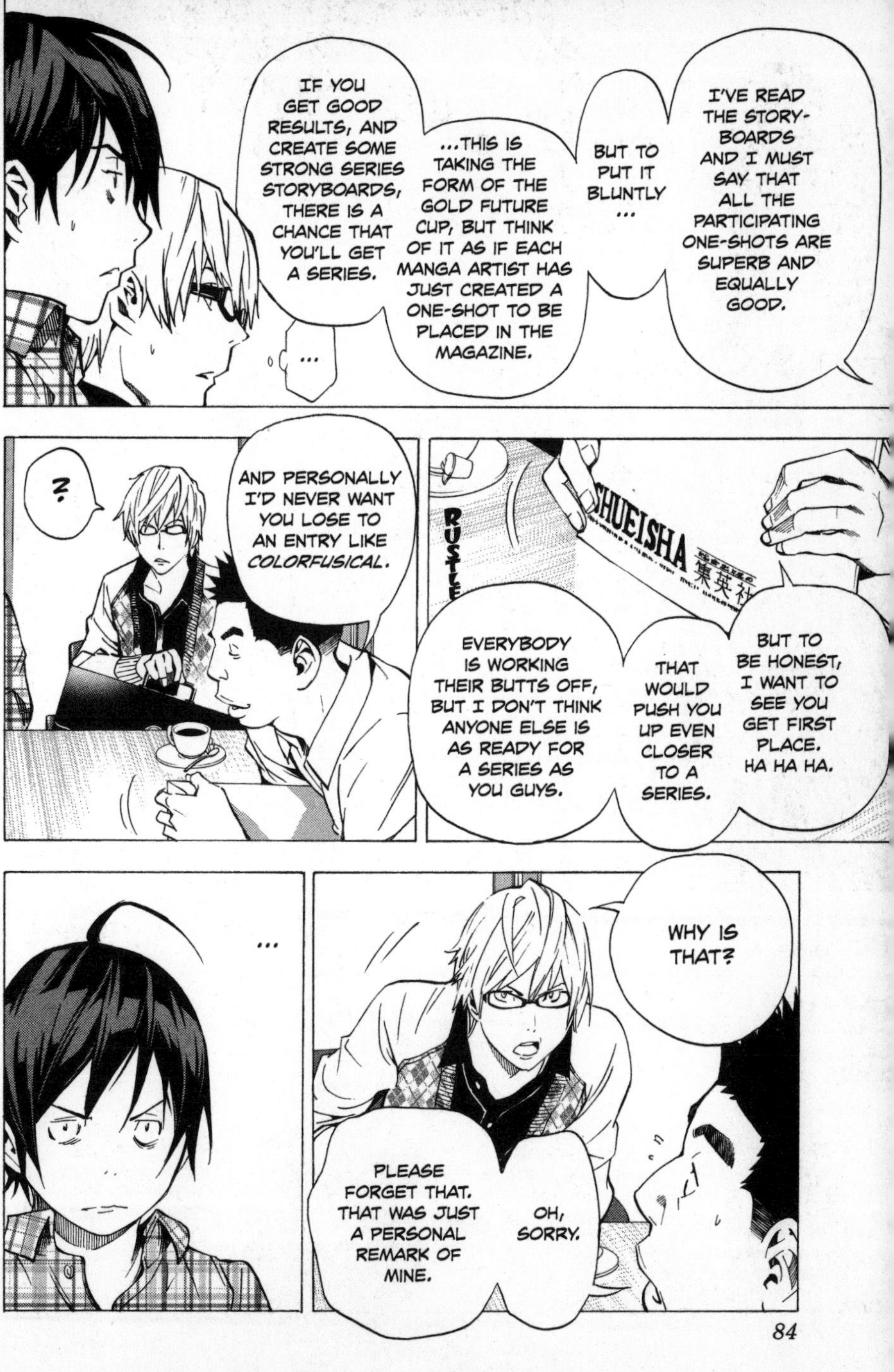
I'VE READ THE STORY-BOARDS AND I MUST SAY THAT ALL THE PARTICIPATING ONE-SHOTS ARE SUPERB AND EQUALLY GOOD.
BUT TO PUT IT BLUNTLY ...
...THIS IS TAKING THE FORM OF THE GOLD FUTURE CUP, BUT THINK OF IT AS IF EACH MANGA ARTIST HAS JUST CREATED A ONE-SHOT TO BE PLACED IN THE MAGAZINE.
IF YOU GET GOOD RESULTS, AND CREATE SOME STRONG SERIES STORYBOARDS, THERE IS A CHANCE THAT YOU'LL GET A SERIES.
...
SHUEISHA 集英社
RUSTLE
BUT TO BE HONEST, I WANT TO SEE YOU GET FIRST PLACE. HA HA HA.
THAT WOULD PUSH YOU UP EVEN CLOSER TO A SERIES.
EVERYBODY IS WORKING THEIR BUTTS OFF, BUT I DON'T THINK ANYONE ELSE IS AS READY FOR A SERIES AS YOU GUYS.
AND PERSONALLY I'D NEVER WANT YOU LOSE TO AN ENTRY LIKE *COLORFUSICAL*.
?
WHY IS THAT?
OH, SORRY.
PLEASE FORGET THAT. THAT WAS JUST A PERSONAL REMARK OF MINE.
...

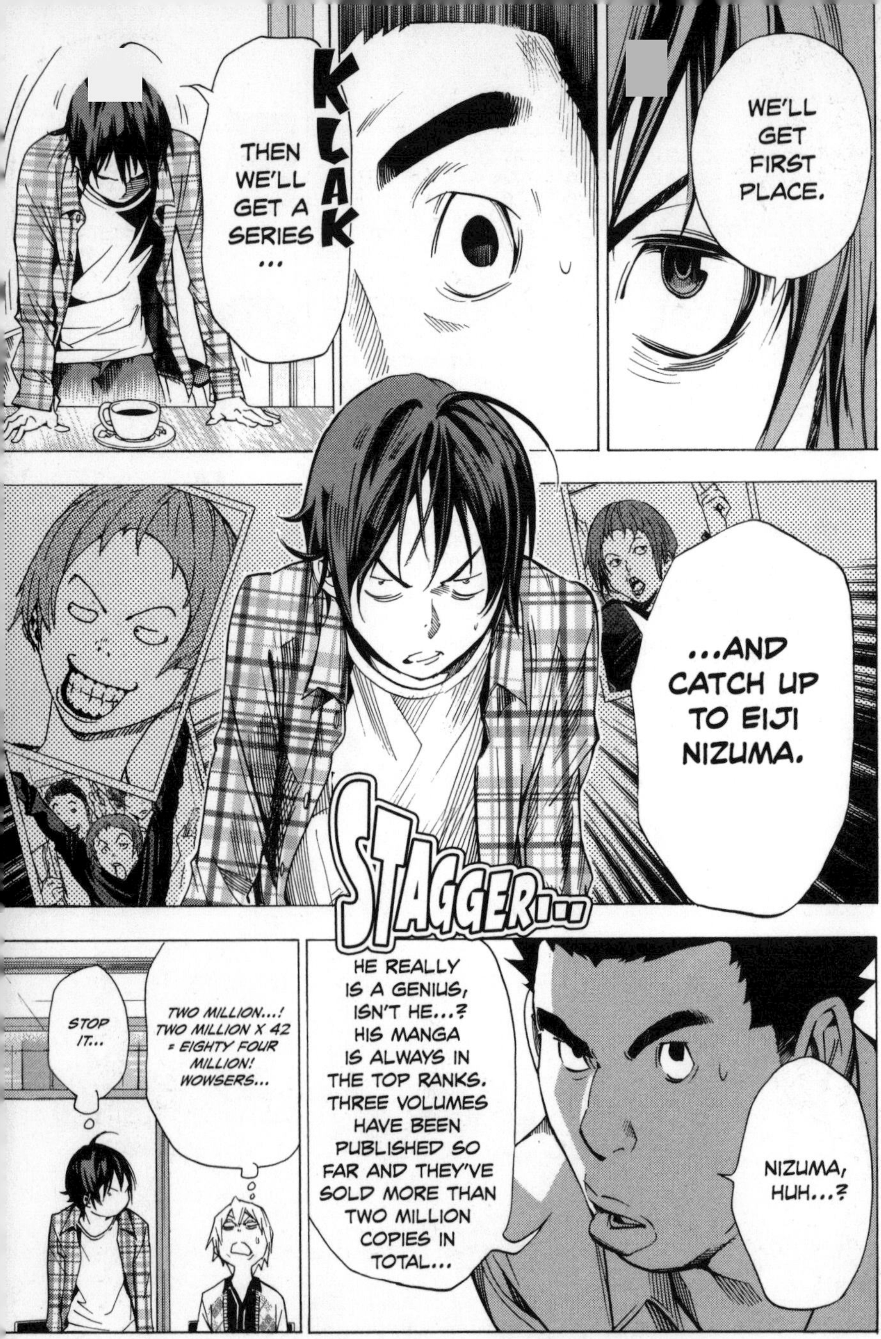
WE'LL GET FIRST PLACE.
KLAK
THEN WE'LL GET A SERIES...
...AND CATCH UP TO EIJI NIZUMA.
STAGGER...
NIZUMA, HUH...?
HE REALLY IS A GENIUS, ISN'T HE...? HIS MANGA IS ALWAYS IN THE TOP RANKS. THREE VOLUMES HAVE BEEN PUBLISHED SO FAR AND THEY'VE SOLD MORE THAN TWO MILLION COPIES IN TOTAL...
TWO MILLION...! TWO MILLION X 42 = EIGHTY FOUR MILLION! WOWSERS...
STOP IT...

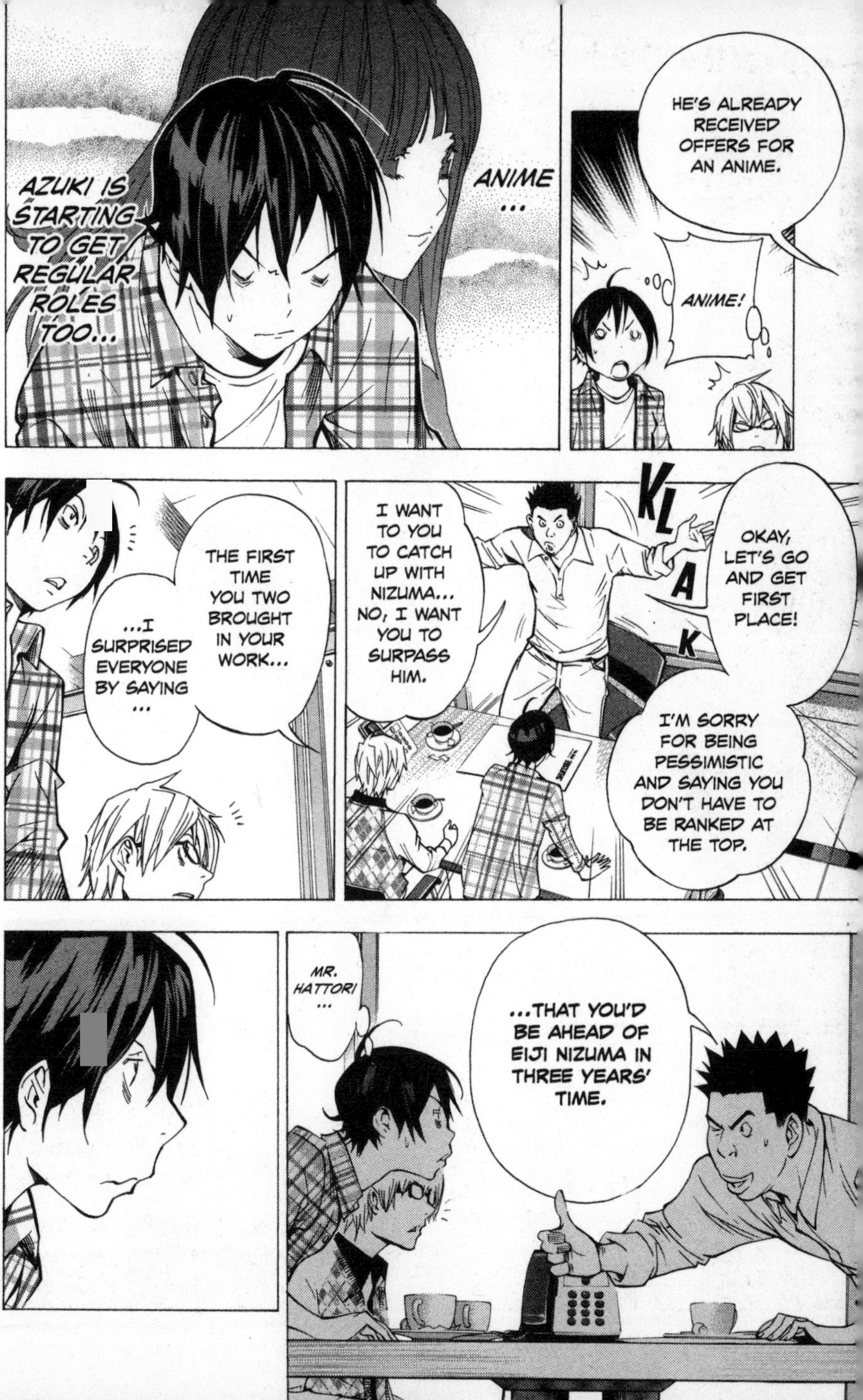
HE'S ALREADY RECEIVED OFFERS FOR AN ANIME.
ANIME!
ANIME ...
AZUKI IS STARTING TO GET REGULAR ROLES TOO...
KLAK
OKAY, LET'S GO AND GET FIRST PLACE!
I'M SORRY FOR BEING PESSIMISTIC AND SAYING YOU DON'T HAVE TO BE RANKED AT THE TOP.
I WANT TO YOU TO CATCH UP WITH NIZUMA... NO, I WANT YOU TO SURPASS HIM.
THE FIRST TIME YOU TWO BROUGHT IN YOUR WORK...
...I SURPRISED EVERYONE BY SAYING ...
...THAT YOU'D BE AHEAD OF EIJI NIZUMA IN THREE YEARS' TIME.
MR. HATTORI ...

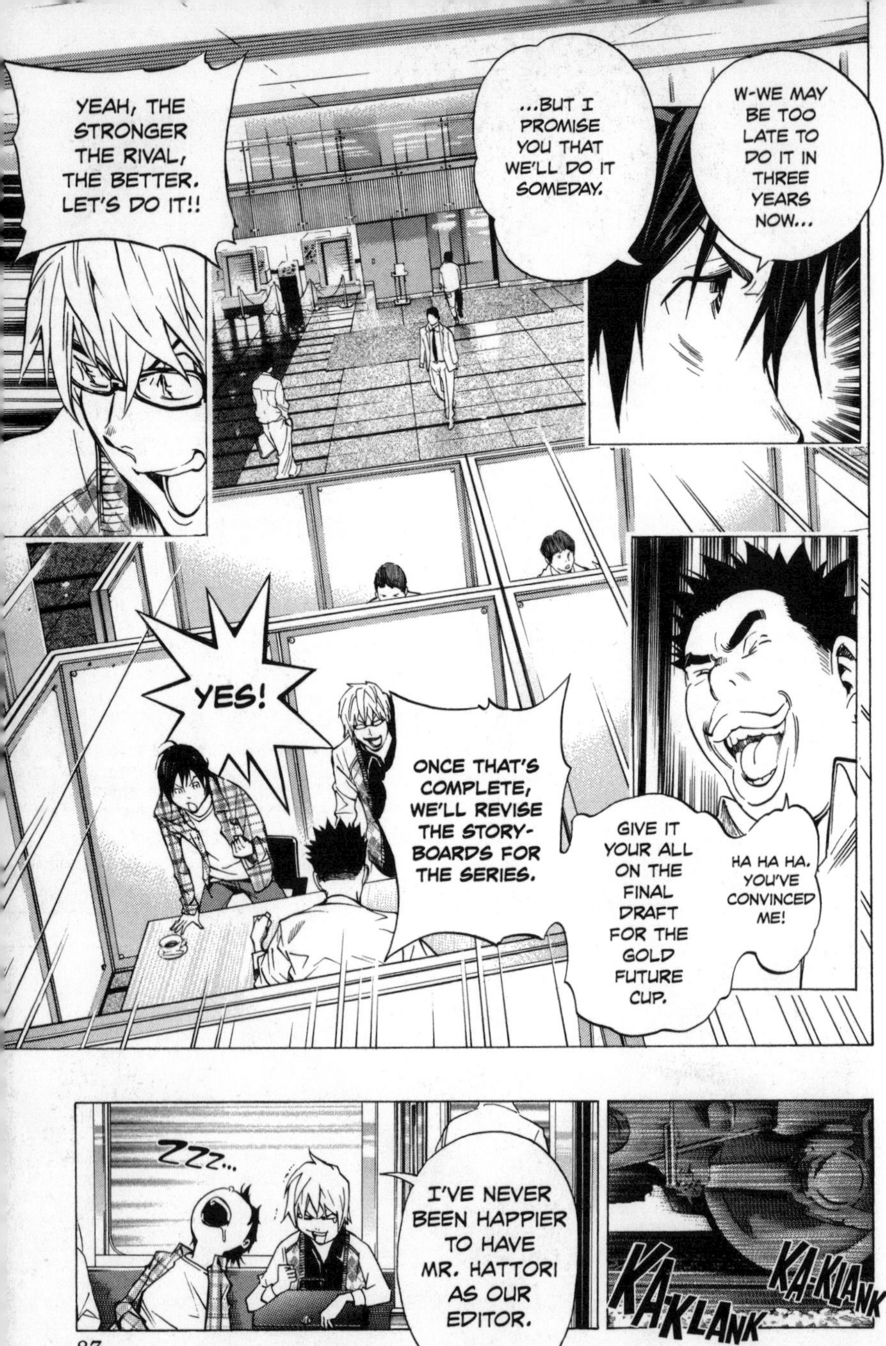
W-WE MAY BE TOO LATE TO DO IT IN THREE YEARS NOW...
...BUT I PROMISE YOU THAT WE'LL DO IT SOMEDAY.
YEAH, THE STRONGER THE RIVAL, THE BETTER. LET'S DO IT!!
HA HA HA. YOU'VE CONVINCED ME!
GIVE IT YOUR ALL ON THE FINAL DRAFT FOR THE GOLD FUTURE CUP.
ONCE THAT'S COMPLETE, WE'LL REVISE THE STORY-BOARDS FOR THE SERIES.
YES!
KA-KLANK
KA-KLANK
I'VE NEVER BEEN HAPPIER TO HAVE MR. HATTORI AS OUR EDITOR.
ZZZ...

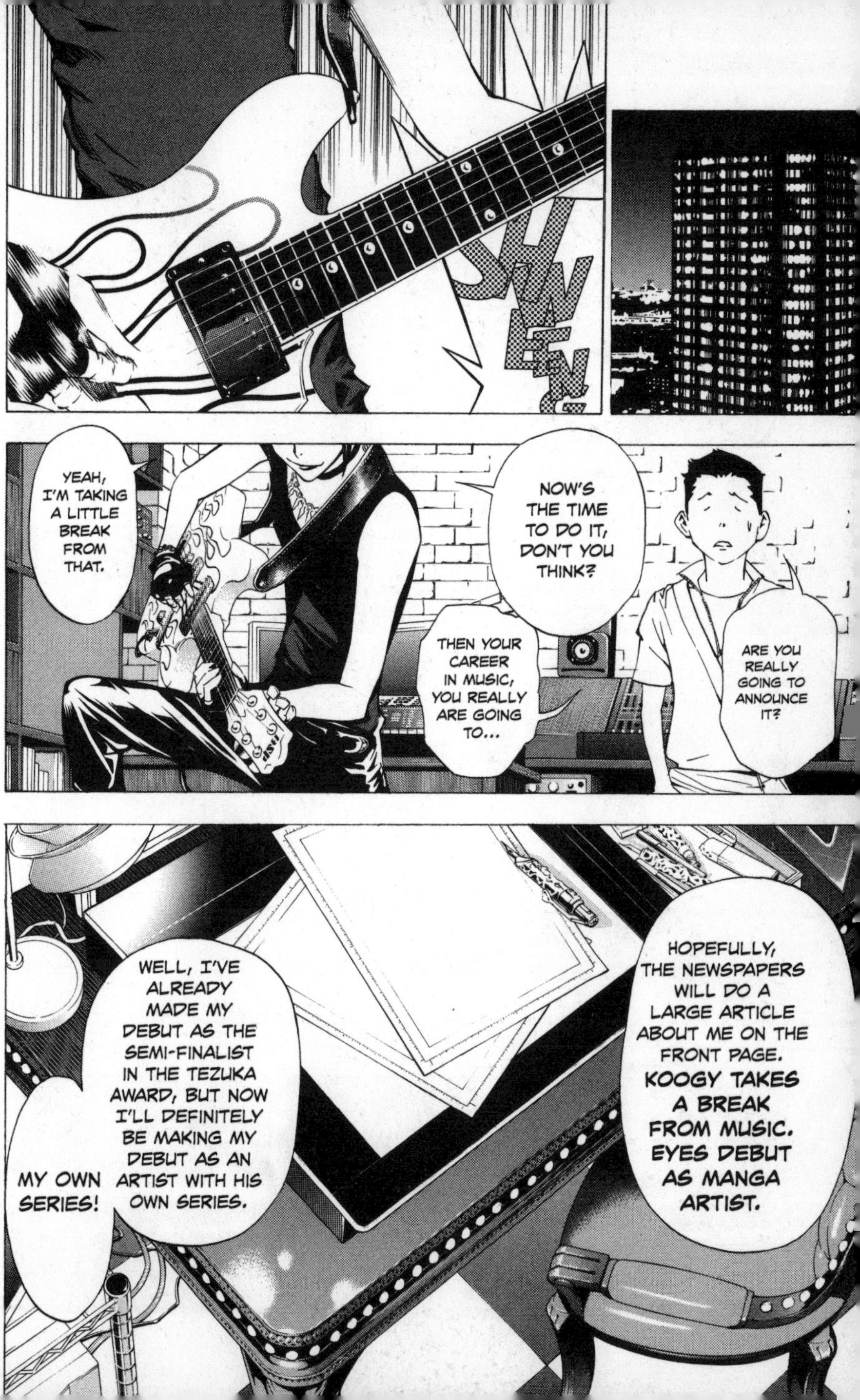
ARE YOU REALLY GOING TO ANNOUNCE IT?
NOW'S THE TIME TO DO IT, DON'T YOU THINK?
THEN YOUR CAREER IN MUSIC, YOU REALLY ARE GOING TO...
YEAH, I'M TAKING A LITTLE BREAK FROM THAT.
HOPEFULLY, THE NEWSPAPERS WILL DO A LARGE ARTICLE ABOUT ME ON THE FRONT PAGE. KOOGY TAKES A BREAK FROM MUSIC. EYES DEBUT AS MANGA ARTIST.
WELL, I'VE ALREADY MADE MY DEBUT AS THE SEMI-FINALIST IN THE TEZUKA AWARD, BUT NOW I'LL DEFINITELY BE MAKING MY DEBUT AS AN ARTIST WITH HIS OWN SERIES.
MY OWN SERIES!

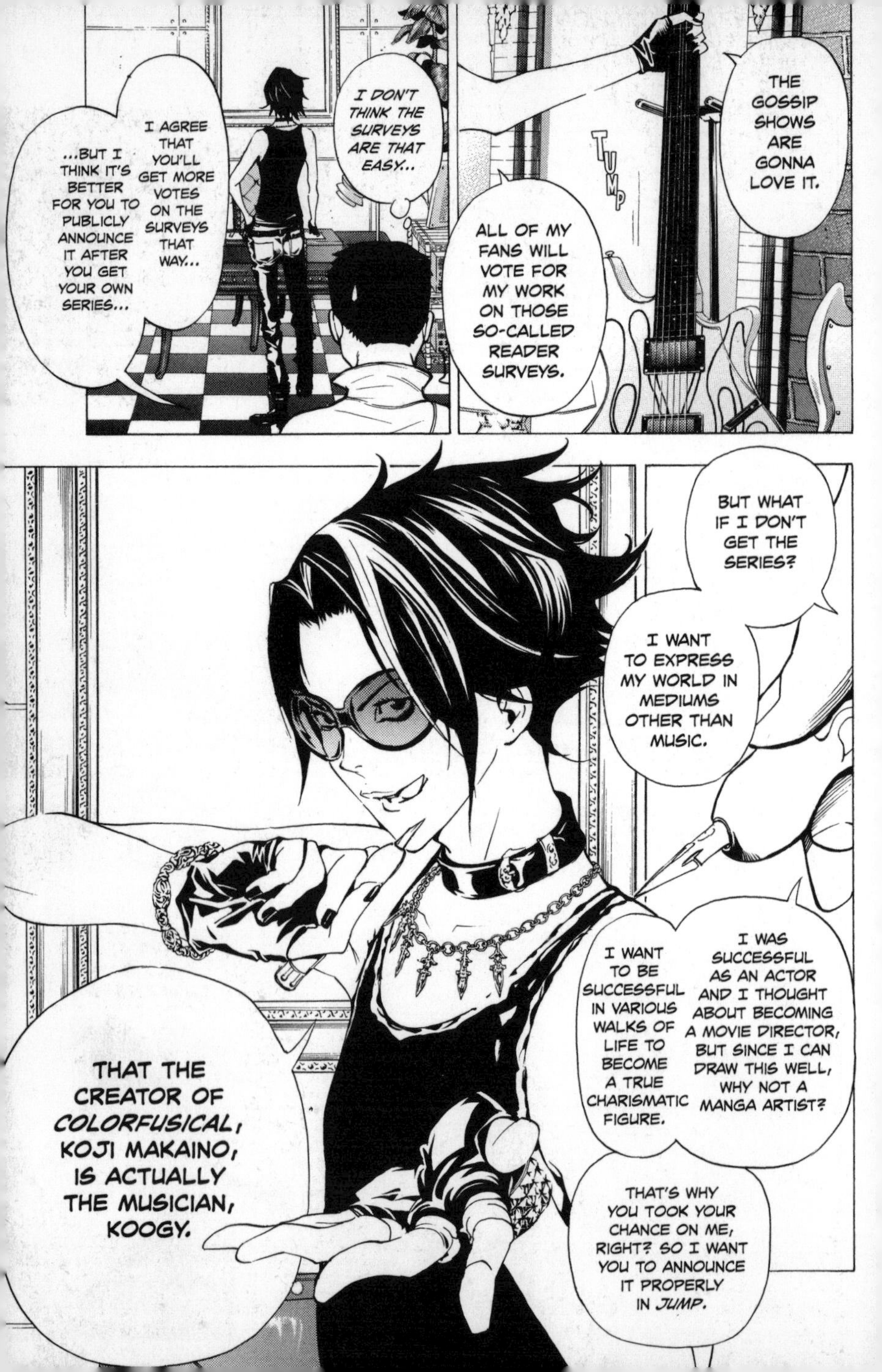
THE GOSSIP SHOWS ARE GONNA LOVE IT.
TUMP
ALL OF MY FANS WILL VOTE FOR MY WORK ON THOSE SO-CALLED READER SURVEYS.
I DON'T THINK THE SURVEYS ARE THAT EASY...
I AGREE THAT YOU'LL GET MORE VOTES ON THE SURVEYS THAT WAY...
...BUT I THINK IT'S BETTER FOR YOU TO PUBLICLY ANNOUNCE IT AFTER YOU GET YOUR OWN SERIES...
BUT WHAT IF I DON'T GET THE SERIES?
I WANT TO EXPRESS MY WORLD IN MEDIUMS OTHER THAN MUSIC.
I WAS SUCCESSFUL AS AN ACTOR AND I THOUGHT ABOUT BECOMING A MOVIE DIRECTOR, BUT SINCE I CAN DRAW THIS WELL, WHY NOT A MANGA ARTIST?
I WANT TO BE SUCCESSFUL IN VARIOUS WALKS OF LIFE TO BECOME A TRUE CHARISMATIC FIGURE.
THAT'S WHY YOU TOOK YOUR CHANCE ON ME, RIGHT? SO I WANT YOU TO ANNOUNCE IT PROPERLY IN *JUMP*.
THAT THE CREATOR OF *COLORFUSICAL*, KOJI MAKAINO, IS ACTUALLY THE MUSICIAN, KOOGY.

OHBA'S STORYBOARD

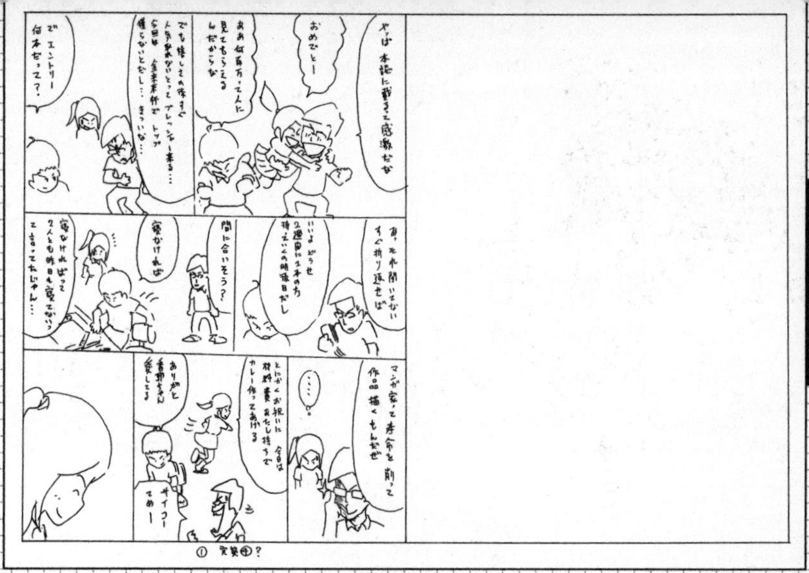

OBATA'S STORYBOARD

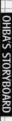

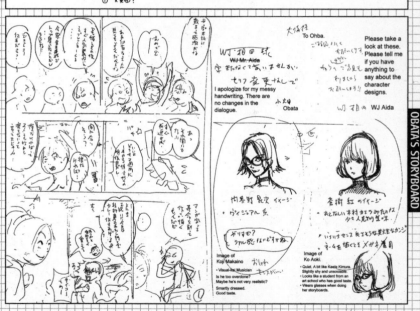

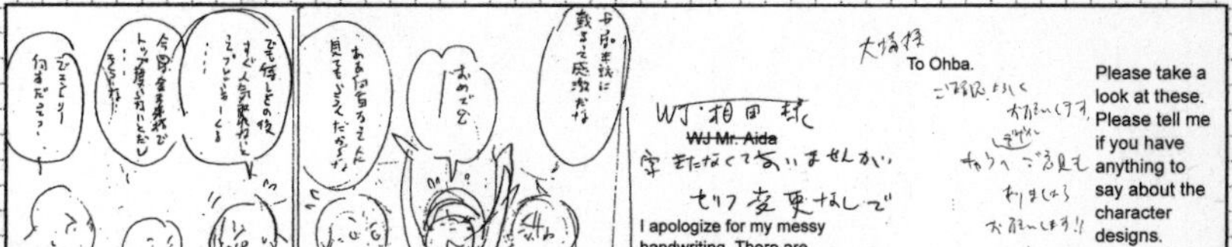
To Ohba.
Please take a look at these. Please tell me if you have anything to say about the character designs.
WJ Aida
WJ Mr. Aida
I apologize for my messy handwriting. There are no changes in the dialogue.
Obata
Image of Koji Makaino
• Visual-kei Musician
Is he too overdone? Maybe he's not very realistic?
Smartly dressed. Good taste.
Image of Ko Aoki.
• Quiet. A bit like Kaela Kimura. Slightly shy and unsociable.
• Looks like a student from an art school who has good taste.
• Wears glasses when doing her storyboards.

COMPLETE!

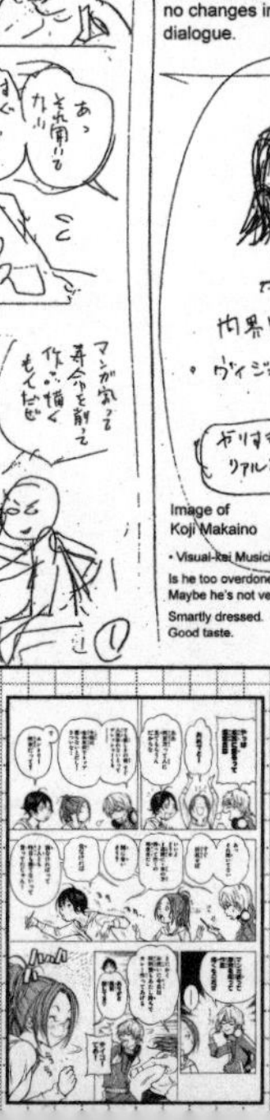

*CREATOR STORYBOARDS AND FINISHED PAGES IN JAPANESE

BAKUMAN。 vol.4

"Until the Final Draft Is Complete"

Chapter 29, pp. 71

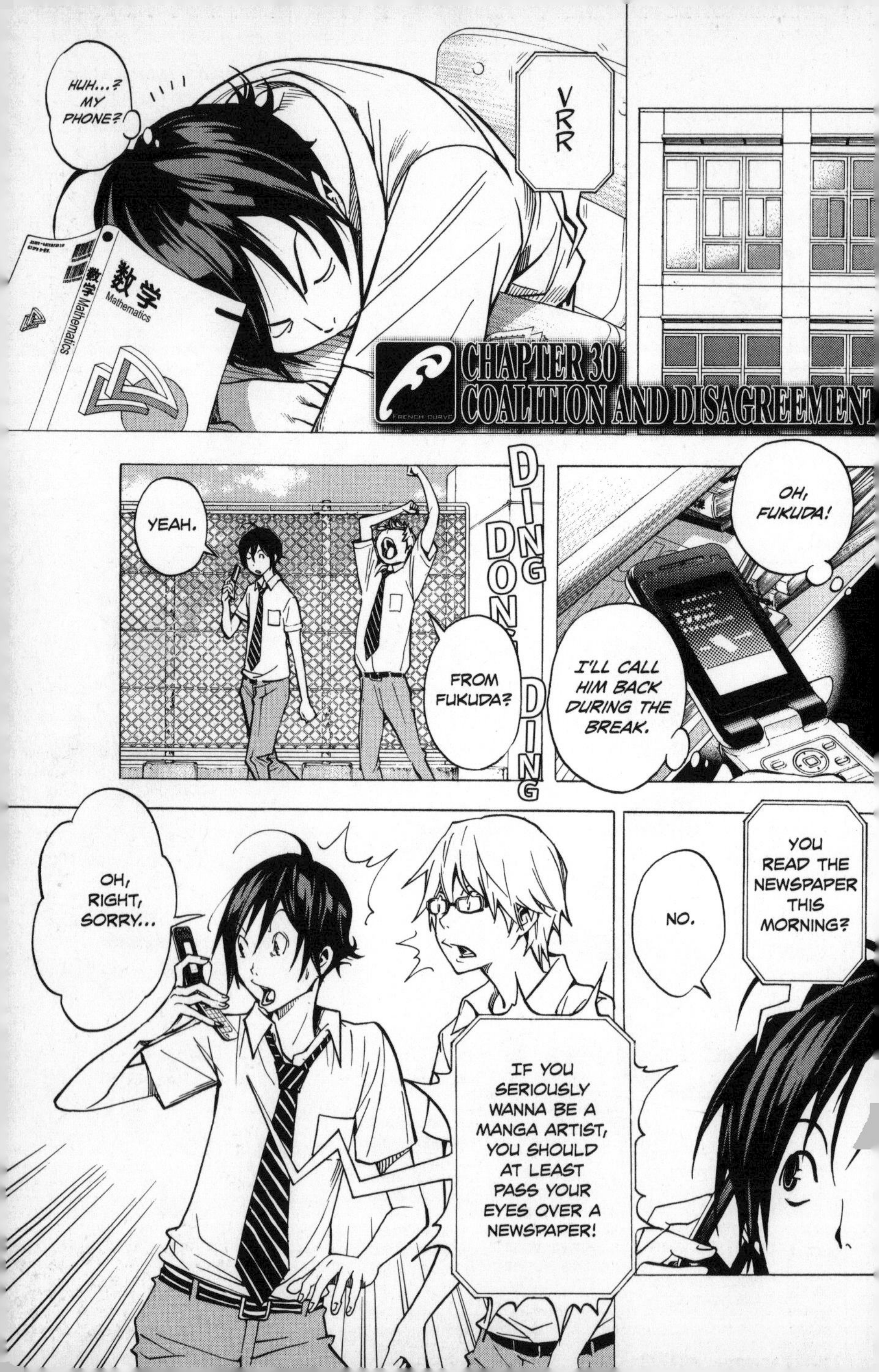
CHAPTER 30
COALITION AND DISAGREEMENT
FRENCH CURVE
VRR
HUH...? MY PHONE?
数学
Mathematics
OH, FUKUDA!
I'LL CALL HIM BACK DURING THE BREAK.
DING DONG DING DING
FROM FUKUDA?
YEAH.
YOU READ THE NEWSPAPER THIS MORNING?
NO.
IF YOU SERIOUSLY WANNA BE A MANGA ARTIST, YOU SHOULD AT LEAST PASS YOUR EYES OVER A NEWSPAPER!
OH, RIGHT, SORRY...

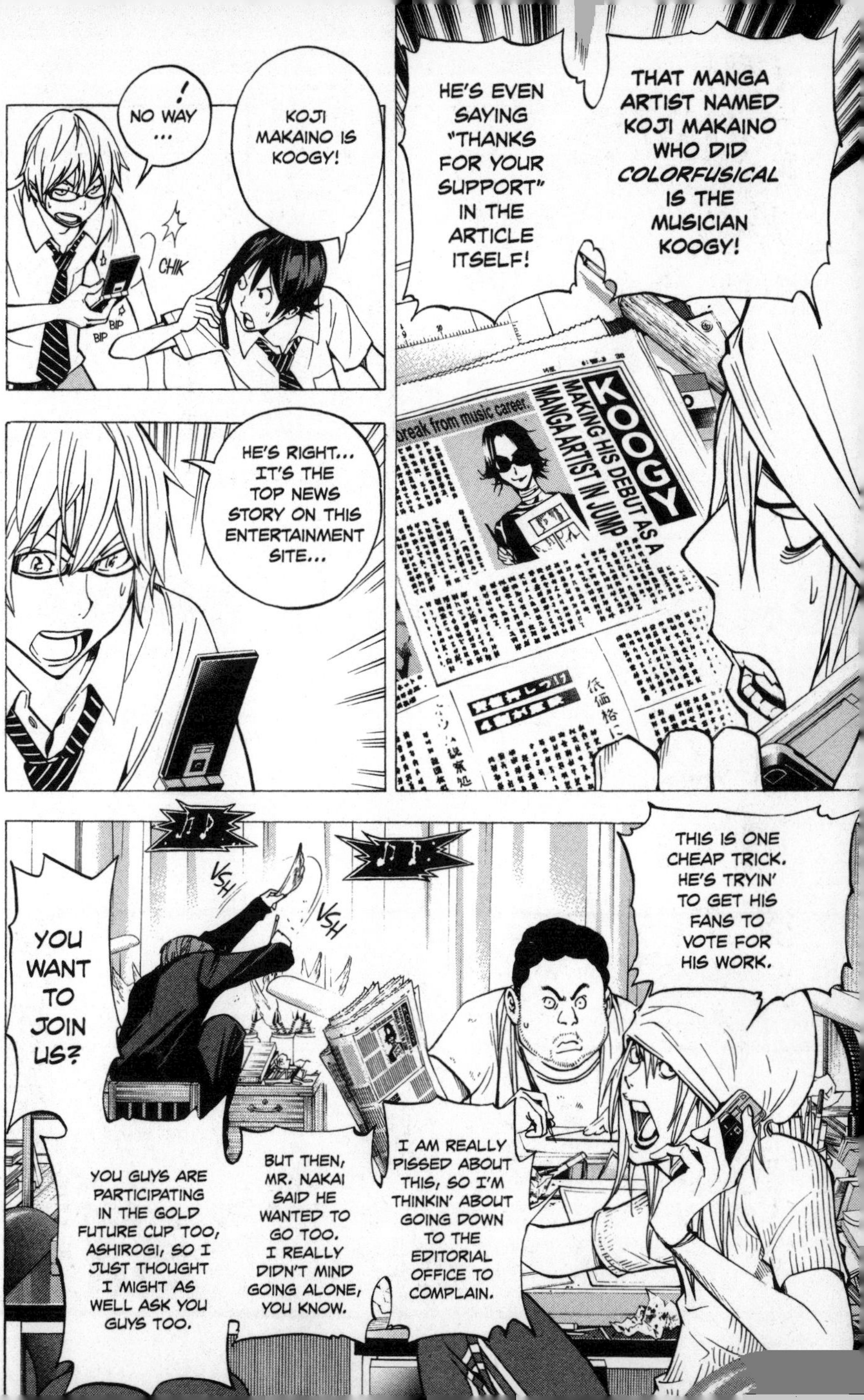
THAT MANGA ARTIST NAMED KOJI MAKAINO WHO DID *COLORFUSICAL* IS THE MUSICIAN KOOGY!
HE'S EVEN SAYING "THANKS FOR YOUR SUPPORT" IN THE ARTICLE ITSELF!
KOOGY
MAKING HIS DEBUT AS A MANGA ARTIST IN JUMP
KOJI MAKAINO IS KOOGY!
! NO WAY ...
CHIK
BIP
BIP
HE'S RIGHT... IT'S THE TOP NEWS STORY ON THIS ENTERTAINMENT SITE...
THIS IS ONE CHEAP TRICK. HE'S TRYIN' TO GET HIS FANS TO VOTE FOR HIS WORK.
VSH
VSH
I AM REALLY PISSED ABOUT THIS, SO I'M THINKIN' ABOUT GOING DOWN TO THE EDITORIAL OFFICE TO COMPLAIN.
BUT THEN, MR. NAKAI SAID HE WANTED TO GO TOO. I REALLY DIDN'T MIND GOING ALONE, YOU KNOW.
YOU GUYS ARE PARTICIPATING IN THE GOLD FUTURE CUP TOO, ASHIROGI, SO I JUST THOUGHT I MIGHT AS WELL ASK YOU GUYS TOO.
YOU WANT TO JOIN US?

READ THIS WAY

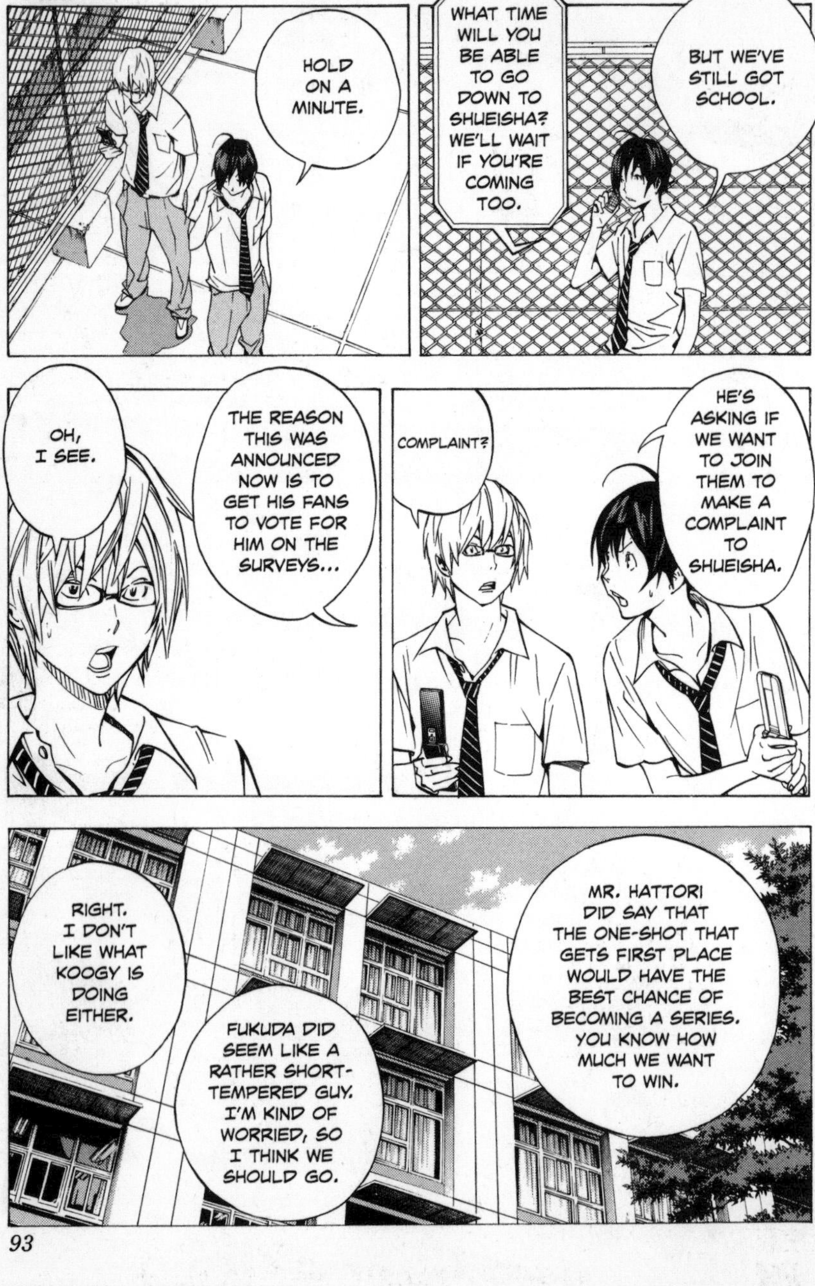
BUT WE'VE STILL GOT SCHOOL.
WHAT TIME WILL YOU BE ABLE TO GO DOWN TO SHUEISHA? WE'LL WAIT IF YOU'RE COMING TOO.
HOLD ON A MINUTE.
HE'S ASKING IF WE WANT TO JOIN THEM TO MAKE A COMPLAINT TO SHUEISHA.
COMPLAINT?
THE REASON THIS WAS ANNOUNCED NOW IS TO GET HIS FANS TO VOTE FOR HIM ON THE SURVEYS...
OH, I SEE.
MR. HATTORI DID SAY THAT THE ONE-SHOT THAT GETS FIRST PLACE WOULD HAVE THE BEST CHANCE OF BECOMING A SERIES. YOU KNOW HOW MUCH WE WANT TO WIN.
FUKUDA DID SEEM LIKE A RATHER SHORT-TEMPERED GUY. I'M KIND OF WORRIED, SO I THINK WE SHOULD GO.
RIGHT. I DON'T LIKE WHAT KOOGY IS DOING EITHER.

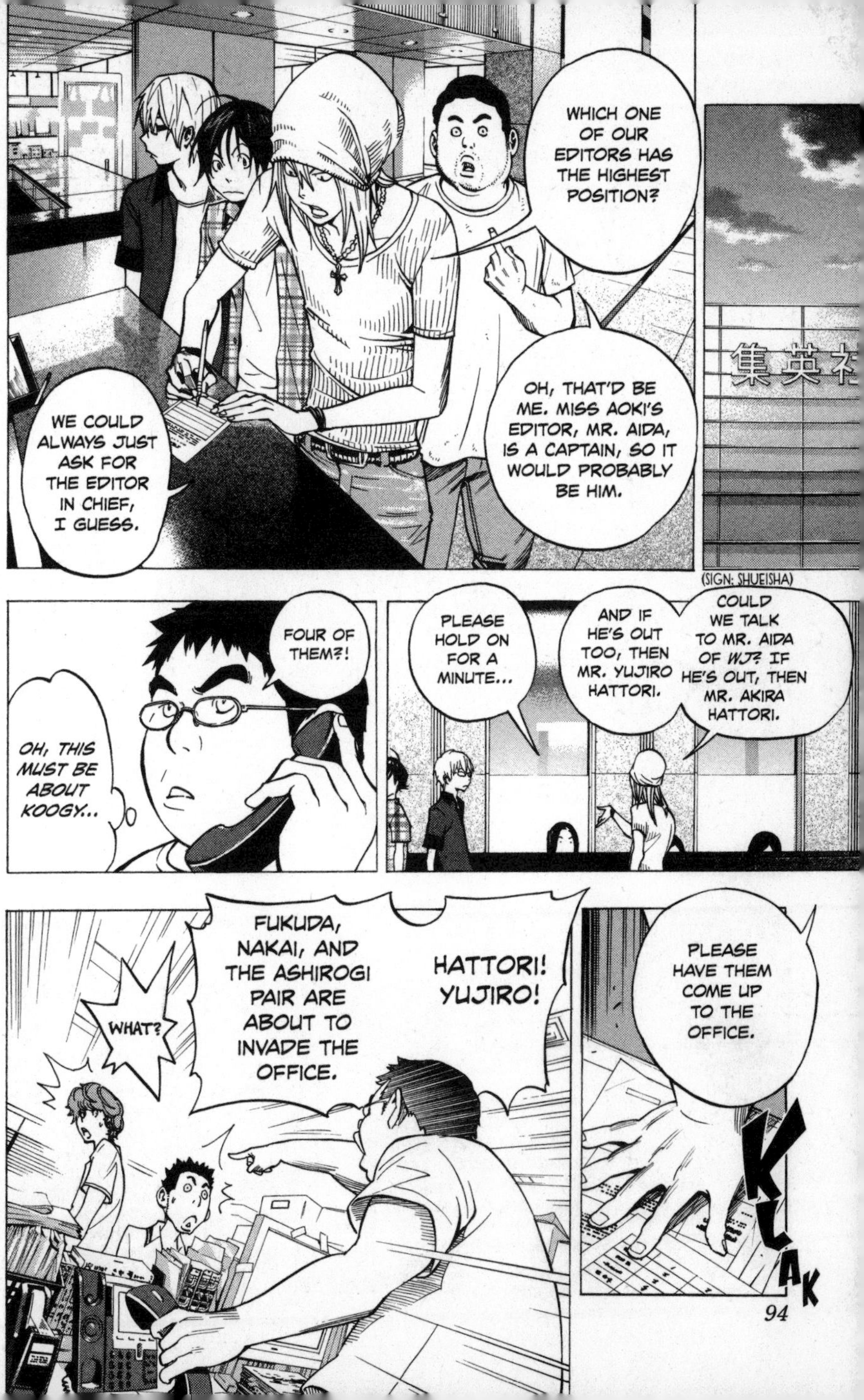
集英社
(SIGN: SHUEISHA)
WHICH ONE OF OUR EDITORS HAS THE HIGHEST POSITION?
OH, THAT'D BE ME. MISS AOKI'S EDITOR, MR. AIDA, IS A CAPTAIN, SO IT WOULD PROBABLY BE HIM.
WE COULD ALWAYS JUST ASK FOR THE EDITOR IN CHIEF, I GUESS.
COULD WE TALK TO MR. AIDA OF *WJ*? IF HE'S OUT, THEN MR. AKIRA HATTORI.
AND IF HE'S OUT TOO, THEN MR. YUJIRO HATTORI.
PLEASE HOLD ON FOR A MINUTE...
FOUR OF THEM?!
OH, THIS MUST BE ABOUT KOOGY...
PLEASE HAVE THEM COME UP TO THE OFFICE.
KLAK
HATTORI! YUJIRO!
FUKUDA, NAKAI, AND THE ASHIROGI PAIR ARE ABOUT TO INVADE THE OFFICE.
WHAT?

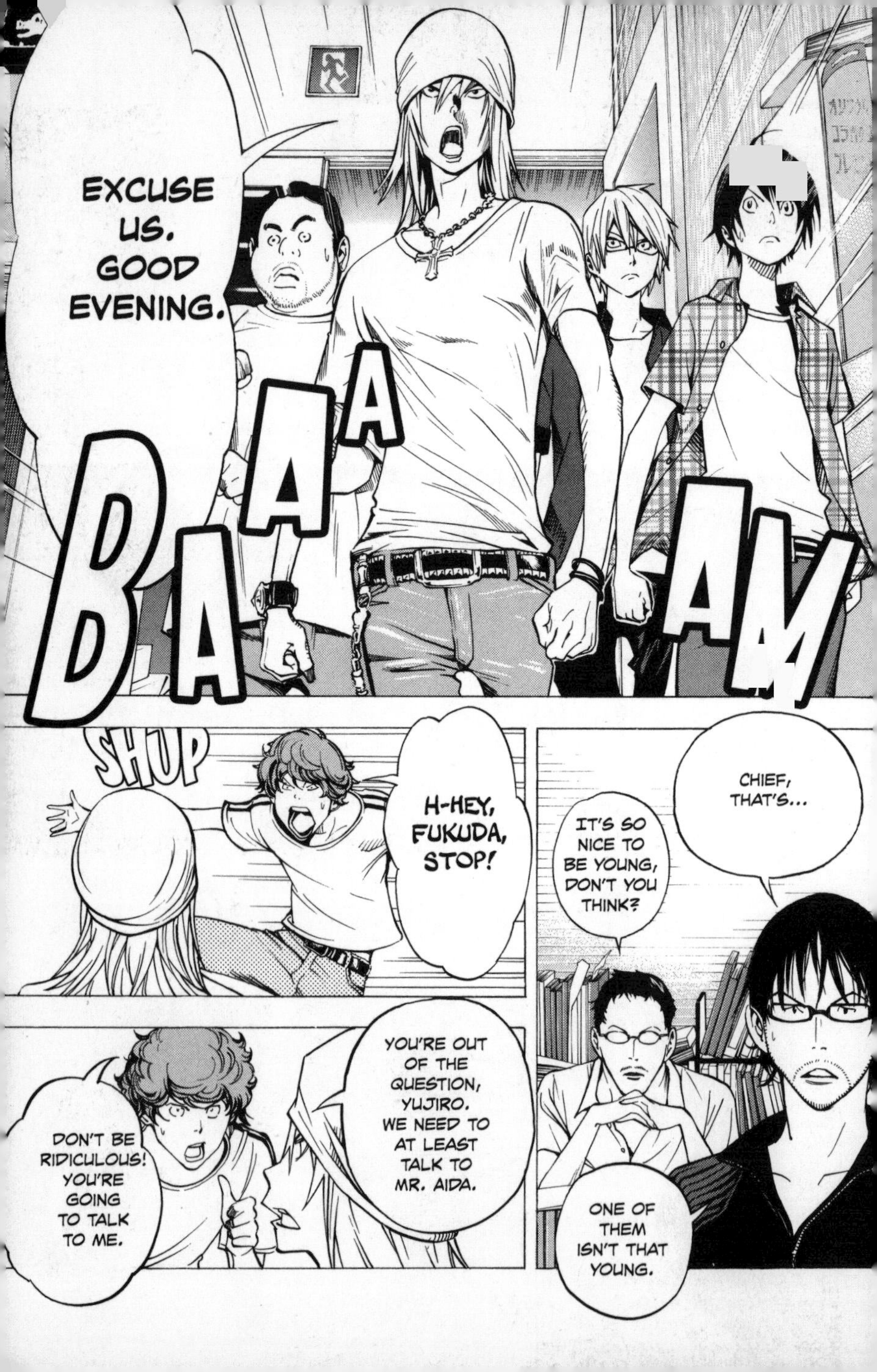
EXCUSE US. GOOD EVENING.
BAAAAM
CHIEF, THAT'S...
IT'S SO NICE TO BE YOUNG, DON'T YOU THINK?
ONE OF THEM ISN'T THAT YOUNG.
SHUP
H-HEY, FUKUDA, STOP!
YOU'RE OUT OF THE QUESTION, YUJIRO. WE NEED TO AT LEAST TALK TO MR. AIDA.
DON'T BE RIDICULOUS! YOU'RE GOING TO TALK TO ME.

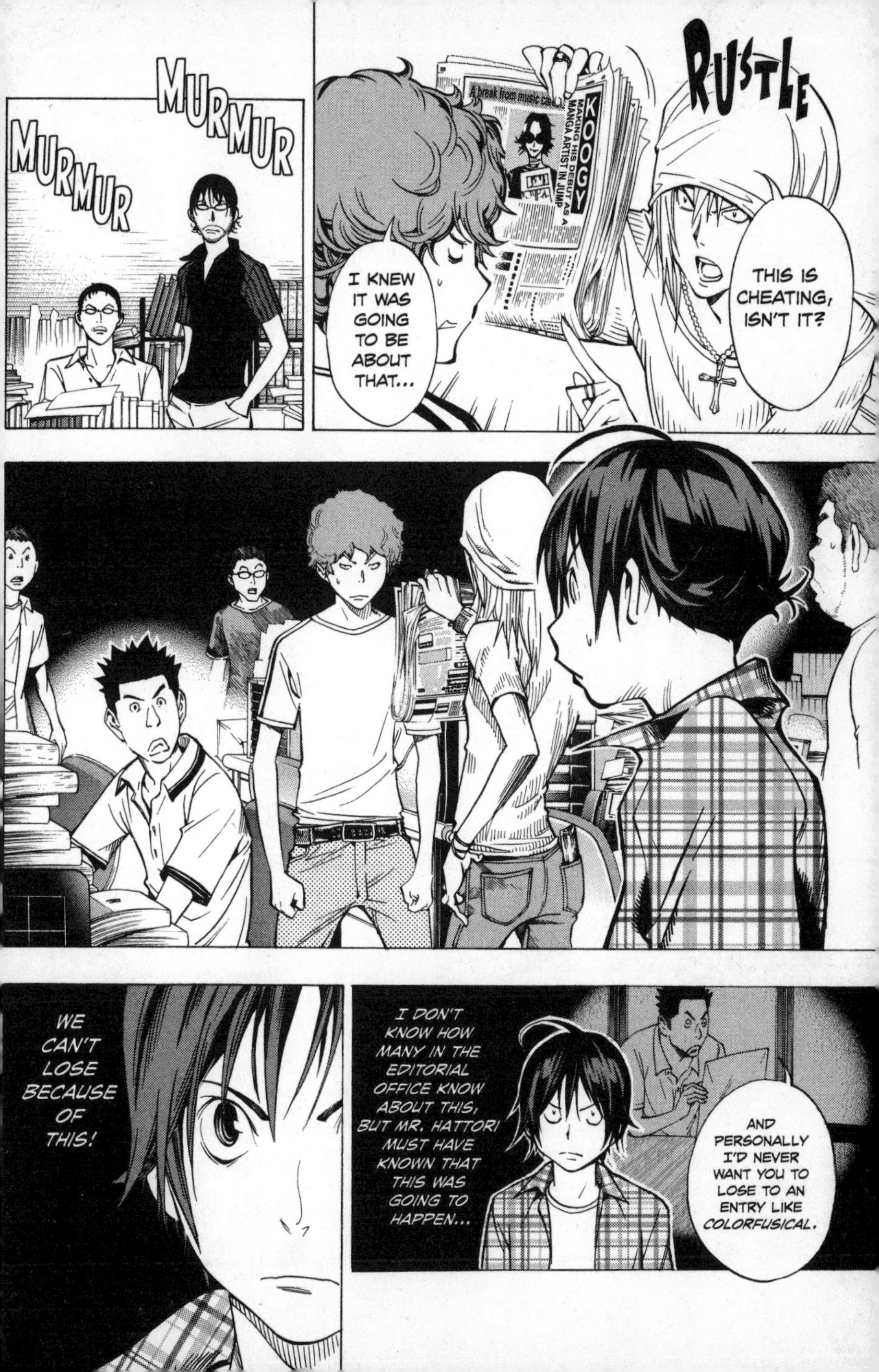
RUSTLE
KOOGY
MAKING HIS DEBUT AS A MANGA ARTIST IN JUMP
THIS IS CHEATING, ISN'T IT?
I KNEW IT WAS GOING TO BE ABOUT THAT...
MURMUR
MURMUR
I DON'T KNOW HOW MANY IN THE EDITORIAL OFFICE KNOW ABOUT THIS, BUT MR. HATTORI MUST HAVE KNOWN THAT THIS WAS GOING TO HAPPEN...
AND PERSONALLY I'D NEVER WANT YOU TO LOSE TO AN ENTRY LIKE *COLORFUSICAL*.
WE CAN'T LOSE BECAUSE OF THIS!

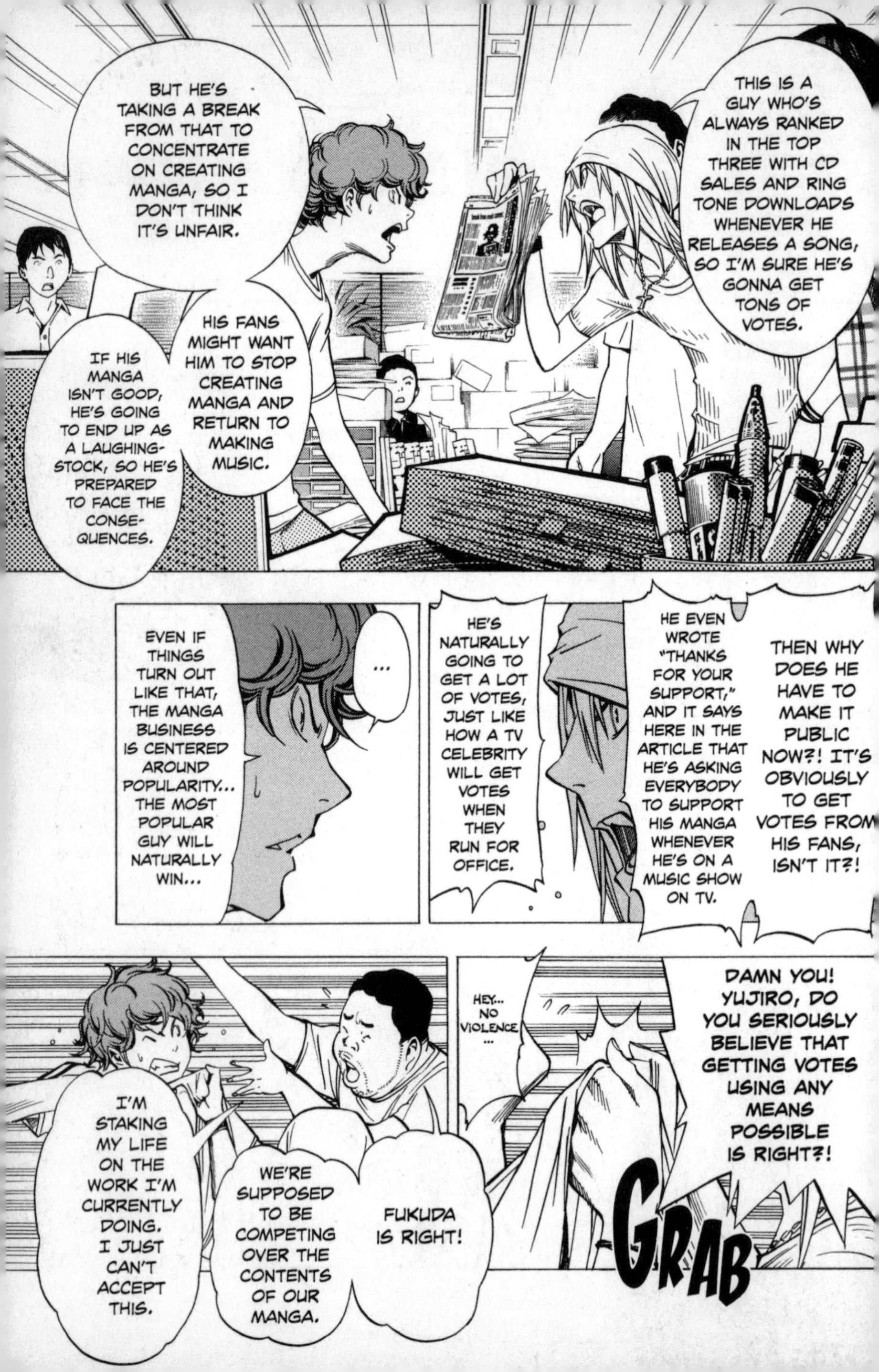
THIS IS A GUY WHO'S ALWAYS RANKED IN THE TOP THREE WITH CD SALES AND RING TONE DOWNLOADS WHENEVER HE RELEASES A SONG, SO I'M SURE HE'S GONNA GET TONS OF VOTES.
BUT HE'S TAKING A BREAK FROM THAT TO CONCENTRATE ON CREATING MANGA, SO I DON'T THINK IT'S UNFAIR.
HIS FANS MIGHT WANT HIM TO STOP CREATING MANGA AND RETURN TO MAKING MUSIC.
IF HIS MANGA ISN'T GOOD, HE'S GOING TO END UP AS A LAUGHING-STOCK, SO HE'S PREPARED TO FACE THE CONSE-QUENCES.
THEN WHY DOES HE HAVE TO MAKE IT PUBLIC NOW?! IT'S OBVIOUSLY TO GET VOTES FROM HIS FANS, ISN'T IT?!
HE EVEN WROTE "THANKS FOR YOUR SUPPORT," AND IT SAYS HERE IN THE ARTICLE THAT HE'S ASKING EVERYBODY TO SUPPORT HIS MANGA WHENEVER HE'S ON A MUSIC SHOW ON TV.
HE'S NATURALLY GOING TO GET A LOT OF VOTES, JUST LIKE HOW A TV CELEBRITY WILL GET VOTES WHEN THEY RUN FOR OFFICE.
...
EVEN IF THINGS TURN OUT LIKE THAT, THE MANGA BUSINESS IS CENTERED AROUND POPULARITY... THE MOST POPULAR GUY WILL NATURALLY WIN...
DAMN YOU! YUJIRO, DO YOU SERIOUSLY BELIEVE THAT GETTING VOTES USING ANY MEANS POSSIBLE IS RIGHT?!
GRAB
HEY... NO VIOLENCE...
FUKUDA IS RIGHT!
WE'RE SUPPOSED TO BE COMPETING OVER THE CONTENTS OF OUR MANGA.
I'M STAKING MY LIFE ON THE WORK I'M CURRENTLY DOING. I JUST CAN'T ACCEPT THIS.

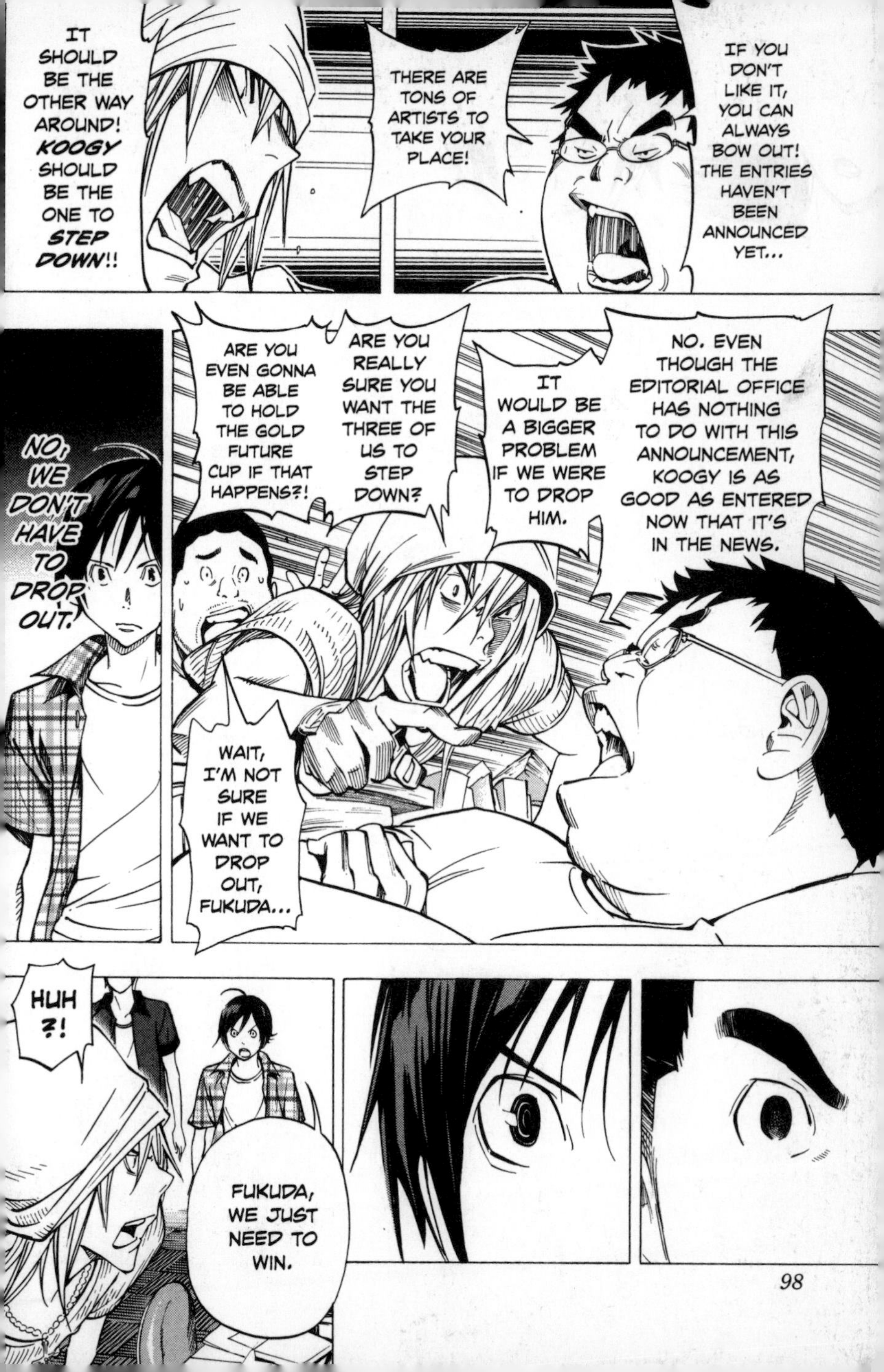
IF YOU DON'T LIKE IT, YOU CAN ALWAYS BOW OUT! THE ENTRIES HAVEN'T BEEN ANNOUNCED YET...
THERE ARE TONS OF ARTISTS TO TAKE YOUR PLACE!
IT SHOULD BE THE OTHER WAY AROUND! KOOGY SHOULD BE THE ONE TO STEP DOWN!!
NO. EVEN THOUGH THE EDITORIAL OFFICE HAS NOTHING TO DO WITH THIS ANNOUNCEMENT, KOOGY IS AS GOOD AS ENTERED NOW THAT IT'S IN THE NEWS.
IT WOULD BE A BIGGER PROBLEM IF WE WERE TO DROP HIM.
ARE YOU REALLY SURE YOU WANT THE THREE OF US TO STEP DOWN?
ARE YOU EVEN GONNA BE ABLE TO HOLD THE GOLD FUTURE CUP IF THAT HAPPENS?!
WAIT, I'M NOT SURE IF WE WANT TO DROP OUT, FUKUDA...
NO, WE DON'T HAVE TO DROP OUT.
HUH?!
FUKUDA, WE JUST NEED TO WIN.

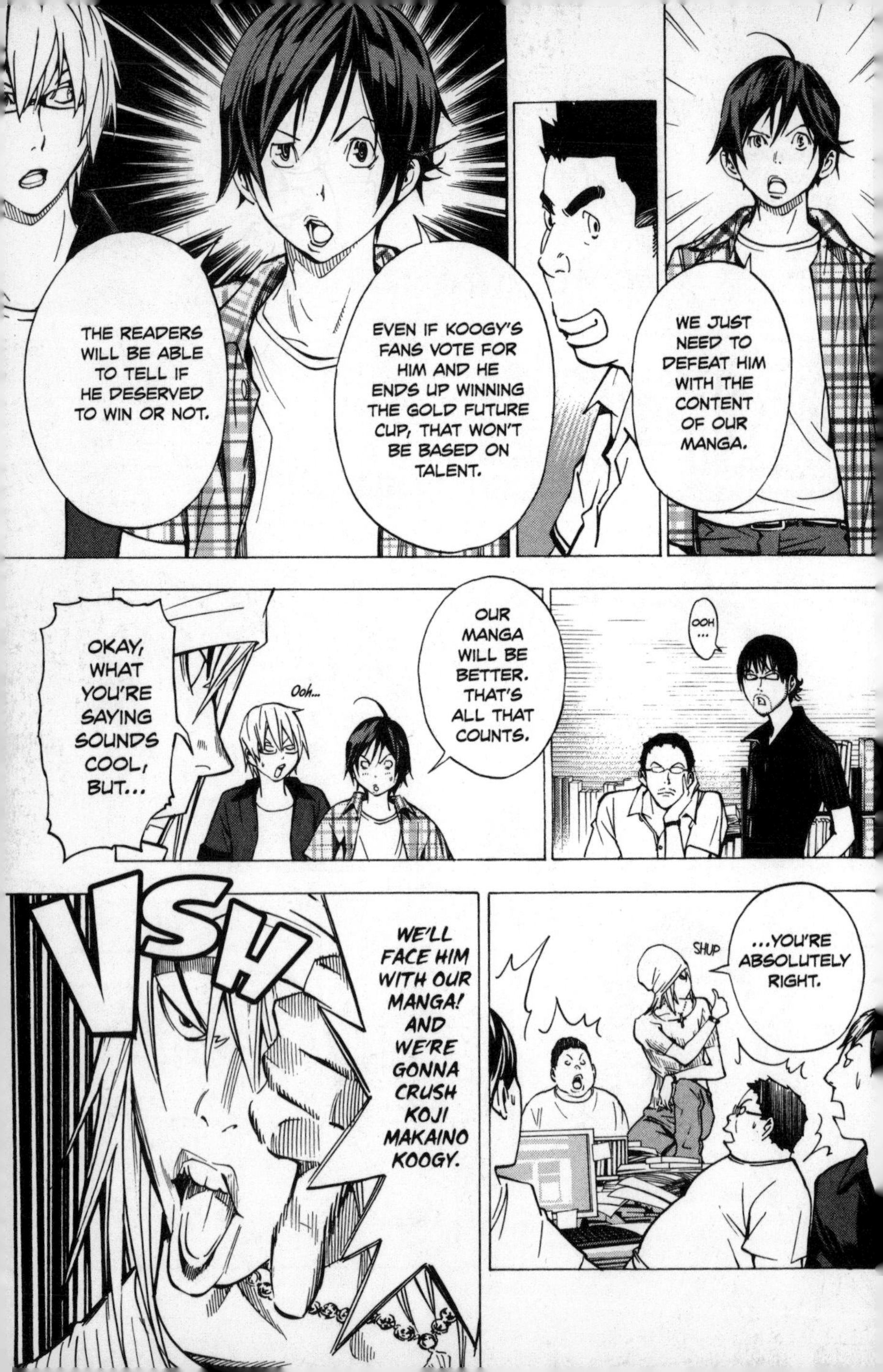

WE JUST NEED TO DEFEAT HIM WITH THE CONTENT OF OUR MANGA.
EVEN IF KOOGY'S FANS VOTE FOR HIM AND HE ENDS UP WINNING THE GOLD FUTURE CUP, THAT WON'T BE BASED ON TALENT.
THE READERS WILL BE ABLE TO TELL IF HE DESERVED TO WIN OR NOT.
OOH...
OUR MANGA WILL BE BETTER. THAT'S ALL THAT COUNTS.
Ooh...
OKAY, WHAT YOU'RE SAYING SOUNDS COOL, BUT...
...YOU'RE ABSOLUTELY RIGHT.
SHUP
VSH
WE'LL FACE HIM WITH OUR MANGA! AND WE'RE GONNA CRUSH KOJI MAKAINO KOOGY.

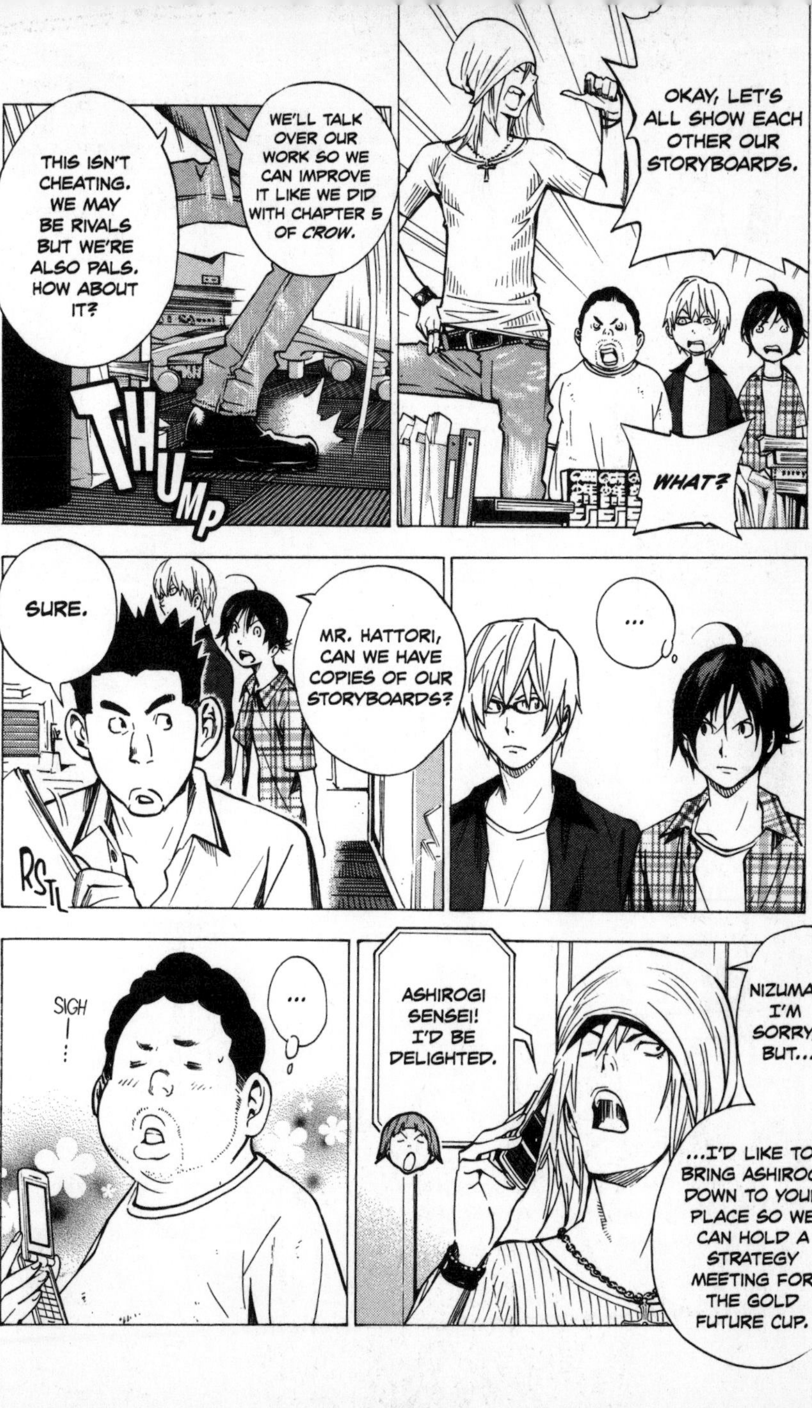
OKAY, LET'S ALL SHOW EACH OTHER OUR STORYBOARDS.
WHAT?
WE'LL TALK OVER OUR WORK SO WE CAN IMPROVE IT LIKE WE DID WITH CHAPTER 5 OF *CROW*.
THIS ISN'T CHEATING. WE MAY BE RIVALS BUT WE'RE ALSO PALS. HOW ABOUT IT?
THUMP
...
MR. HATTORI, CAN WE HAVE COPIES OF OUR STORYBOARDS?
SURE.
RSTL
NIZUMA, I'M SORRY, BUT...
...I'D LIKE TO BRING ASHIROGI DOWN TO YOUR PLACE SO WE CAN HOLD A STRATEGY MEETING FOR THE GOLD FUTURE CUP.
ASHIROGI SENSEI! I'D BE DELIGHTED.
...
SIGH

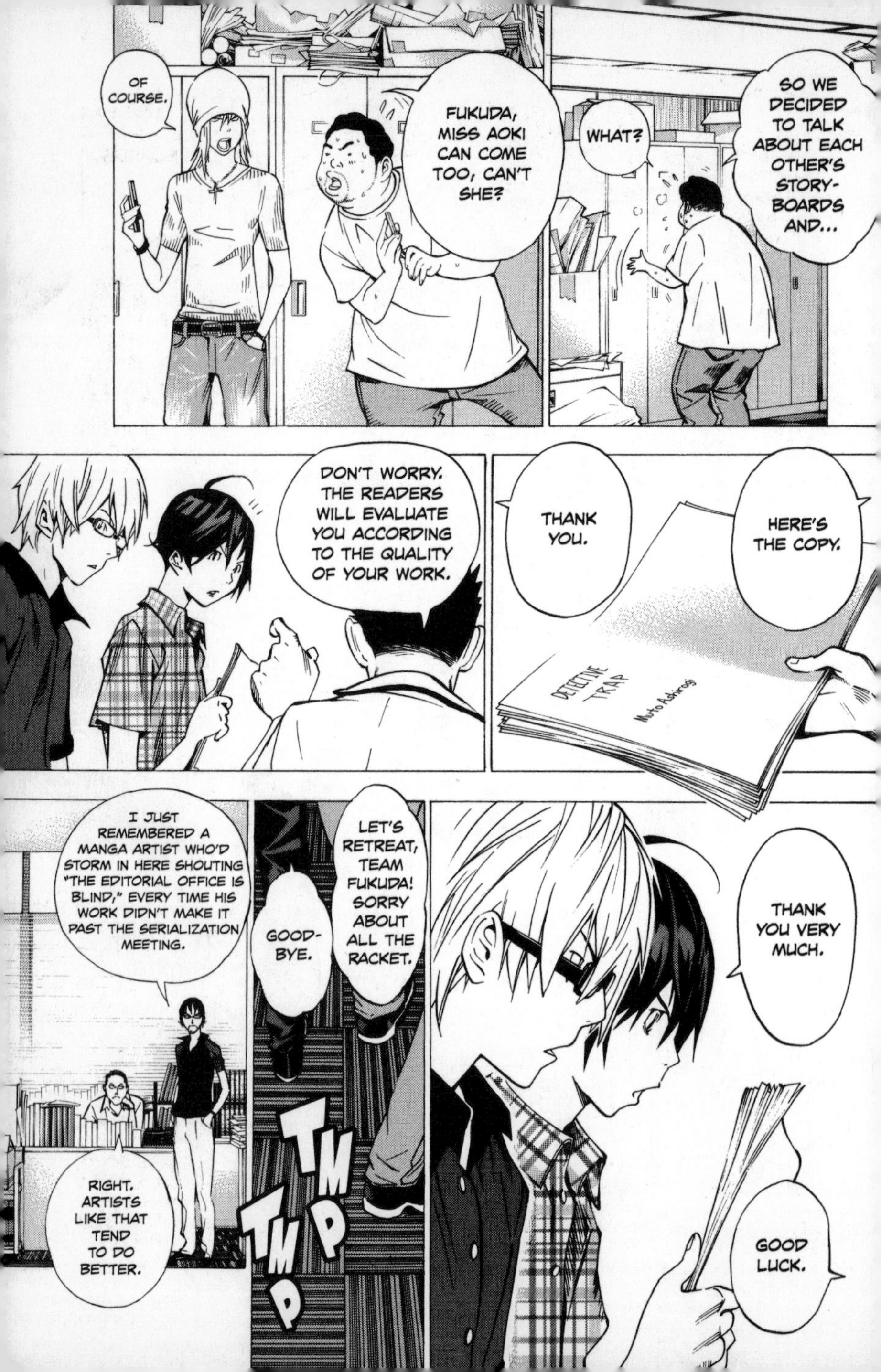
SO WE DECIDED TO TALK ABOUT EACH OTHER'S STORY-BOARDS AND...
WHAT?
FUKUDA, MISS AOKI CAN COME TOO, CAN'T SHE?
OF COURSE.
HERE'S THE COPY.
THANK YOU.
DETECTIVE TRAP
Muto Ashirogi
DON'T WORRY. THE READERS WILL EVALUATE YOU ACCORDING TO THE QUALITY OF YOUR WORK.
THANK YOU VERY MUCH.
GOOD LUCK.
LET'S RETREAT, TEAM FUKUDA! SORRY ABOUT ALL THE RACKET.
GOOD-BYE.
TMP
TMP
I JUST REMEMBERED A MANGA ARTIST WHO'D STORM IN HERE SHOUTING "THE EDITORIAL OFFICE IS BLIND," EVERY TIME HIS WORK DIDN'T MAKE IT PAST THE SERIALIZATION MEETING.
RIGHT. ARTISTS LIKE THAT TEND TO DO BETTER.

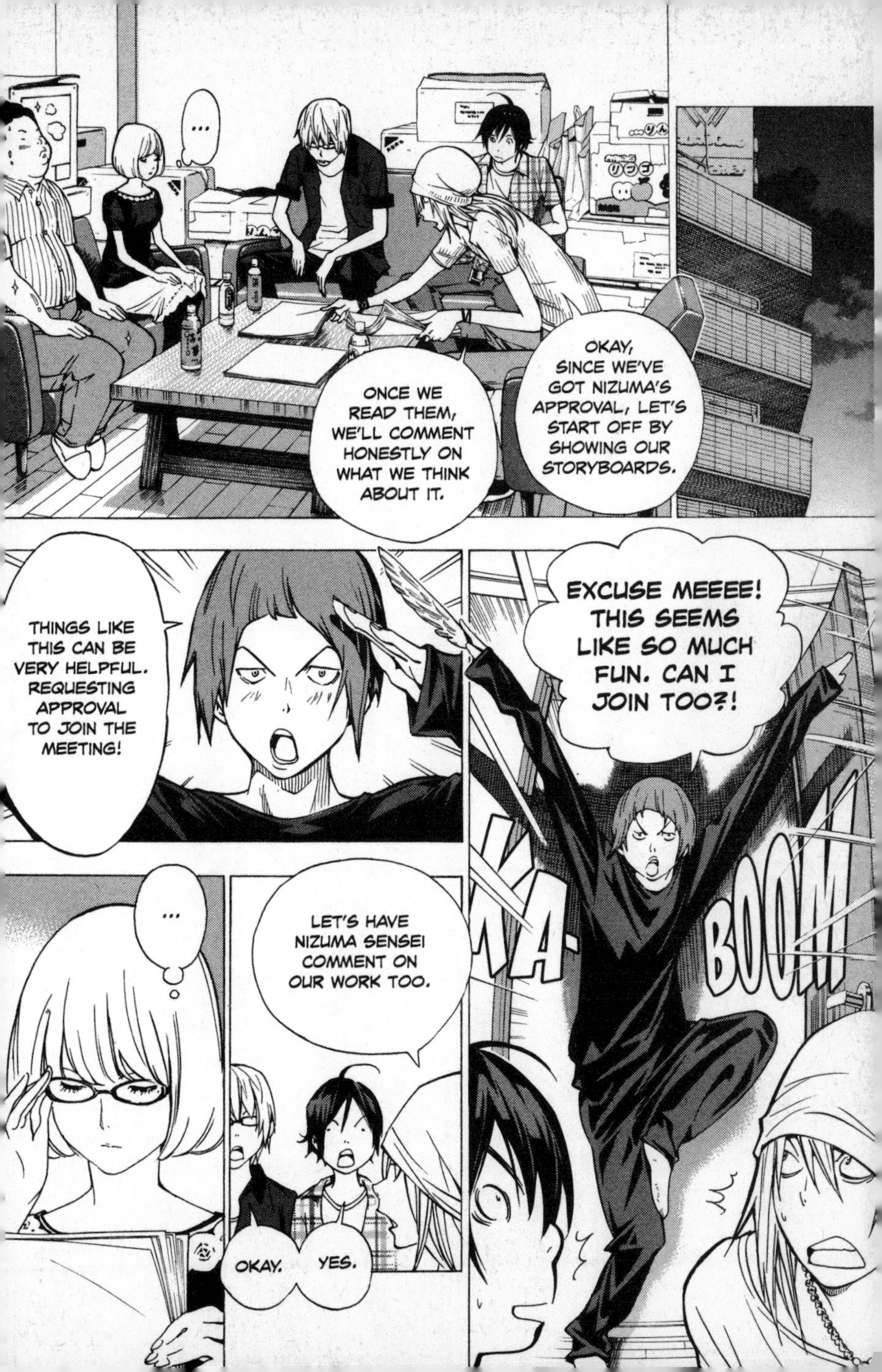
OKAY, SINCE WE'VE GOT NIZUMA'S APPROVAL, LET'S START OFF BY SHOWING OUR STORYBOARDS.
ONCE WE READ THEM, WE'LL COMMENT HONESTLY ON WHAT WE THINK ABOUT IT.
...
EXCUSE MEEEE! THIS SEEMS LIKE SO MUCH FUN. CAN I JOIN TOO?!
BOOM
THINGS LIKE THIS CAN BE VERY HELPFUL. REQUESTING APPROVAL TO JOIN THE MEETING!
LET'S HAVE NIZUMA SENSEI COMMENT ON OUR WORK TOO.
YES.
OKAY.
...

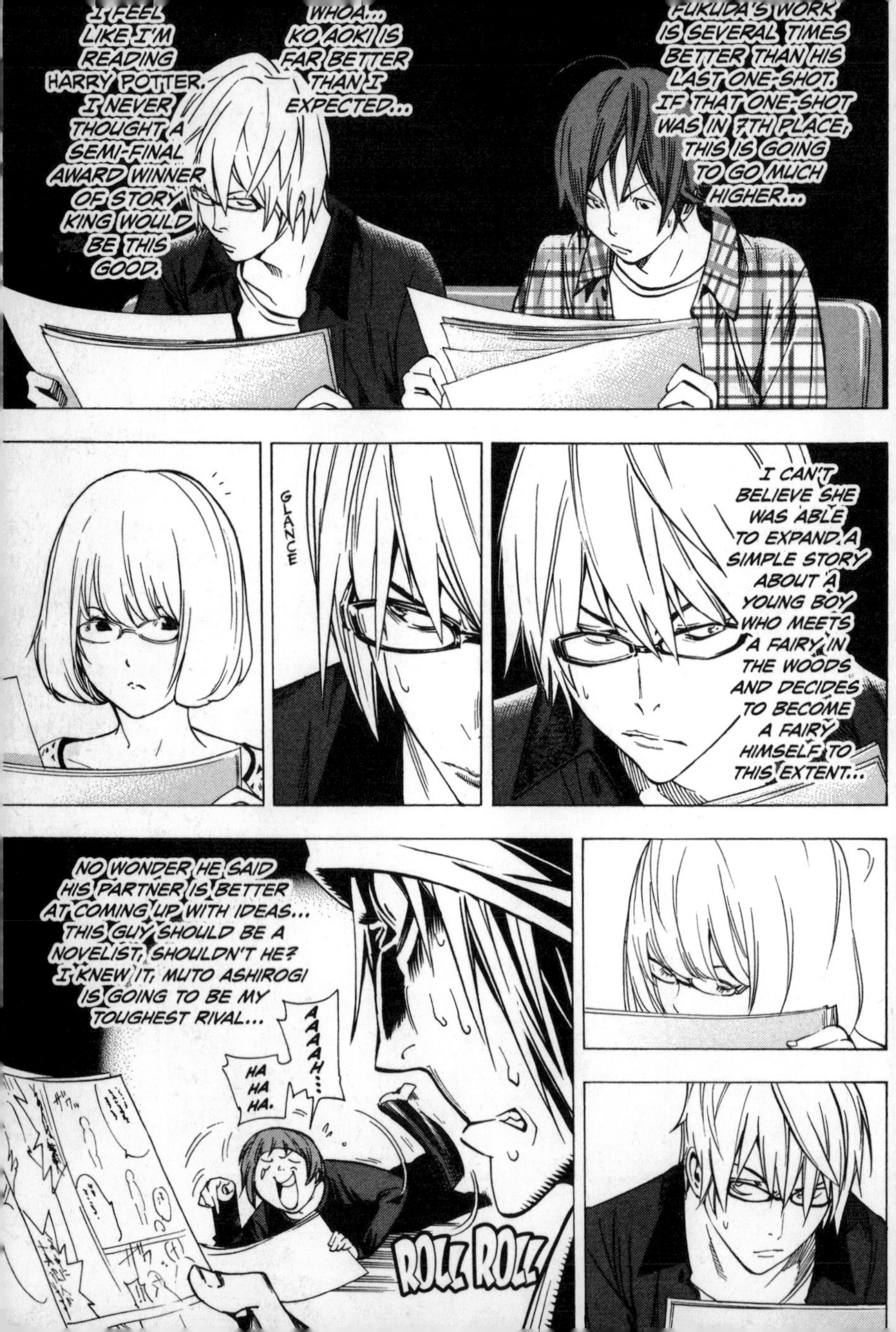

FUKUDA'S WORK IS SEVERAL TIMES BETTER THAN HIS LAST ONE-SHOT. IF THAT ONE-SHOT WAS IN 7TH PLACE, THIS IS GOING TO GO MUCH HIGHER...
WHOA... KO AOKI IS FAR BETTER THAN I EXPECTED...
I FEEL LIKE I'M READING HARRY POTTER. I NEVER THOUGHT A SEMI-FINAL AWARD WINNER OF STORY KING WOULD BE THIS GOOD.
I CAN'T BELIEVE SHE WAS ABLE TO EXPAND A SIMPLE STORY ABOUT A YOUNG BOY WHO MEETS A FAIRY IN THE WOODS AND DECIDES TO BECOME A FAIRY HIMSELF TO THIS EXTENT...
GLANCE
NO WONDER HE SAID HIS PARTNER IS BETTER AT COMING UP WITH IDEAS... THIS GUY SHOULD BE A NOVELIST, SHOULDN'T HE? I KNEW IT, MUTO ASHIROGI IS GOING TO BE MY TOUGHEST RIVAL...
AAAAAH...
HA HA HA.
ROLL ROLL

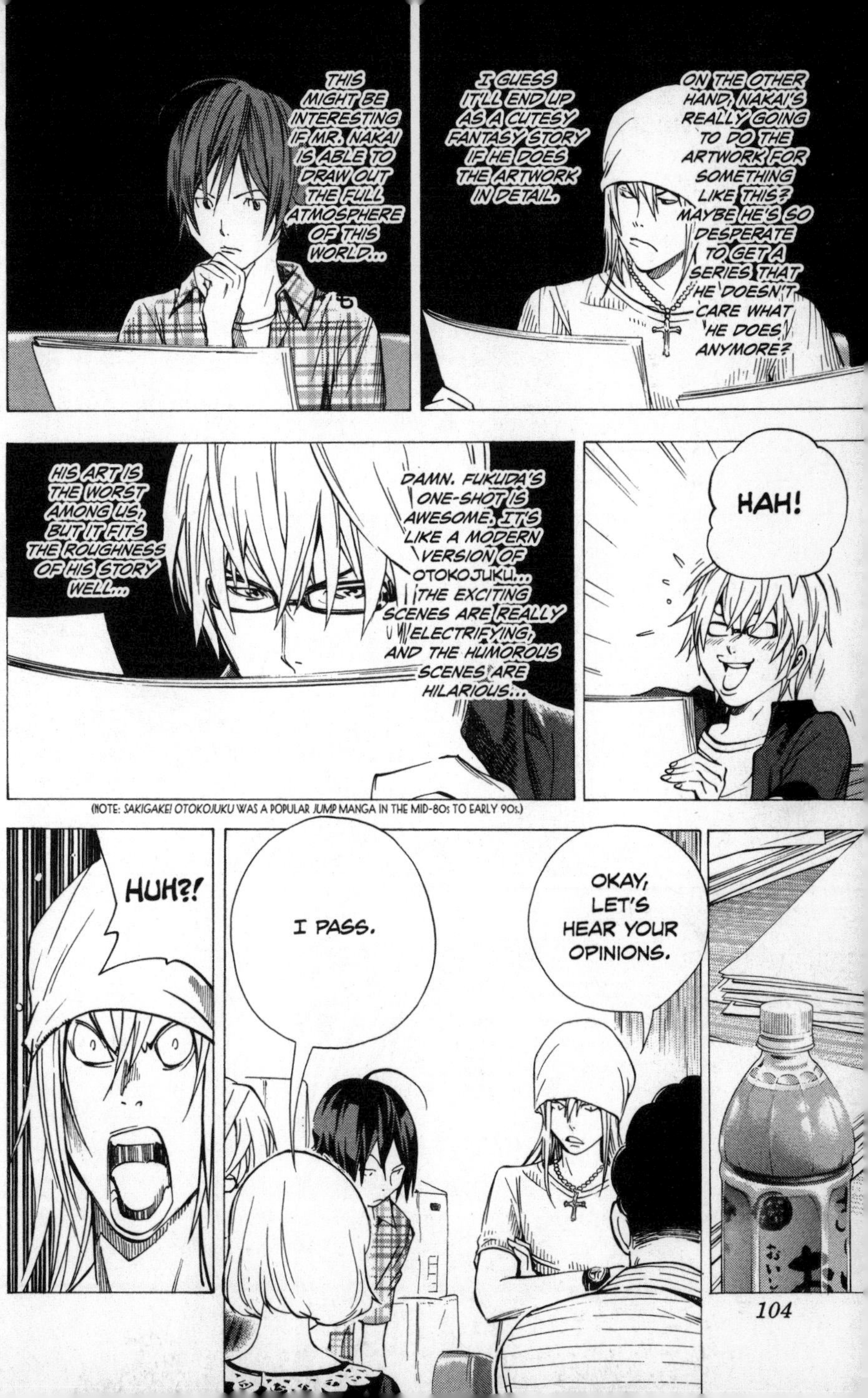
ON THE OTHER HAND, NAKAI'S REALLY GOING TO DO THE ARTWORK FOR SOMETHING LIKE THIS? MAYBE HE'S SO DESPERATE TO GET A SERIES THAT HE DOESN'T CARE WHAT HE DOES ANYMORE?
I GUESS IT'LL END UP AS A CUTESY FANTASY STORY IF HE DOES THE ARTWORK IN DETAIL.
THIS MIGHT BE INTERESTING IF MR. NAKAI IS ABLE TO DRAW OUT THE FULL ATMOSPHERE OF THIS WORLD...
HAH!
DAMN. FUKUDA'S ONE-SHOT IS AWESOME. IT'S LIKE A MODERN VERSION OF OTOKOJUKU... THE EXCITING SCENES ARE REALLY ELECTRIFYING, AND THE HUMOROUS SCENES ARE HILARIOUS...
HIS ART IS THE WORST AMONG US, BUT IT FITS THE ROUGHNESS OF HIS STORY WELL...
OKAY, LET'S HEAR YOUR OPINIONS.
I PASS.
HUH?!

(NOTE: *SAKIGAKE! OTOKOJUKU* WAS A POPULAR *JUMP* MANGA IN THE MID-80s TO EARLY 90s.)

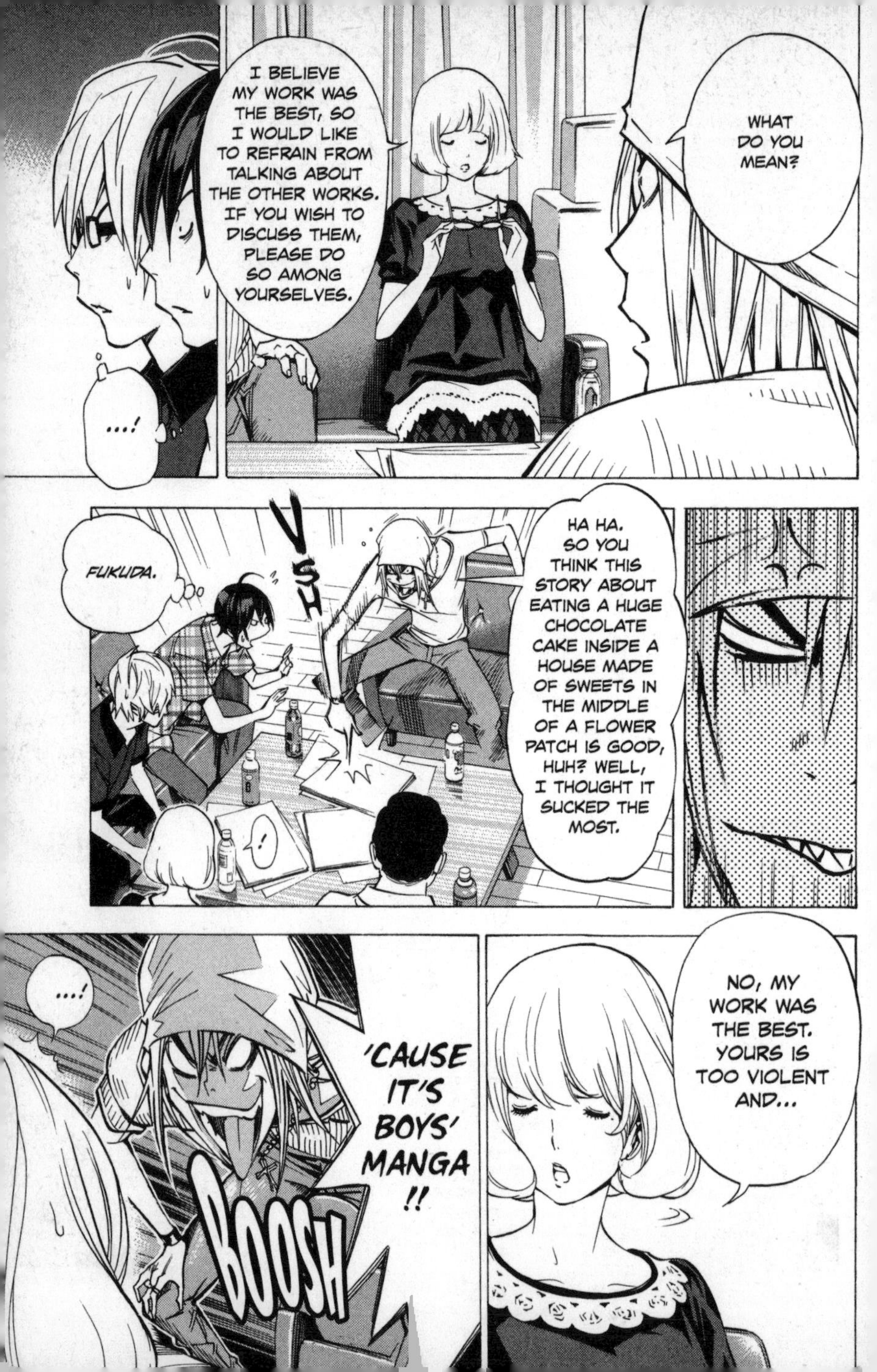
WHAT DO YOU MEAN?
I BELIEVE MY WORK WAS THE BEST, SO I WOULD LIKE TO REFRAIN FROM TALKING ABOUT THE OTHER WORKS. IF YOU WISH TO DISCUSS THEM, PLEASE DO SO AMONG YOURSELVES.
...!
HA HA. SO YOU THINK THIS STORY ABOUT EATING A HUGE CHOCOLATE CAKE INSIDE A HOUSE MADE OF SWEETS IN THE MIDDLE OF A FLOWER PATCH IS GOOD, HUH? WELL, I THOUGHT IT SUCKED THE MOST.
VSH
FUKUDA.
!
NO, MY WORK WAS THE BEST. YOURS IS TOO VIOLENT AND...
...!
'CAUSE IT'S BOYS' MANGA!!
BOOSH

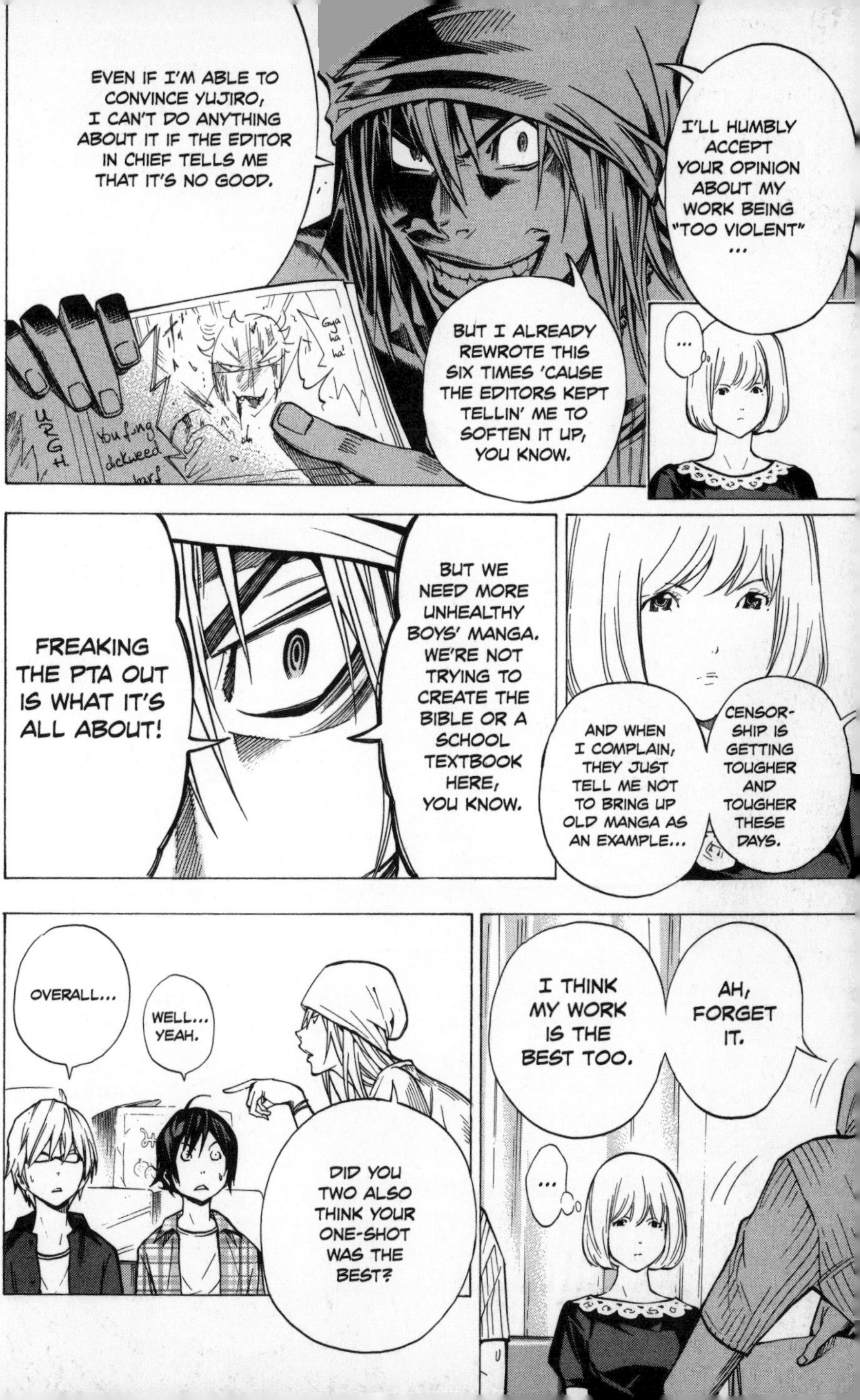
I'LL HUMBLY ACCEPT YOUR OPINION ABOUT MY WORK BEING "TOO VIOLENT"...
BUT I ALREADY REWROTE THIS SIX TIMES 'CAUSE THE EDITORS KEPT TELLIN' ME TO SOFTEN IT UP, YOU KNOW.
EVEN IF I'M ABLE TO CONVINCE YUJIRO, I CAN'T DO ANYTHING ABOUT IT IF THE EDITOR IN CHIEF TELLS ME THAT IT'S NO GOOD.
...
CENSOR-SHIP IS GETTING TOUGHER AND TOUGHER THESE DAYS.
AND WHEN I COMPLAIN, THEY JUST TELL ME NOT TO BRING UP OLD MANGA AS AN EXAMPLE...
BUT WE NEED MORE UNHEALTHY BOYS' MANGA. WE'RE NOT TRYING TO CREATE THE BIBLE OR A SCHOOL TEXTBOOK HERE, YOU KNOW.
FREAKING THE PTA OUT IS WHAT IT'S ALL ABOUT!
AH, FORGET IT.
I THINK MY WORK IS THE BEST TOO.
...
DID YOU TWO ALSO THINK YOUR ONE-SHOT WAS THE BEST?
WELL... YEAH.
OVERALL...

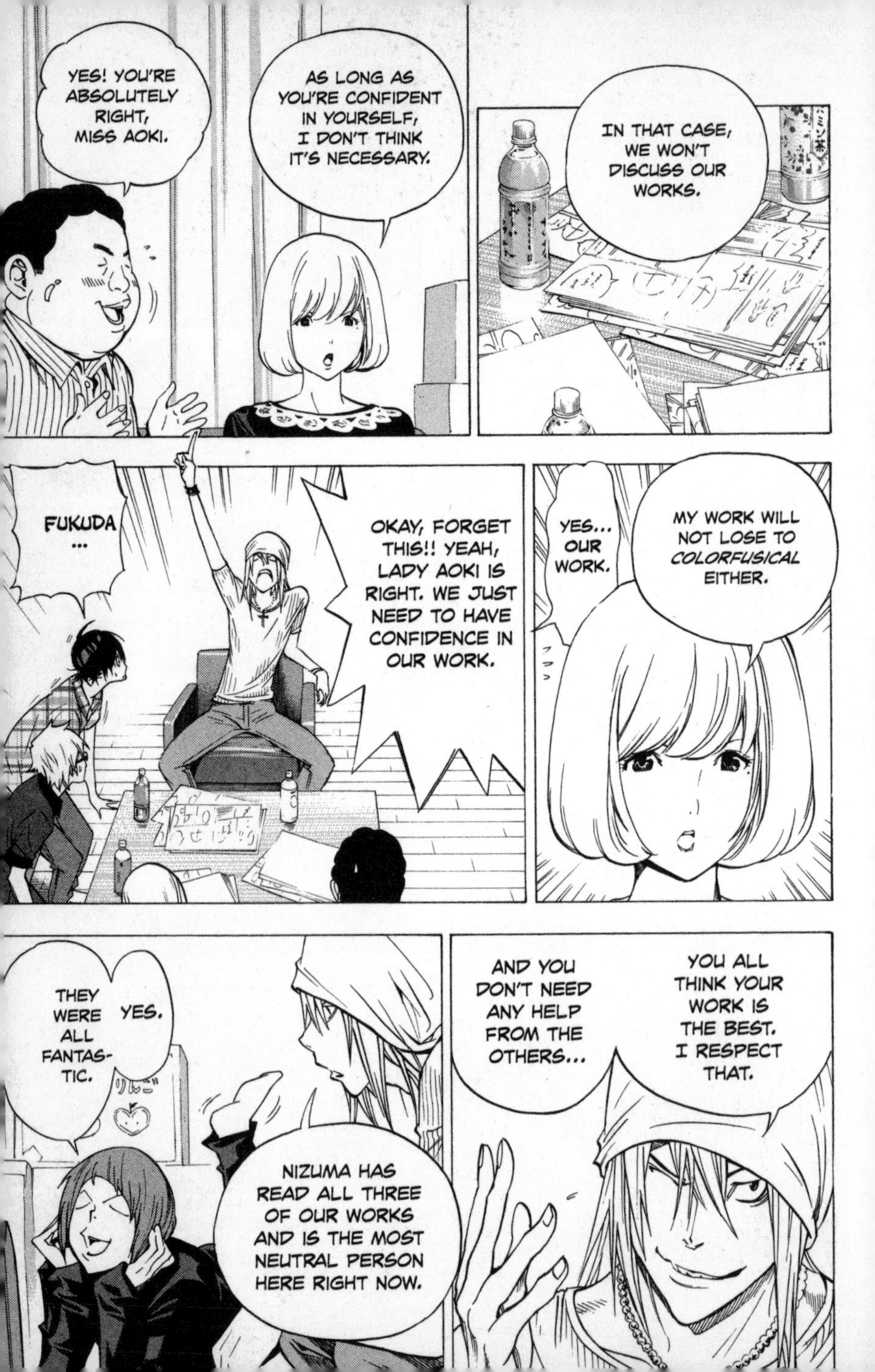
IN THAT CASE, WE WON'T DISCUSS OUR WORKS.
AS LONG AS YOU'RE CONFIDENT IN YOURSELF, I DON'T THINK IT'S NECESSARY.
YES! YOU'RE ABSOLUTELY RIGHT, MISS AOKI.
MY WORK WILL NOT LOSE TO *COLORFUSICAL* EITHER.
YES... OUR WORK.
OKAY, FORGET THIS!! YEAH, LADY AOKI IS RIGHT. WE JUST NEED TO HAVE CONFIDENCE IN OUR WORK.
FUKUDA...
YOU ALL THINK YOUR WORK IS THE BEST. I RESPECT THAT.
AND YOU DON'T NEED ANY HELP FROM THE OTHERS...
YES.
THEY WERE ALL FANTASTIC.
NIZUMA HAS READ ALL THREE OF OUR WORKS AND IS THE MOST NEUTRAL PERSON HERE RIGHT NOW.

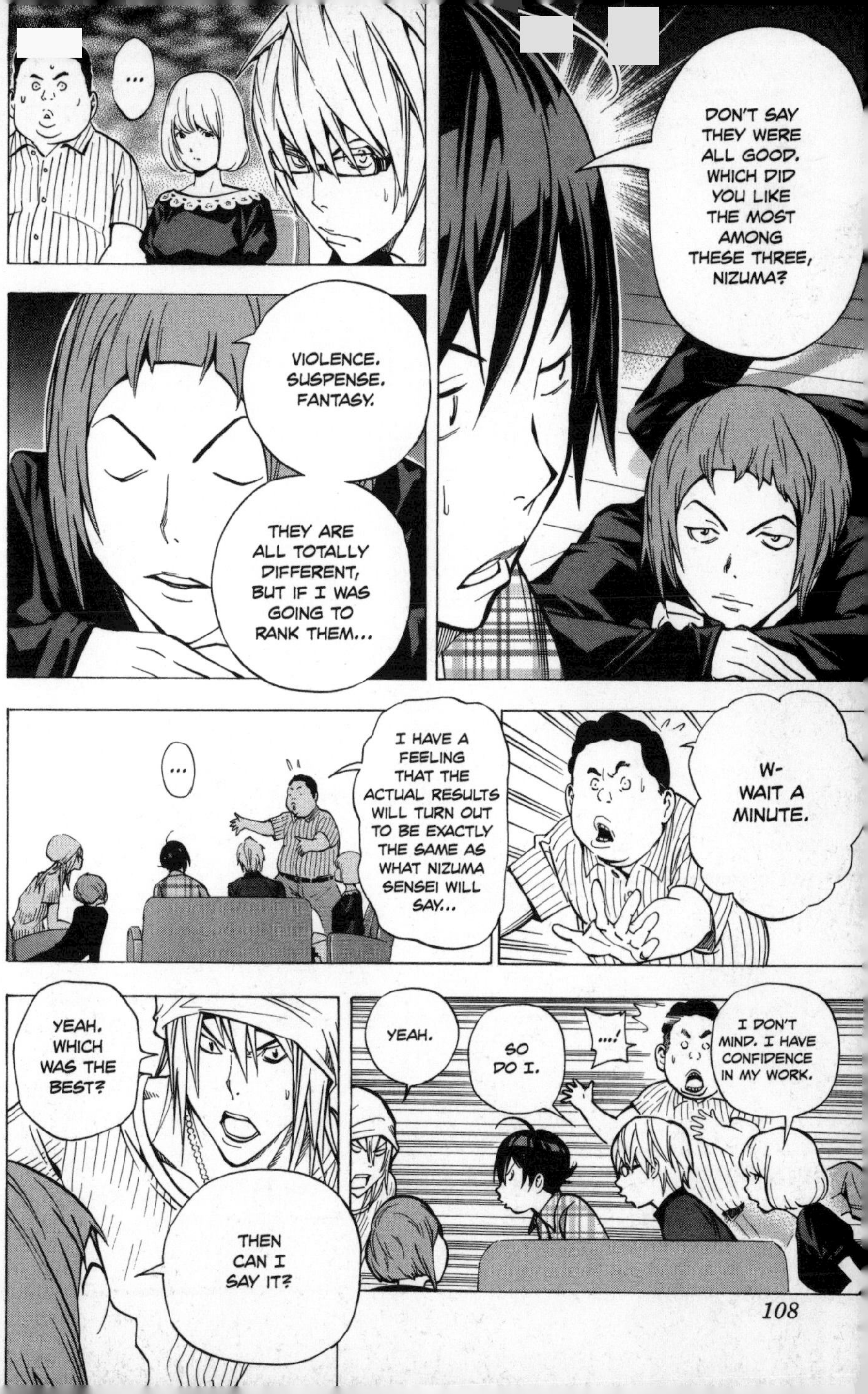
DON'T SAY THEY WERE ALL GOOD. WHICH DID YOU LIKE THE MOST AMONG THESE THREE, NIZUMA?
...
VIOLENCE. SUSPENSE. FANTASY.
THEY ARE ALL TOTALLY DIFFERENT, BUT IF I WAS GOING TO RANK THEM...
W- WAIT A MINUTE.
I HAVE A FEELING THAT THE ACTUAL RESULTS WILL TURN OUT TO BE EXACTLY THE SAME AS WHAT NIZUMA SENSEI WILL SAY...
...
I DON'T MIND. I HAVE CONFIDENCE IN MY WORK.
....!
SO DO I.
YEAH.
YEAH. WHICH WAS THE BEST?
THEN CAN I SAY IT?

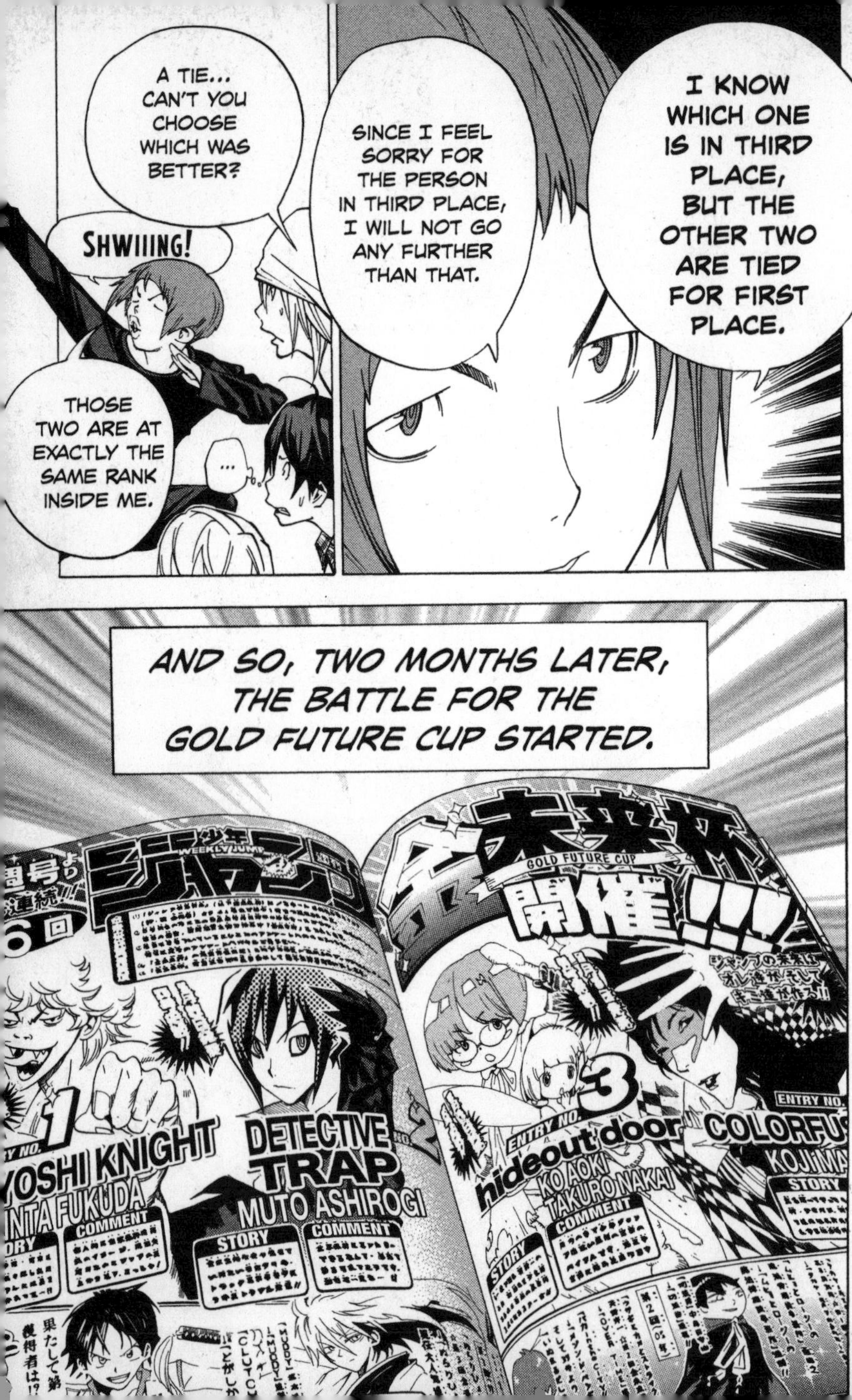

I KNOW WHICH ONE IS IN THIRD PLACE, BUT THE OTHER TWO ARE TIED FOR FIRST PLACE.
SINCE I FEEL SORRY FOR THE PERSON IN THIRD PLACE, I WILL NOT GO ANY FURTHER THAN THAT.
A TIE... CAN'T YOU CHOOSE WHICH WAS BETTER?
SHWIIING!
THOSE TWO ARE AT EXACTLY THE SAME RANK INSIDE ME.
...
AND SO, TWO MONTHS LATER, THE BATTLE FOR THE GOLD FUTURE CUP STARTED.
GOLD FUTURE CUP
開催!!!
WEEKLY JUMP
ENTRY NO.
COLORFU
STORY
ENTRY NO. 3
hideout door
KO AOKI
TAKURO NAKAI
COMMENT
STORY
DETECTIVE TRAP
MUTO ASHIROGI
STORY
COMMENT
YOSHI KNIGHT
INTA FUKUDA
COMMENT

OHBA'S STORYBOARD

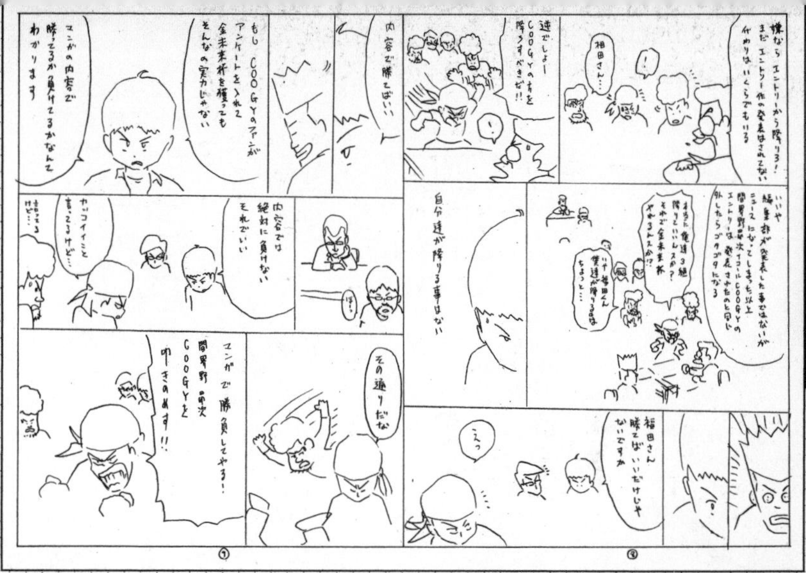

嫌ならエントリーから降りろ！
まだエントリー作の発表はされてない
代わりはいくらでもいる
！
相田さん…
逆でしょー COOGYの方を降ろすべきだ!!
！
いいや 編集部が発表した事ではないが ニュースになってしまった以上 外したらゴタゴタになる
間界野次エントリーは発表されたのと同じ
まさか俺達3組降りていいんですか？ それで金未来杯やるんですか!?
いや… 福田さん 僕達が降りるのは ちょっと…
自分達が降りる事はない
福田さん 勝てばいいだけじゃないですか
えっ
内容で勝てばいい
もし COOGYのファンがアンケートを入れて 金未来杯を獲っても そんなの実力じゃない
マンガの内容で 勝ってるか負けてるかなんて わかります
内容では 絶対に負けない それでいい
ぼー…
カッコイイこと 言ってるけど…
言ってるけど…
その通りだな
マンガで勝負してやる！ 間界野の次 COOGYを 叩きのめす!!

OBATA'S STORYBOARD

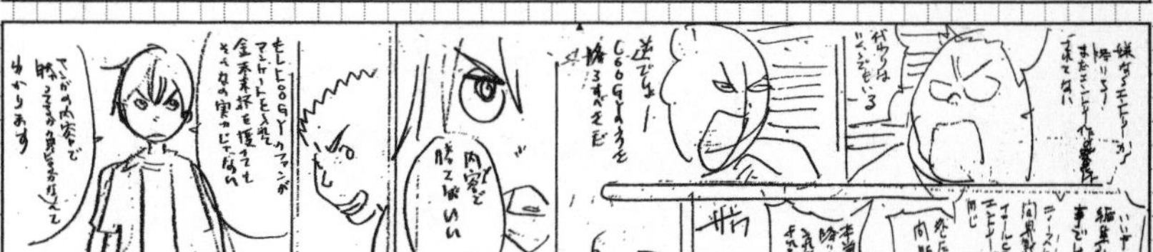

COMPLETE!

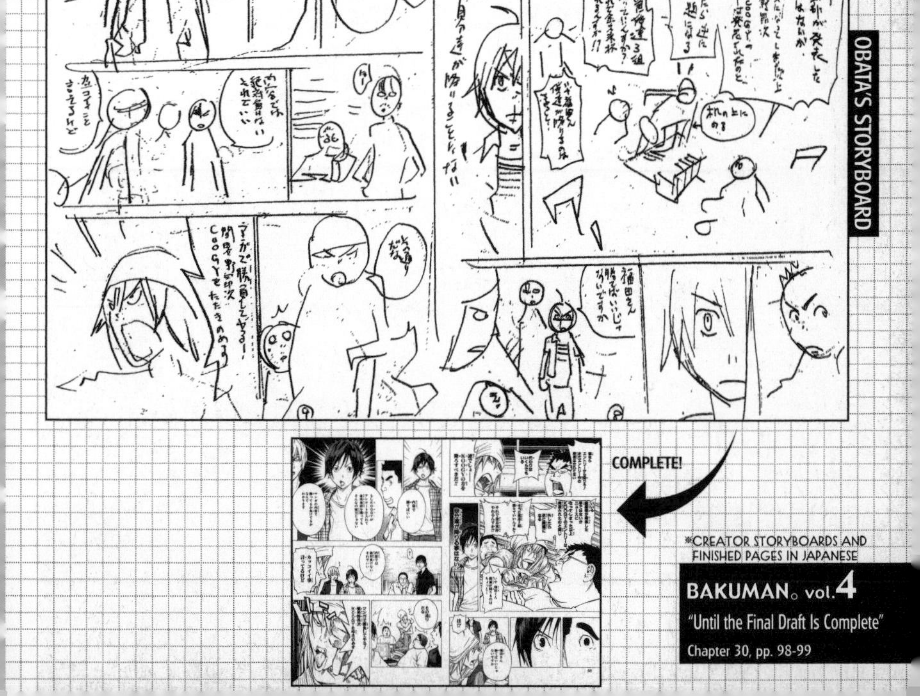

※CREATOR STORYBOARDS AND FINISHED PAGES IN JAPANESE

BAKUMAN。 vol.4

"Until the Final Draft Is Complete"

Chapter 30, pp. 98-99

AUGUST 9, MONDAY

JUMP DOUBLE ISSUE 37-38

JUMP GOLD FUTURE CUP ENTRY NUMBER 1

KIYOSHI KNIGHT

BY SHINTA FUKUDA

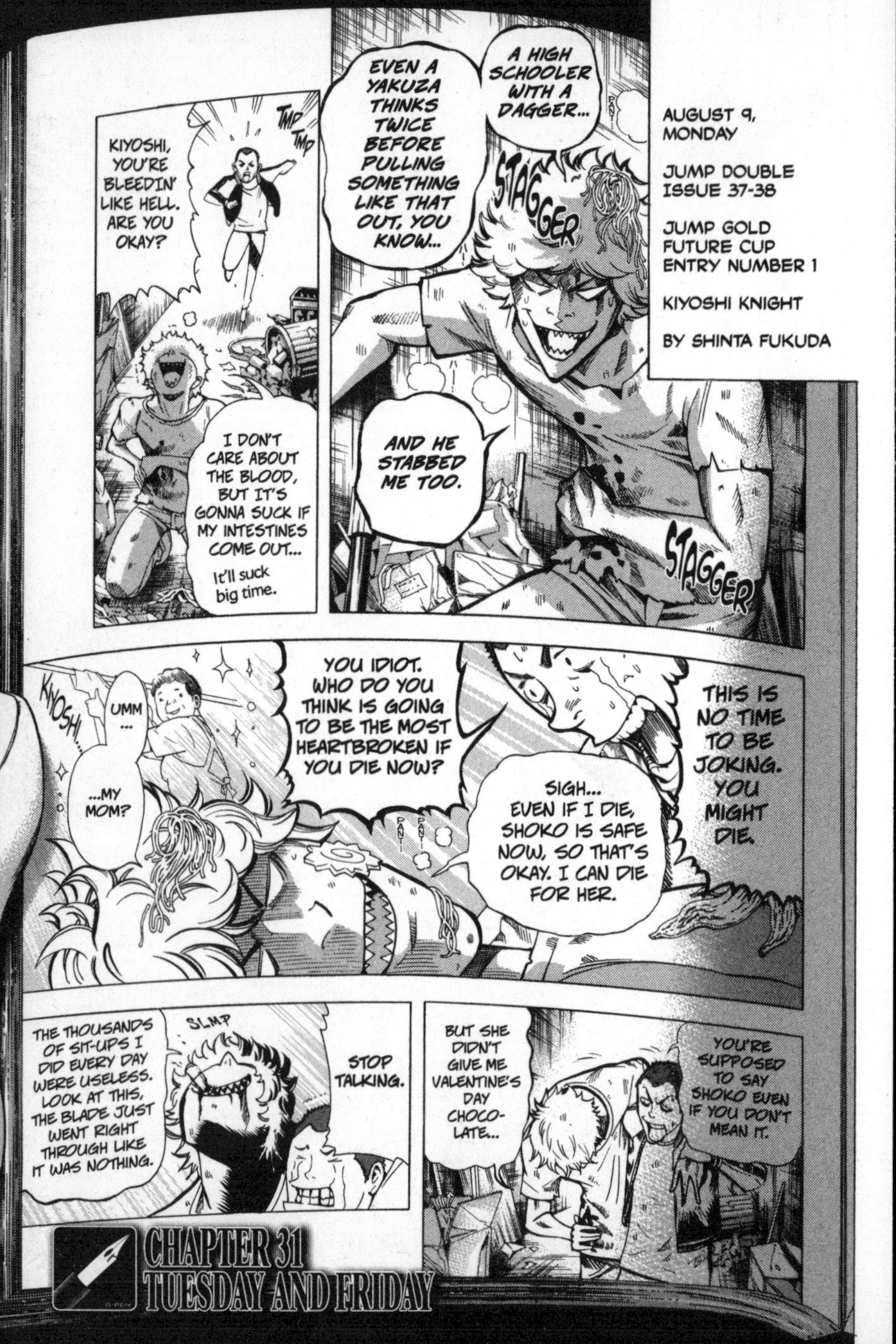
A HIGH SCHOOLER WITH A DAGGER...
EVEN A YAKUZA THINKS TWICE BEFORE PULLING SOMETHING LIKE THAT OUT, YOU KNOW...
PANT...
STAGGER
AND HE STABBED ME TOO.
STAGGER
TMP TMP
KIYOSHI, YOU'RE BLEEDIN' LIKE HELL. ARE YOU OKAY?
I DON'T CARE ABOUT THE BLOOD, BUT IT'S GONNA SUCK IF MY INTESTINES COME OUT...
It'll suck big time.
THIS IS NO TIME TO BE JOKING. YOU MIGHT DIE.
SIGH... EVEN IF I DIE, SHOKO IS SAFE NOW, SO THAT'S OKAY. I CAN DIE FOR HER.
YOU IDIOT. WHO DO YOU THINK IS GOING TO BE THE MOST HEARTBROKEN IF YOU DIE NOW?
PANT... PANT...
KIYOSHI...
UMM ...
...MY MOM?
YOU'RE SUPPOSED TO SAY SHOKO EVEN IF YOU DON'T MEAN IT.
BUT SHE DIDN'T GIVE ME VALENTINE'S DAY CHOCO-LATE...
STOP TALKING.
SLMP
THE THOUSANDS OF SIT-UPS I DID EVERY DAY WERE USELESS. LOOK AT THIS, THE BLADE JUST WENT RIGHT THROUGH LIKE IT WAS NOTHING.

CHAPTER 31
TUESDAY AND FRIDAY

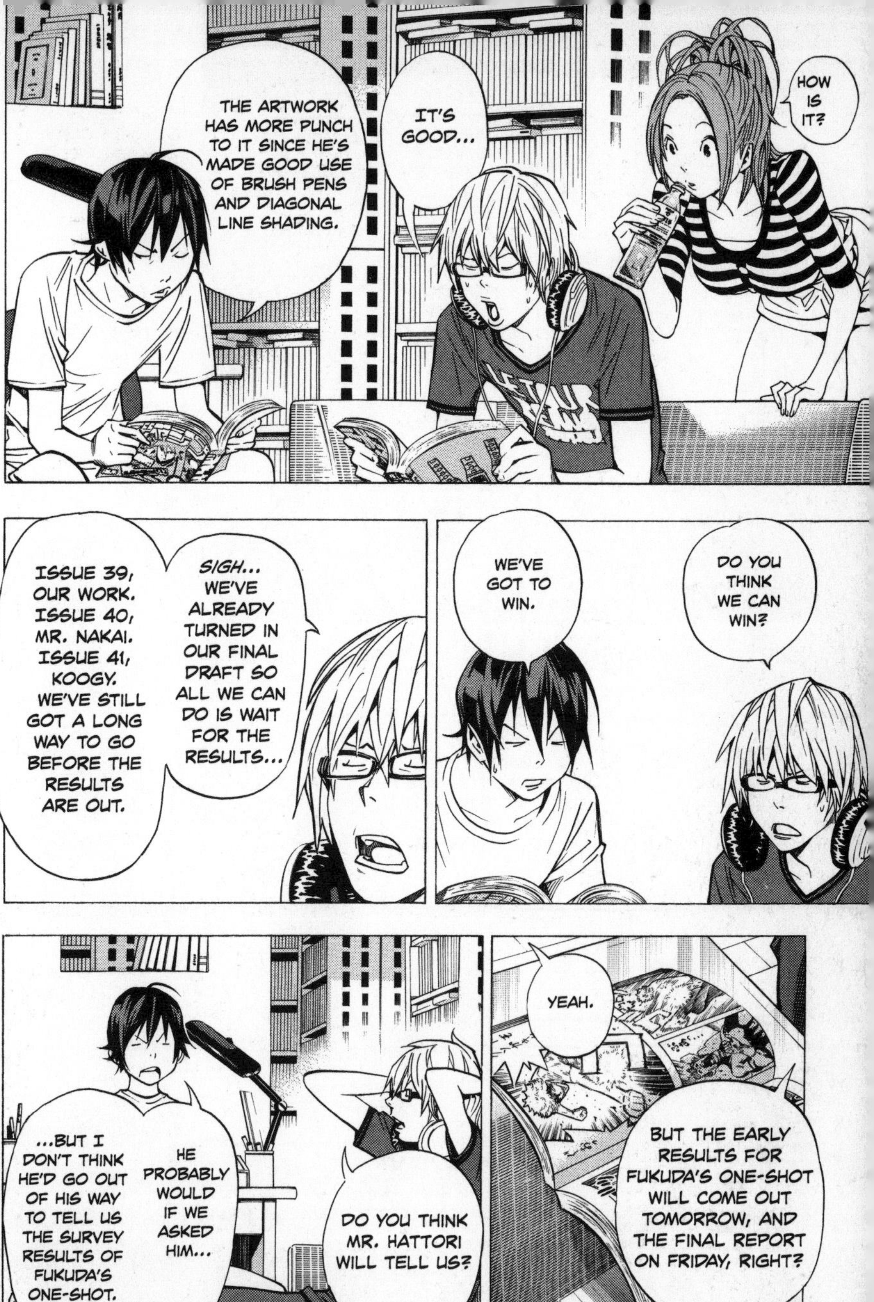
HOW IS IT?
IT'S GOOD...
THE ARTWORK HAS MORE PUNCH TO IT SINCE HE'S MADE GOOD USE OF BRUSH PENS AND DIAGONAL LINE SHADING.
DO YOU THINK WE CAN WIN?
WE'VE GOT TO WIN.
SIGH... WE'VE ALREADY TURNED IN OUR FINAL DRAFT SO ALL WE CAN DO IS WAIT FOR THE RESULTS...
ISSUE 39, OUR WORK. ISSUE 40, MR. NAKAI. ISSUE 41, KOOGY. WE'VE STILL GOT A LONG WAY TO GO BEFORE THE RESULTS ARE OUT.
BUT THE EARLY RESULTS FOR FUKUDA'S ONE-SHOT WILL COME OUT TOMORROW, AND THE FINAL REPORT ON FRIDAY, RIGHT?
YEAH.
DO YOU THINK MR. HATTORI WILL TELL US?
HE PROBABLY WOULD IF WE ASKED HIM...
...BUT I DON'T THINK HE'D GO OUT OF HIS WAY TO TELL US THE SURVEY RESULTS OF FUKUDA'S ONE-SHOT.

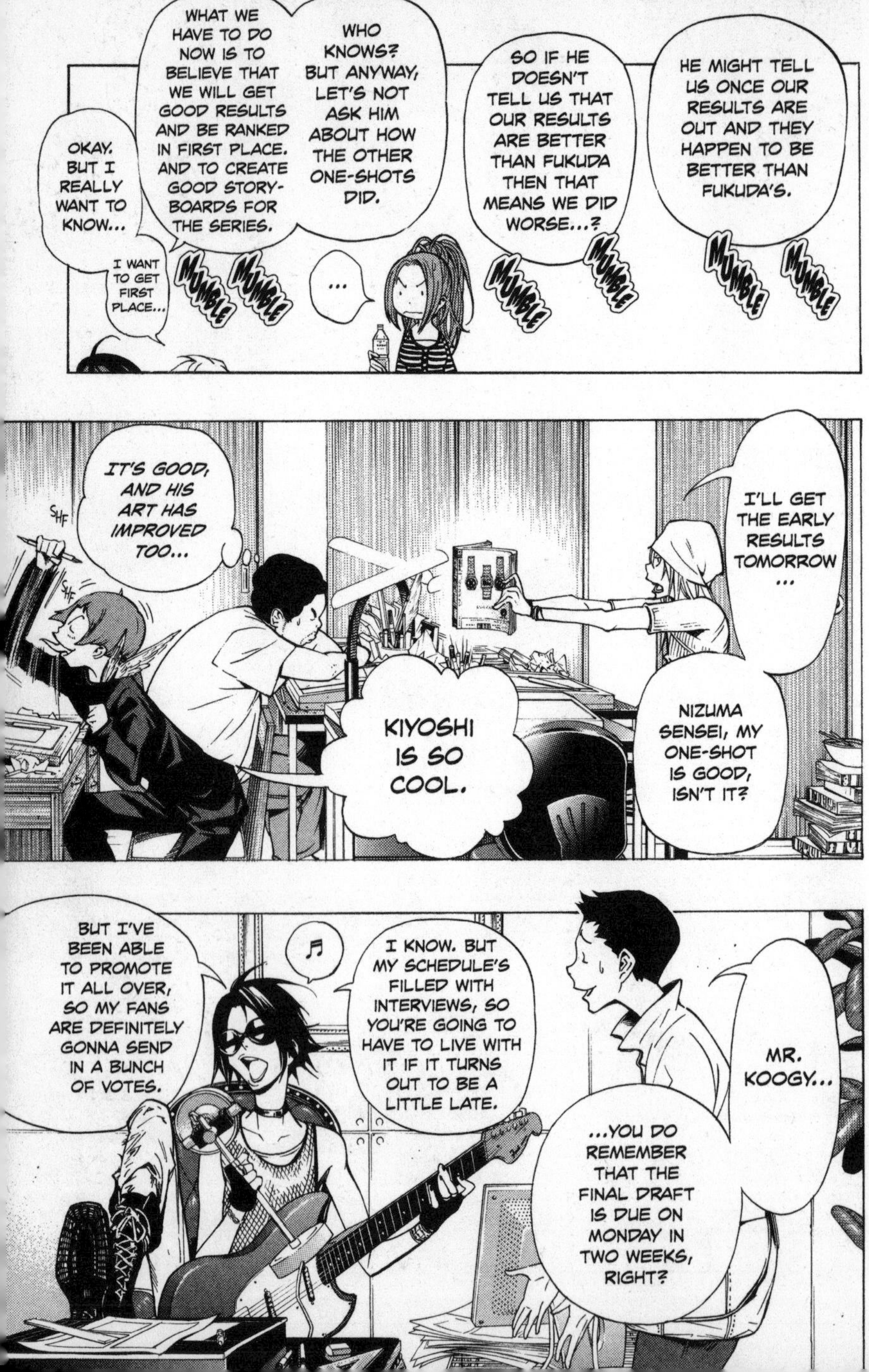
HE MIGHT TELL US ONCE OUR RESULTS ARE OUT AND THEY HAPPEN TO BE BETTER THAN FUKUDA'S.
MUMBLE
MUMBLE
SO IF HE DOESN'T TELL US THAT OUR RESULTS ARE BETTER THAN FUKUDA THEN THAT MEANS WE DID WORSE...?
MUMBLE
MUMBLE
WHO KNOWS? BUT ANYWAY, LET'S NOT ASK HIM ABOUT HOW THE OTHER ONE-SHOTS DID.
...
WHAT WE HAVE TO DO NOW IS TO BELIEVE THAT WE WILL GET GOOD RESULTS AND BE RANKED IN FIRST PLACE. AND TO CREATE GOOD STORY-BOARDS FOR THE SERIES.
MUMBLE
MUMBLE
OKAY. BUT I REALLY WANT TO KNOW...
I WANT TO GET FIRST PLACE...
I'LL GET THE EARLY RESULTS TOMORROW...
NIZUMA SENSEI, MY ONE-SHOT IS GOOD, ISN'T IT?
KIYOSHI IS SO COOL.
IT'S GOOD, AND HIS ART HAS IMPROVED TOO...
SHF
SHF
MR. KOOGY...
...YOU DO REMEMBER THAT THE FINAL DRAFT IS DUE ON MONDAY IN TWO WEEKS, RIGHT?
I KNOW. BUT MY SCHEDULE'S FILLED WITH INTERVIEWS, SO YOU'RE GOING TO HAVE TO LIVE WITH IT IF IT TURNS OUT TO BE A LITTLE LATE.
♫
BUT I'VE BEEN ABLE TO PROMOTE IT ALL OVER, SO MY FANS ARE DEFINITELY GONNA SEND IN A BUNCH OF VOTES.

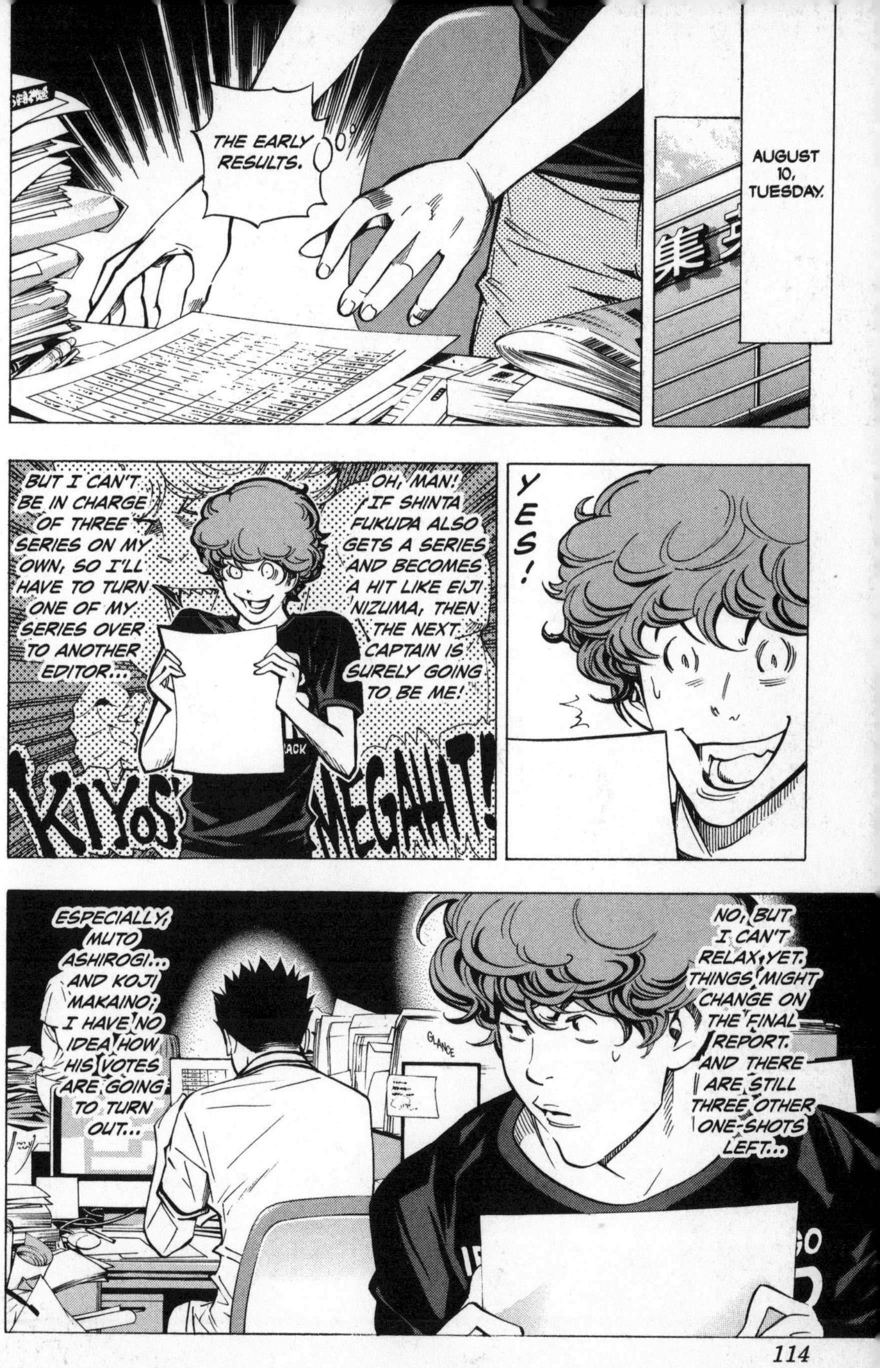
AUGUST 10, TUESDAY.
THE EARLY RESULTS.
YES!
OH, MAN! IF SHINTA FUKUDA ALSO GETS A SERIES AND BECOMES A HIT LIKE EIJI NIZUMA, THEN THE NEXT CAPTAIN IS SURELY GOING TO BE ME!
BUT I CAN'T BE IN CHARGE OF THREE SERIES ON MY OWN, SO I'LL HAVE TO TURN ONE OF MY SERIES OVER TO ANOTHER EDITOR...
MEGAHIT!
KIYOS
NO, BUT I CAN'T RELAX YET. THINGS MIGHT CHANGE ON THE FINAL REPORT. AND THERE ARE STILL THREE OTHER ONE-SHOTS LEFT...
GLANCE
ESPECIALLY, MUTO ASHIROGI... AND KOJI MAKAINO; I HAVE NO IDEA HOW HIS VOTES ARE GOING TO TURN OUT...

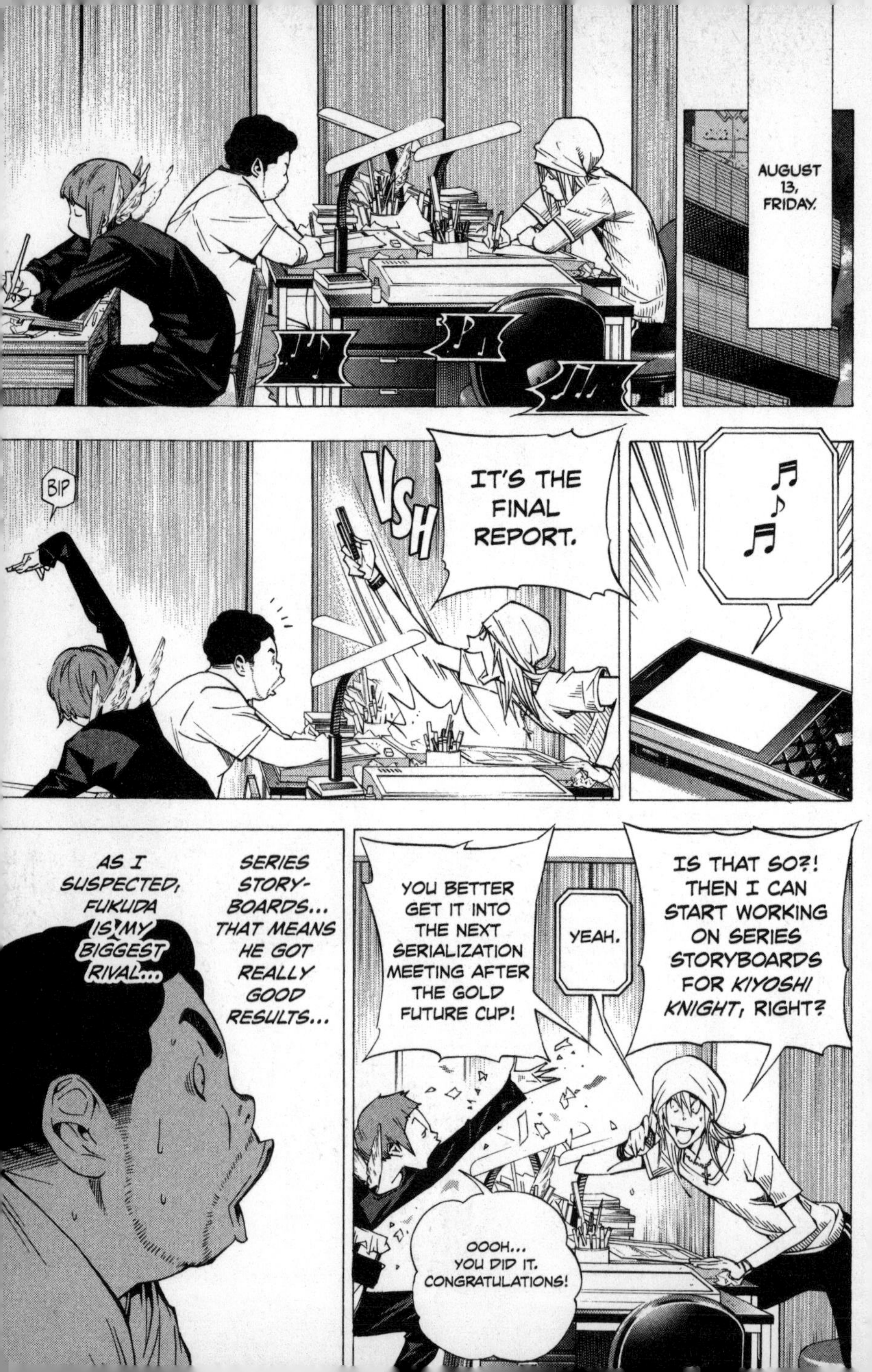
AUGUST 13, FRIDAY.
IT'S THE FINAL REPORT.
VSH
BIP
IS THAT SO?! THEN I CAN START WORKING ON SERIES STORYBOARDS FOR *KIYOSHI KNIGHT*, RIGHT?
YEAH.
YOU BETTER GET IT INTO THE NEXT SERIALIZATION MEETING AFTER THE GOLD FUTURE CUP!
OOOH... YOU DID IT. CONGRATULATIONS!
SERIES STORYBOARDS... THAT MEANS HE GOT REALLY GOOD RESULTS...
AS I SUSPECTED, FUKUDA IS MY BIGGEST RIVAL...

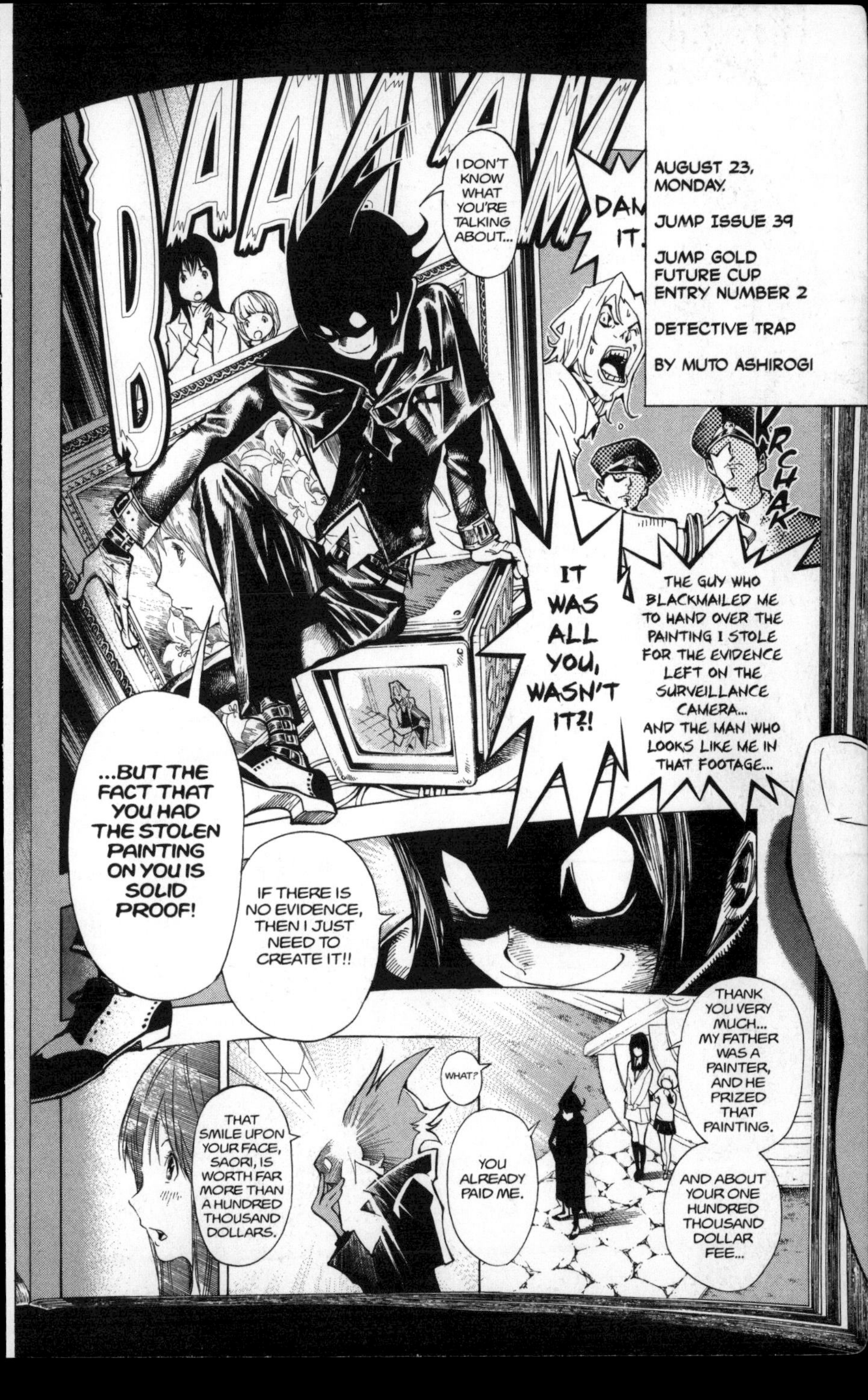
AUGUST 23, MONDAY.
JUMP ISSUE 39
JUMP GOLD FUTURE CUP ENTRY NUMBER 2
DETECTIVE TRAP
BY MUTO ASHIROGI
DAM IT.
I DON'T KNOW WHAT YOU'RE TALKING ABOUT...
KRCHAK
THE GUY WHO BLACKMAILED ME TO HAND OVER THE PAINTING I STOLE FOR THE EVIDENCE LEFT ON THE SURVEILLANCE CAMERA... AND THE MAN WHO LOOKS LIKE ME IN THAT FOOTAGE...
IT WAS ALL YOU, WASN'T IT?!
...BUT THE FACT THAT YOU HAD THE STOLEN PAINTING ON YOU IS SOLID PROOF!
IF THERE IS NO EVIDENCE, THEN I JUST NEED TO CREATE IT!!
THANK YOU VERY MUCH... MY FATHER WAS A PAINTER, AND HE PRIZED THAT PAINTING.
AND ABOUT YOUR ONE HUNDRED THOUSAND DOLLAR FEE...
YOU ALREADY PAID ME.
WHAT?
THAT SMILE UPON YOUR FACE, SAORI, IS WORTH FAR MORE THAN A HUNDRED THOUSAND DOLLARS.

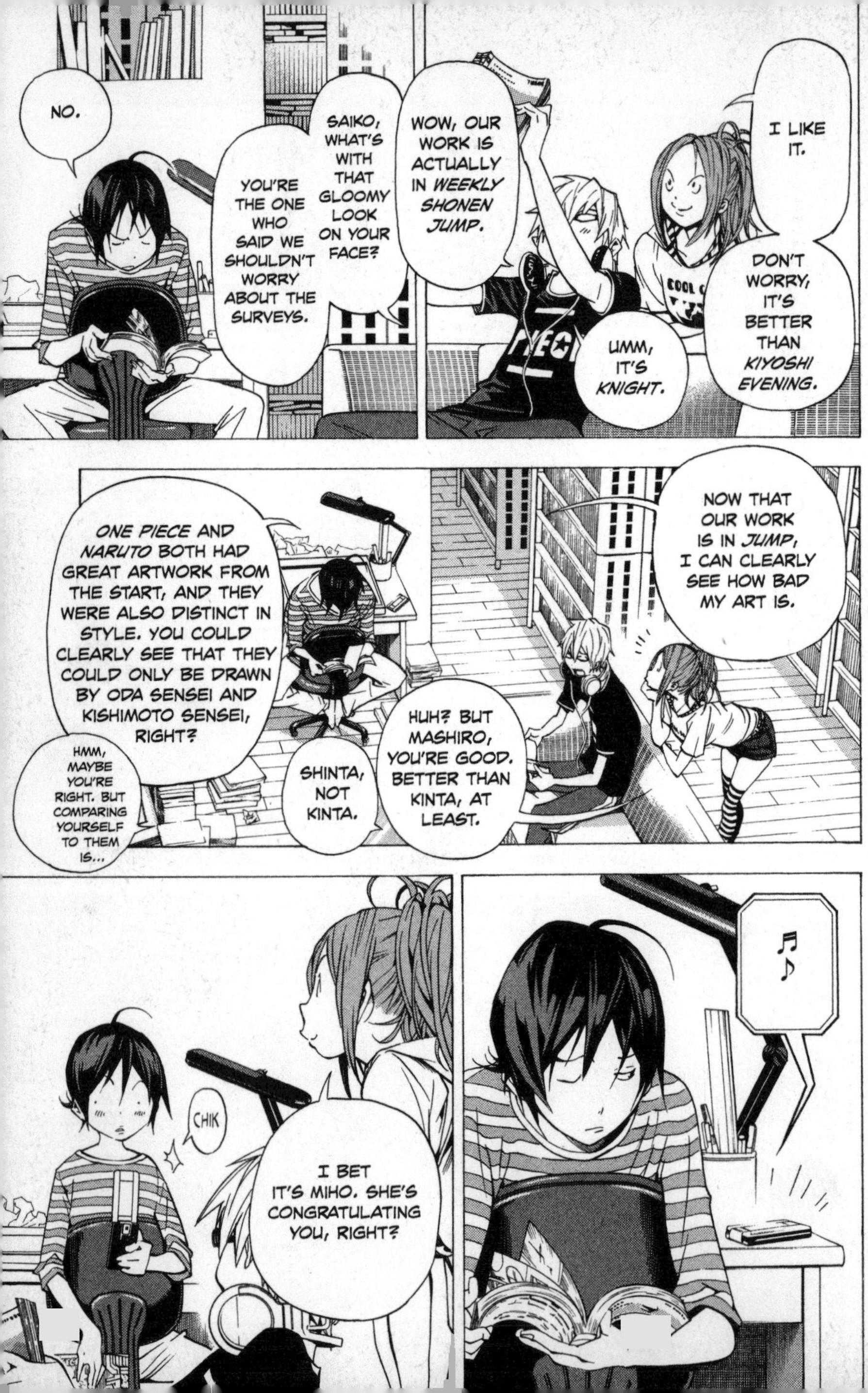
I LIKE IT.
WOW, OUR WORK IS ACTUALLY IN *WEEKLY SHONEN JUMP*.
DON'T WORRY, IT'S BETTER THAN *KIYOSHI EVENING*.
UMM, IT'S *KNIGHT*.
SAIKO, WHAT'S WITH THAT GLOOMY LOOK ON YOUR FACE?
YOU'RE THE ONE WHO SAID WE SHOULDN'T WORRY ABOUT THE SURVEYS.
NO.
NOW THAT OUR WORK IS IN *JUMP*, I CAN CLEARLY SEE HOW BAD MY ART IS.
HUH? BUT MASHIRO, YOU'RE GOOD. BETTER THAN KINTA, AT LEAST.
SHINTA, NOT KINTA.
ONE PIECE AND *NARUTO* BOTH HAD GREAT ARTWORK FROM THE START, AND THEY WERE ALSO DISTINCT IN STYLE. YOU COULD CLEARLY SEE THAT THEY COULD ONLY BE DRAWN BY ODA SENSEI AND KISHIMOTO SENSEI, RIGHT?
HMM, MAYBE YOU'RE RIGHT. BUT COMPARING YOURSELF TO THEM IS...
♬ ♪
I BET IT'S MIHO. SHE'S CONGRATULATING YOU, RIGHT?
CHIK

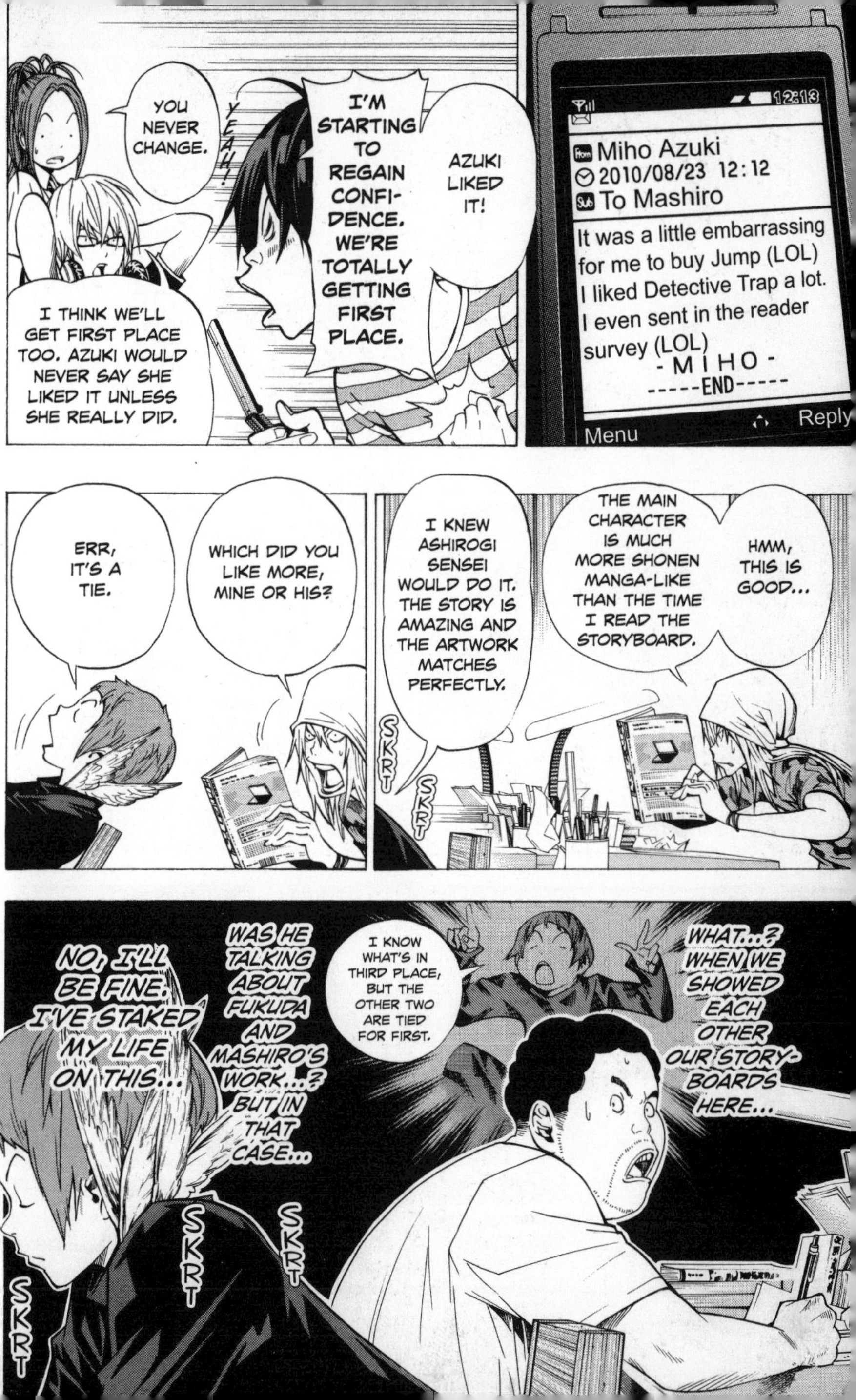
12:13
Miho Azuki
2010/08/23 12:12
To Mashiro
It was a little embarrassing for me to buy Jump (LOL) I liked Detective Trap a lot. I even sent in the reader survey (LOL)
-MIHO-
-----END-----
Menu
Reply
AZUKI LIKED IT!
I'M STARTING TO REGAIN CONFIDENCE. WE'RE TOTALLY GETTING FIRST PLACE.
YEAH!
YOU NEVER CHANGE.
I THINK WE'LL GET FIRST PLACE TOO. AZUKI WOULD NEVER SAY SHE LIKED IT UNLESS SHE REALLY DID.
HMM, THIS IS GOOD...
THE MAIN CHARACTER IS MUCH MORE SHONEN MANGA-LIKE THAN THE TIME I READ THE STORYBOARD.
I KNEW ASHIROGI SENSEI WOULD DO IT. THE STORY IS AMAZING AND THE ARTWORK MATCHES PERFECTLY.
SKRT
SKRT
WHICH DID YOU LIKE MORE, MINE OR HIS?
ERR, IT'S A TIE.
WHAT...? WHEN WE SHOWED EACH OTHER OUR STORYBOARDS HERE...
I KNOW WHAT'S IN THIRD PLACE, BUT THE OTHER TWO ARE TIED FOR FIRST.
WAS HE TALKING ABOUT FUKUDA AND MASHIRO'S WORK...? BUT IN THAT CASE...
NO, I'LL BE FINE. I'VE STAKED MY LIFE ON THIS...
SKRT
SKRT
SKRT

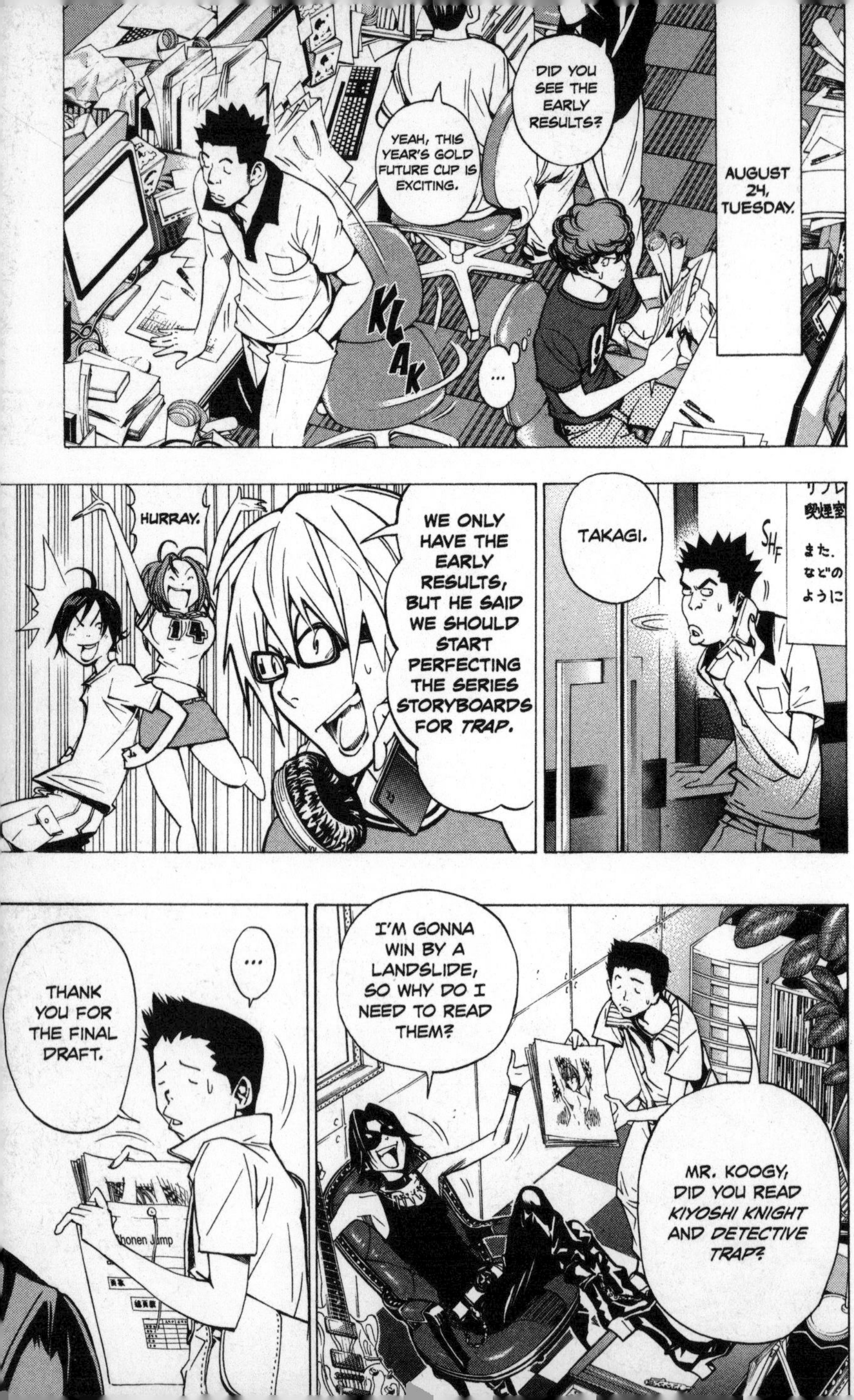
AUGUST 24, TUESDAY.
DID YOU SEE THE EARLY RESULTS?
YEAH, THIS YEAR'S GOLD FUTURE CUP IS EXCITING.
KLAK
...
TAKAGI.
SHF
WE ONLY HAVE THE EARLY RESULTS, BUT HE SAID WE SHOULD START PERFECTING THE SERIES STORYBOARDS FOR *TRAP*.
HURRAY.
MR. KOOGY, DID YOU READ *KIYOSHI KNIGHT* AND *DETECTIVE TRAP*?
I'M GONNA WIN BY A LANDSLIDE, SO WHY DO I NEED TO READ THEM?
...
THANK YOU FOR THE FINAL DRAFT.

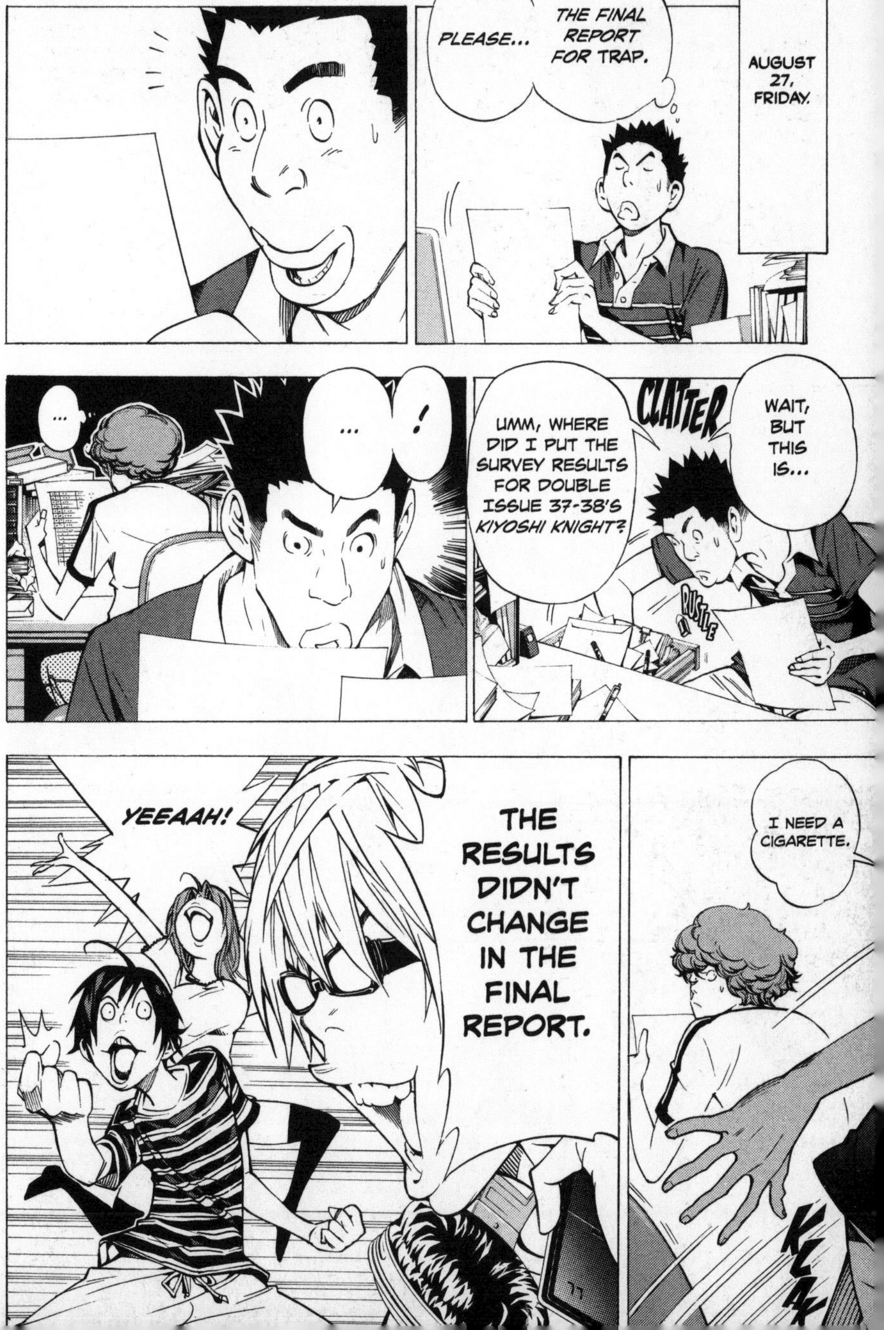
AUGUST 27, FRIDAY.
PLEASE... THE FINAL REPORT FOR TRAP.
WAIT, BUT THIS IS...
CLATTER
UMM, WHERE DID I PUT THE SURVEY RESULTS FOR DOUBLE ISSUE 37-38'S *KIYOSHI KNIGHT*?
RUSTLE
!
...
...
I NEED A CIGARETTE.
KLAK
THE RESULTS DIDN'T CHANGE IN THE FINAL REPORT.
YEEAAH!

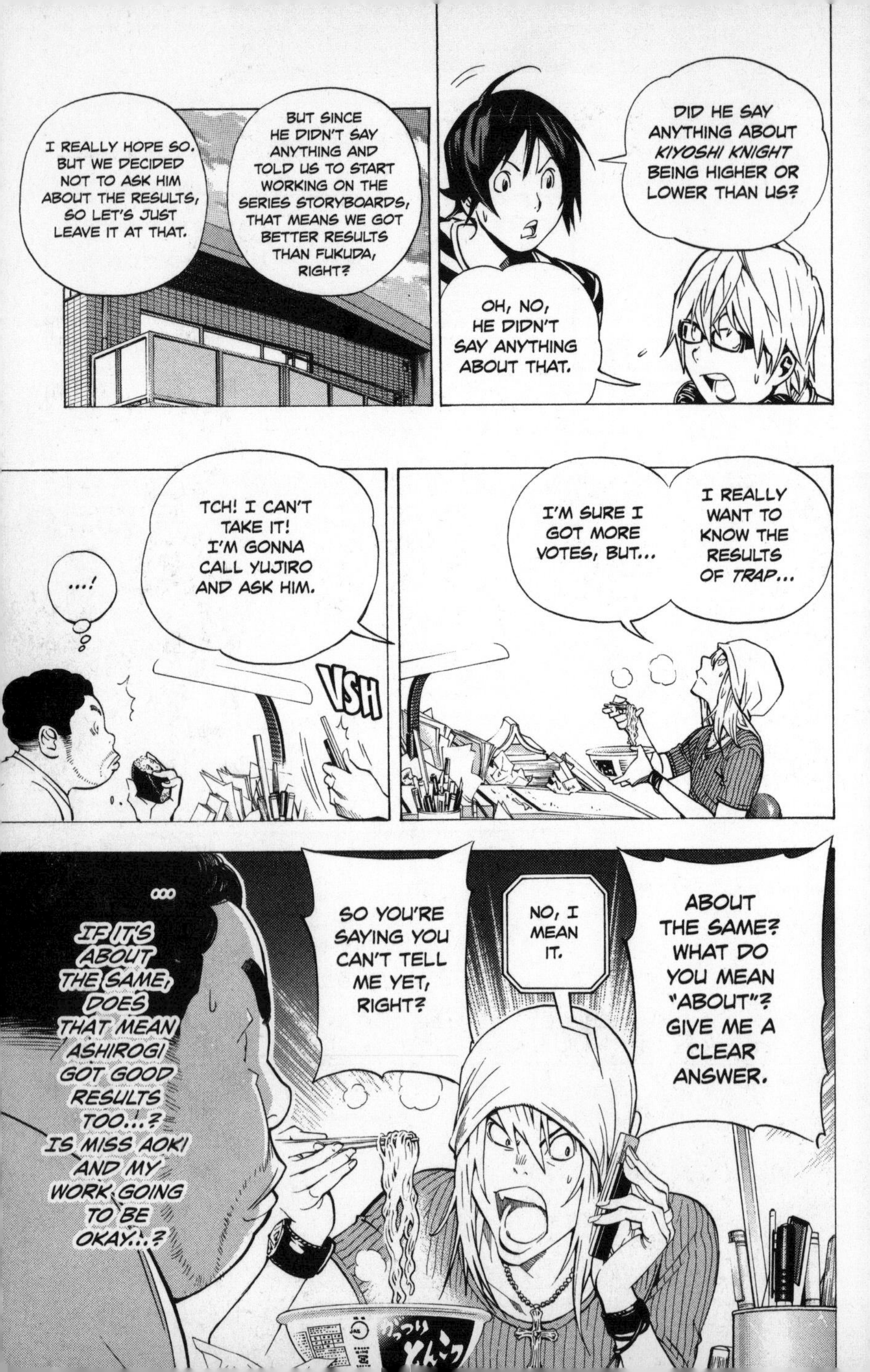
DID HE SAY ANYTHING ABOUT *KIYOSHI KNIGHT* BEING HIGHER OR LOWER THAN US?
OH, NO, HE DIDN'T SAY ANYTHING ABOUT THAT.
BUT SINCE HE DIDN'T SAY ANYTHING AND TOLD US TO START WORKING ON THE SERIES STORYBOARDS, THAT MEANS WE GOT BETTER RESULTS THAN FUKUDA, RIGHT?
I REALLY HOPE SO. BUT WE DECIDED NOT TO ASK HIM ABOUT THE RESULTS, SO LET'S JUST LEAVE IT AT THAT.
I REALLY WANT TO KNOW THE RESULTS OF *TRAP*...
I'M SURE I GOT MORE VOTES, BUT...
TCH! I CAN'T TAKE IT! I'M GONNA CALL YUJIRO AND ASK HIM.
VSH
...!
ABOUT THE SAME? WHAT DO YOU MEAN "ABOUT"? GIVE ME A CLEAR ANSWER.
NO, I MEAN IT.
SO YOU'RE SAYING YOU CAN'T TELL ME YET, RIGHT?
...
IF IT'S ABOUT THE SAME, DOES THAT MEAN ASHIROGI GOT GOOD RESULTS TOO...? IS MISS AOKI AND MY WORK GOING TO BE OKAY...?

AUGUST 30, MONDAY

JUMP ISSUE 40

JUMP GOLD FUTURE CUP ENTRY NUMBER 3

HIDEOUT DOOR

STORY BY KO AOKI, ART BY TAKURO NAKAI

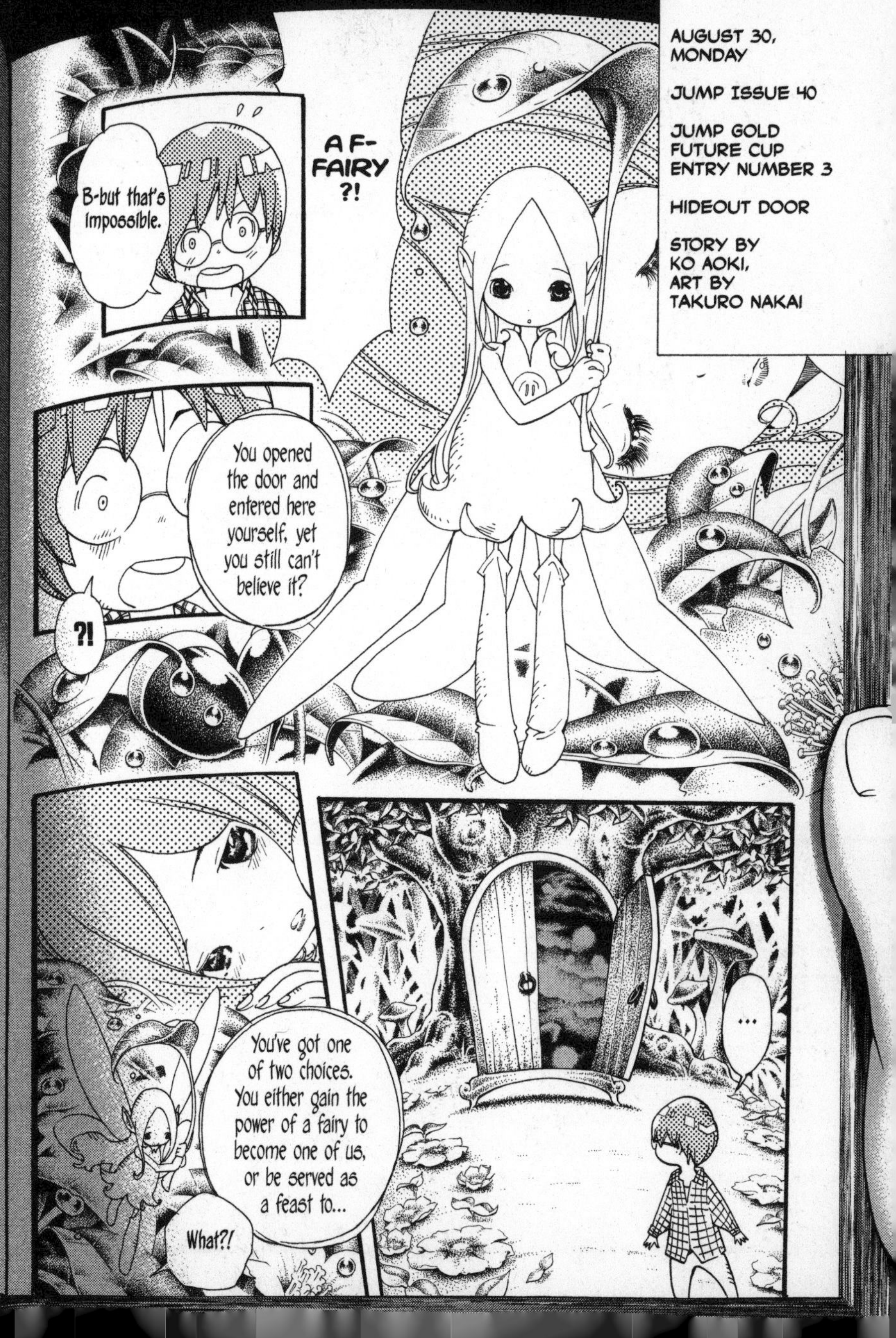
A F-FAIRY ?!
B-but that's impossible.
You opened the door and entered here yourself, yet you still can't believe it?
?!
...
You've got one of two choices. You either gain the power of a fairy to become one of us, or be served as a feast to...
What?!

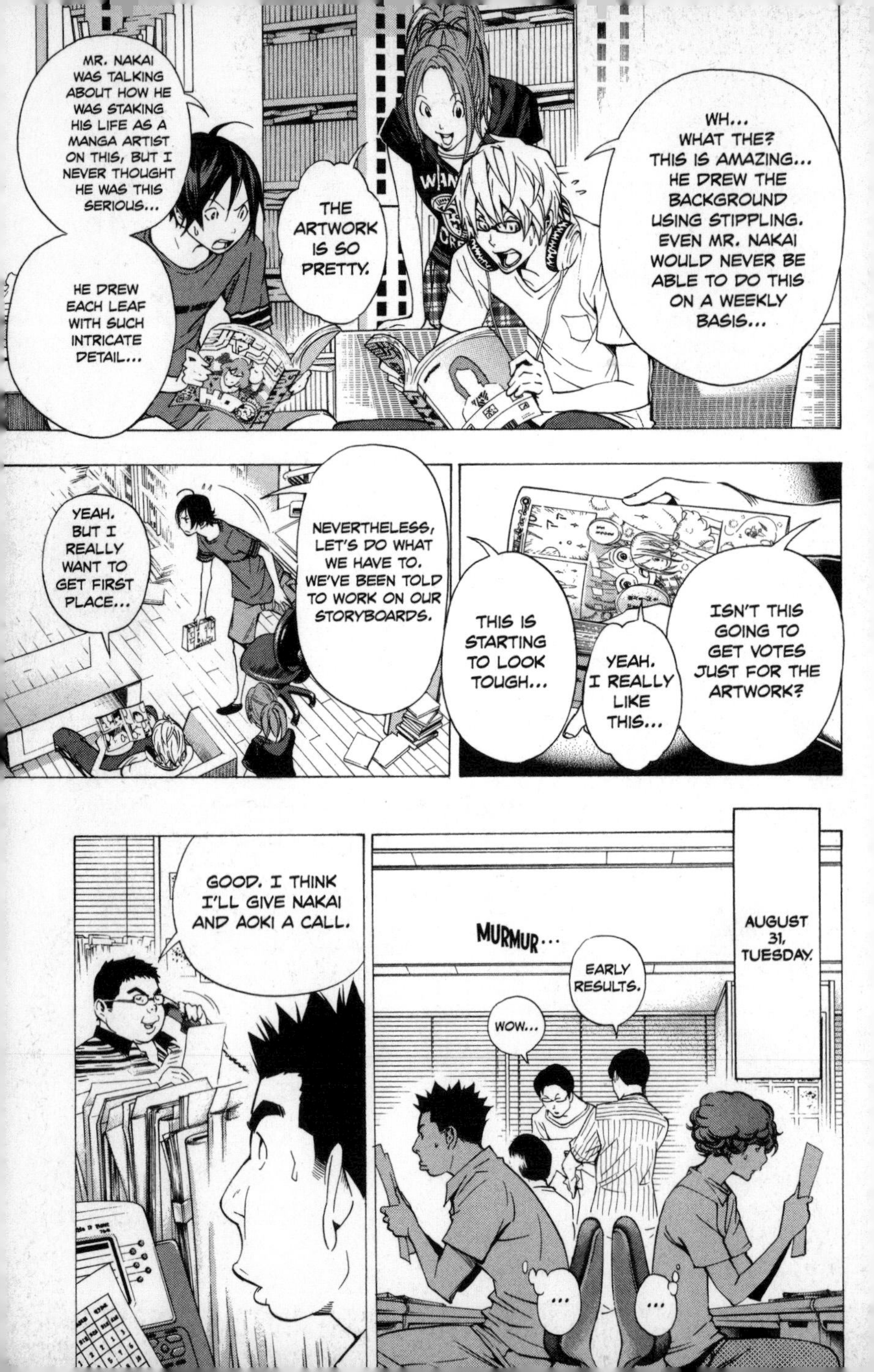
WH... WHAT THE? THIS IS AMAZING... HE DREW THE BACKGROUND USING STIPPLING. EVEN MR. NAKAI WOULD NEVER BE ABLE TO DO THIS ON A WEEKLY BASIS...
THE ARTWORK IS SO PRETTY.
MR. NAKAI WAS TALKING ABOUT HOW HE WAS STAKING HIS LIFE AS A MANGA ARTIST ON THIS, BUT I NEVER THOUGHT HE WAS THIS SERIOUS...
HE DREW EACH LEAF WITH SUCH INTRICATE DETAIL...
ISN'T THIS GOING TO GET VOTES JUST FOR THE ARTWORK?
YEAH. I REALLY LIKE THIS...
THIS IS STARTING TO LOOK TOUGH...
NEVERTHELESS, LET'S DO WHAT WE HAVE TO. WE'VE BEEN TOLD TO WORK ON OUR STORYBOARDS.
YEAH. BUT I REALLY WANT TO GET FIRST PLACE...
AUGUST 31, TUESDAY.
MURMUR...
EARLY RESULTS.
WOW...
...
...
GOOD. I THINK I'LL GIVE NAKAI AND AOKI A CALL.

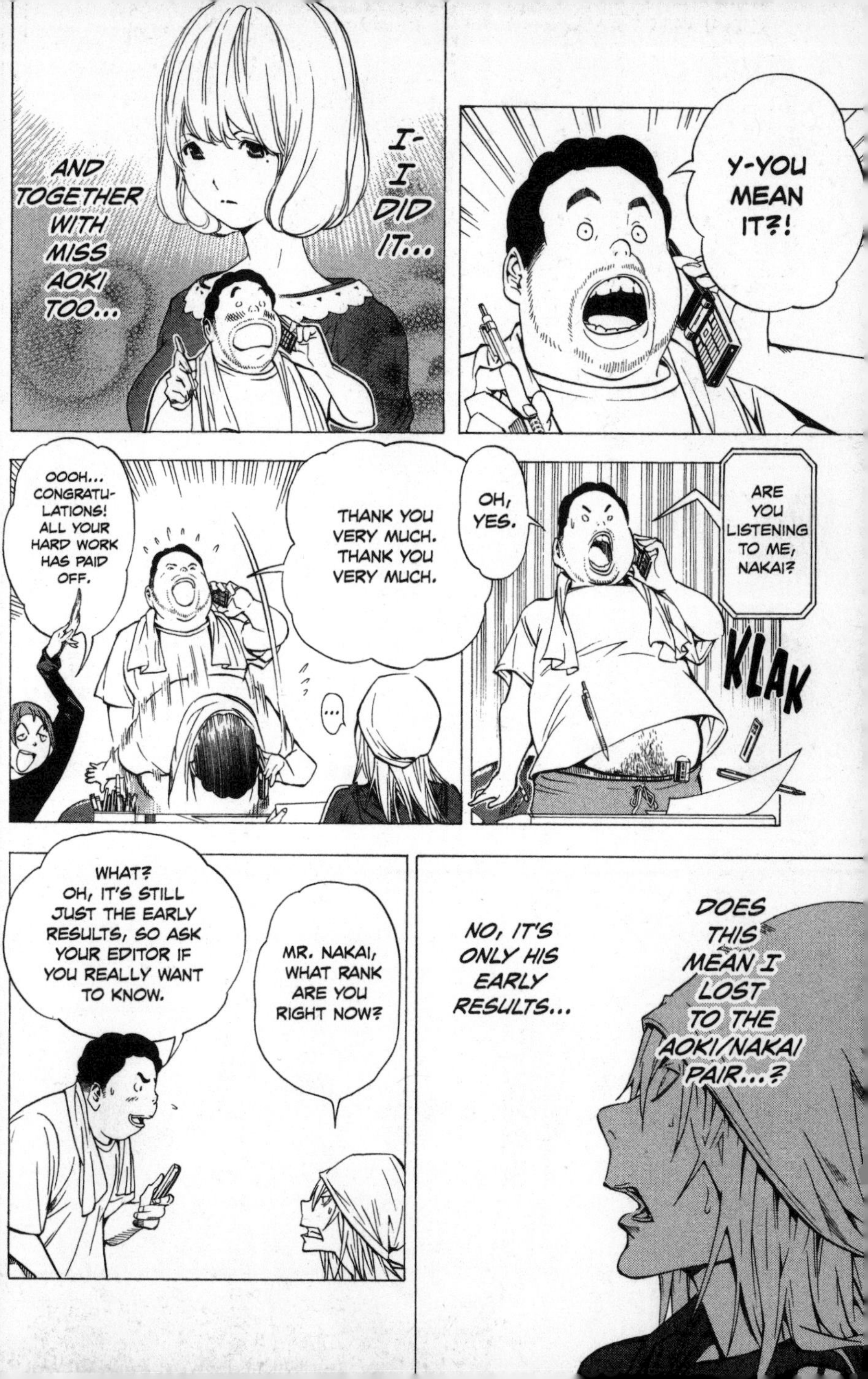
Y-YOU MEAN IT?!
I- I DID IT...
AND TOGETHER WITH MISS AOKI TOO...
ARE YOU LISTENING TO ME, NAKAI?
KLAK
OH, YES.
THANK YOU VERY MUCH. THANK YOU VERY MUCH.
OOOH... CONGRATU-LATIONS! ALL YOUR HARD WORK HAS PAID OFF.
...
DOES THIS MEAN I LOST TO THE AOKI/NAKAI PAIR...?
NO, IT'S ONLY HIS EARLY RESULTS...
MR. NAKAI, WHAT RANK ARE YOU RIGHT NOW?
WHAT? OH, IT'S STILL JUST THE EARLY RESULTS, SO ASK YOUR EDITOR IF YOU REALLY WANT TO KNOW.

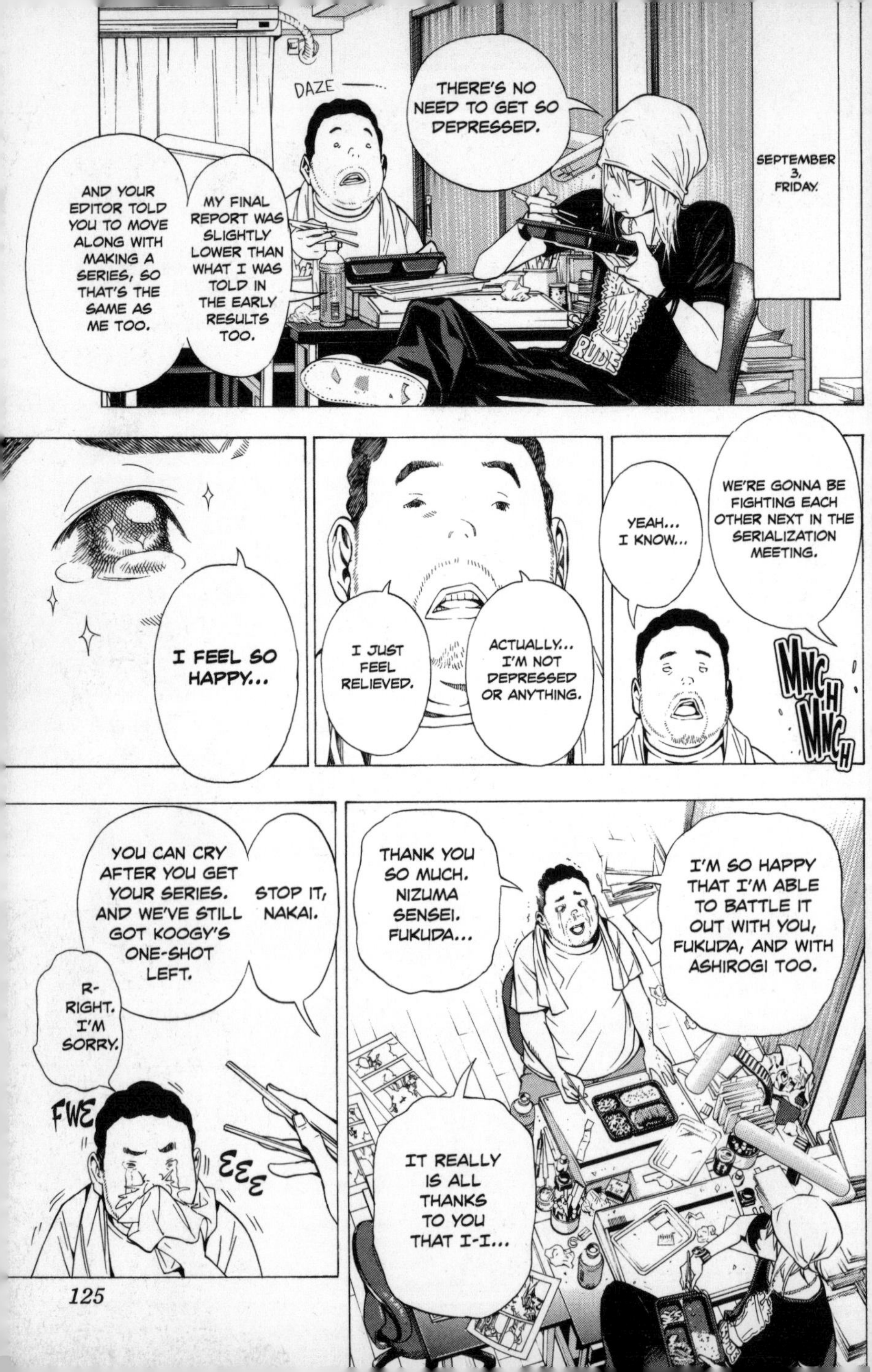
SEPTEMBER 3, FRIDAY.
THERE'S NO NEED TO GET SO DEPRESSED.
DAZE
MY FINAL REPORT WAS SLIGHTLY LOWER THAN WHAT I WAS TOLD IN THE EARLY RESULTS TOO.
AND YOUR EDITOR TOLD YOU TO MOVE ALONG WITH MAKING A SERIES, SO THAT'S THE SAME AS ME TOO.
WE'RE GONNA BE FIGHTING EACH OTHER NEXT IN THE SERIALIZATION MEETING.
YEAH... I KNOW...
MNCH MNCH
ACTUALLY... I'M NOT DEPRESSED OR ANYTHING.
I JUST FEEL RELIEVED.
I FEEL SO HAPPY...
I'M SO HAPPY THAT I'M ABLE TO BATTLE IT OUT WITH YOU, FUKUDA, AND WITH ASHIROGI TOO.
THANK YOU SO MUCH. NIZUMA SENSEI. FUKUDA...
IT REALLY IS ALL THANKS TO YOU THAT I-I...
STOP IT, NAKAI.
YOU CAN CRY AFTER YOU GET YOUR SERIES. AND WE'VE STILL GOT KOOGY'S ONE-SHOT LEFT.
R-RIGHT. I'M SORRY.
FWE
EEE

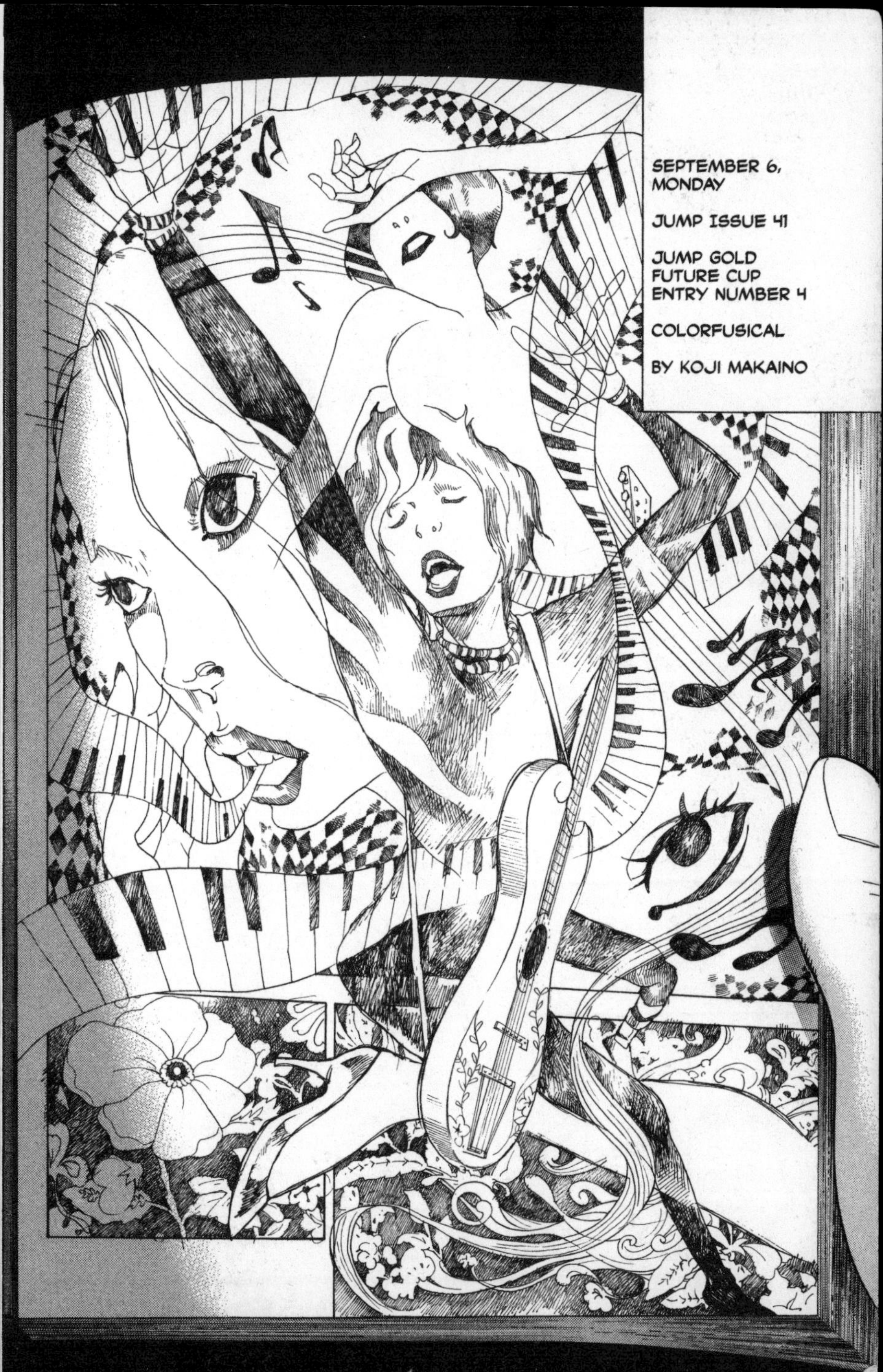
SEPTEMBER 6, MONDAY
JUMP ISSUE 41
JUMP GOLD FUTURE CUP ENTRY NUMBER 4
COLORFUSICAL
BY KOJI MAKAINO

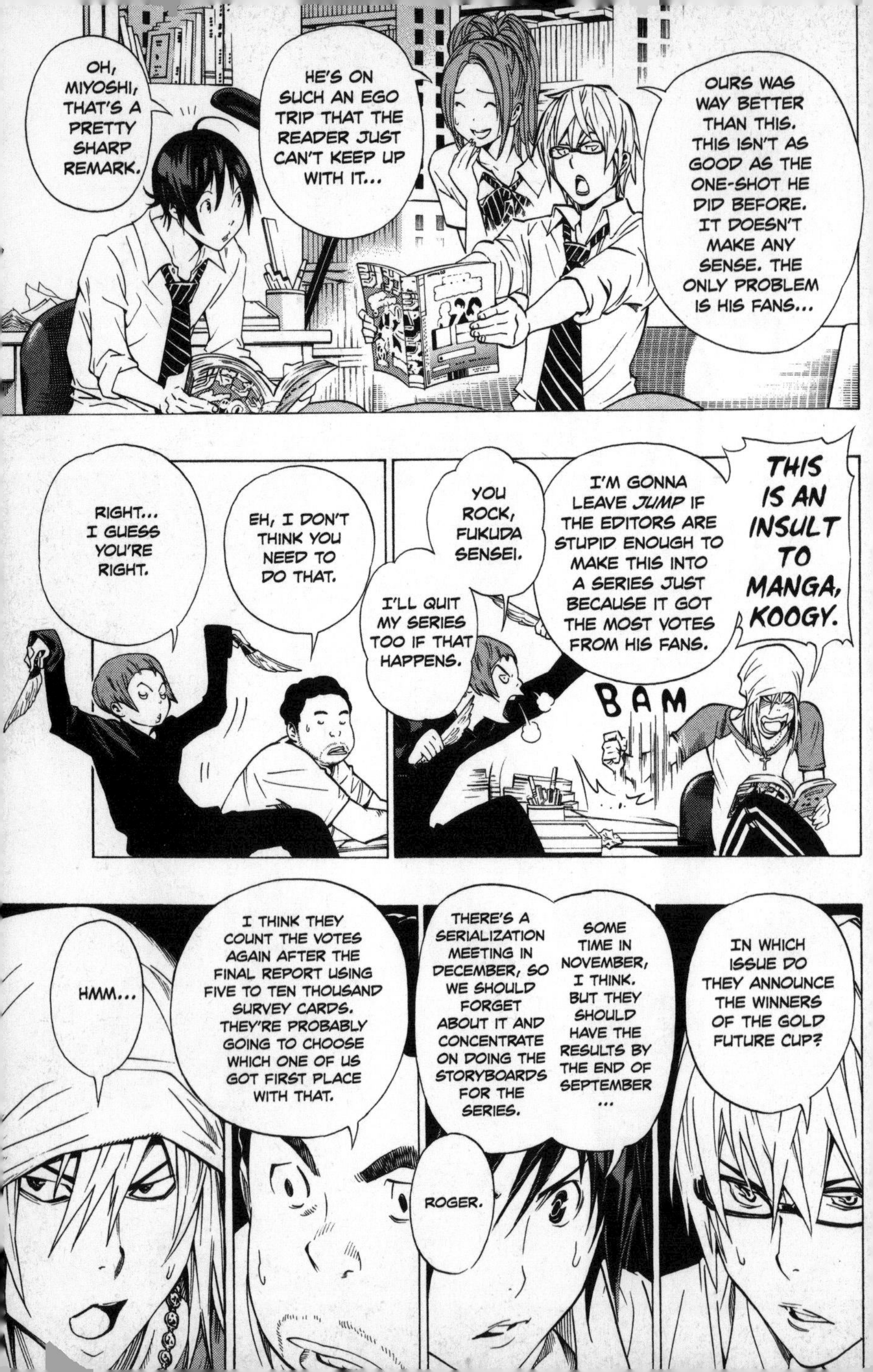
OURS WAS WAY BETTER THAN THIS. THIS ISN'T AS GOOD AS THE ONE-SHOT HE DID BEFORE. IT DOESN'T MAKE ANY SENSE. THE ONLY PROBLEM IS HIS FANS...
HE'S ON SUCH AN EGO TRIP THAT THE READER JUST CAN'T KEEP UP WITH IT...
OH, MIYOSHI, THAT'S A PRETTY SHARP REMARK.
THIS IS AN INSULT TO MANGA, KOOGY.
BAM
I'M GONNA LEAVE *JUMP* IF THE EDITORS ARE STUPID ENOUGH TO MAKE THIS INTO A SERIES JUST BECAUSE IT GOT THE MOST VOTES FROM HIS FANS.
YOU ROCK, FUKUDA SENSEI.
I'LL QUIT MY SERIES TOO IF THAT HAPPENS.
EH, I DON'T THINK YOU NEED TO DO THAT.
RIGHT... I GUESS YOU'RE RIGHT.
IN WHICH ISSUE DO THEY ANNOUNCE THE WINNERS OF THE GOLD FUTURE CUP?
SOME TIME IN NOVEMBER, I THINK. BUT THEY SHOULD HAVE THE RESULTS BY THE END OF SEPTEMBER...
THERE'S A SERIALIZATION MEETING IN DECEMBER, SO WE SHOULD FORGET ABOUT IT AND CONCENTRATE ON DOING THE STORYBOARDS FOR THE SERIES.
ROGER.
I THINK THEY COUNT THE VOTES AGAIN AFTER THE FINAL REPORT USING FIVE TO TEN THOUSAND SURVEY CARDS. THEY'RE PROBABLY GOING TO CHOOSE WHICH ONE OF US GOT FIRST PLACE WITH THAT.
HMM...

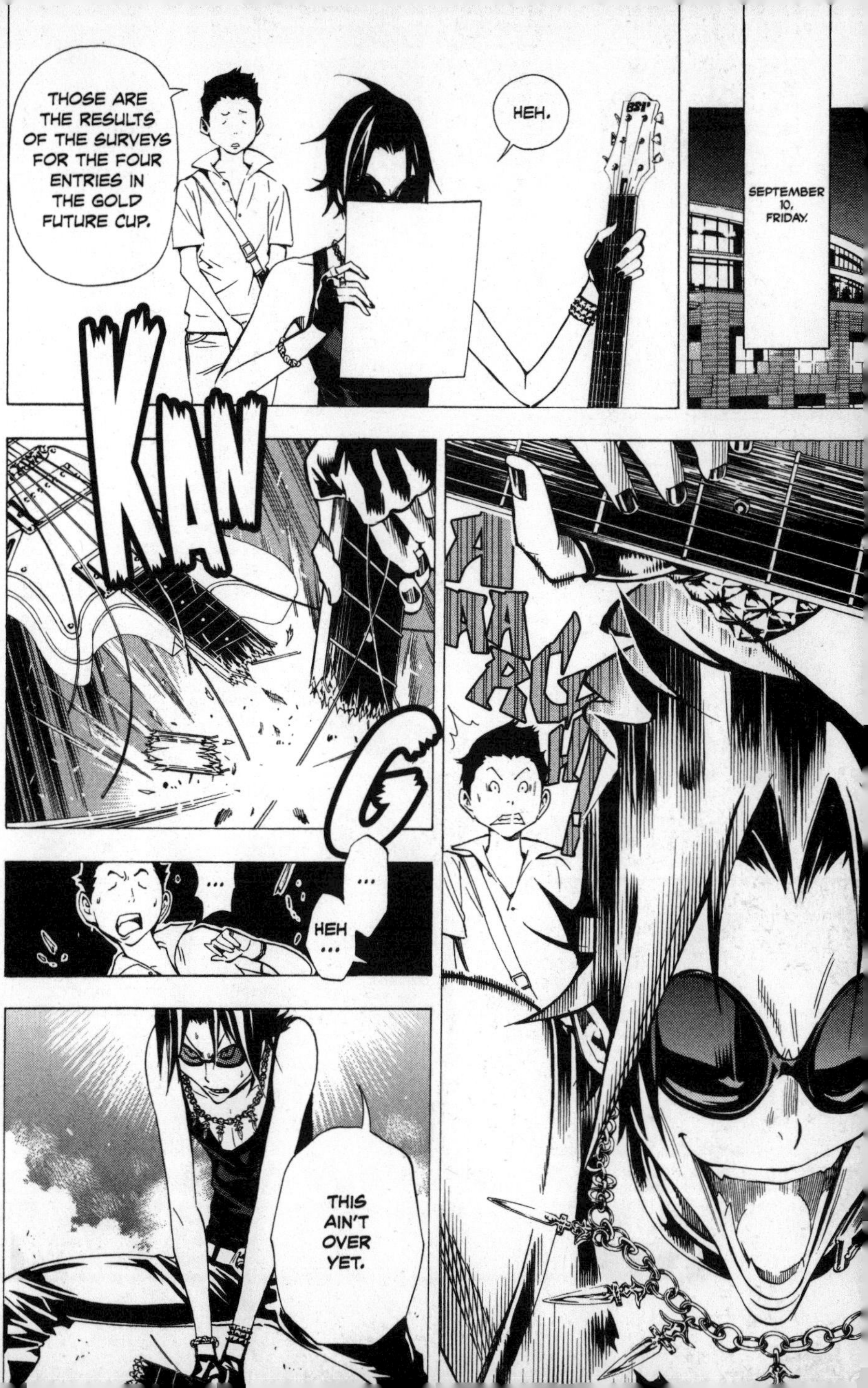
SEPTEMBER 10, FRIDAY.
THOSE ARE THE RESULTS OF THE SURVEYS FOR THE FOUR ENTRIES IN THE GOLD FUTURE CUP.
HEH.
AAAARGH!
KAN
G
...
...
HEH ...
THIS AIN'T OVER YET.

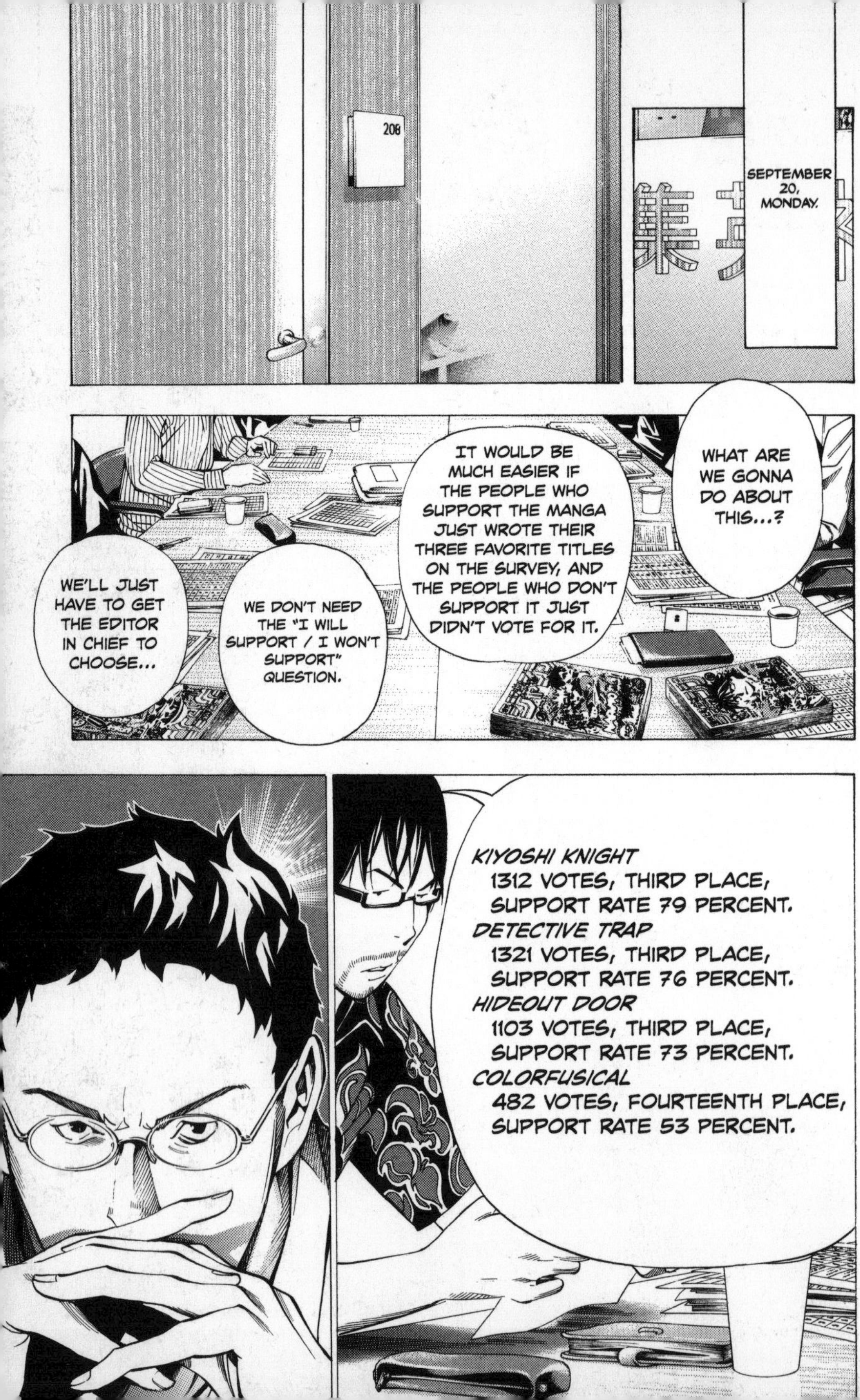
SEPTEMBER 20, MONDAY.
WHAT ARE WE GONNA DO ABOUT THIS...?
IT WOULD BE MUCH EASIER IF THE PEOPLE WHO SUPPORT THE MANGA JUST WROTE THEIR THREE FAVORITE TITLES ON THE SURVEY, AND THE PEOPLE WHO DON'T SUPPORT IT JUST DIDN'T VOTE FOR IT.
WE DON'T NEED THE "I WILL SUPPORT / I WON'T SUPPORT" QUESTION.
WE'LL JUST HAVE TO GET THE EDITOR IN CHIEF TO CHOOSE...
KIYOSHI KNIGHT 1312 VOTES, THIRD PLACE, SUPPORT RATE 79 PERCENT. *DETECTIVE TRAP* 1321 VOTES, THIRD PLACE, SUPPORT RATE 76 PERCENT. *HIDEOUT DOOR* 1103 VOTES, THIRD PLACE, SUPPORT RATE 73 PERCENT. *COLORFUSICAL* 482 VOTES, FOURTEENTH PLACE, SUPPORT RATE 53 PERCENT.

OHBA'S STORYBOARD

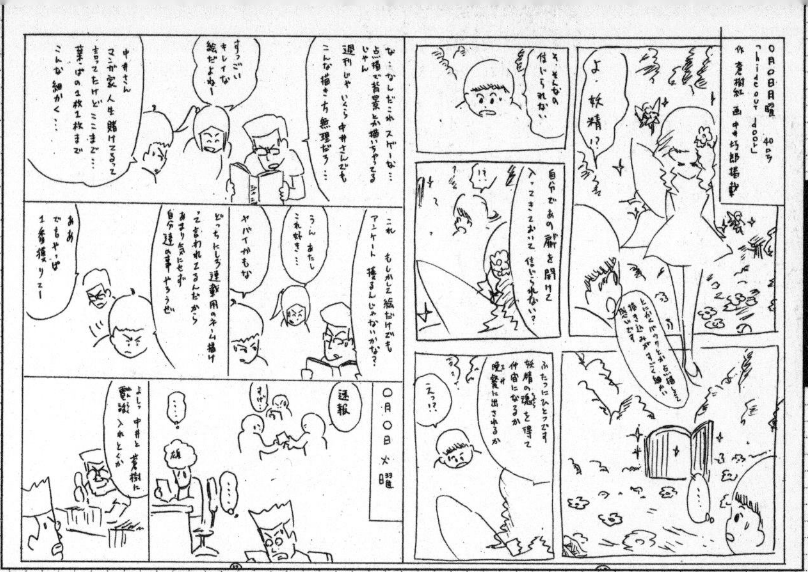

○月○日月曜 40号「hide out door」作 青樹紅 画 中井巧朗 掲載
よ・妖精!?
そ、そんなの信じられない
自分であの扉を開けて入ってきておいて信じられない?
!?
えっ!?
……
な…なんだこれスゲーな…点描で背景とか描いちゃってるじゃん 週刊じゃいくら中井さんでもこんな描き方無理だろ…
すっごいキレイな絵だよね～
中井さんマンガ家人生賭けてるって言ってたけどここまで…葉っぱの1枚1枚までこんな細かく…
これもしかして絵だけでもアンケート獲るんじゃないかな?
うんあたしこれ好き…
ヤバイかもな
どっちにしろ連載用のネーム描けって言われてるんだから あまり気にせず自分達の事やろうぜ
ああでもやっぱ1番獲りてー
○月○日火曜
速報
……
よしっ中井と青樹に電話入れとくか
……

OBATA'S STORYBOARD

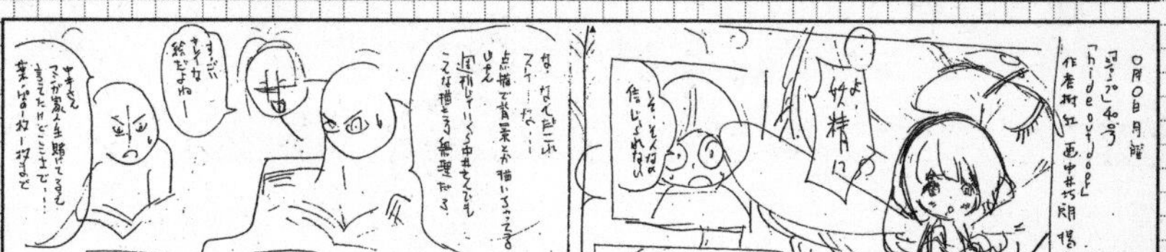

COMPLETE!

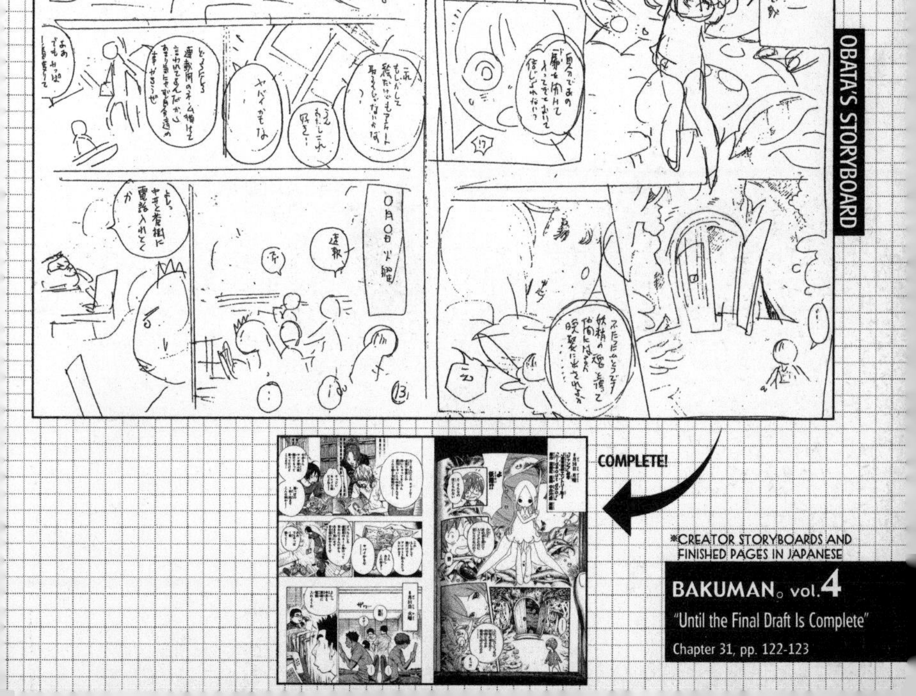

*CREATOR STORYBOARDS AND FINISHED PAGES IN JAPANESE

BAKUMAN。vol.4

"Until the Final Draft Is Complete"

Chapter 31, pp. 122-123

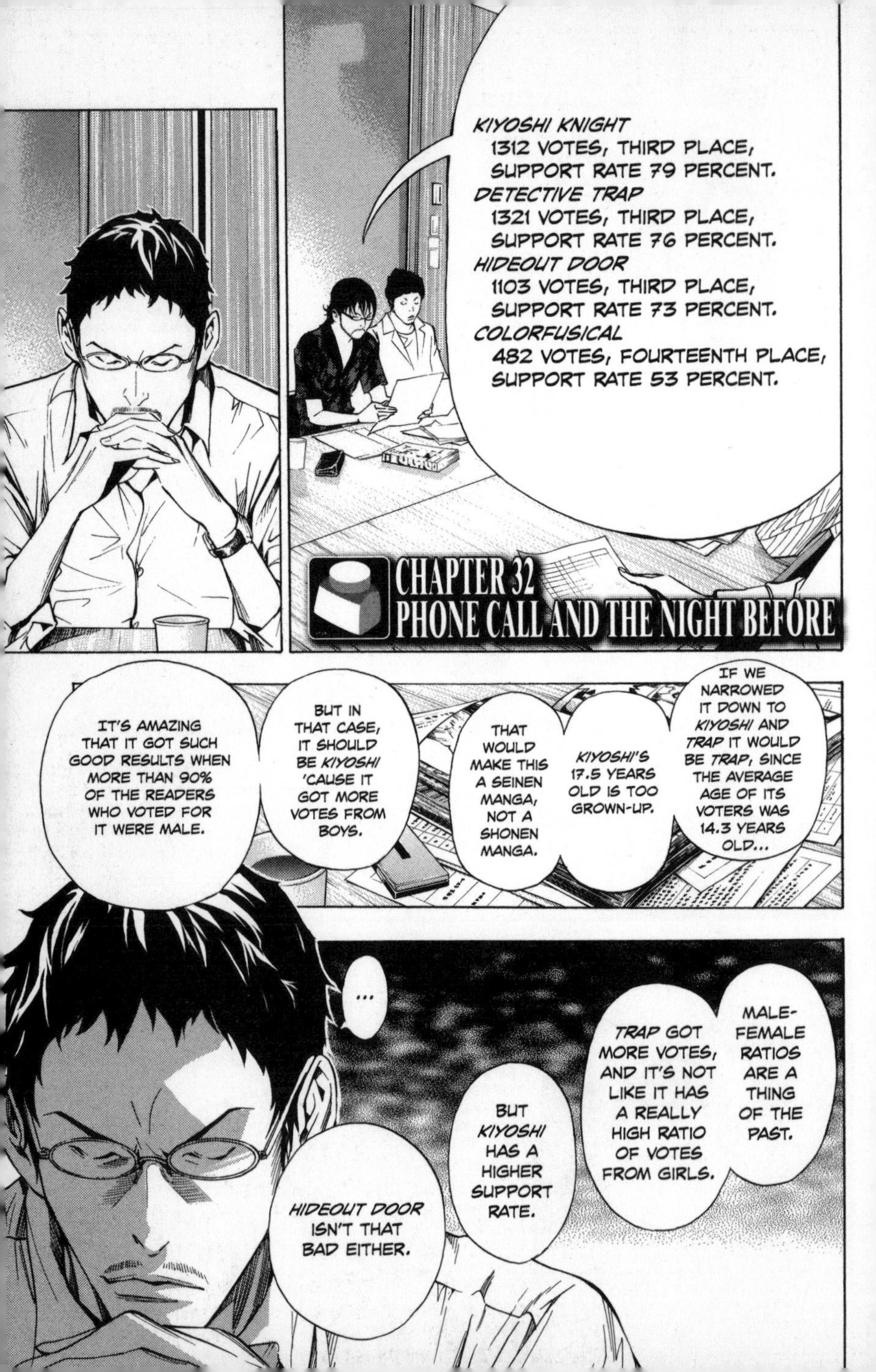
KIYOSHI KNIGHT 1312 VOTES, THIRD PLACE, SUPPORT RATE 79 PERCENT. DETECTIVE TRAP 1321 VOTES, THIRD PLACE, SUPPORT RATE 76 PERCENT. HIDEOUT DOOR 1103 VOTES, THIRD PLACE, SUPPORT RATE 73 PERCENT. COLORFUSICAL 482 VOTES, FOURTEENTH PLACE, SUPPORT RATE 53 PERCENT.
CHAPTER 32
PHONE CALL AND THE NIGHT BEFORE
IF WE NARROWED IT DOWN TO KIYOSHI AND TRAP IT WOULD BE TRAP, SINCE THE AVERAGE AGE OF ITS VOTERS WAS 14.3 YEARS OLD...
KIYOSHI'S 17.5 YEARS OLD IS TOO GROWN-UP.
THAT WOULD MAKE THIS A SEINEN MANGA, NOT A SHONEN MANGA.
BUT IN THAT CASE, IT SHOULD BE KIYOSHI 'CAUSE IT GOT MORE VOTES FROM BOYS.
IT'S AMAZING THAT IT GOT SUCH GOOD RESULTS WHEN MORE THAN 90% OF THE READERS WHO VOTED FOR IT WERE MALE.
MALE-FEMALE RATIOS ARE A THING OF THE PAST.
TRAP GOT MORE VOTES, AND IT'S NOT LIKE IT HAS A REALLY HIGH RATIO OF VOTES FROM GIRLS.
BUT KIYOSHI HAS A HIGHER SUPPORT RATE.
...
HIDEOUT DOOR ISN'T THAT BAD EITHER.

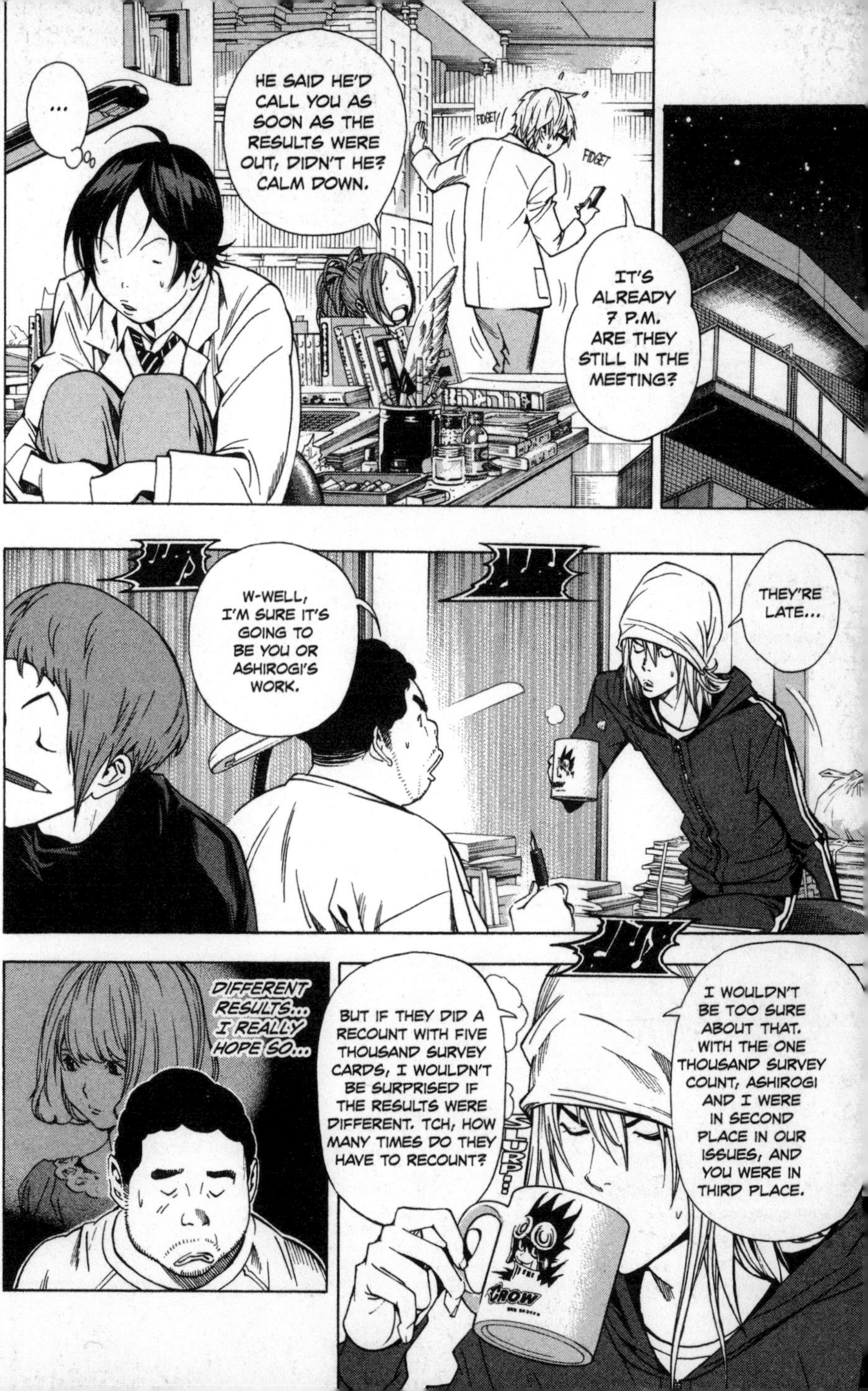
FIDGET
FIDGET
IT'S ALREADY 7 P.M. ARE THEY STILL IN THE MEETING?
HE SAID HE'D CALL YOU AS SOON AS THE RESULTS WERE OUT, DIDN'T HE? CALM DOWN.
...
THEY'RE LATE...
W-WELL, I'M SURE IT'S GOING TO BE YOU OR ASHIROGI'S WORK.
I WOULDN'T BE TOO SURE ABOUT THAT. WITH THE ONE THOUSAND SURVEY COUNT, ASHIROGI AND I WERE IN SECOND PLACE IN OUR ISSUES, AND YOU WERE IN THIRD PLACE.
SLURP...
BUT IF THEY DID A RECOUNT WITH FIVE THOUSAND SURVEY CARDS, I WOULDN'T BE SURPRISED IF THE RESULTS WERE DIFFERENT. TCH, HOW MANY TIMES DO THEY HAVE TO RECOUNT?
DIFFERENT RESULTS... I REALLY HOPE SO...

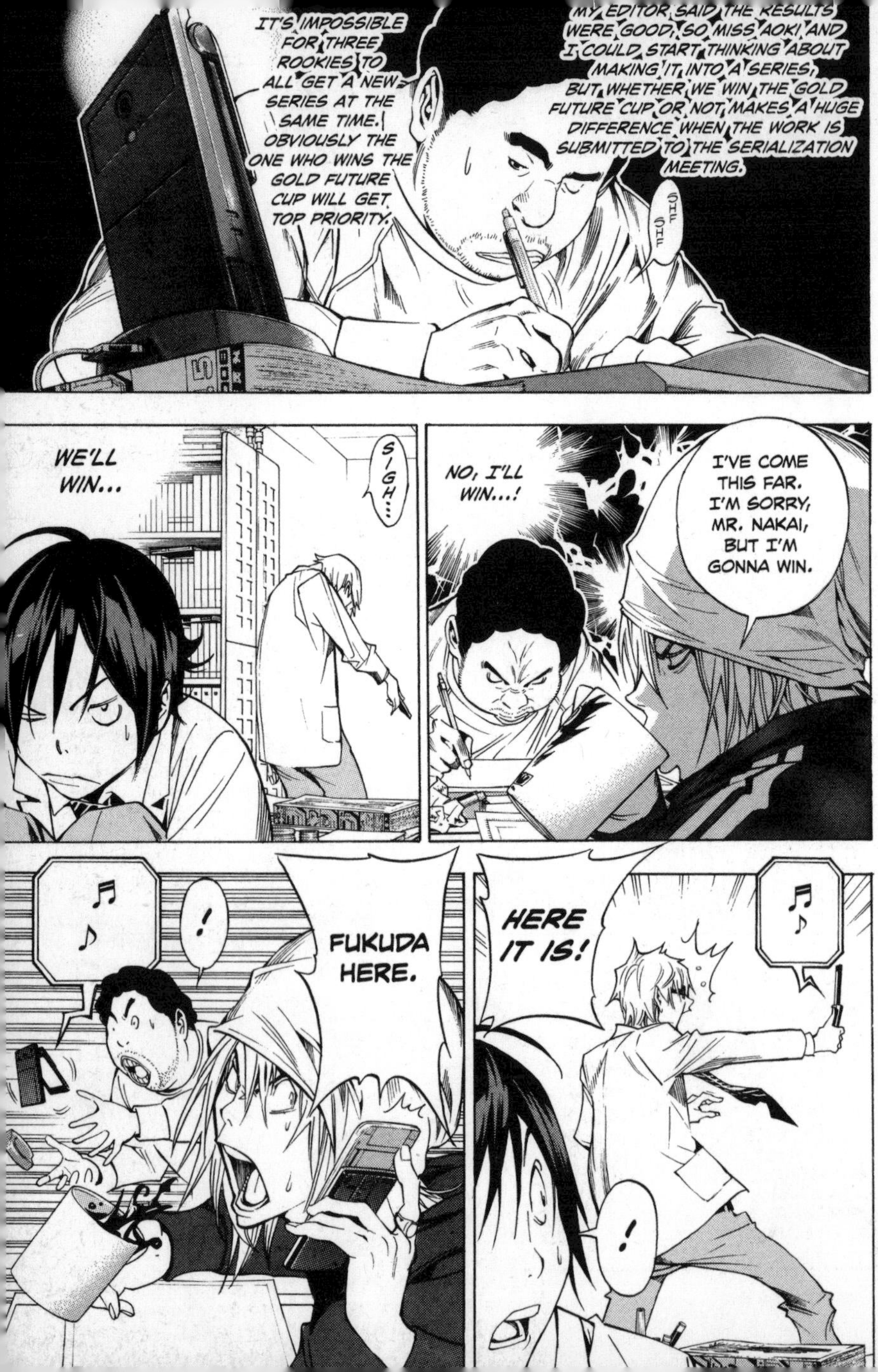

MY EDITOR SAID THE RESULTS WERE GOOD, SO MISS AOKI AND I COULD START THINKING ABOUT MAKING IT INTO A SERIES, BUT WHETHER WE WIN THE GOLD FUTURE CUP OR NOT MAKES A HUGE DIFFERENCE WHEN THE WORK IS SUBMITTED TO THE SERIALIZATION MEETING.
IT'S IMPOSSIBLE FOR THREE ROOKIES TO ALL GET A NEW SERIES AT THE SAME TIME. OBVIOUSLY THE ONE WHO WINS THE GOLD FUTURE CUP WILL GET TOP PRIORITY.
SHF SHF
I'VE COME THIS FAR. I'M SORRY, MR. NAKAI, BUT I'M GONNA WIN.
NO, I'LL WIN...!
SIGH...
WE'LL WIN...
♫ ♪
HERE IT IS!
!
FUKUDA HERE.
!
♫ ♪

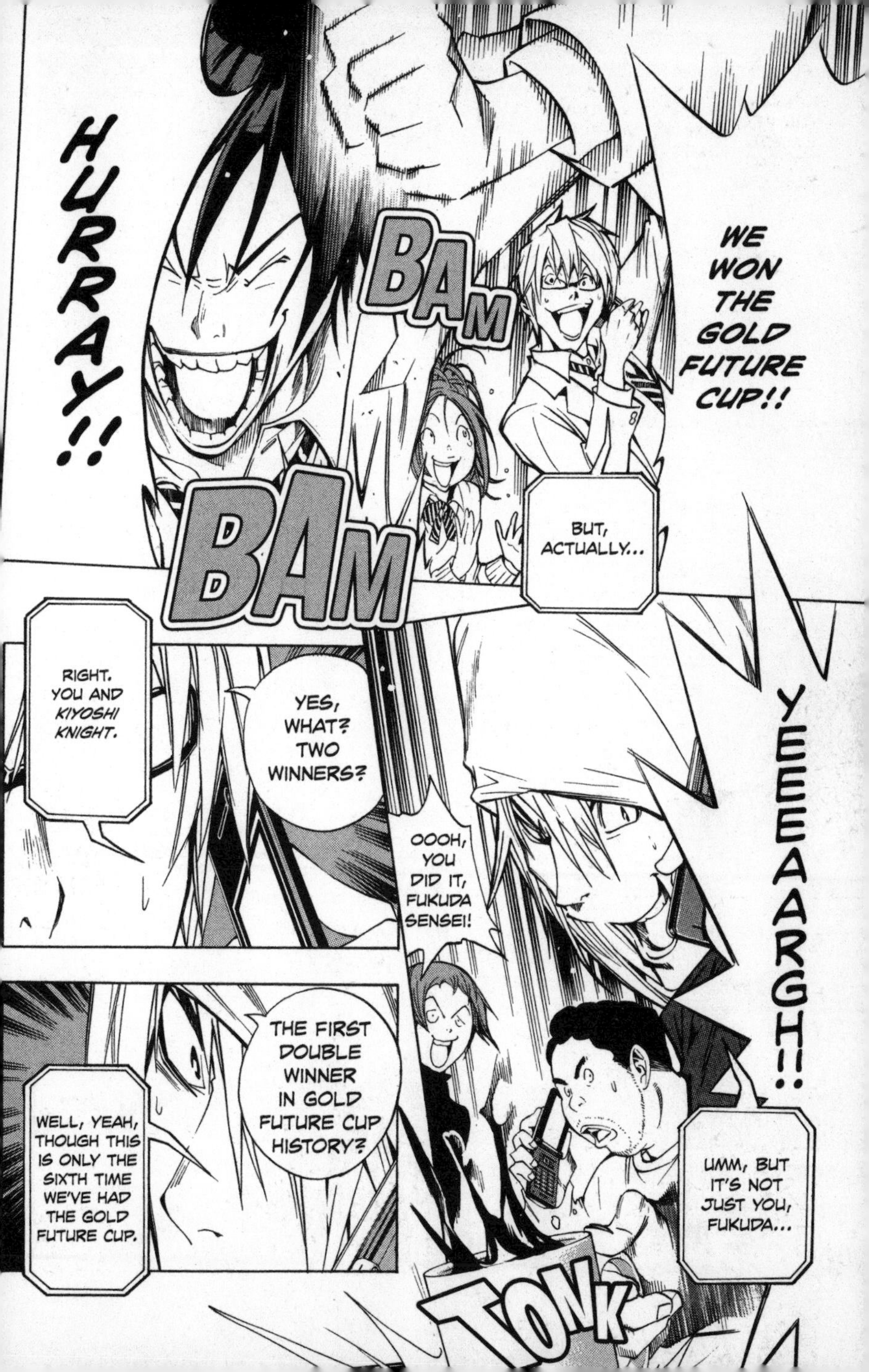
WE WON THE GOLD FUTURE CUP!!
BAM
HURRAY!!
BAM
BUT, ACTUALLY...
YEEEAARGH!!
OOOH, YOU DID IT, FUKUDA SENSEI!
UMM, BUT IT'S NOT JUST YOU, FUKUDA...
TONK
YES, WHAT? TWO WINNERS?
RIGHT. YOU AND *KIYOSHI KNIGHT*.
THE FIRST DOUBLE WINNER IN GOLD FUTURE CUP HISTORY?
WELL, YEAH, THOUGH THIS IS ONLY THE SIXTH TIME WE'VE HAD THE GOLD FUTURE CUP.

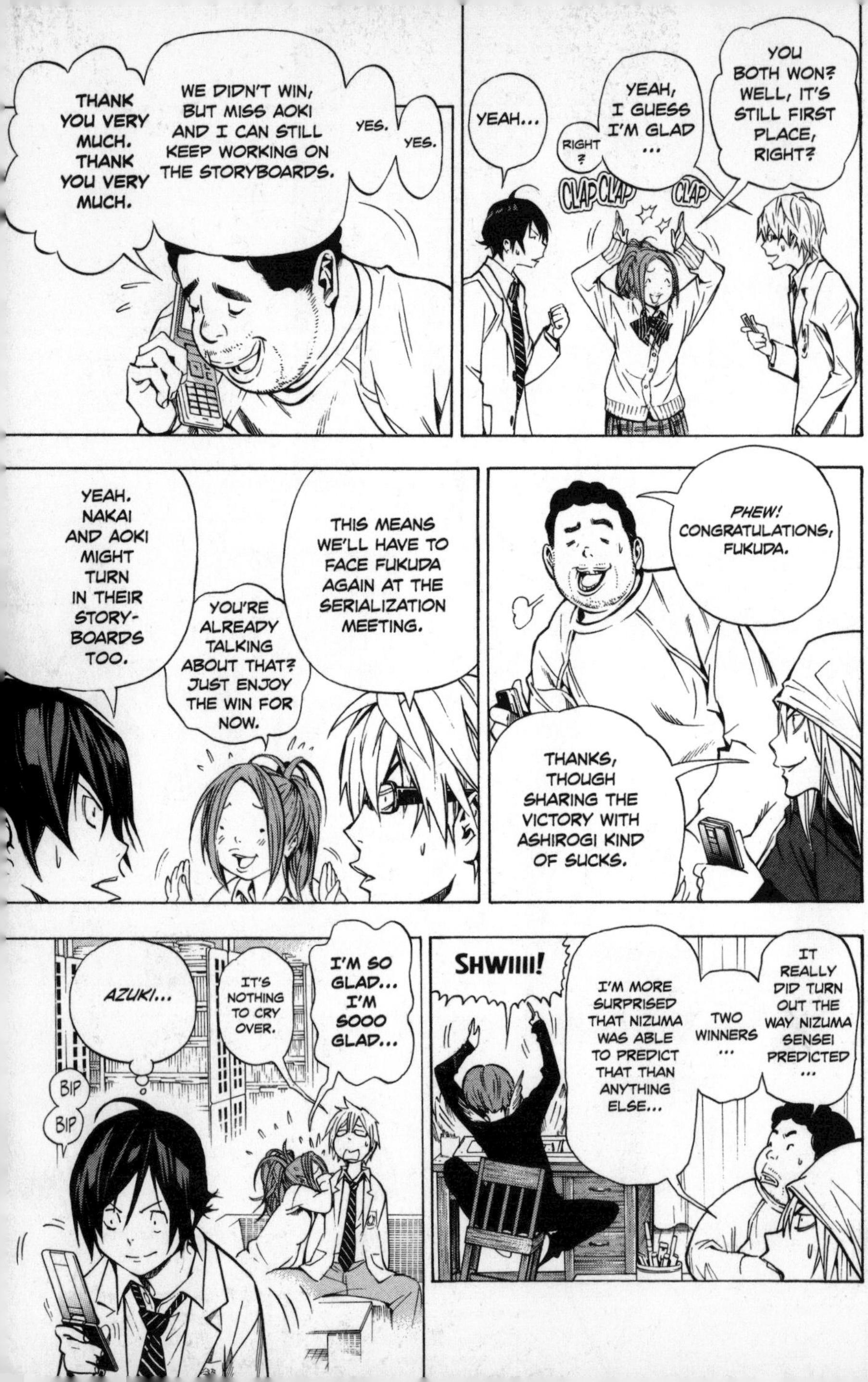
YOU BOTH WON? WELL, IT'S STILL FIRST PLACE, RIGHT?
YEAH, I GUESS I'M GLAD...
RIGHT?
CLAP CLAP
CLAP
YEAH...
YES.
YES.
WE DIDN'T WIN, BUT MISS AOKI AND I CAN STILL KEEP WORKING ON THE STORYBOARDS.
THANK YOU VERY MUCH. THANK YOU VERY MUCH.
PHEW! CONGRATULATIONS, FUKUDA.
THANKS, THOUGH SHARING THE VICTORY WITH ASHIROGI KIND OF SUCKS.
THIS MEANS WE'LL HAVE TO FACE FUKUDA AGAIN AT THE SERIALIZATION MEETING.
YOU'RE ALREADY TALKING ABOUT THAT? JUST ENJOY THE WIN FOR NOW.
YEAH. NAKAI AND AOKI MIGHT TURN IN THEIR STORY-BOARDS TOO.
IT REALLY DID TURN OUT THE WAY NIZUMA SENSEI PREDICTED...
TWO WINNERS...
I'M MORE SURPRISED THAT NIZUMA WAS ABLE TO PREDICT THAT THAN ANYTHING ELSE...
SHWIIII!
I'M SO GLAD... I'M SOOO GLAD...
IT'S NOTHING TO CRY OVER.
AZUKI...
BIP
BIP

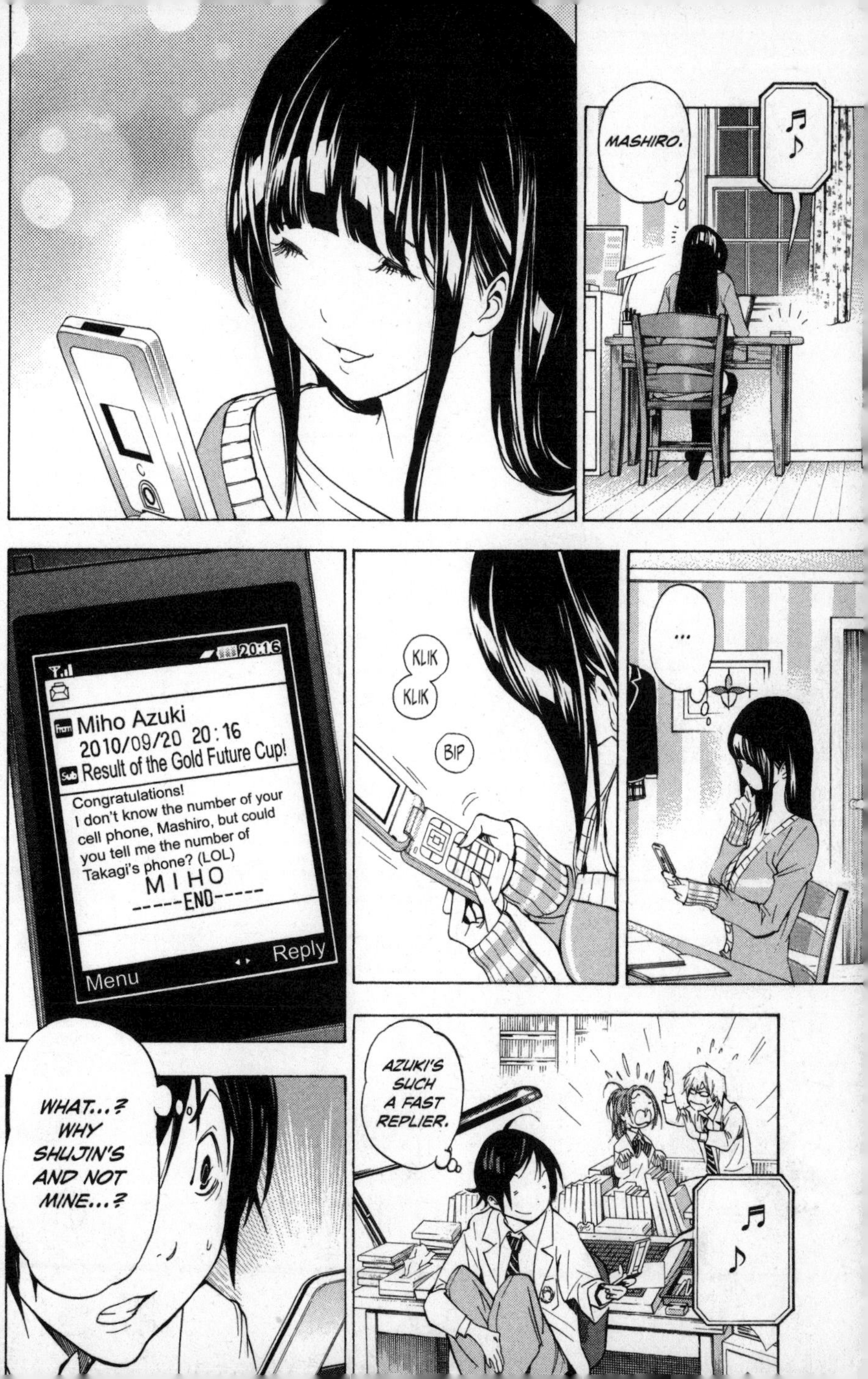
MASHIRO.
...
KLIK
KLIK
BIP
20:16
From Miho Azuki
2010/09/20 20:16
Sub Result of the Gold Future Cup!
Congratulations!
I don't know the number of your cell phone, Mashiro, but could you tell me the number of Takagi's phone? (LOL)
MIHO
-----END-----
Reply
Menu
AZUKI'S SUCH A FAST REPLIER.
WHAT...? WHY SHUJIN'S AND NOT MINE...?

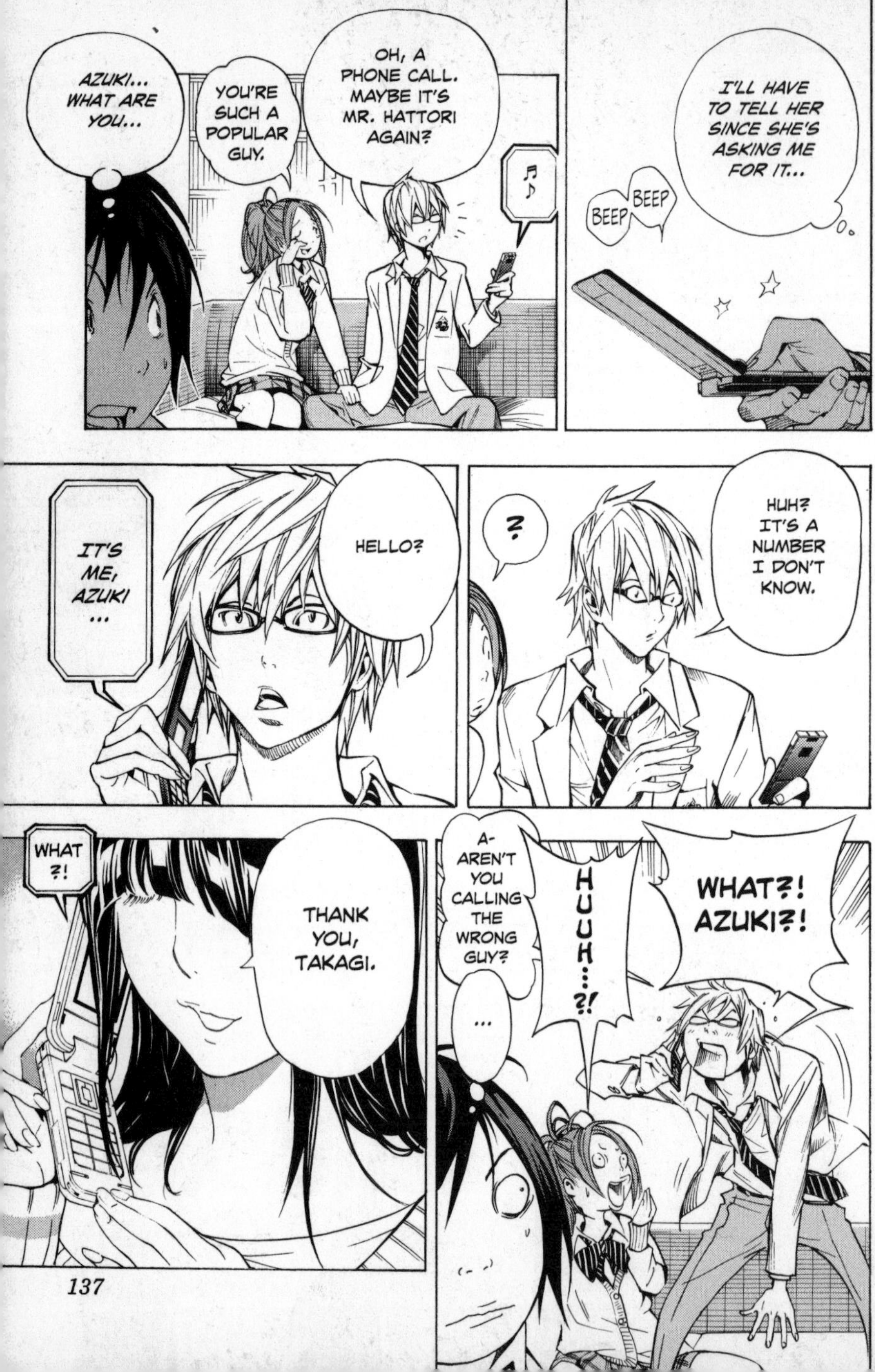
I'LL HAVE TO TELL HER SINCE SHE'S ASKING ME FOR IT...
BEEP
BEEP
OH, A PHONE CALL. MAYBE IT'S MR. HATTORI AGAIN?
♪
YOU'RE SUCH A POPULAR GUY.
AZUKI... WHAT ARE YOU...
HUH? IT'S A NUMBER I DON'T KNOW.
?
HELLO?
IT'S ME, AZUKI ...
WHAT?! AZUKI?!
HUUH...?!
A-AREN'T YOU CALLING THE WRONG GUY?
...
THANK YOU, TAKAGI.
WHAT?!

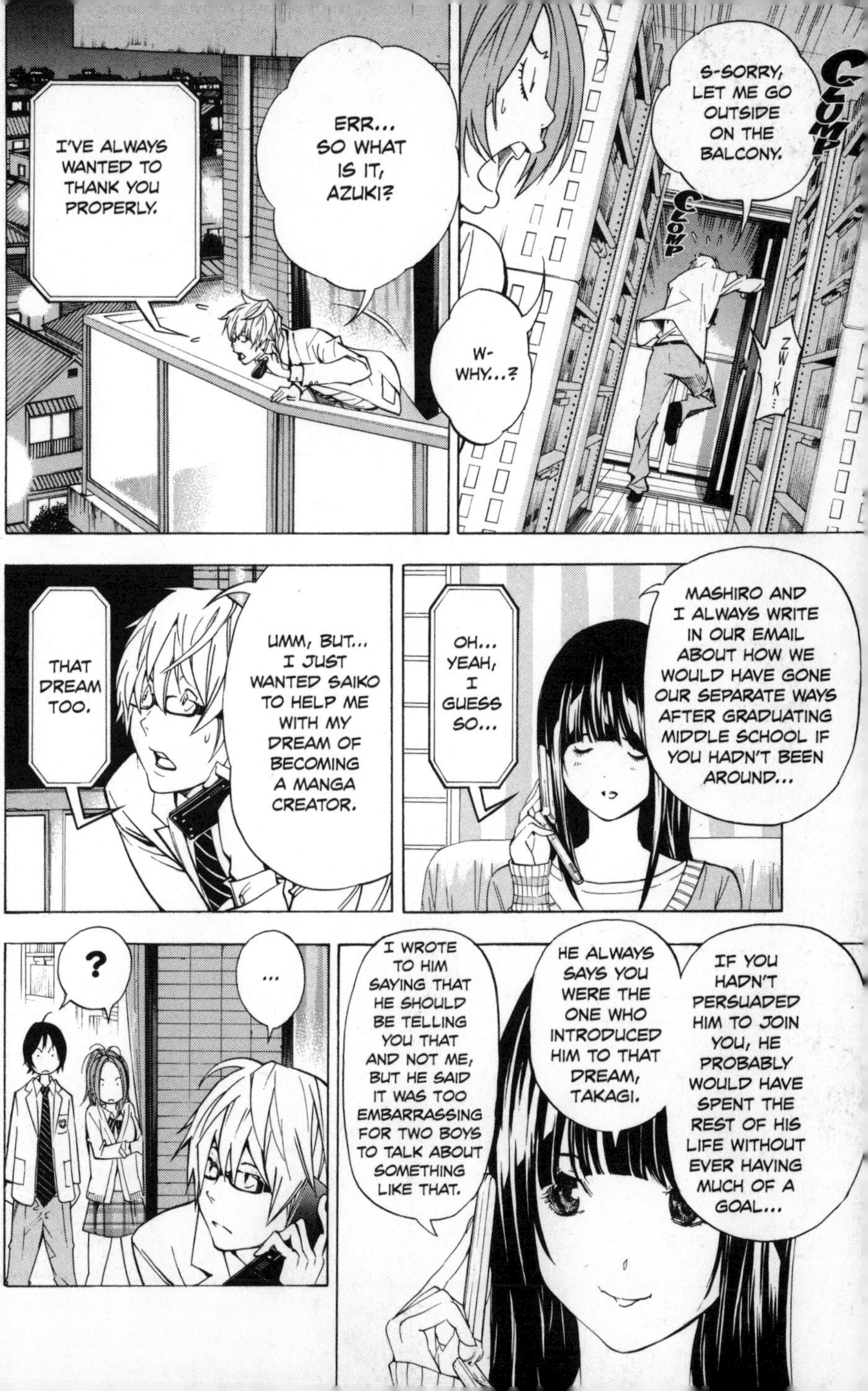
S-SORRY, LET ME GO OUTSIDE ON THE BALCONY.
CLUMP
CLOMP
ZWIK...
W-WHY...?
ERR... SO WHAT IS IT, AZUKI?
I'VE ALWAYS WANTED TO THANK YOU PROPERLY.
MASHIRO AND I ALWAYS WRITE IN OUR EMAIL ABOUT HOW WE WOULD HAVE GONE OUR SEPARATE WAYS AFTER GRADUATING MIDDLE SCHOOL IF YOU HADN'T BEEN AROUND...
OH... YEAH, I GUESS SO...
UMM, BUT... I JUST WANTED SAIKO TO HELP ME WITH MY DREAM OF BECOMING A MANGA CREATOR.
THAT DREAM TOO.
IF YOU HADN'T PERSUADED HIM TO JOIN YOU, HE PROBABLY WOULD HAVE SPENT THE REST OF HIS LIFE WITHOUT EVER HAVING MUCH OF A GOAL...
HE ALWAYS SAYS YOU WERE THE ONE WHO INTRODUCED HIM TO THAT DREAM, TAKAGI.
I WROTE TO HIM SAYING THAT HE SHOULD BE TELLING YOU THAT AND NOT ME, BUT HE SAID IT WAS TOO EMBARRASSING FOR TWO BOYS TO TALK ABOUT SOMETHING LIKE THAT.
...
?

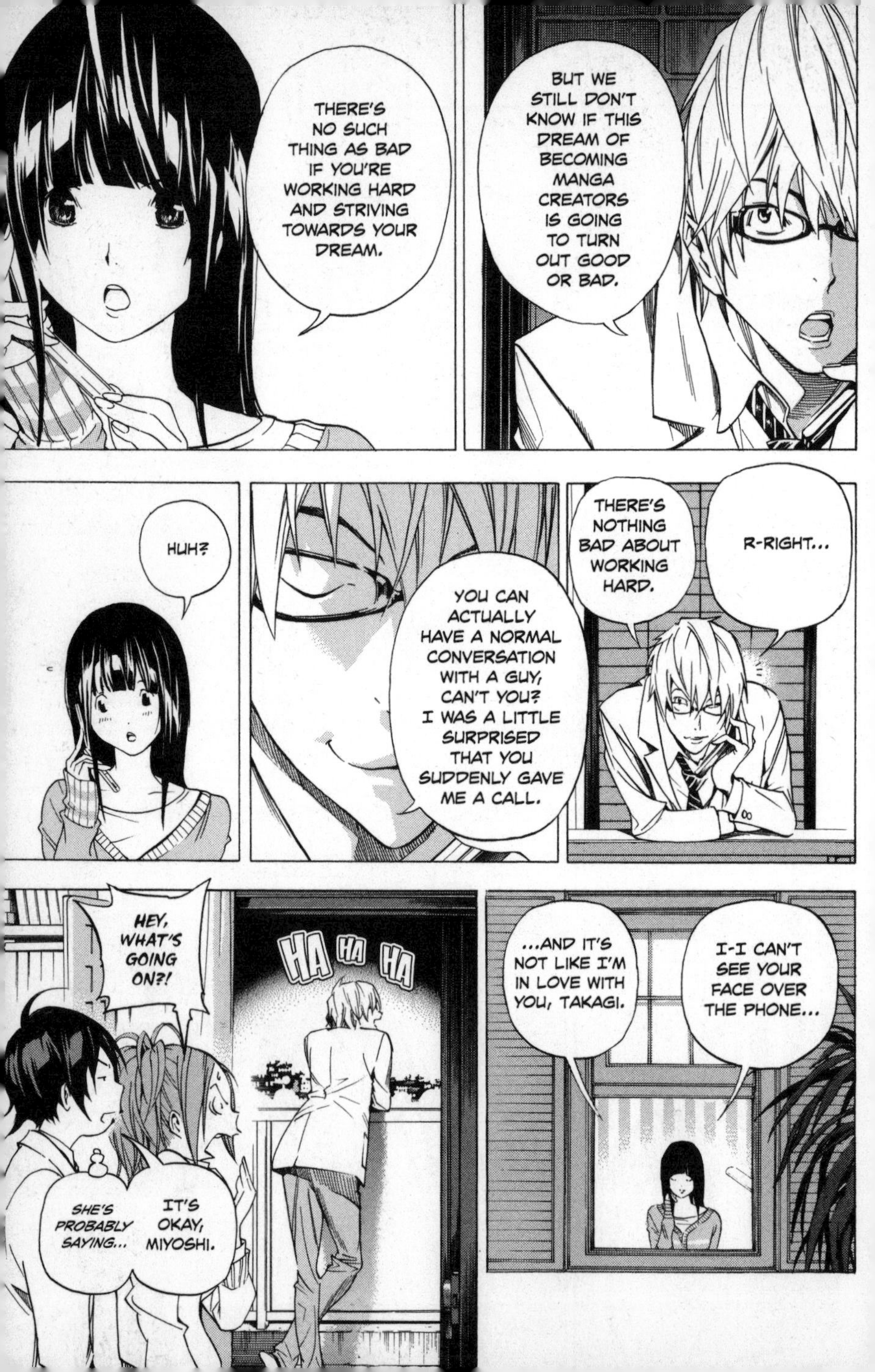
BUT WE STILL DON'T KNOW IF THIS DREAM OF BECOMING MANGA CREATORS IS GOING TO TURN OUT GOOD OR BAD.
THERE'S NO SUCH THING AS BAD IF YOU'RE WORKING HARD AND STRIVING TOWARDS YOUR DREAM.
R-RIGHT...
THERE'S NOTHING BAD ABOUT WORKING HARD.
YOU CAN ACTUALLY HAVE A NORMAL CONVERSATION WITH A GUY, CAN'T YOU? I WAS A LITTLE SURPRISED THAT YOU SUDDENLY GAVE ME A CALL.
HUH?
I-I CAN'T SEE YOUR FACE OVER THE PHONE...
...AND IT'S NOT LIKE I'M IN LOVE WITH YOU, TAKAGI.
HA HA HA
HEY, WHAT'S GOING ON?!
IT'S OKAY, MIYOSHI.
SHE'S PROBABLY SAYING...

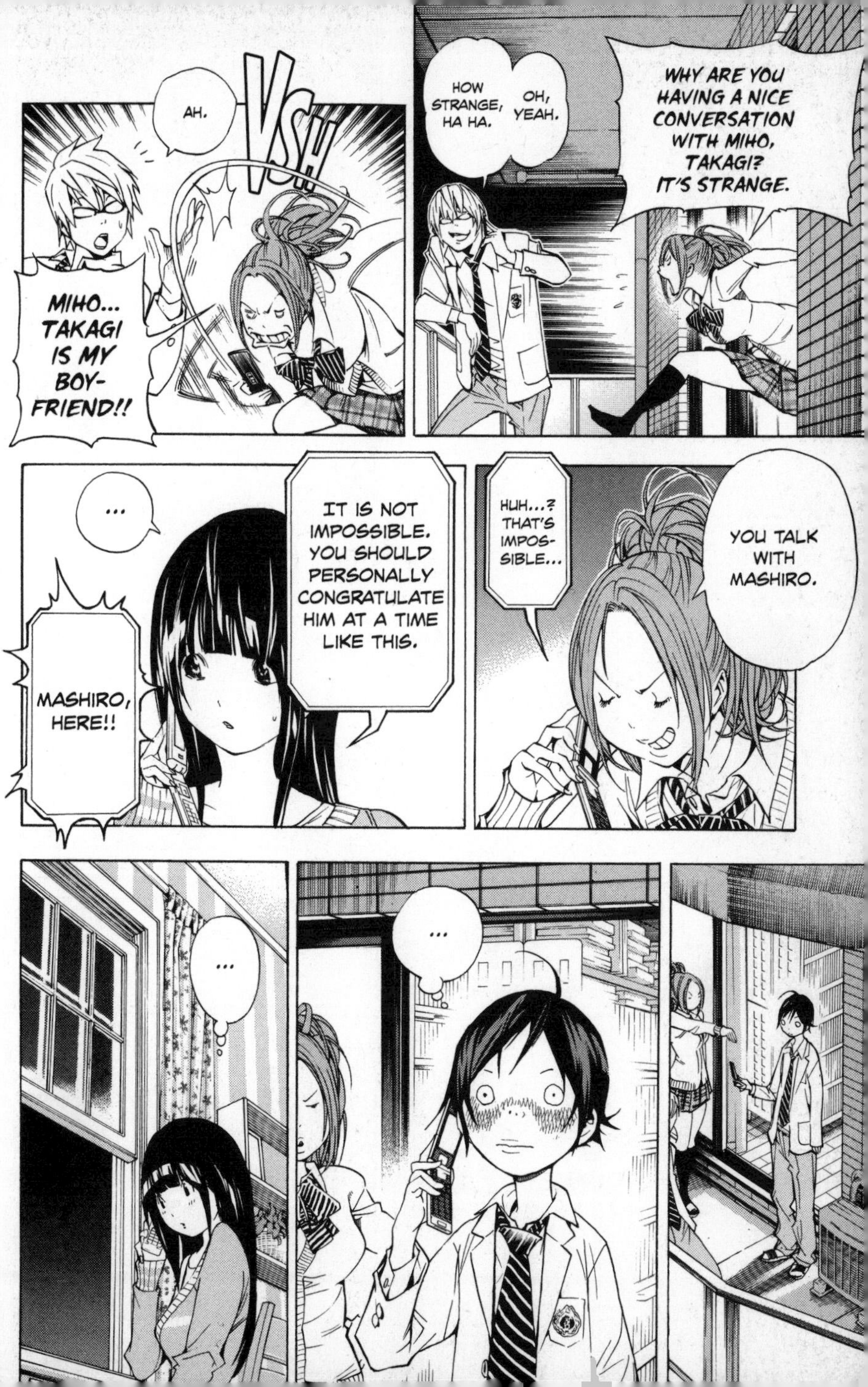
WHY ARE YOU HAVING A NICE CONVERSATION WITH MIHO, TAKAGI? IT'S STRANGE.
OH, YEAH.
HOW STRANGE, HA HA.
AH.
VSH
MIHO... TAKAGI IS MY BOY-FRIEND!!
YOU TALK WITH MASHIRO.
HUH...? THAT'S IMPOS-SIBLE...
IT IS NOT IMPOSSIBLE. YOU SHOULD PERSONALLY CONGRATULATE HIM AT A TIME LIKE THIS.
...
MASHIRO, HERE!!
...
...

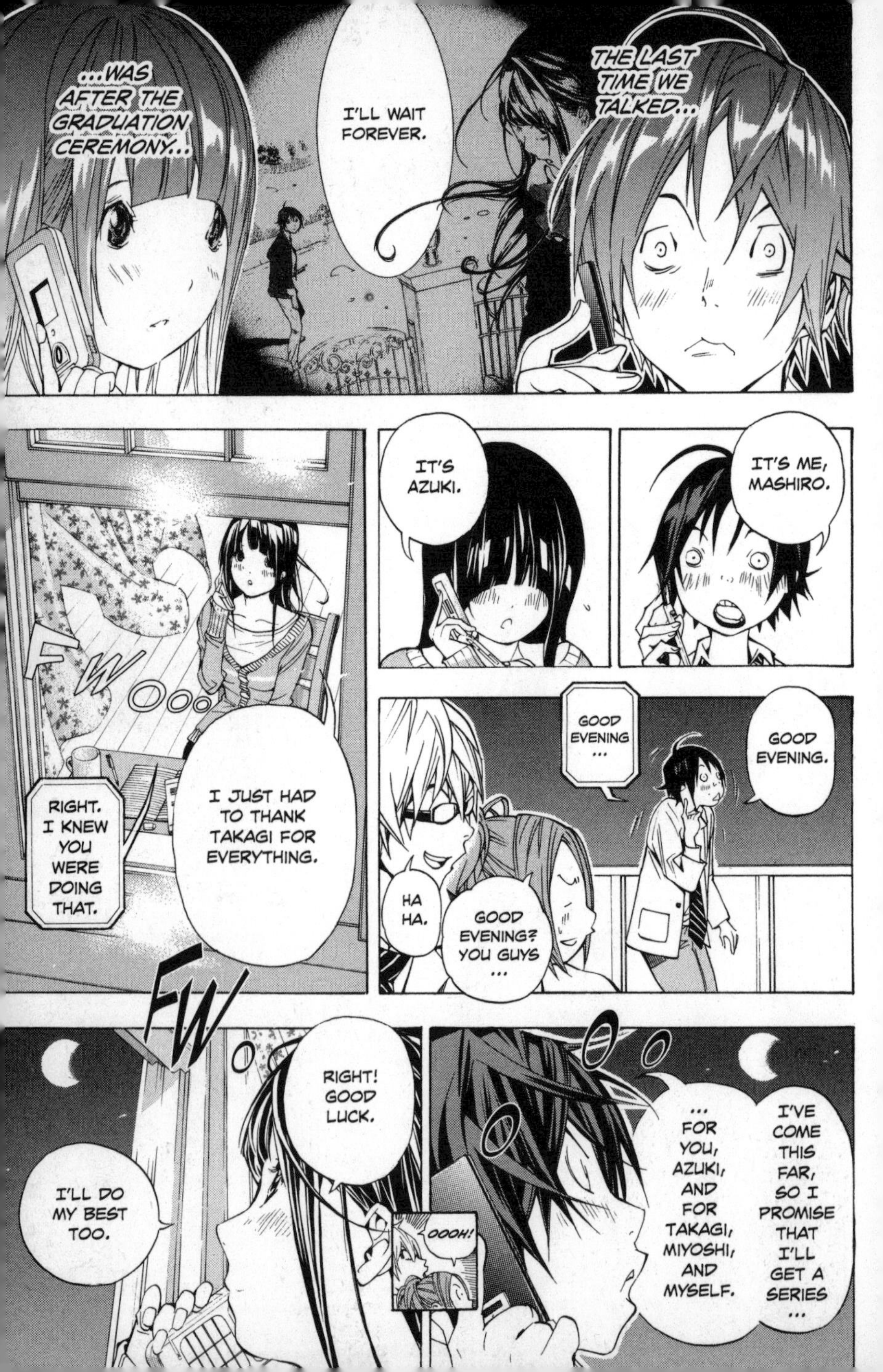
THE LAST TIME WE TALKED...
I'LL WAIT FOREVER.
...WAS AFTER THE GRADUATION CEREMONY...
IT'S ME, MASHIRO.
IT'S AZUKI.
GOOD EVENING.
GOOD EVENING ...
HA HA.
GOOD EVENING? YOU GUYS ...
FWOOO
I JUST HAD TO THANK TAKAGI FOR EVERYTHING.
RIGHT. I KNEW YOU WERE DOING THAT.
I'VE COME THIS FAR, SO I PROMISE THAT I'LL GET A SERIES ...
... FOR YOU, AZUKI, AND FOR TAKAGI, MIYOSHI, AND MYSELF.
OOOH!
FWOOO
RIGHT! GOOD LUCK.
I'LL DO MY BEST TOO.

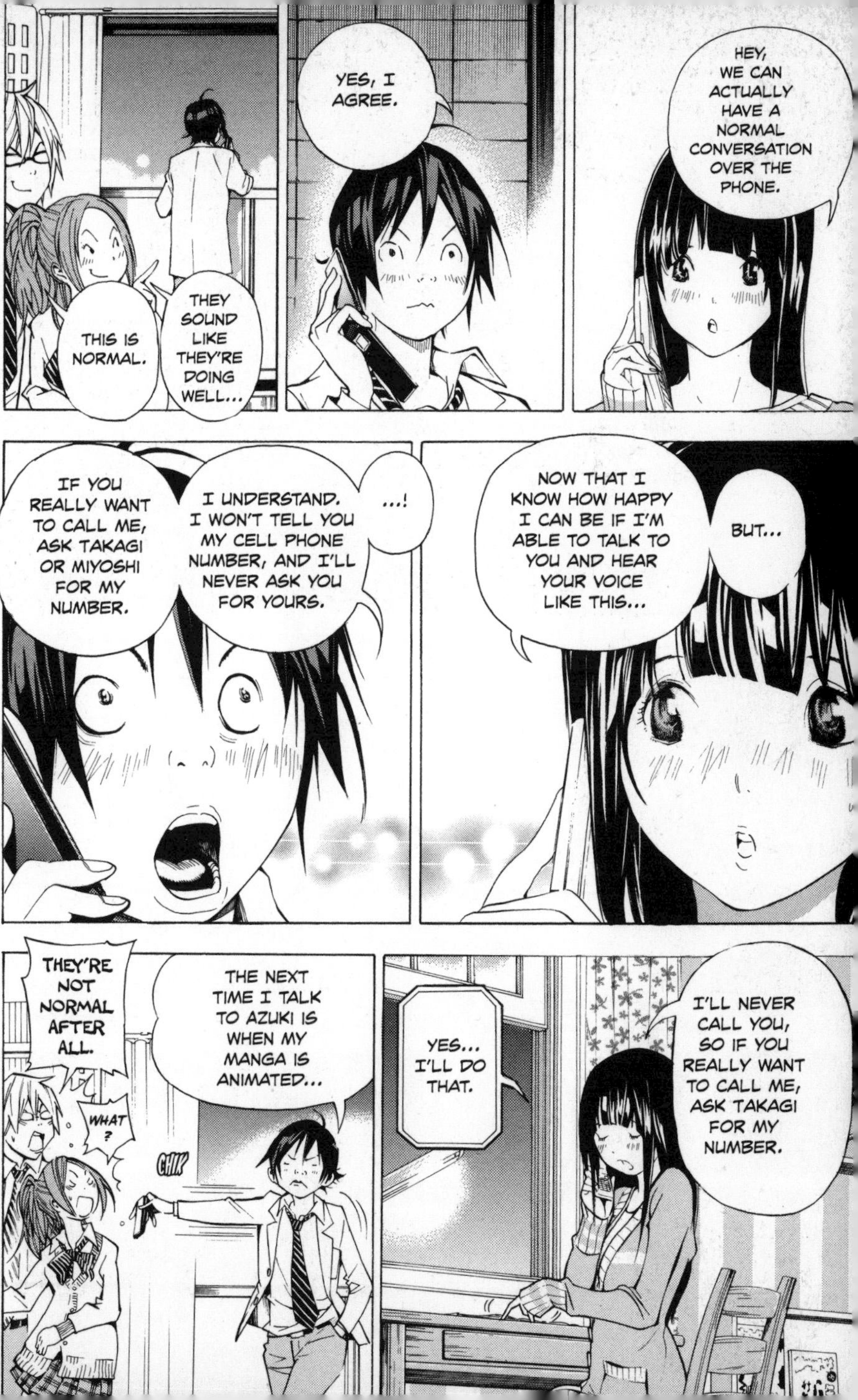
HEY, WE CAN ACTUALLY HAVE A NORMAL CONVERSATION OVER THE PHONE.
YES, I AGREE.
THEY SOUND LIKE THEY'RE DOING WELL...
THIS IS NORMAL.
BUT...
NOW THAT I KNOW HOW HAPPY I CAN BE IF I'M ABLE TO TALK TO YOU AND HEAR YOUR VOICE LIKE THIS...
...!
I UNDERSTAND. I WON'T TELL YOU MY CELL PHONE NUMBER, AND I'LL NEVER ASK YOU FOR YOURS.
IF YOU REALLY WANT TO CALL ME, ASK TAKAGI OR MIYOSHI FOR MY NUMBER.
I'LL NEVER CALL YOU, SO IF YOU REALLY WANT TO CALL ME, ASK TAKAGI FOR MY NUMBER.
YES... I'LL DO THAT.
THE NEXT TIME I TALK TO AZUKI IS WHEN MY MANGA IS ANIMATED...
THEY'RE NOT NORMAL AFTER ALL.
WHAT?
CHIK

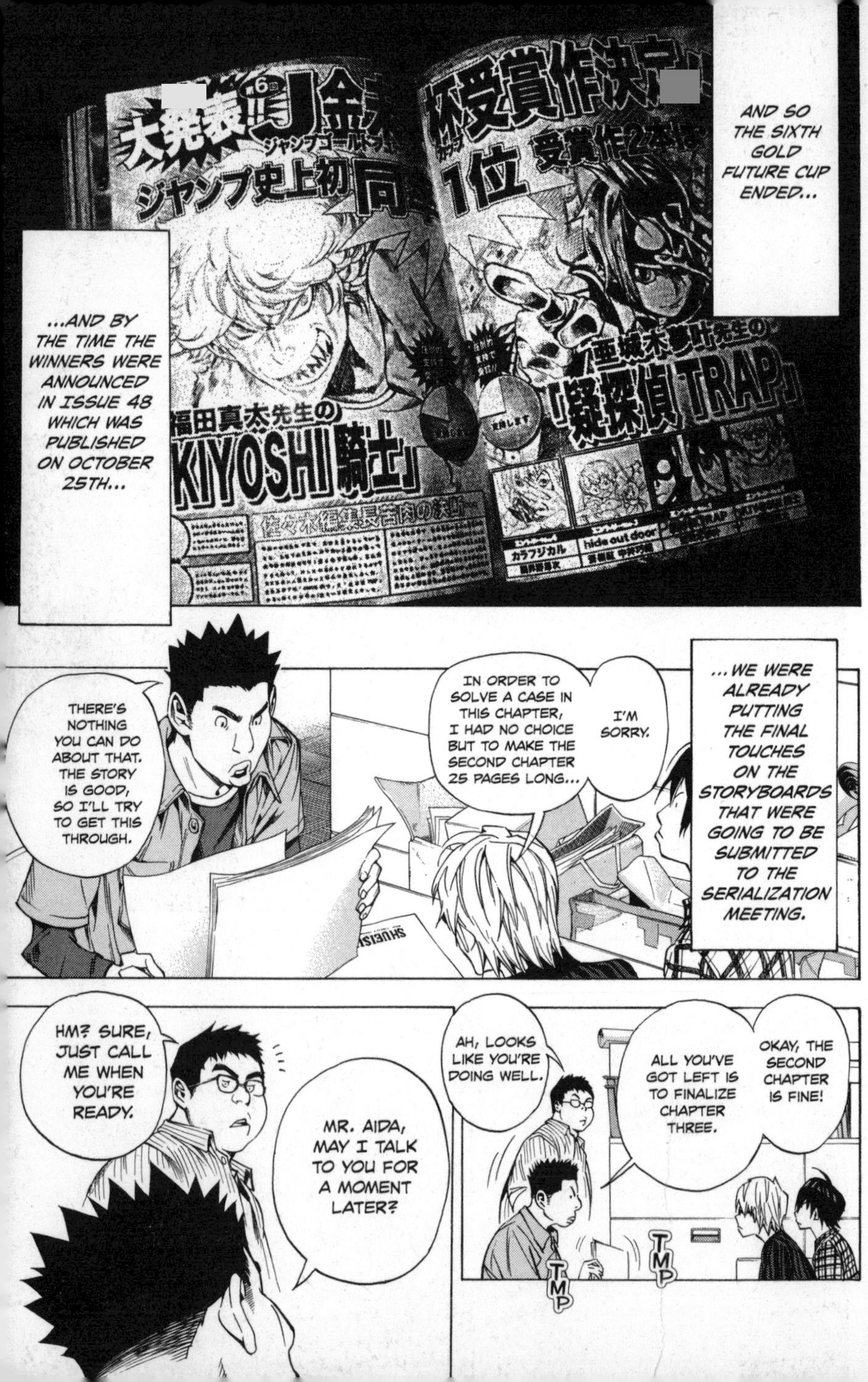
AND SO THE SIXTH GOLD FUTURE CUP ENDED...
...AND BY THE TIME THE WINNERS WERE ANNOUNCED IN ISSUE 48 WHICH WAS PUBLISHED ON OCTOBER 25TH...
大発表!!
ジャンプ史上初
1位
受賞作2本!?
亜城木夢叶先生の
『疑探偵TRAP』
福田真太先生の
『KIYOSHI騎士』
hide out door
カラフジカル
...WE WERE ALREADY PUTTING THE FINAL TOUCHES ON THE STORYBOARDS THAT WERE GOING TO BE SUBMITTED TO THE SERIALIZATION MEETING.
I'M SORRY.
IN ORDER TO SOLVE A CASE IN THIS CHAPTER, I HAD NO CHOICE BUT TO MAKE THE SECOND CHAPTER 25 PAGES LONG...
THERE'S NOTHING YOU CAN DO ABOUT THAT. THE STORY IS GOOD, SO I'LL TRY TO GET THIS THROUGH.
SHUEISHA
OKAY, THE SECOND CHAPTER IS FINE!
ALL YOU'VE GOT LEFT IS TO FINALIZE CHAPTER THREE.
AH, LOOKS LIKE YOU'RE DOING WELL.
TMP
TMP
MR. AIDA, MAY I TALK TO YOU FOR A MOMENT LATER?
HM? SURE, JUST CALL ME WHEN YOU'RE READY.

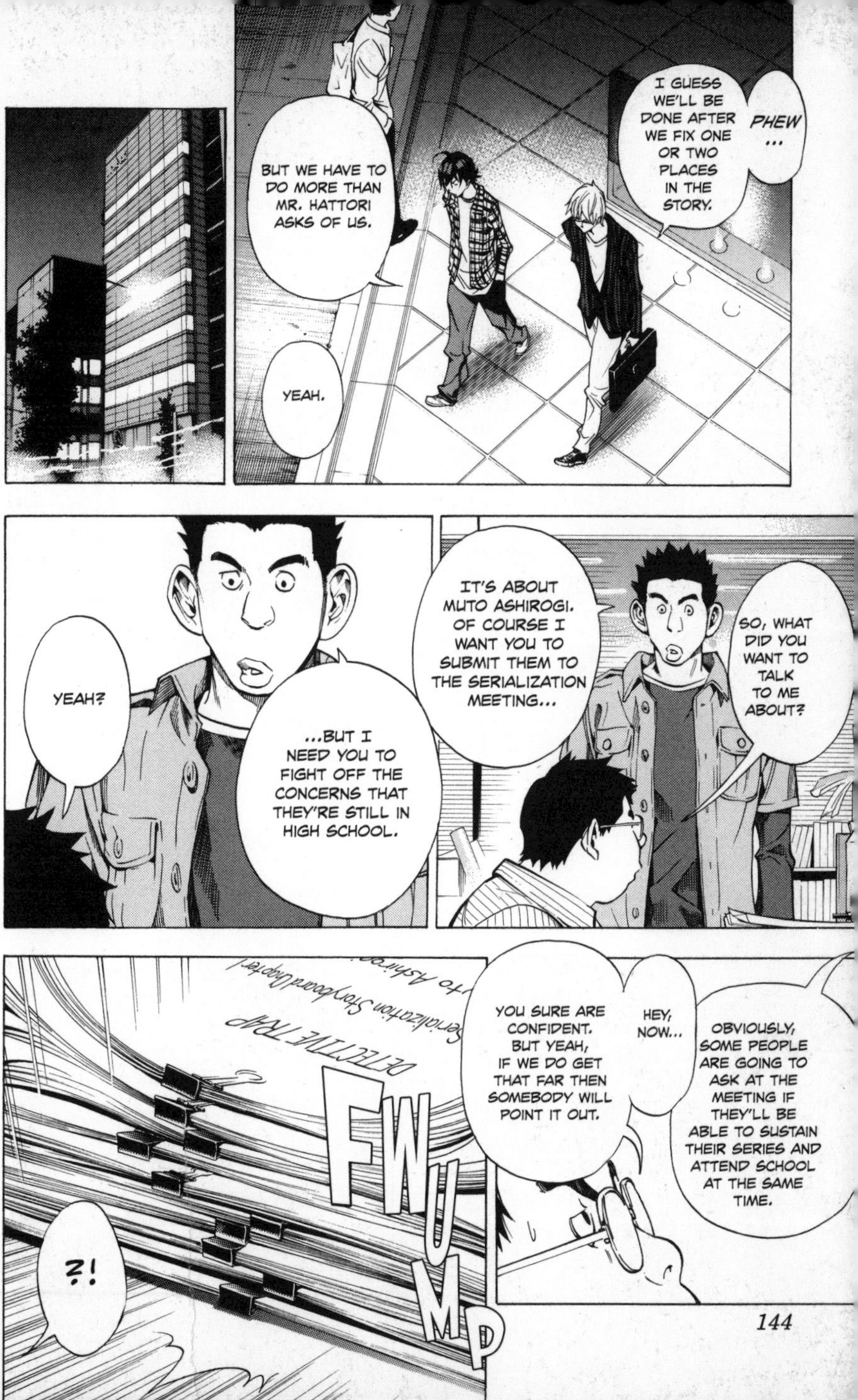
PHEW...
I GUESS WE'LL BE DONE AFTER WE FIX ONE OR TWO PLACES IN THE STORY.
BUT WE HAVE TO DO MORE THAN MR. HATTORI ASKS OF US.
YEAH.
SO, WHAT DID YOU WANT TO TALK TO ME ABOUT?
IT'S ABOUT MUTO ASHIROGI. OF COURSE I WANT YOU TO SUBMIT THEM TO THE SERIALIZATION MEETING...
...BUT I NEED YOU TO FIGHT OFF THE CONCERNS THAT THEY'RE STILL IN HIGH SCHOOL.
YEAH?
OBVIOUSLY, SOME PEOPLE ARE GOING TO ASK AT THE MEETING IF THEY'LL BE ABLE TO SUSTAIN THEIR SERIES AND ATTEND SCHOOL AT THE SAME TIME.
HEY, NOW...
YOU SURE ARE CONFIDENT. BUT YEAH, IF WE DO GET THAT FAR THEN SOMEBODY WILL POINT IT OUT.
DETECTIVE TRAP
FWUMP
?!

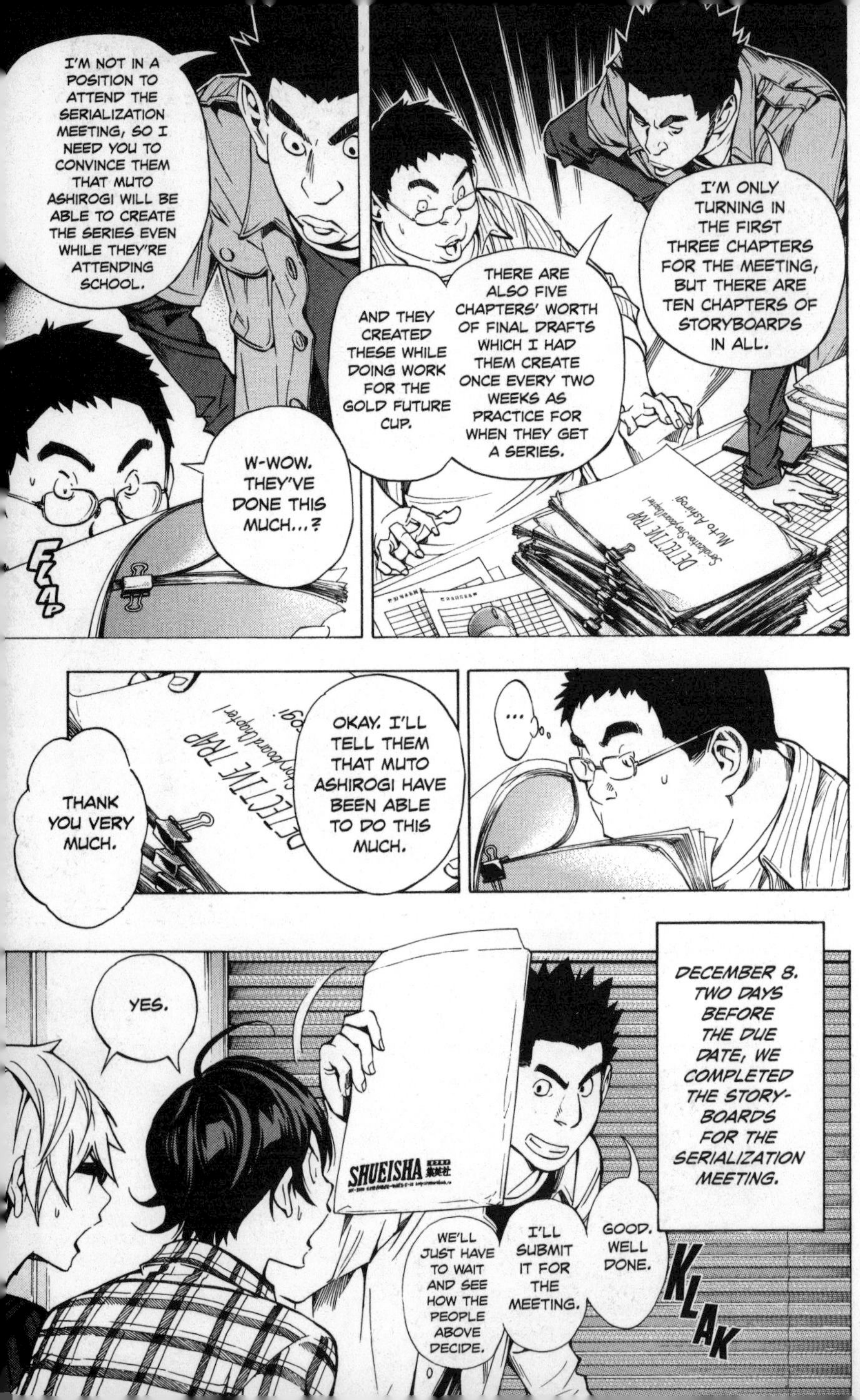
I'M ONLY TURNING IN THE FIRST THREE CHAPTERS FOR THE MEETING, BUT THERE ARE TEN CHAPTERS OF STORYBOARDS IN ALL.
THERE ARE ALSO FIVE CHAPTERS' WORTH OF FINAL DRAFTS WHICH I HAD THEM CREATE ONCE EVERY TWO WEEKS AS PRACTICE FOR WHEN THEY GET A SERIES.
AND THEY CREATED THESE WHILE DOING WORK FOR THE GOLD FUTURE CUP.
I'M NOT IN A POSITION TO ATTEND THE SERIALIZATION MEETING, SO I NEED YOU TO CONVINCE THEM THAT MUTO ASHIROGI WILL BE ABLE TO CREATE THE SERIES EVEN WHILE THEY'RE ATTENDING SCHOOL.
W-WOW. THEY'VE DONE THIS MUCH...?
FLAP
...
OKAY. I'LL TELL THEM THAT MUTO ASHIROGI HAVE BEEN ABLE TO DO THIS MUCH.
THANK YOU VERY MUCH.
DECEMBER 8. TWO DAYS BEFORE THE DUE DATE, WE COMPLETED THE STORY-BOARDS FOR THE SERIALIZATION MEETING.
GOOD. WELL DONE.
KLAK
I'LL SUBMIT IT FOR THE MEETING.
WE'LL JUST HAVE TO WAIT AND SEE HOW THE PEOPLE ABOVE DECIDE.
SHUEISHA
YES.

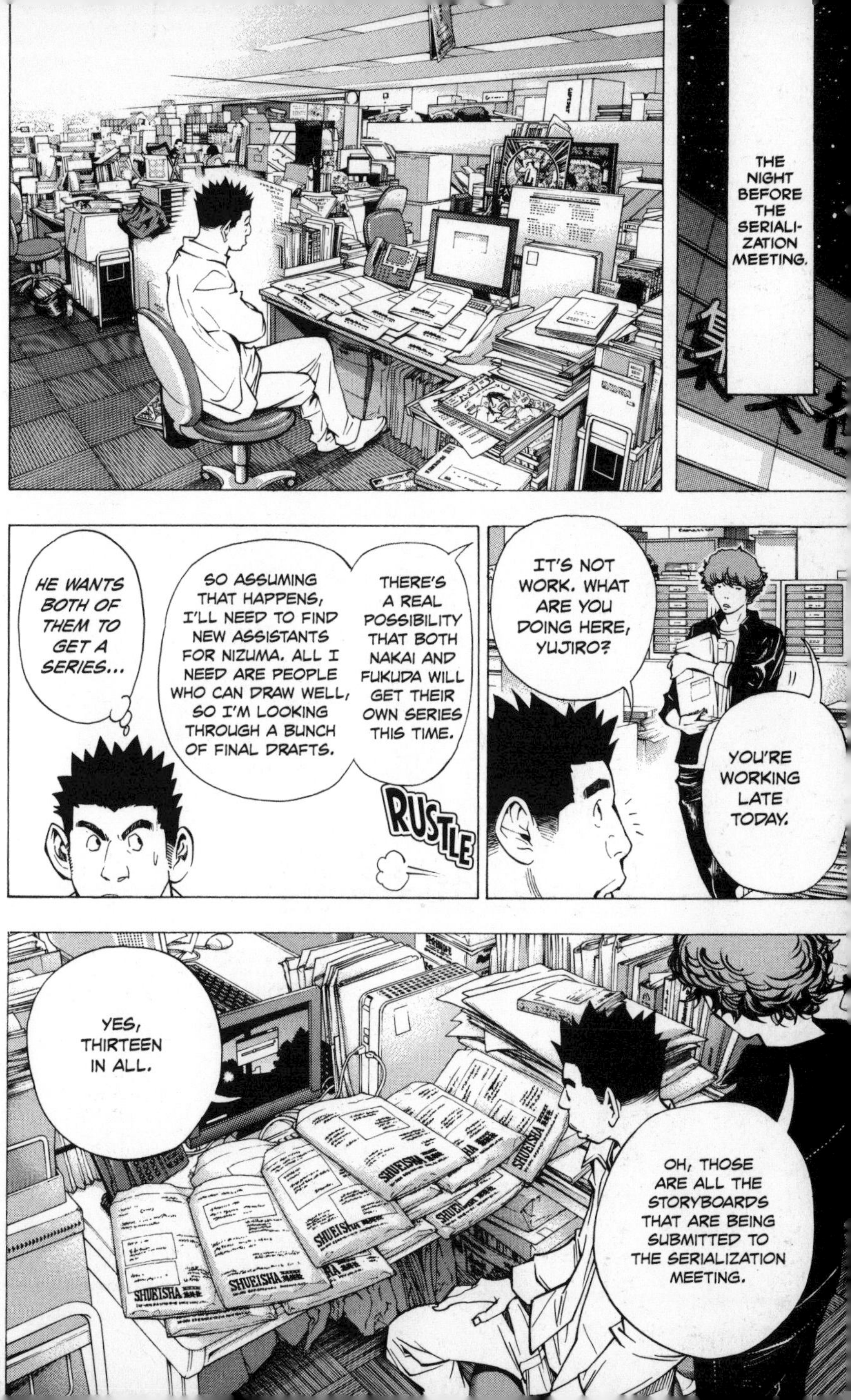
THE NIGHT BEFORE THE SERIALIZATION MEETING.
YOU'RE WORKING LATE TODAY.
IT'S NOT WORK. WHAT ARE YOU DOING HERE, YUJIRO?
THERE'S A REAL POSSIBILITY THAT BOTH NAKAI AND FUKUDA WILL GET THEIR OWN SERIES THIS TIME.
SO ASSUMING THAT HAPPENS, I'LL NEED TO FIND NEW ASSISTANTS FOR NIZUMA. ALL I NEED ARE PEOPLE WHO CAN DRAW WELL, SO I'M LOOKING THROUGH A BUNCH OF FINAL DRAFTS.
RUSTLE
HE WANTS BOTH OF THEM TO GET A SERIES...
OH, THOSE ARE ALL THE STORYBOARDS THAT ARE BEING SUBMITTED TO THE SERIALIZATION MEETING.
YES, THIRTEEN IN ALL.

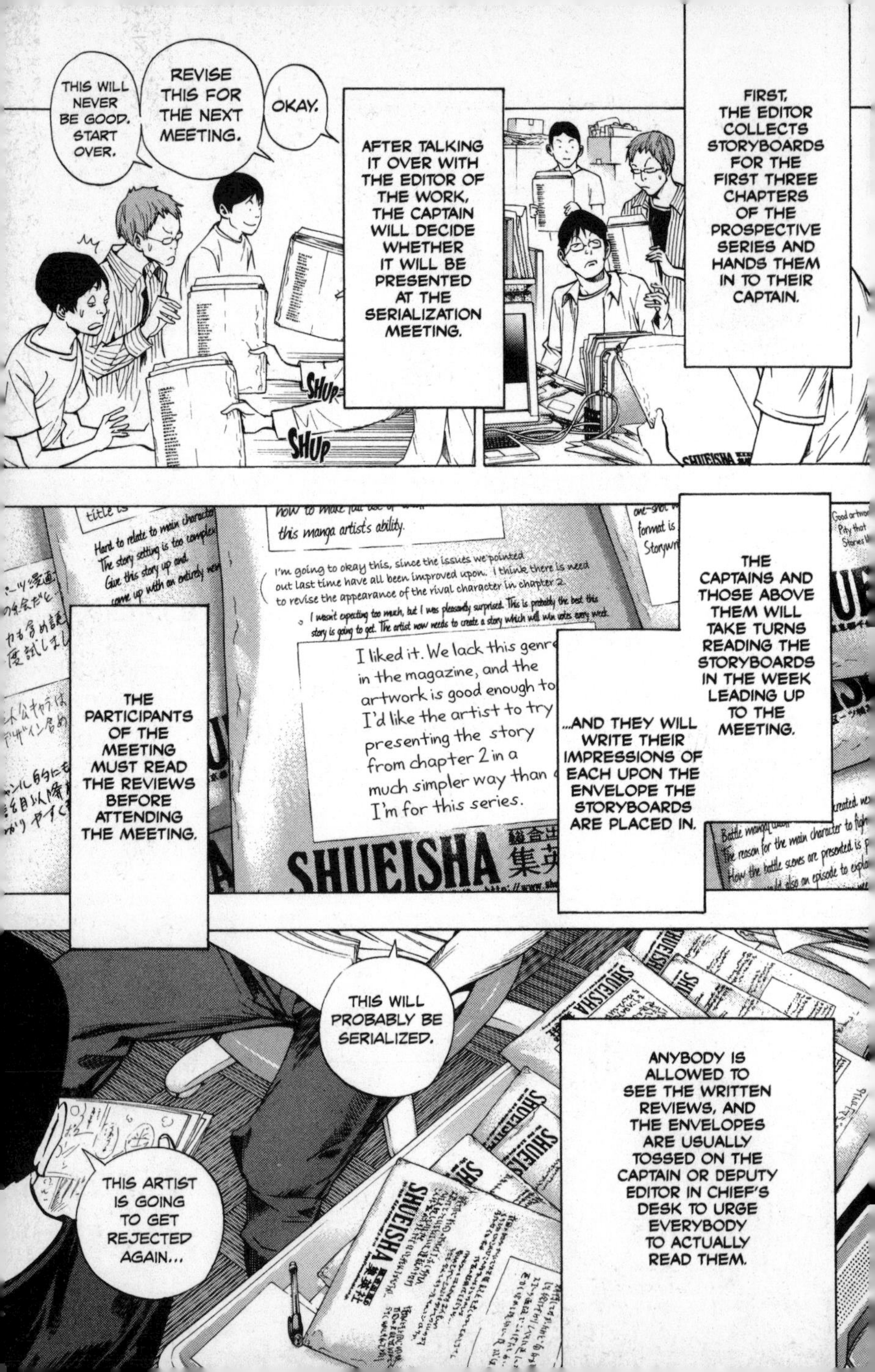
FIRST, THE EDITOR COLLECTS STORYBOARDS FOR THE FIRST THREE CHAPTERS OF THE PROSPECTIVE SERIES AND HANDS THEM IN TO THEIR CAPTAIN.
AFTER TALKING IT OVER WITH THE EDITOR OF THE WORK, THE CAPTAIN WILL DECIDE WHETHER IT WILL BE PRESENTED AT THE SERIALIZATION MEETING.
OKAY.
REVISE THIS FOR THE NEXT MEETING.
THIS WILL NEVER BE GOOD. START OVER.
SHUP
SHUP
THE CAPTAINS AND THOSE ABOVE THEM WILL TAKE TURNS READING THE STORYBOARDS IN THE WEEK LEADING UP TO THE MEETING.
...AND THEY WILL WRITE THEIR IMPRESSIONS OF EACH UPON THE ENVELOPE THE STORYBOARDS ARE PLACED IN.
this manga artist's ability.
I'm going to okay this, since the issues we pointed out last time have all been improved upon. I think there is need to revise the appearance of the rival character in chapter 2.
I wasn't expecting too much, but I was pleasantly surprised. This is probably the best this story is going to get. The artist now needs to create a story which will win votes every week.
I liked it. We lack this genre in the magazine, and the artwork is good enough to I'd like the artist to try presenting the story from chapter 2 in a much simpler way than I'm for this series.
Hard to relate to main character The story setting is too complex Give this story up and
SHUEISHA
THE PARTICIPANTS OF THE MEETING MUST READ THE REVIEWS BEFORE ATTENDING THE MEETING.
ANYBODY IS ALLOWED TO SEE THE WRITTEN REVIEWS, AND THE ENVELOPES ARE USUALLY TOSSED ON THE CAPTAIN OR DEPUTY EDITOR IN CHIEF'S DESK TO URGE EVERYBODY TO ACTUALLY READ THEM.
THIS WILL PROBABLY BE SERIALIZED.
THIS ARTIST IS GOING TO GET REJECTED AGAIN...

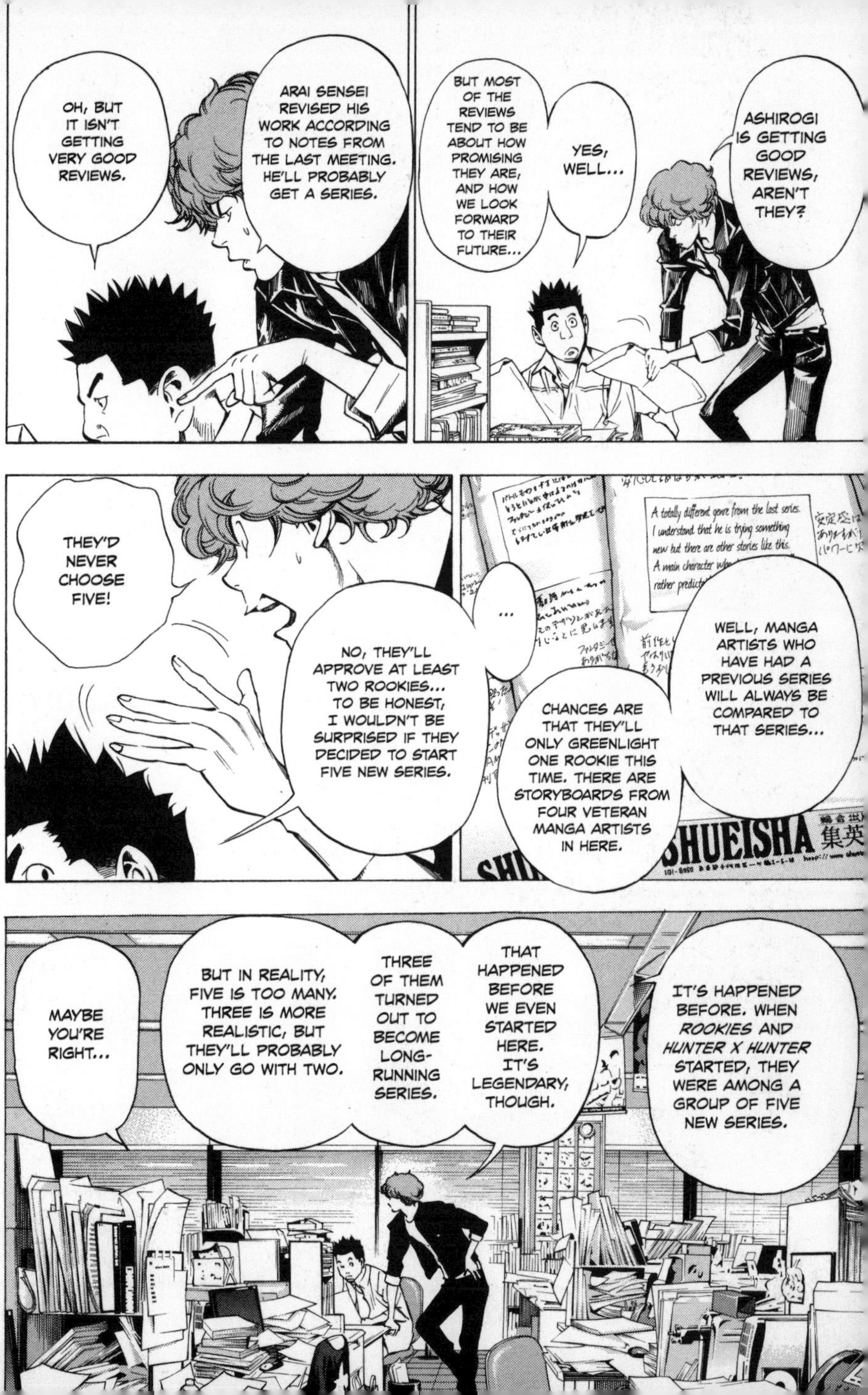
ASHIROGI IS GETTING GOOD REVIEWS, AREN'T THEY?
YES, WELL...
BUT MOST OF THE REVIEWS TEND TO BE ABOUT HOW PROMISING THEY ARE, AND HOW WE LOOK FORWARD TO THEIR FUTURE...
ARAI SENSEI REVISED HIS WORK ACCORDING TO NOTES FROM THE LAST MEETING. HE'LL PROBABLY GET A SERIES.
OH, BUT IT ISN'T GETTING VERY GOOD REVIEWS.
A totally different genre from the last series.
I understand that he is trying something
new but there are other stories like this.
WELL, MANGA ARTISTS WHO HAVE HAD A PREVIOUS SERIES WILL ALWAYS BE COMPARED TO THAT SERIES...
CHANCES ARE THAT THEY'LL ONLY GREENLIGHT ONE ROOKIE THIS TIME. THERE ARE STORYBOARDS FROM FOUR VETERAN MANGA ARTISTS IN HERE.
SHUEISHA 集英
...
NO, THEY'LL APPROVE AT LEAST TWO ROOKIES... TO BE HONEST, I WOULDN'T BE SURPRISED IF THEY DECIDED TO START FIVE NEW SERIES.
THEY'D NEVER CHOOSE FIVE!
IT'S HAPPENED BEFORE. WHEN *ROOKIES* AND *HUNTER X HUNTER* STARTED, THEY WERE AMONG A GROUP OF FIVE NEW SERIES.
THAT HAPPENED BEFORE WE EVEN STARTED HERE. IT'S LEGENDARY, THOUGH.
THREE OF THEM TURNED OUT TO BECOME LONG-RUNNING SERIES.
BUT IN REALITY, FIVE IS TOO MANY. THREE IS MORE REALISTIC, BUT THEY'LL PROBABLY ONLY GO WITH TWO.
MAYBE YOU'RE RIGHT...

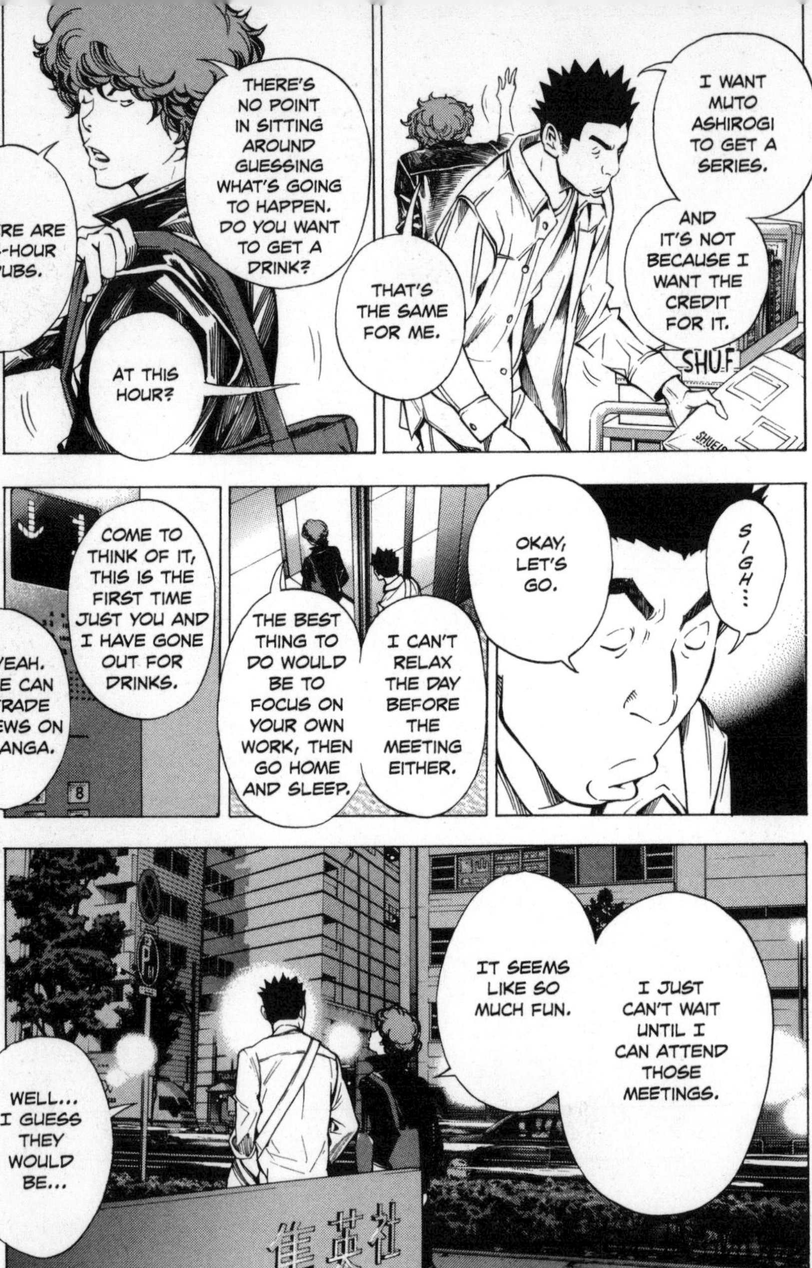
I WANT MUTO ASHIROGI TO GET A SERIES.
AND IT'S NOT BECAUSE I WANT THE CREDIT FOR IT.
SHUF
THAT'S THE SAME FOR ME.
THERE'S NO POINT IN SITTING AROUND GUESSING WHAT'S GOING TO HAPPEN. DO YOU WANT TO GET A DRINK?
AT THIS HOUR?
THERE ARE 24-HOUR PUBS.
SIGH...
OKAY, LET'S GO.
I CAN'T RELAX THE DAY BEFORE THE MEETING EITHER.
THE BEST THING TO DO WOULD BE TO FOCUS ON YOUR OWN WORK, THEN GO HOME AND SLEEP.
COME TO THINK OF IT, THIS IS THE FIRST TIME JUST YOU AND I HAVE GONE OUT FOR DRINKS.
YEAH. WE CAN TRADE VIEWS ON MANGA.
I JUST CAN'T WAIT UNTIL I CAN ATTEND THOSE MEETINGS.
IT SEEMS LIKE SO MUCH FUN.
WELL... I GUESS THEY WOULD BE...
集英社
(SIGN: SHUEISHA)

OHBA'S STORYBOARD

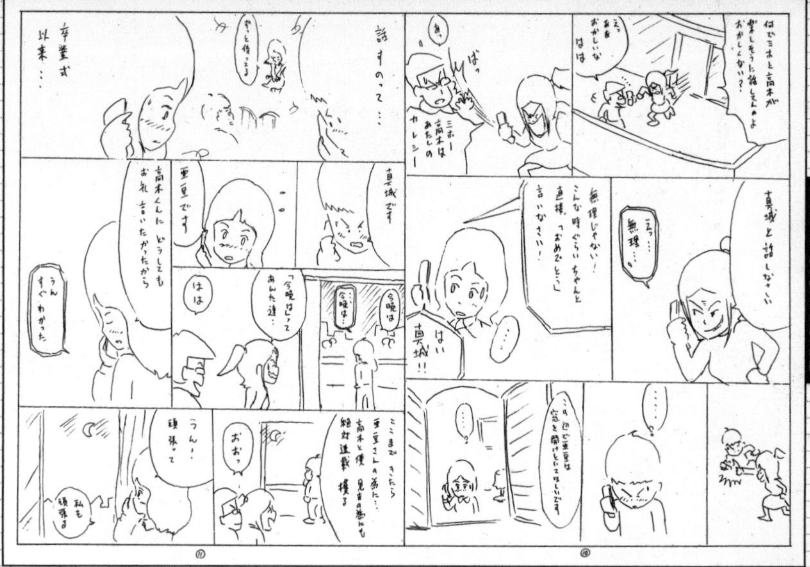
何でミホと高木が楽しそうに話してんのよ おかしくない?
えっ ああ おかしいな はは
ばっ
ミホー 高木はあたしのカレシー
あ、
真城と話しなさい
えっ… 無理…
無理じゃない! こんな時ぐらいちゃんと直接「おめでとう」言いなさい!
…
はい 真城!!
……
……
…?
話すのって…
卒業式以来…
真城です
…
亜豆です
高木くんにどうしてもお礼言いたかったから
今晩は
今晩は…
「今晩は」ってあんた達…
はは
うん すぐわかった
ここまできたら亜豆さんの為に…高木と僕 見吉の為にも絶対連載摂る
おおっ
うん! 頑張って
私も頑張る

OBATA'S STORYBOARD

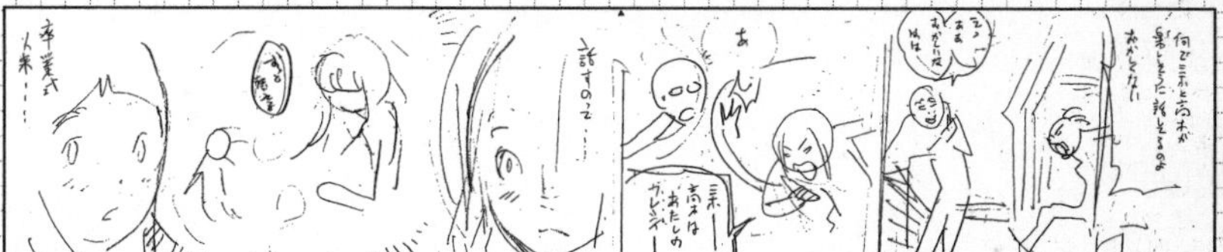
何で三ホと高木が楽しそうに話してるのよ おかしくない
えっ ああ おかしいな はは
あ
ミホー 高木はあたしのカレシー
真城と話しなさい
えっ… 無理…
無理じゃない こんな時ぐらいちゃんと直接「おめでとう」言いなさい
はい 真城
……
……
話すのって…
卒業式以来…
真城です
亜豆です
高木くんどうしてもお礼言いたかったから
今晩は
今晩は…
今晩はってあんた達
はは
うん すぐわかった
うん! 頑張って
私も頑張る

COMPLETE!

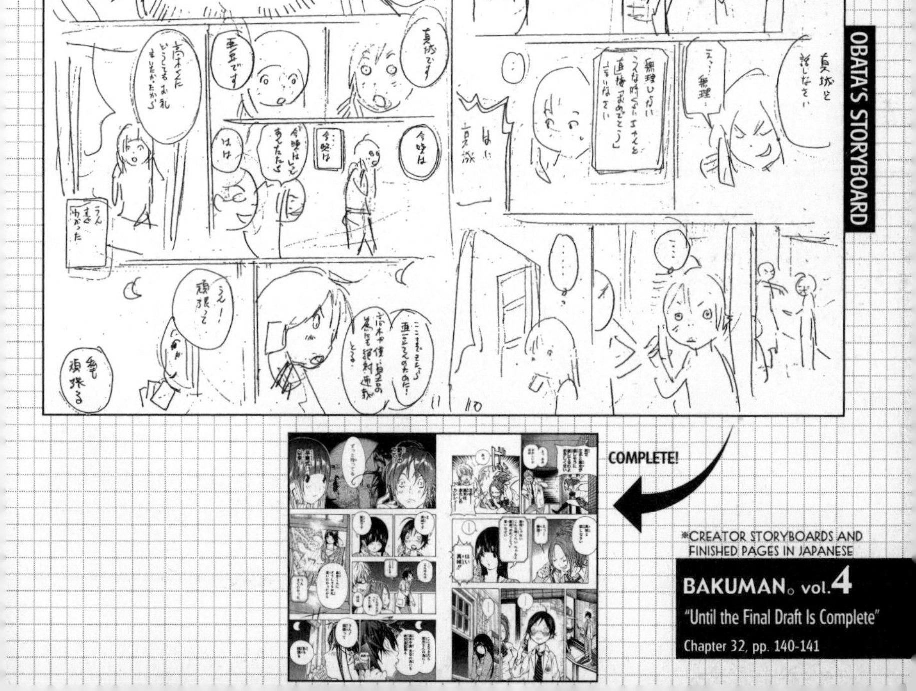

※CREATOR STORYBOARDS AND FINISHED PAGES IN JAPANESE

BAKUMAN。 vol.4

"Until the Final Draft Is Complete"

Chapter 32, pp. 140-141

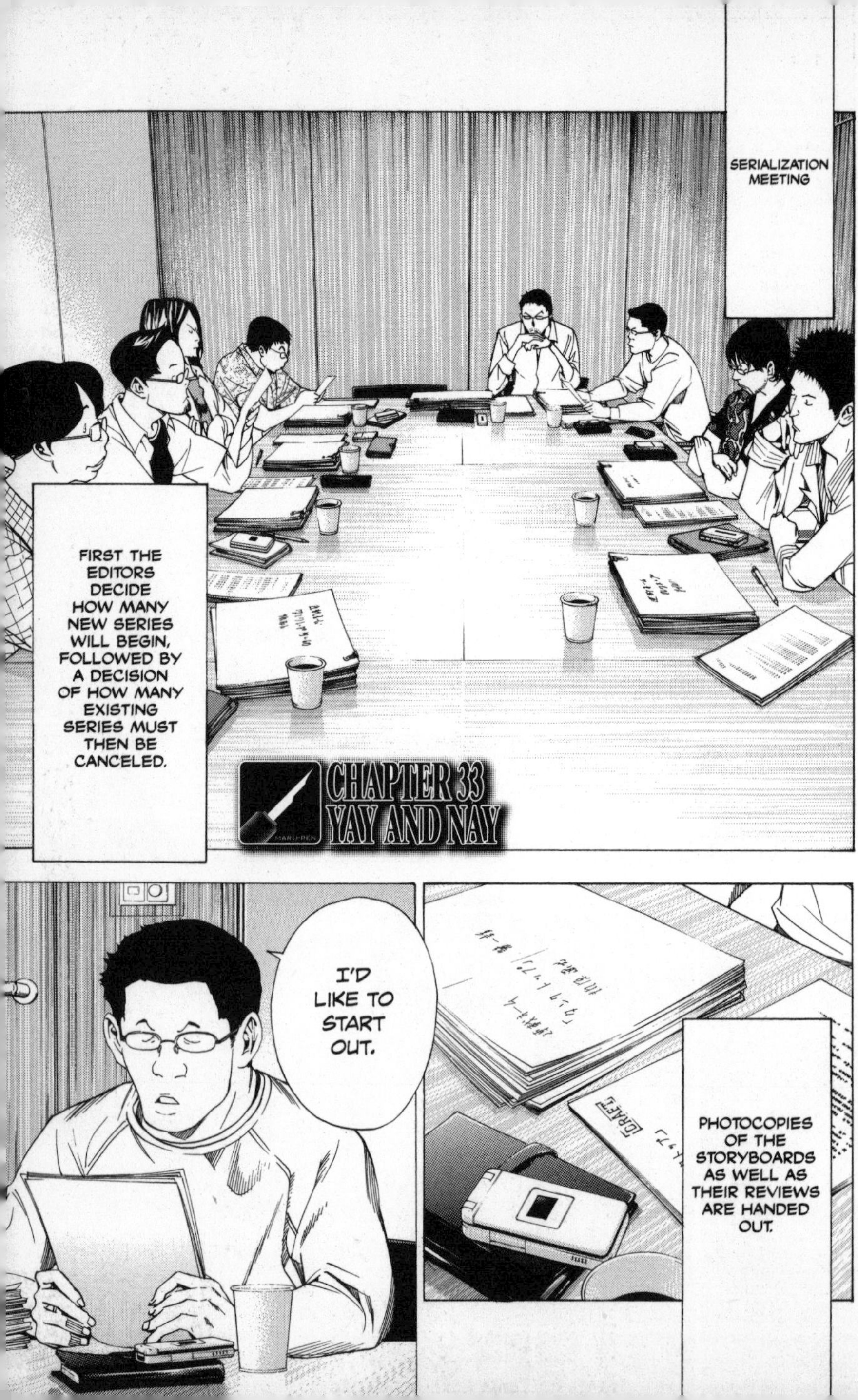
SERIALIZATION MEETING
FIRST THE EDITORS DECIDE HOW MANY NEW SERIES WILL BEGIN, FOLLOWED BY A DECISION OF HOW MANY EXISTING SERIES MUST THEN BE CANCELED.
CHAPTER 33
YAY AND NAY
PHOTOCOPIES OF THE STORYBOARDS AS WELL AS THEIR REVIEWS ARE HANDED OUT.
I'D LIKE TO START OUT.

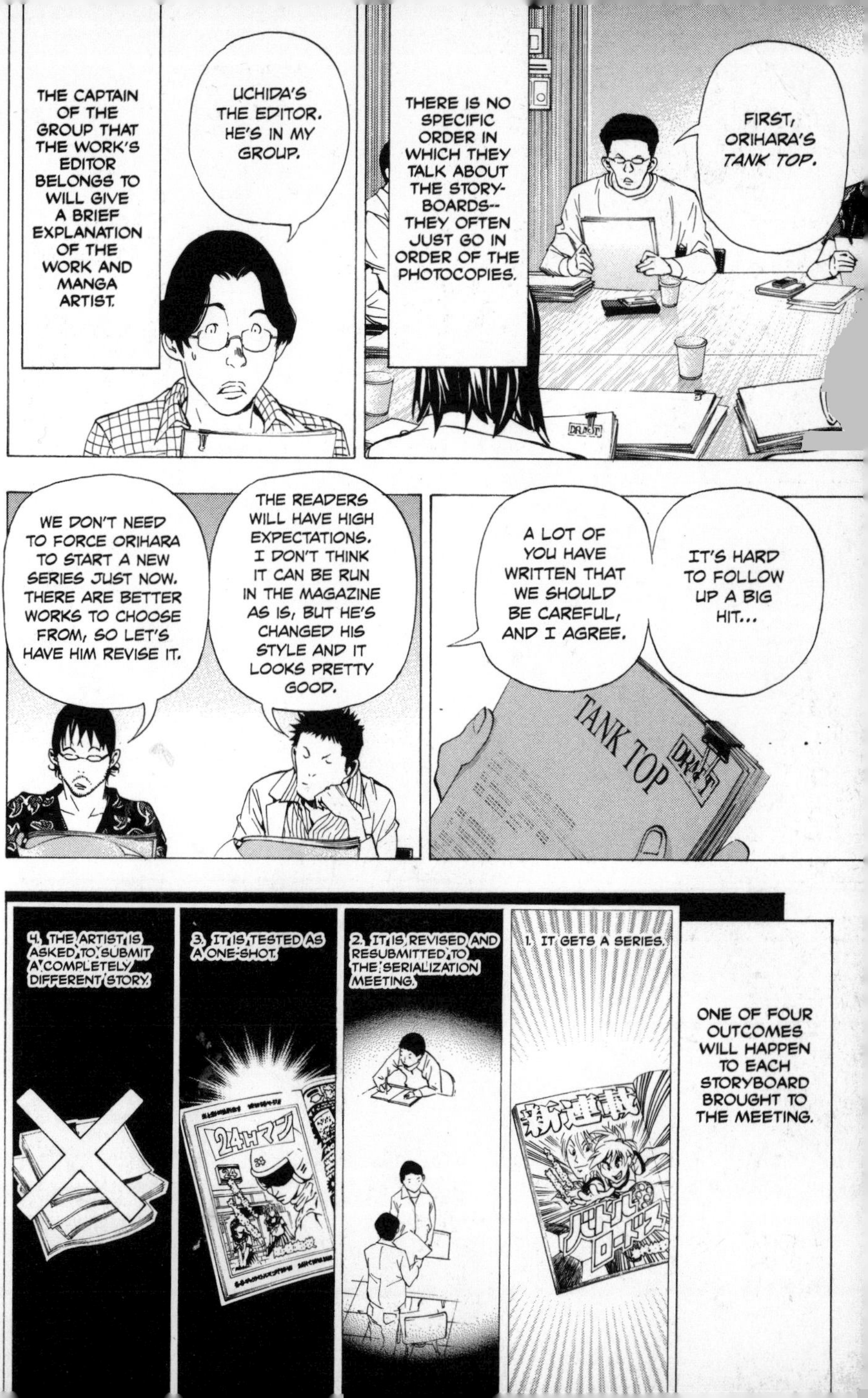
FIRST, ORIHARA'S *TANK TOP*.
THERE IS NO SPECIFIC ORDER IN WHICH THEY TALK ABOUT THE STORYBOARDS-- THEY OFTEN JUST GO IN ORDER OF THE PHOTOCOPIES.
UCHIDA'S THE EDITOR. HE'S IN MY GROUP.
THE CAPTAIN OF THE GROUP THAT THE WORK'S EDITOR BELONGS TO WILL GIVE A BRIEF EXPLANATION OF THE WORK AND MANGA ARTIST.
IT'S HARD TO FOLLOW UP A BIG HIT...
A LOT OF YOU HAVE WRITTEN THAT WE SHOULD BE CAREFUL, AND I AGREE.
TANK TOP
THE READERS WILL HAVE HIGH EXPECTATIONS. I DON'T THINK IT CAN BE RUN IN THE MAGAZINE AS IS, BUT HE'S CHANGED HIS STYLE AND IT LOOKS PRETTY GOOD.
WE DON'T NEED TO FORCE ORIHARA TO START A NEW SERIES JUST NOW. THERE ARE BETTER WORKS TO CHOOSE FROM, SO LET'S HAVE HIM REVISE IT.
ONE OF FOUR OUTCOMES WILL HAPPEN TO EACH STORYBOARD BROUGHT TO THE MEETING.
1. IT GETS A SERIES.
新連載
2. IT IS REVISED AND RESUBMITTED TO THE SERIALIZATION MEETING.
3. IT IS TESTED AS A ONE-SHOT.
24Hマン
4. THE ARTIST IS ASKED TO SUBMIT A COMPLETELY DIFFERENT STORY.

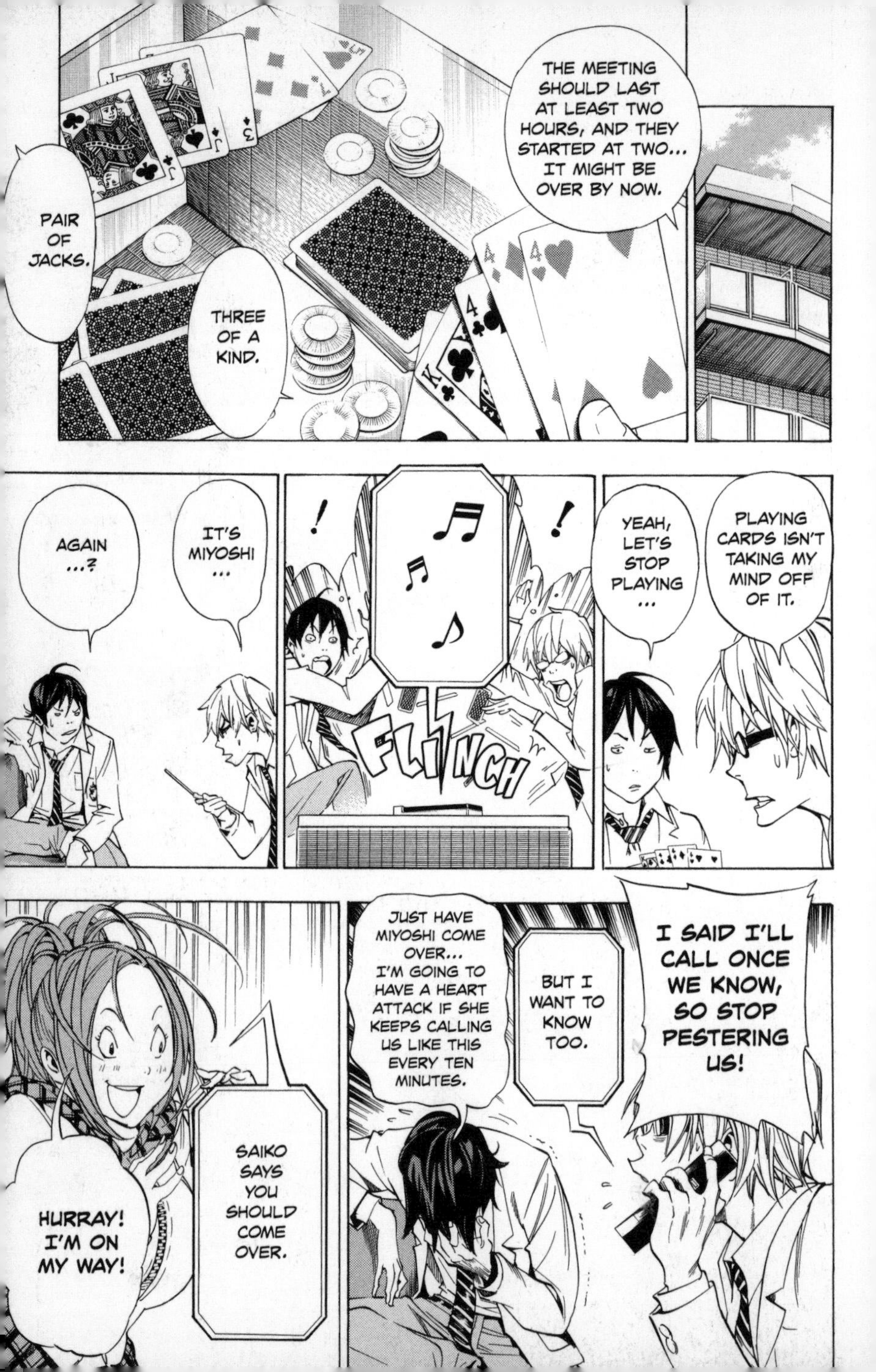
THE MEETING SHOULD LAST AT LEAST TWO HOURS, AND THEY STARTED AT TWO... IT MIGHT BE OVER BY NOW.
THREE OF A KIND.
PAIR OF JACKS.
PLAYING CARDS ISN'T TAKING MY MIND OFF OF IT.
YEAH, LET'S STOP PLAYING...
!
!
FLINCH
IT'S MIYOSHI...
AGAIN...?
I SAID I'LL CALL ONCE WE KNOW, SO STOP PESTERING US!
BUT I WANT TO KNOW TOO.
JUST HAVE MIYOSHI COME OVER... I'M GOING TO HAVE A HEART ATTACK IF SHE KEEPS CALLING US LIKE THIS EVERY TEN MINUTES.
SAIKO SAYS YOU SHOULD COME OVER.
HURRAY! I'M ON MY WAY!

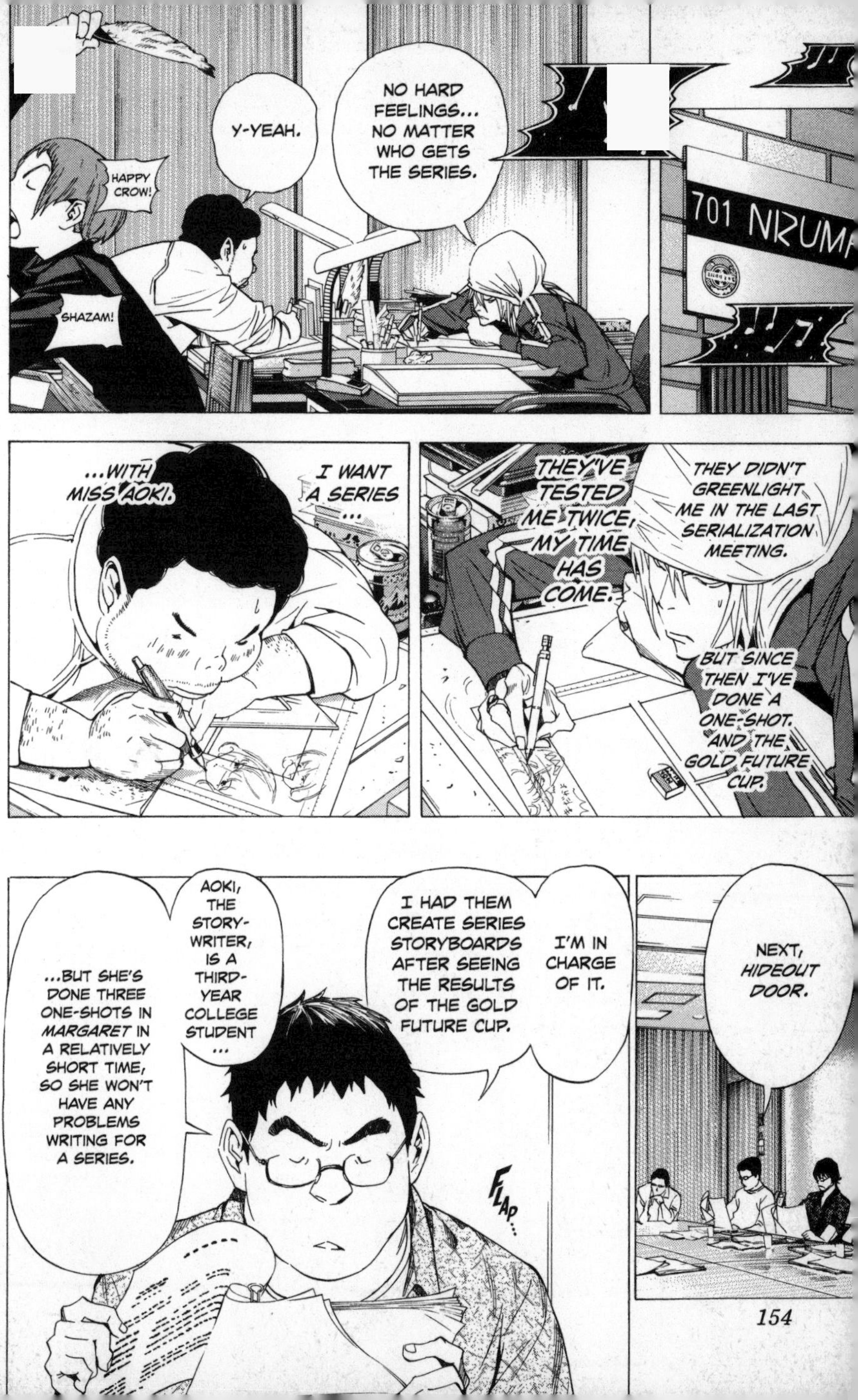
701 NIZUM
NO HARD FEELINGS... NO MATTER WHO GETS THE SERIES.
Y-YEAH.
HAPPY CROW!
SHAZAM!
THEY DIDN'T GREENLIGHT ME IN THE LAST SERIALIZATION MEETING.
THEY'VE TESTED ME TWICE. MY TIME HAS COME.
BUT SINCE THEN I'VE DONE A ONE-SHOT. AND THE GOLD FUTURE CUP.
I WANT A SERIES ...
...WITH MISS AOKI.
NEXT, HIDEOUT DOOR.
I'M IN CHARGE OF IT.
I HAD THEM CREATE SERIES STORYBOARDS AFTER SEEING THE RESULTS OF THE GOLD FUTURE CUP.
AOKI, THE STORY-WRITER, IS A THIRD-YEAR COLLEGE STUDENT ...
...BUT SHE'S DONE THREE ONE-SHOTS IN *MARGARET* IN A RELATIVELY SHORT TIME, SO SHE WON'T HAVE ANY PROBLEMS WRITING FOR A SERIES.
FLAP...

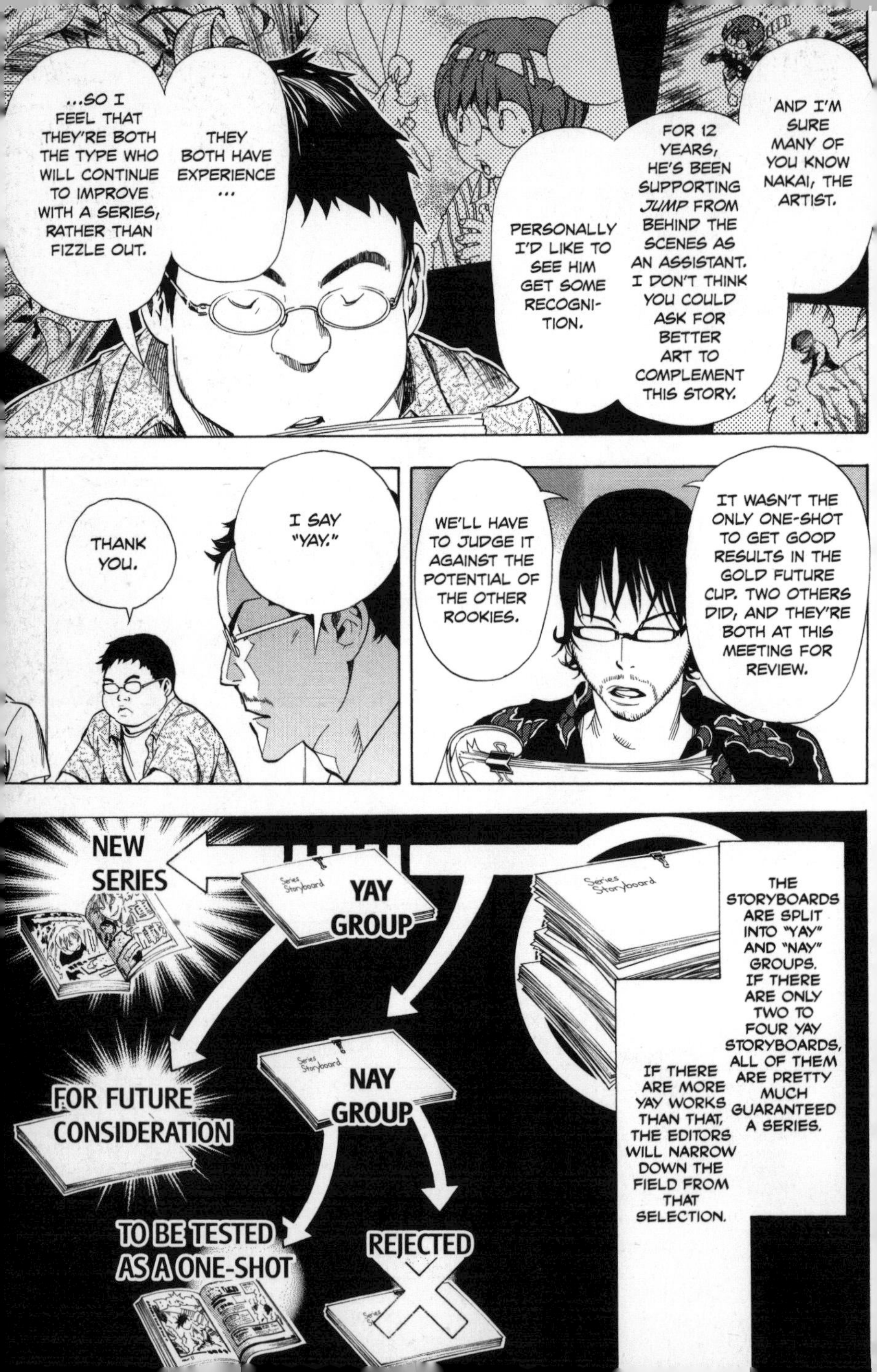
AND I'M SURE MANY OF YOU KNOW NAKAI, THE ARTIST.
FOR 12 YEARS, HE'S BEEN SUPPORTING *JUMP* FROM BEHIND THE SCENES AS AN ASSISTANT. I DON'T THINK YOU COULD ASK FOR BETTER ART TO COMPLEMENT THIS STORY.
PERSONALLY I'D LIKE TO SEE HIM GET SOME RECOGNITION.
THEY BOTH HAVE EXPERIENCE...
...SO I FEEL THAT THEY'RE BOTH THE TYPE WHO WILL CONTINUE TO IMPROVE WITH A SERIES, RATHER THAN FIZZLE OUT.
IT WASN'T THE ONLY ONE-SHOT TO GET GOOD RESULTS IN THE GOLD FUTURE CUP. TWO OTHERS DID, AND THEY'RE BOTH AT THIS MEETING FOR REVIEW.
WE'LL HAVE TO JUDGE IT AGAINST THE POTENTIAL OF THE OTHER ROOKIES.
I SAY "YAY."
THANK YOU.
THE STORYBOARDS ARE SPLIT INTO "YAY" AND "NAY" GROUPS. IF THERE ARE ONLY TWO TO FOUR YAY STORYBOARDS, ALL OF THEM ARE PRETTY MUCH GUARANTEED A SERIES.
IF THERE ARE MORE YAY WORKS THAN THAT, THE EDITORS WILL NARROW DOWN THE FIELD FROM THAT SELECTION.
Series Storyboard
YAY GROUP
NEW SERIES
NAY GROUP
FOR FUTURE CONSIDERATION
REJECTED
TO BE TESTED AS A ONE-SHOT

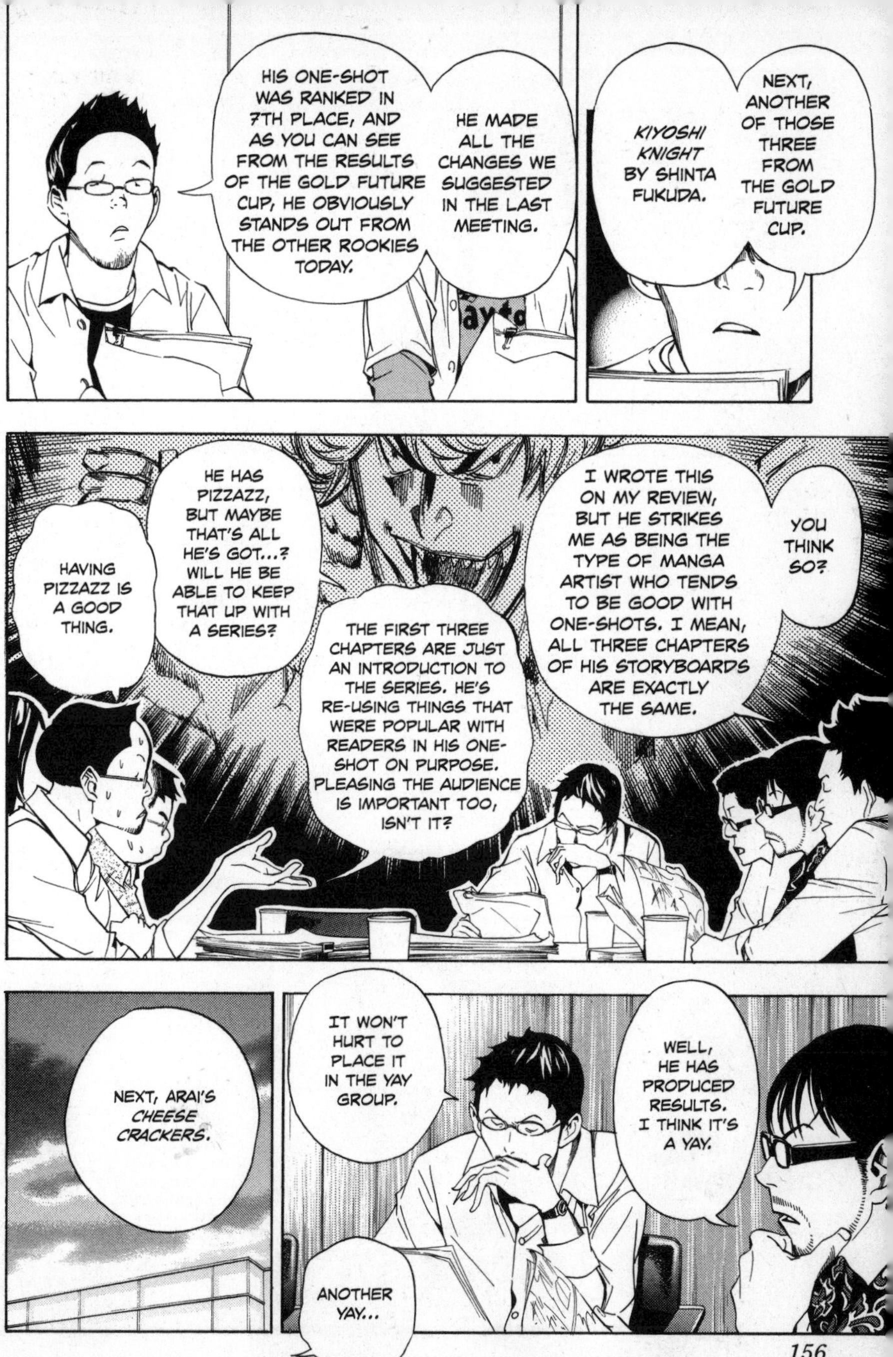
NEXT, ANOTHER OF THOSE THREE FROM THE GOLD FUTURE CUP.
KIYOSHI KNIGHT BY SHINTA FUKUDA.
HE MADE ALL THE CHANGES WE SUGGESTED IN THE LAST MEETING.
HIS ONE-SHOT WAS RANKED IN 7TH PLACE, AND AS YOU CAN SEE FROM THE RESULTS OF THE GOLD FUTURE CUP, HE OBVIOUSLY STANDS OUT FROM THE OTHER ROOKIES TODAY.
YOU THINK SO?
I WROTE THIS ON MY REVIEW, BUT HE STRIKES ME AS BEING THE TYPE OF MANGA ARTIST WHO TENDS TO BE GOOD WITH ONE-SHOTS. I MEAN, ALL THREE CHAPTERS OF HIS STORYBOARDS ARE EXACTLY THE SAME.
THE FIRST THREE CHAPTERS ARE JUST AN INTRODUCTION TO THE SERIES. HE'S RE-USING THINGS THAT WERE POPULAR WITH READERS IN HIS ONE-SHOT ON PURPOSE. PLEASING THE AUDIENCE IS IMPORTANT TOO, ISN'T IT?
HE HAS PIZZAZZ, BUT MAYBE THAT'S ALL HE'S GOT...? WILL HE BE ABLE TO KEEP THAT UP WITH A SERIES?
HAVING PIZZAZZ IS A GOOD THING.
WELL, HE HAS PRODUCED RESULTS. I THINK IT'S A YAY.
IT WON'T HURT TO PLACE IT IN THE YAY GROUP.
ANOTHER YAY...
NEXT, ARAI'S *CHEESE CRACKERS*.

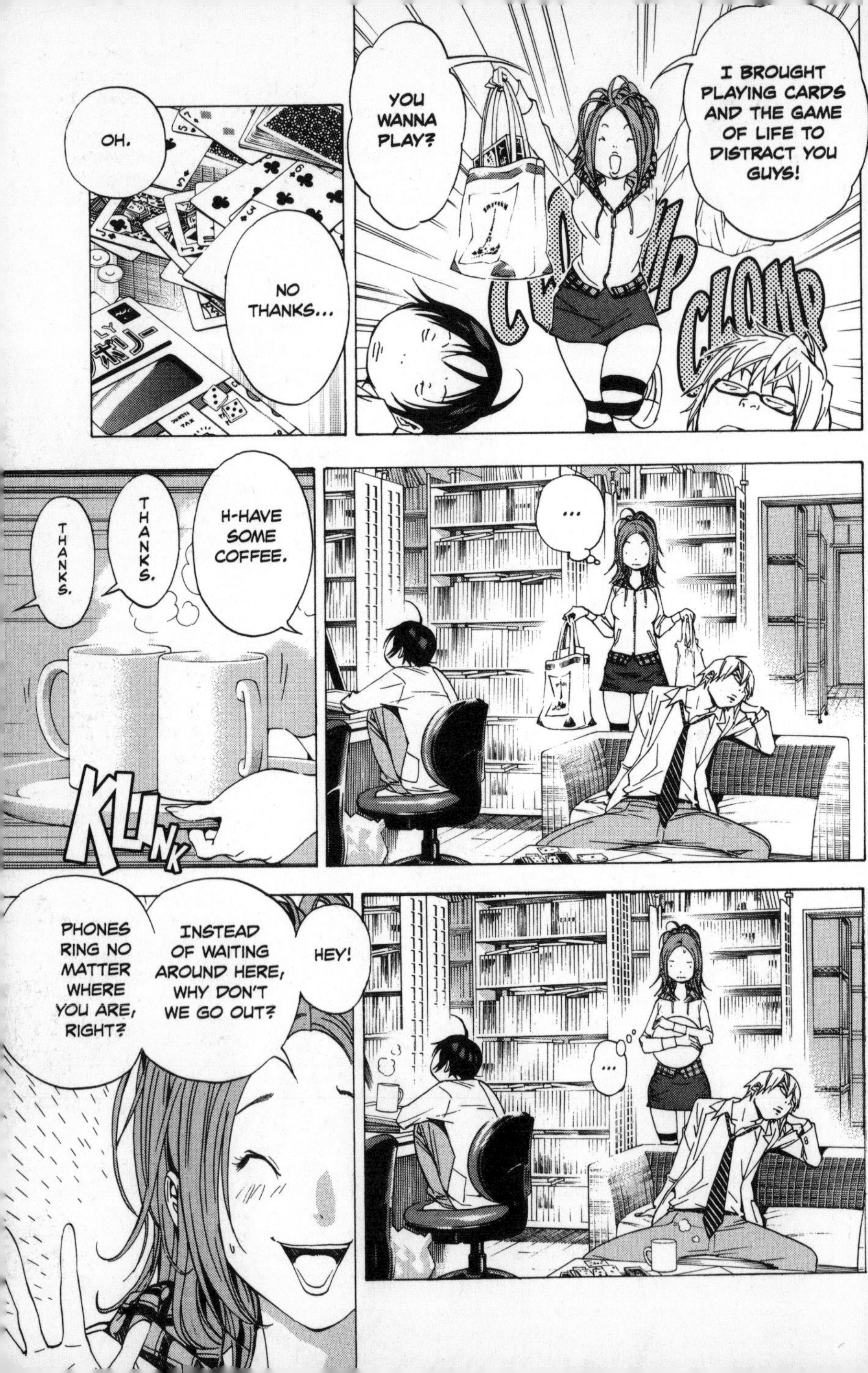
I BROUGHT PLAYING CARDS AND THE GAME OF LIFE TO DISTRACT YOU GUYS!
CLOMP
CLOMP
YOU WANNA PLAY?
NO THANKS...
OH.
...
H-HAVE SOME COFFEE.
THANKS.
THANKS.
KLUNK
...
HEY!
INSTEAD OF WAITING AROUND HERE, WHY DON'T WE GO OUT?
PHONES RING NO MATTER WHERE YOU ARE, RIGHT?

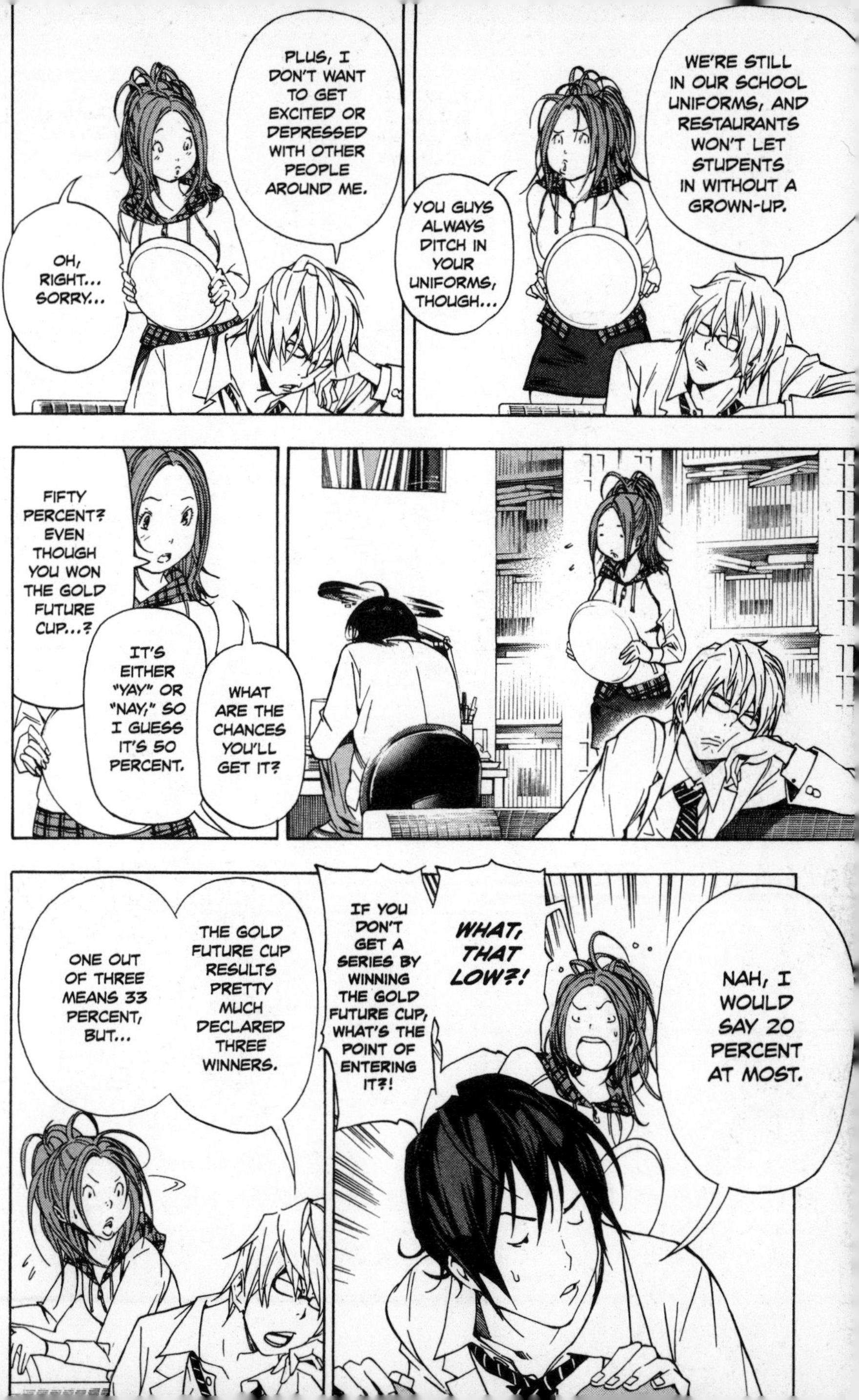
WE'RE STILL IN OUR SCHOOL UNIFORMS, AND RESTAURANTS WON'T LET STUDENTS IN WITHOUT A GROWN-UP.
YOU GUYS ALWAYS DITCH IN YOUR UNIFORMS, THOUGH...
PLUS, I DON'T WANT TO GET EXCITED OR DEPRESSED WITH OTHER PEOPLE AROUND ME.
OH, RIGHT... SORRY...
WHAT ARE THE CHANCES YOU'LL GET IT?
IT'S EITHER "YAY" OR "NAY," SO I GUESS IT'S 50 PERCENT.
FIFTY PERCENT? EVEN THOUGH YOU WON THE GOLD FUTURE CUP...?
NAH, I WOULD SAY 20 PERCENT AT MOST.
WHAT, THAT LOW?!
IF YOU DON'T GET A SERIES BY WINNING THE GOLD FUTURE CUP, WHAT'S THE POINT OF ENTERING IT?!
THE GOLD FUTURE CUP RESULTS PRETTY MUCH DECLARED THREE WINNERS.
ONE OUT OF THREE MEANS 33 PERCENT, BUT...

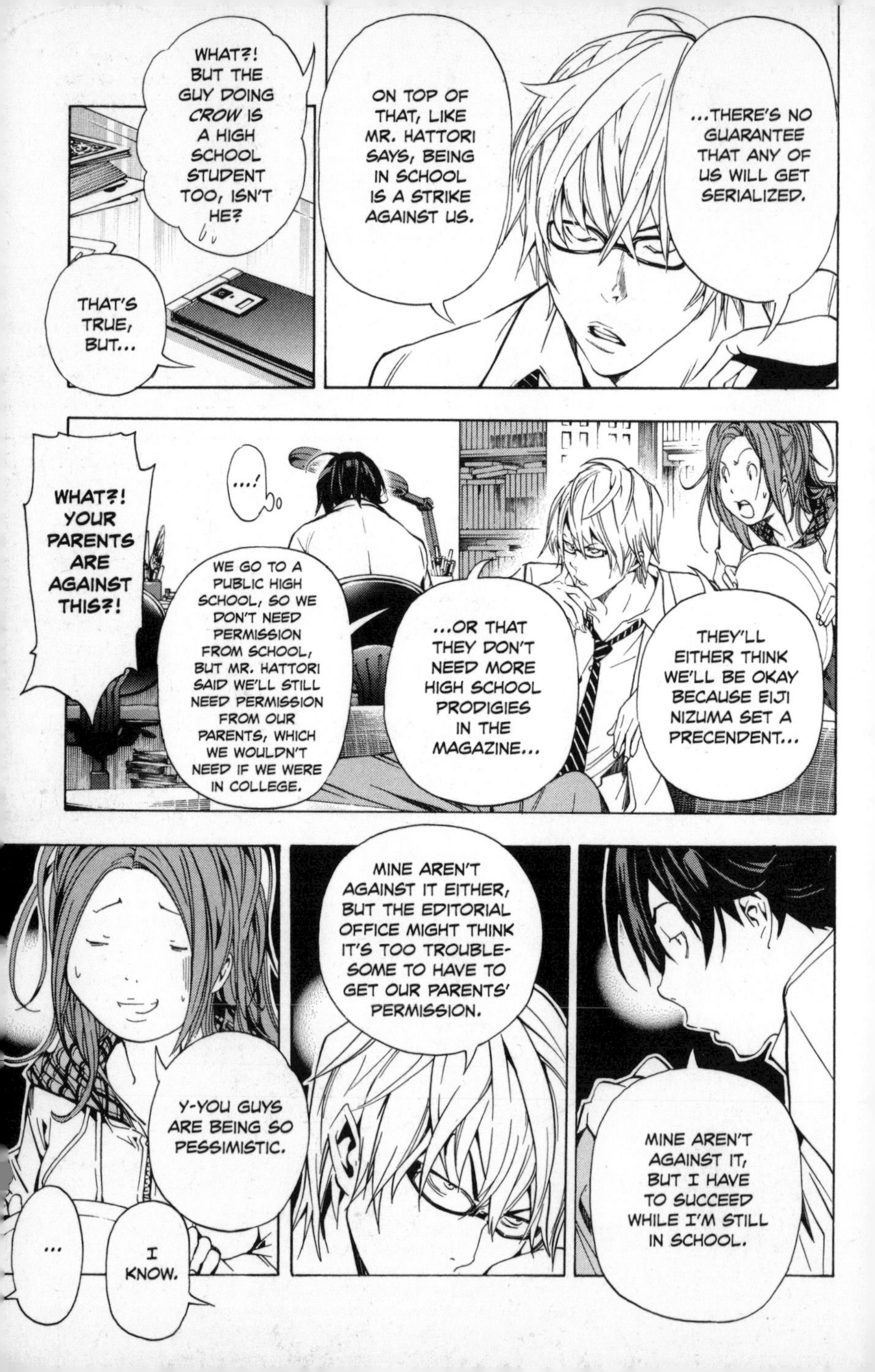
...THERE'S NO GUARANTEE THAT ANY OF US WILL GET SERIALIZED.
ON TOP OF THAT, LIKE MR. HATTORI SAYS, BEING IN SCHOOL IS A STRIKE AGAINST US.
WHAT?! BUT THE GUY DOING *CROW* IS A HIGH SCHOOL STUDENT TOO, ISN'T HE?
THAT'S TRUE, BUT...
THEY'LL EITHER THINK WE'LL BE OKAY BECAUSE EIJI NIZUMA SET A PRECENDENT...
...OR THAT THEY DON'T NEED MORE HIGH SCHOOL PRODIGIES IN THE MAGAZINE...
...!
WE GO TO A PUBLIC HIGH SCHOOL, SO WE DON'T NEED PERMISSION FROM SCHOOL, BUT MR. HATTORI SAID WE'LL STILL NEED PERMISSION FROM OUR PARENTS, WHICH WE WOULDN'T NEED IF WE WERE IN COLLEGE.
WHAT?! YOUR PARENTS ARE AGAINST THIS?!
MINE AREN'T AGAINST IT, BUT I HAVE TO SUCCEED WHILE I'M STILL IN SCHOOL.
MINE AREN'T AGAINST IT EITHER, BUT THE EDITORIAL OFFICE MIGHT THINK IT'S TOO TROUBLE-SOME TO HAVE TO GET OUR PARENTS' PERMISSION.
Y-YOU GUYS ARE BEING SO PESSIMISTIC.
I KNOW.
...

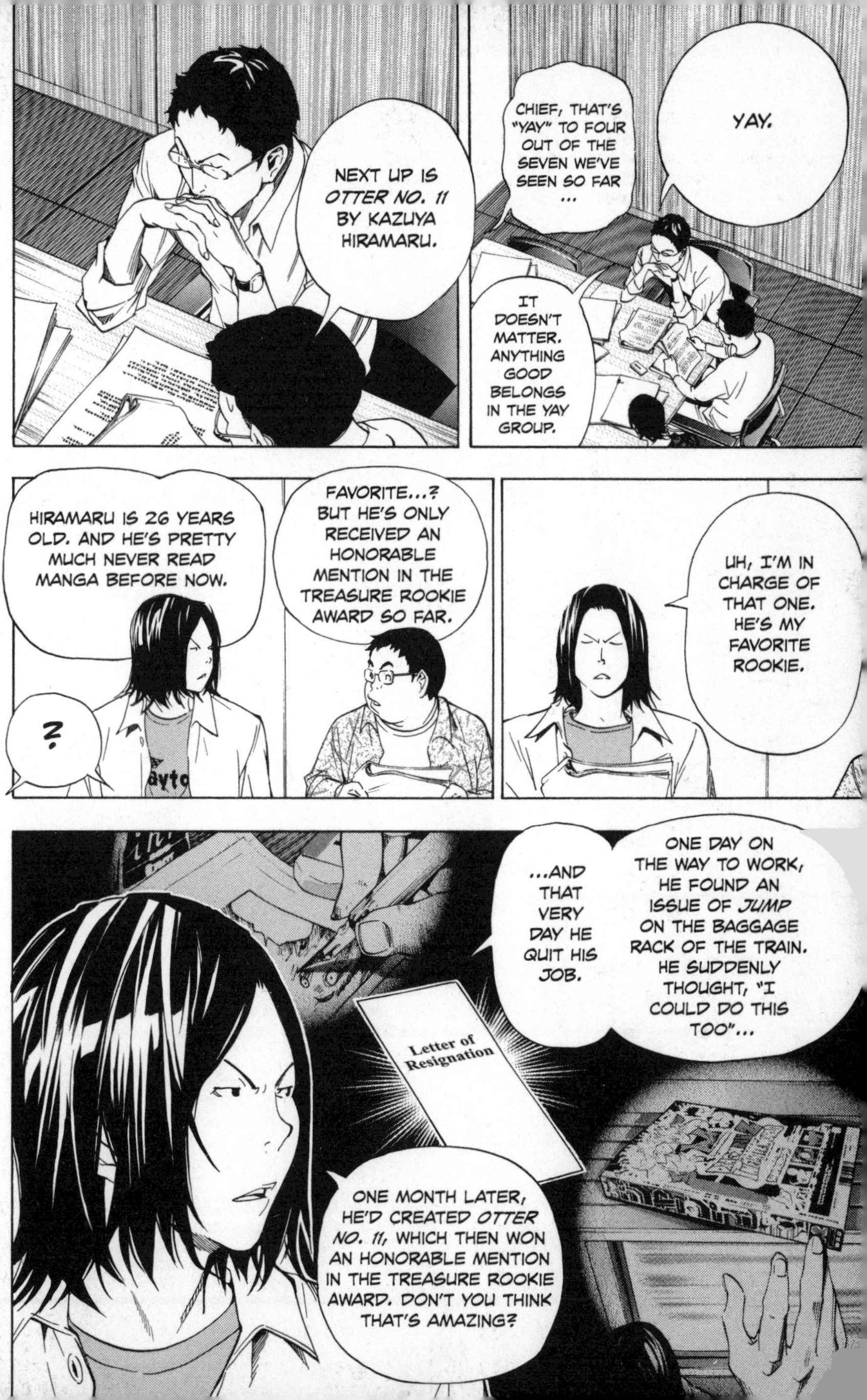
YAY.
CHIEF, THAT'S "YAY" TO FOUR OUT OF THE SEVEN WE'VE SEEN SO FAR ...
IT DOESN'T MATTER. ANYTHING GOOD BELONGS IN THE YAY GROUP.
NEXT UP IS *OTTER NO. 11* BY KAZUYA HIRAMARU.
UH, I'M IN CHARGE OF THAT ONE. HE'S MY FAVORITE ROOKIE.
FAVORITE...? BUT HE'S ONLY RECEIVED AN HONORABLE MENTION IN THE TREASURE ROOKIE AWARD SO FAR.
HIRAMARU IS 26 YEARS OLD. AND HE'S PRETTY MUCH NEVER READ MANGA BEFORE NOW.
?
ONE DAY ON THE WAY TO WORK, HE FOUND AN ISSUE OF *JUMP* ON THE BAGGAGE RACK OF THE TRAIN. HE SUDDENLY THOUGHT, "I COULD DO THIS TOO"...
...AND THAT VERY DAY HE QUIT HIS JOB.
Letter of Resignation
ONE MONTH LATER, HE'D CREATED *OTTER NO. 11,* WHICH THEN WON AN HONORABLE MENTION IN THE TREASURE ROOKIE AWARD. DON'T YOU THINK THAT'S AMAZING?

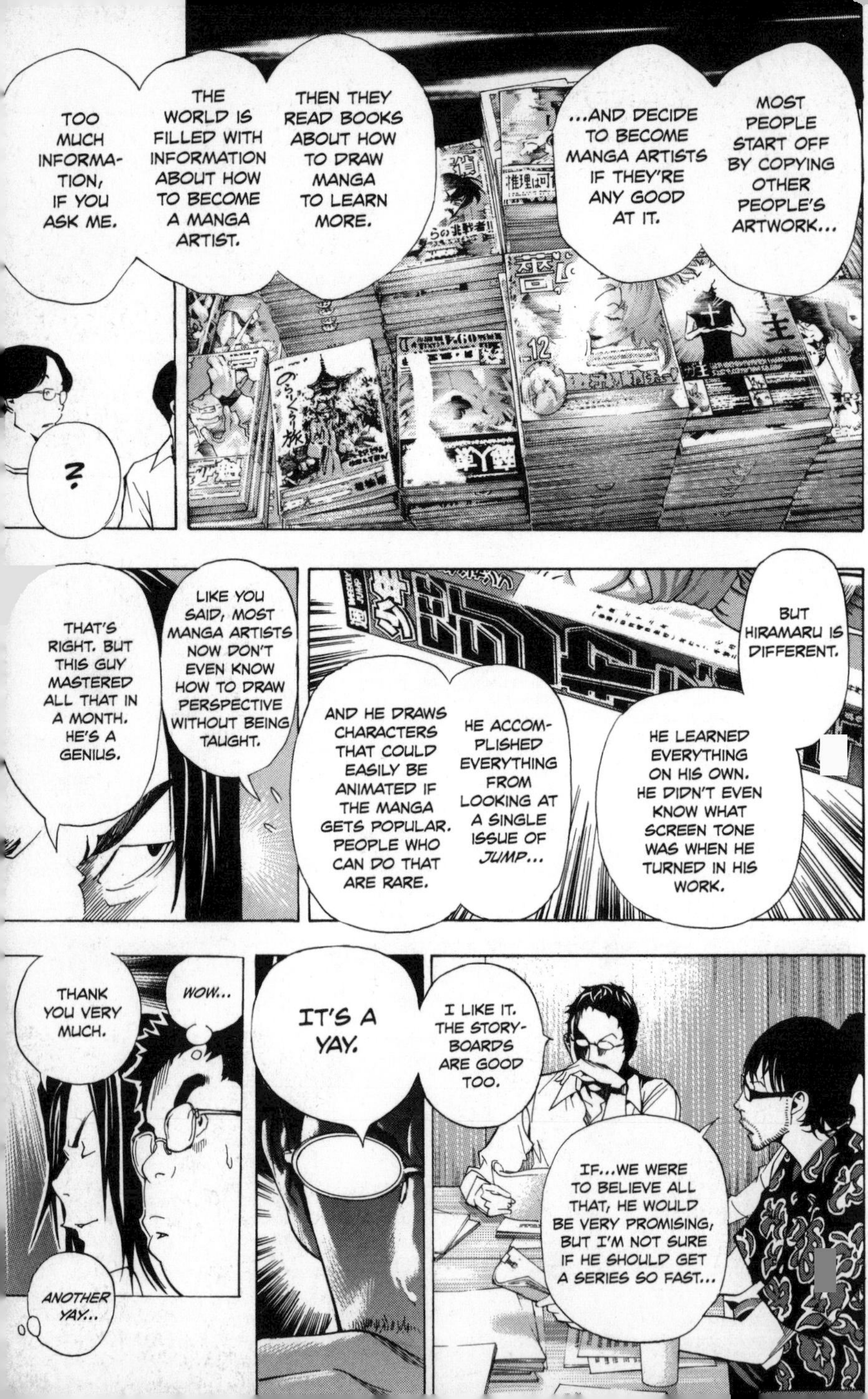
MOST PEOPLE START OFF BY COPYING OTHER PEOPLE'S ARTWORK...
...AND DECIDE TO BECOME MANGA ARTISTS IF THEY'RE ANY GOOD AT IT.
THEN THEY READ BOOKS ABOUT HOW TO DRAW MANGA TO LEARN MORE.
THE WORLD IS FILLED WITH INFORMATION ABOUT HOW TO BECOME A MANGA ARTIST.
TOO MUCH INFORMATION, IF YOU ASK ME.
?
BUT HIRAMARU IS DIFFERENT.
HE LEARNED EVERYTHING ON HIS OWN. HE DIDN'T EVEN KNOW WHAT SCREEN TONE WAS WHEN HE TURNED IN HIS WORK.
HE ACCOMPLISHED EVERYTHING FROM LOOKING AT A SINGLE ISSUE OF *JUMP*...
AND HE DRAWS CHARACTERS THAT COULD EASILY BE ANIMATED IF THE MANGA GETS POPULAR. PEOPLE WHO CAN DO THAT ARE RARE.
LIKE YOU SAID, MOST MANGA ARTISTS NOW DON'T EVEN KNOW HOW TO DRAW PERSPECTIVE WITHOUT BEING TAUGHT.
THAT'S RIGHT. BUT THIS GUY MASTERED ALL THAT IN A MONTH. HE'S A GENIUS.
I LIKE IT. THE STORYBOARDS ARE GOOD TOO.
IF...WE WERE TO BELIEVE ALL THAT, HE WOULD BE VERY PROMISING, BUT I'M NOT SURE IF HE SHOULD GET A SERIES SO FAST...
IT'S A YAY.
WOW...
THANK YOU VERY MUCH.
ANOTHER YAY...

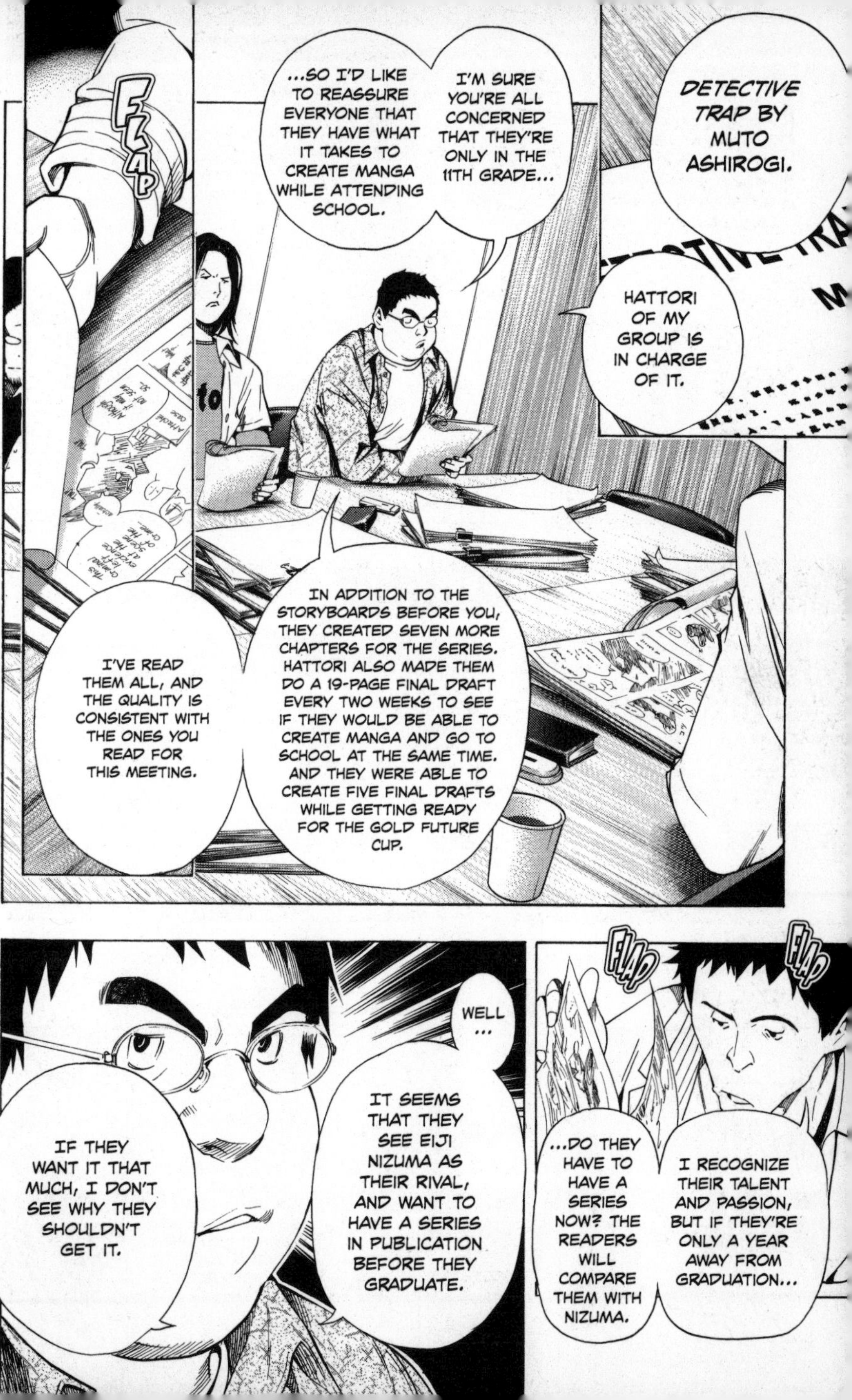
DETECTIVE TRAP BY MUTO ASHIROGI.
HATTORI OF MY GROUP IS IN CHARGE OF IT.
I'M SURE YOU'RE ALL CONCERNED THAT THEY'RE ONLY IN THE 11TH GRADE...
...SO I'D LIKE TO REASSURE EVERYONE THAT THEY HAVE WHAT IT TAKES TO CREATE MANGA WHILE ATTENDING SCHOOL.
IN ADDITION TO THE STORYBOARDS BEFORE YOU, THEY CREATED SEVEN MORE CHAPTERS FOR THE SERIES. HATTORI ALSO MADE THEM DO A 19-PAGE FINAL DRAFT EVERY TWO WEEKS TO SEE IF THEY WOULD BE ABLE TO CREATE MANGA AND GO TO SCHOOL AT THE SAME TIME. AND THEY WERE ABLE TO CREATE FIVE FINAL DRAFTS WHILE GETTING READY FOR THE GOLD FUTURE CUP.
I'VE READ THEM ALL, AND THE QUALITY IS CONSISTENT WITH THE ONES YOU READ FOR THIS MEETING.
FLAP
FLAP
FLAP
I RECOGNIZE THEIR TALENT AND PASSION, BUT IF THEY'RE ONLY A YEAR AWAY FROM GRADUATION...
...DO THEY HAVE TO HAVE A SERIES NOW? THE READERS WILL COMPARE THEM WITH NIZUMA.
WELL...
IT SEEMS THAT THEY SEE EIJI NIZUMA AS THEIR RIVAL, AND WANT TO HAVE A SERIES IN PUBLICATION BEFORE THEY GRADUATE.
IF THEY WANT IT THAT MUCH, I DON'T SEE WHY THEY SHOULDN'T GET IT.

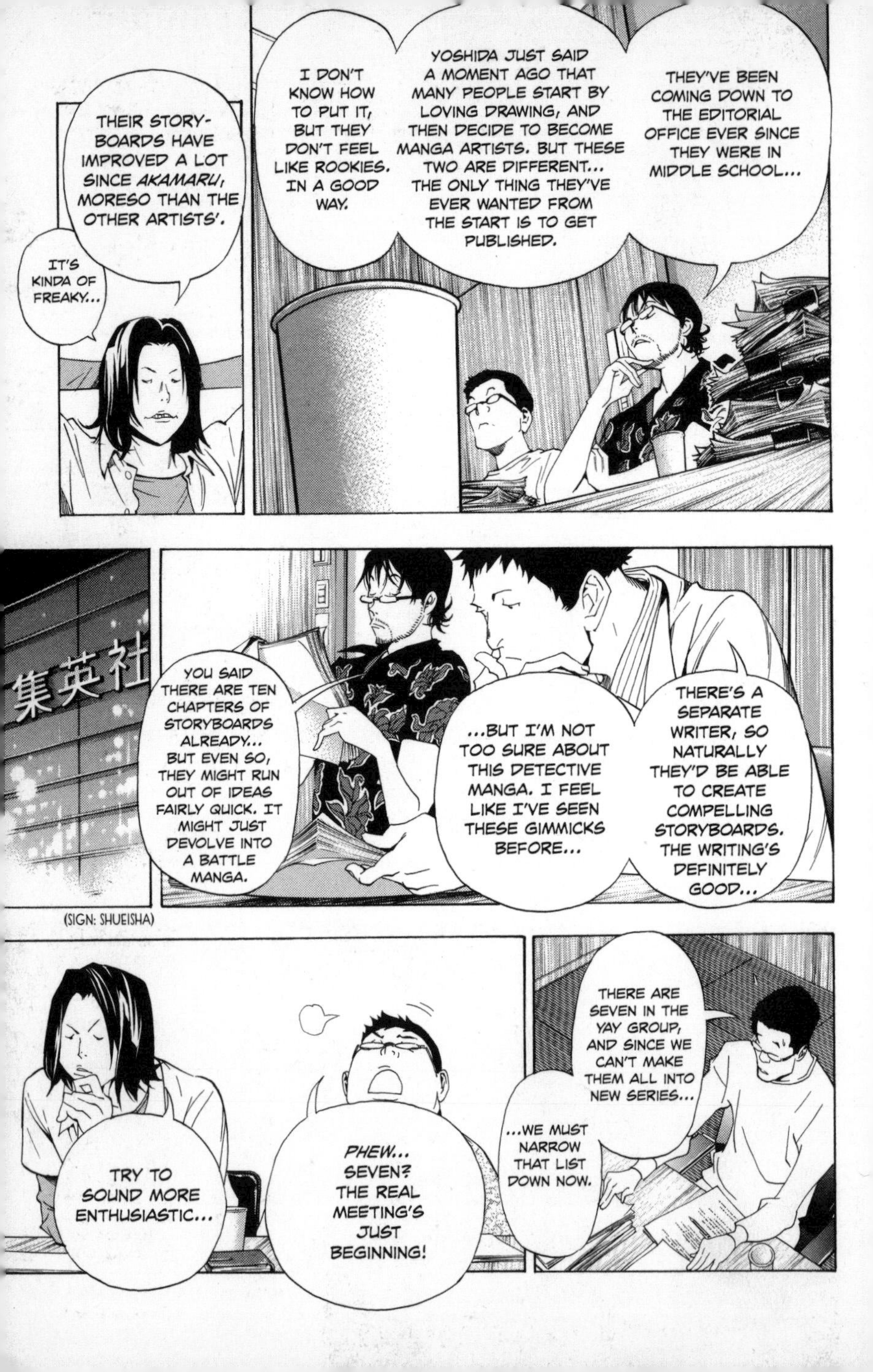

THEY'VE BEEN COMING DOWN TO THE EDITORIAL OFFICE EVER SINCE THEY WERE IN MIDDLE SCHOOL...
YOSHIDA JUST SAID A MOMENT AGO THAT MANY PEOPLE START BY LOVING DRAWING, AND THEN DECIDE TO BECOME MANGA ARTISTS. BUT THESE TWO ARE DIFFERENT... THE ONLY THING THEY'VE EVER WANTED FROM THE START IS TO GET PUBLISHED.
I DON'T KNOW HOW TO PUT IT, BUT THEY DON'T FEEL LIKE ROOKIES. IN A GOOD WAY.
THEIR STORY-BOARDS HAVE IMPROVED A LOT SINCE *AKAMARU*, MORESO THAN THE OTHER ARTISTS'.
IT'S KINDA OF FREAKY...
THERE'S A SEPARATE WRITER, SO NATURALLY THEY'D BE ABLE TO CREATE COMPELLING STORYBOARDS. THE WRITING'S DEFINITELY GOOD...
...BUT I'M NOT TOO SURE ABOUT THIS DETECTIVE MANGA. I FEEL LIKE I'VE SEEN THESE GIMMICKS BEFORE...
YOU SAID THERE ARE TEN CHAPTERS OF STORYBOARDS ALREADY... BUT EVEN SO, THEY MIGHT RUN OUT OF IDEAS FAIRLY QUICK. IT MIGHT JUST DEVOLVE INTO A BATTLE MANGA.
集英社
THERE ARE SEVEN IN THE YAY GROUP, AND SINCE WE CAN'T MAKE THEM ALL INTO NEW SERIES...
...WE MUST NARROW THAT LIST DOWN NOW.
PHEW... SEVEN? THE REAL MEETING'S JUST BEGINNING!
TRY TO SOUND MORE ENTHUSIASTIC...

(SIGN: SHUEISHA)

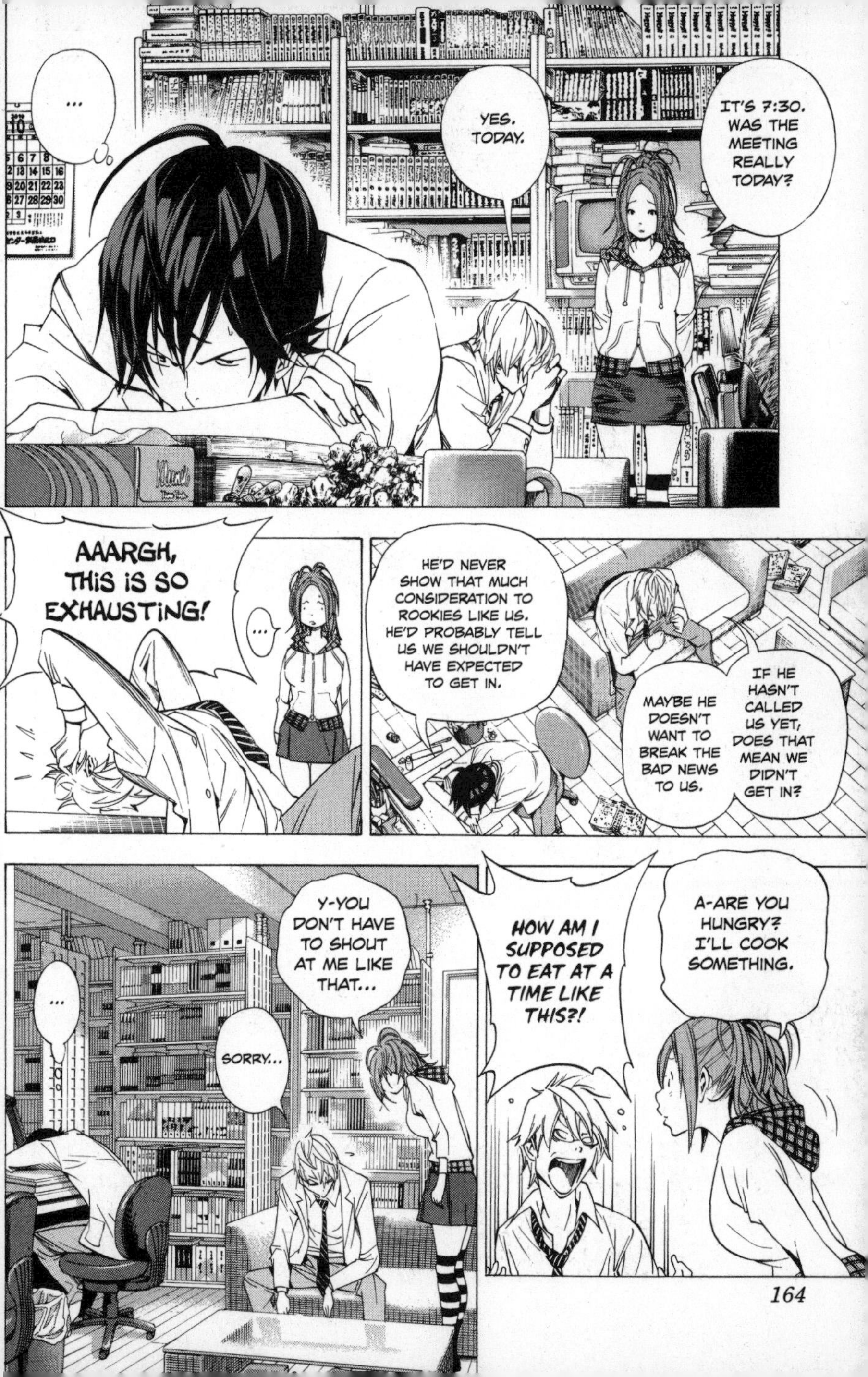
IT'S 7:30. WAS THE MEETING REALLY TODAY?
YES. TODAY.
...
IF HE HASN'T CALLED US YET, DOES THAT MEAN WE DIDN'T GET IN?
MAYBE HE DOESN'T WANT TO BREAK THE BAD NEWS TO US.
HE'D NEVER SHOW THAT MUCH CONSIDERATION TO ROOKIES LIKE US. HE'D PROBABLY TELL US WE SHOULDN'T HAVE EXPECTED TO GET IN.
AAARGH, THIS IS SO EXHAUSTING!
...
A-ARE YOU HUNGRY? I'LL COOK SOMETHING.
HOW AM I SUPPOSED TO EAT AT A TIME LIKE THIS?!
Y-YOU DON'T HAVE TO SHOUT AT ME LIKE THAT...
SORRY...
...

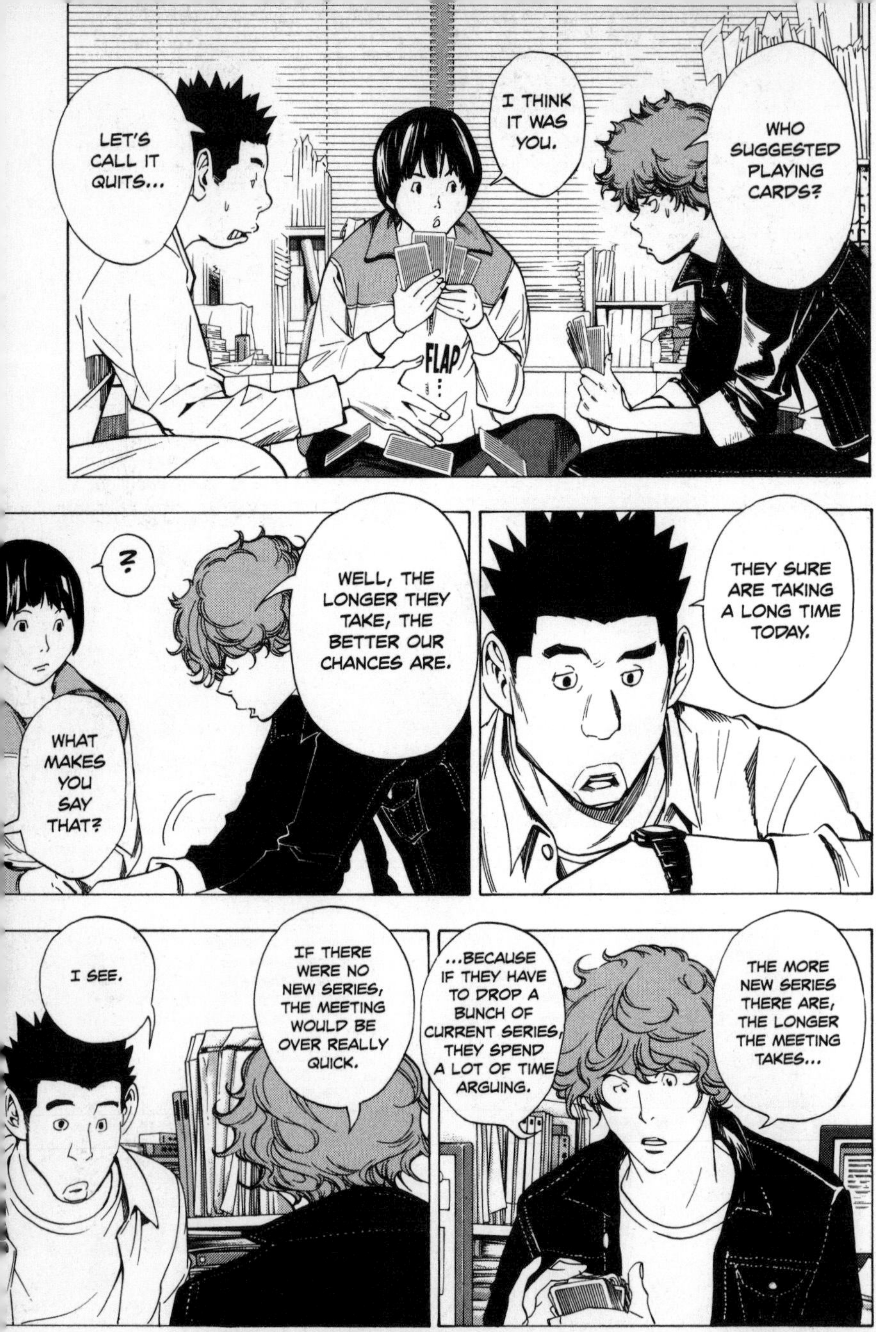
WHO SUGGESTED PLAYING CARDS?
I THINK IT WAS YOU.
LET'S CALL IT QUITS...
FLAP
THEY SURE ARE TAKING A LONG TIME TODAY.
WELL, THE LONGER THEY TAKE, THE BETTER OUR CHANCES ARE.
?
WHAT MAKES YOU SAY THAT?
THE MORE NEW SERIES THERE ARE, THE LONGER THE MEETING TAKES...
...BECAUSE IF THEY HAVE TO DROP A BUNCH OF CURRENT SERIES, THEY SPEND A LOT OF TIME ARGUING.
IF THERE WERE NO NEW SERIES, THE MEETING WOULD BE OVER REALLY QUICK.
I SEE.

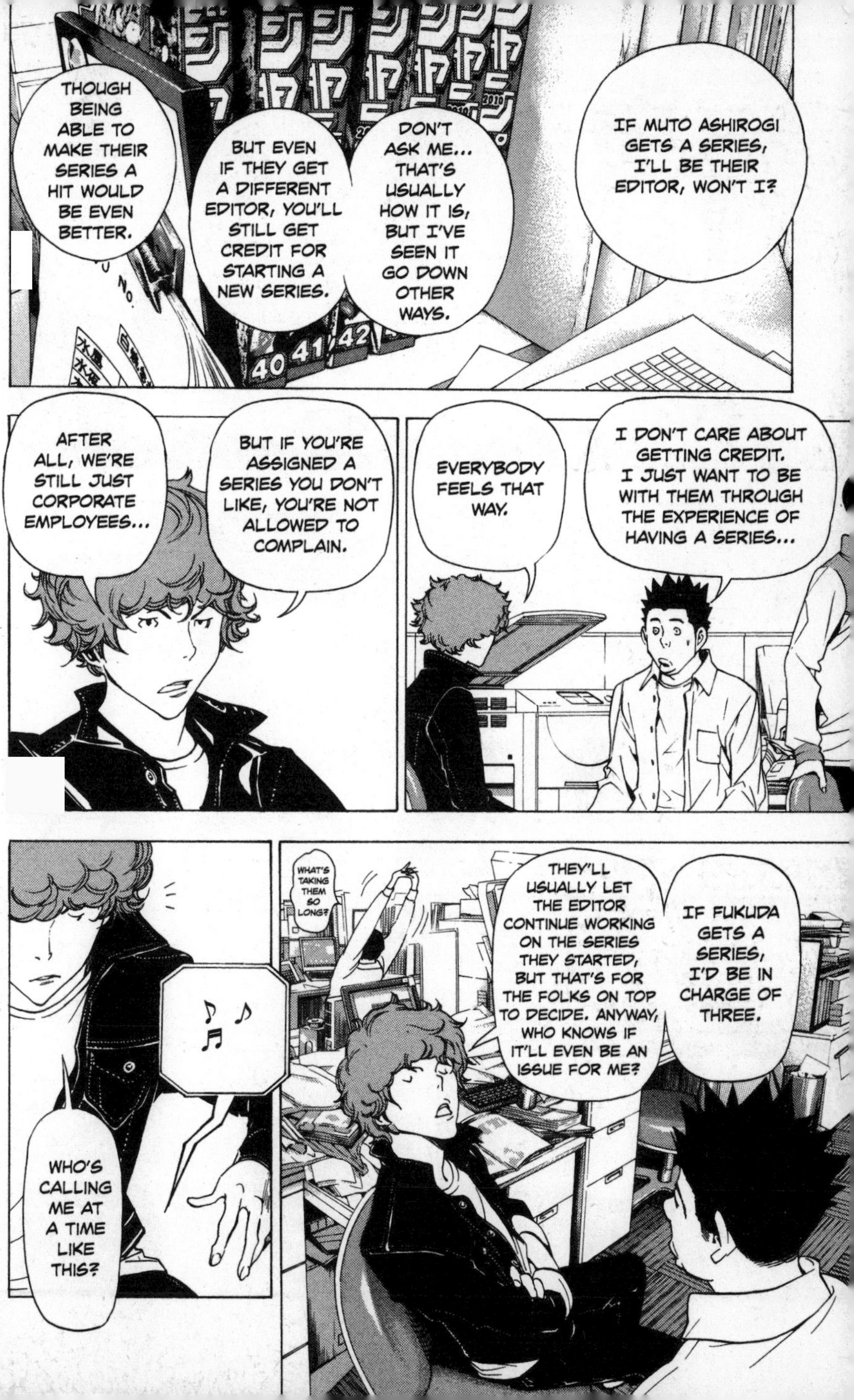
IF MUTO ASHIROGI GETS A SERIES, I'LL BE THEIR EDITOR, WON'T I?
DON'T ASK ME... THAT'S USUALLY HOW IT IS, BUT I'VE SEEN IT GO DOWN OTHER WAYS.
BUT EVEN IF THEY GET A DIFFERENT EDITOR, YOU'LL STILL GET CREDIT FOR STARTING A NEW SERIES.
THOUGH BEING ABLE TO MAKE THEIR SERIES A HIT WOULD BE EVEN BETTER.
I DON'T CARE ABOUT GETTING CREDIT. I JUST WANT TO BE WITH THEM THROUGH THE EXPERIENCE OF HAVING A SERIES...
EVERYBODY FEELS THAT WAY.
BUT IF YOU'RE ASSIGNED A SERIES YOU DON'T LIKE, YOU'RE NOT ALLOWED TO COMPLAIN.
AFTER ALL, WE'RE STILL JUST CORPORATE EMPLOYEES...
IF FUKUDA GETS A SERIES, I'D BE IN CHARGE OF THREE.
THEY'LL USUALLY LET THE EDITOR CONTINUE WORKING ON THE SERIES THEY STARTED, BUT THAT'S FOR THE FOLKS ON TOP TO DECIDE. ANYWAY, WHO KNOWS IF IT'LL EVEN BE AN ISSUE FOR ME?
WHAT'S TAKING THEM SO LONG?
♪ ♪ ♫
WHO'S CALLING ME AT A TIME LIKE THIS?

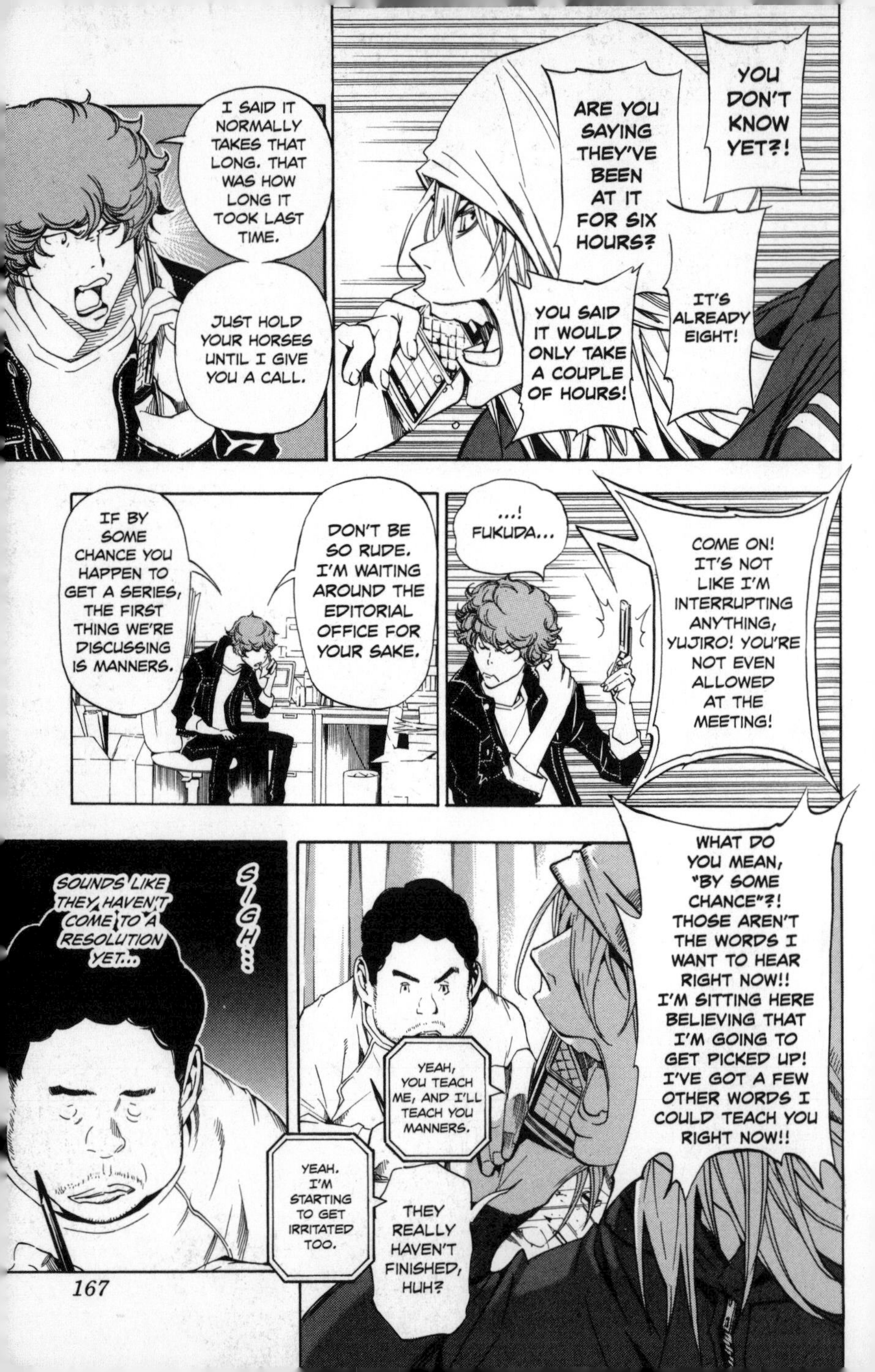
YOU DON'T KNOW YET?!
ARE YOU SAYING THEY'VE BEEN AT IT FOR SIX HOURS?
IT'S ALREADY EIGHT!
YOU SAID IT WOULD ONLY TAKE A COUPLE OF HOURS!
I SAID IT NORMALLY TAKES THAT LONG. THAT WAS HOW LONG IT TOOK LAST TIME.
JUST HOLD YOUR HORSES UNTIL I GIVE YOU A CALL.
COME ON! IT'S NOT LIKE I'M INTERRUPTING ANYTHING, YUJIRO! YOU'RE NOT EVEN ALLOWED AT THE MEETING!
...! FUKUDA...
DON'T BE SO RUDE. I'M WAITING AROUND THE EDITORIAL OFFICE FOR YOUR SAKE.
IF BY SOME CHANCE YOU HAPPEN TO GET A SERIES, THE FIRST THING WE'RE DISCUSSING IS MANNERS.
WHAT DO YOU MEAN, "BY SOME CHANCE"?! THOSE AREN'T THE WORDS I WANT TO HEAR RIGHT NOW!! I'M SITTING HERE BELIEVING THAT I'M GOING TO GET PICKED UP! I'VE GOT A FEW OTHER WORDS I COULD TEACH YOU RIGHT NOW!!
YEAH, YOU TEACH ME, AND I'LL TEACH YOU MANNERS.
THEY REALLY HAVEN'T FINISHED, HUH?
YEAH. I'M STARTING TO GET IRRITATED TOO.
SIGH...
SOUNDS LIKE THEY HAVEN'T COME TO A RESOLUTION YET...

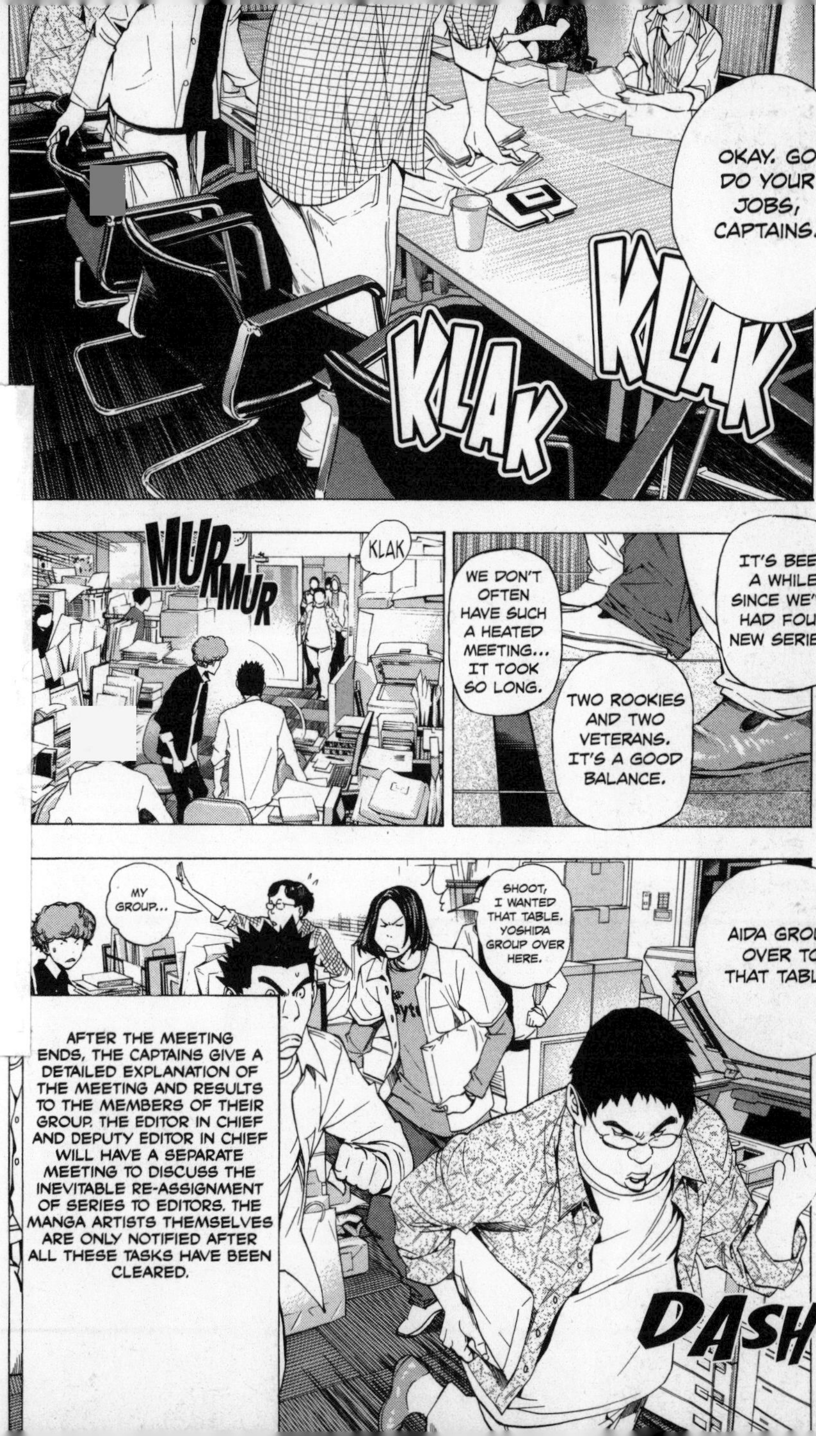
OKAY. GO DO YOUR JOBS, CAPTAINS.
KLAK
KLAK
IT'S BEEN A WHILE SINCE WE'VE HAD FOUR NEW SERIES.
WE DON'T OFTEN HAVE SUCH A HEATED MEETING... IT TOOK SO LONG.
TWO ROOKIES AND TWO VETERANS. IT'S A GOOD BALANCE.
KLAK
MURMUR
AIDA GROUP OVER TO THAT TABLE.
SHOOT, I WANTED THAT TABLE. YOSHIDA GROUP OVER HERE.
MY GROUP...
AFTER THE MEETING ENDS, THE CAPTAINS GIVE A DETAILED EXPLANATION OF THE MEETING AND RESULTS TO THE MEMBERS OF THEIR GROUP. THE EDITOR IN CHIEF AND DEPUTY EDITOR IN CHIEF WILL HAVE A SEPARATE MEETING TO DISCUSS THE INEVITABLE RE-ASSIGNMENT OF SERIES TO EDITORS. THE MANGA ARTISTS THEMSELVES ARE ONLY NOTIFIED AFTER ALL THESE TASKS HAVE BEEN CLEARED.
DASH

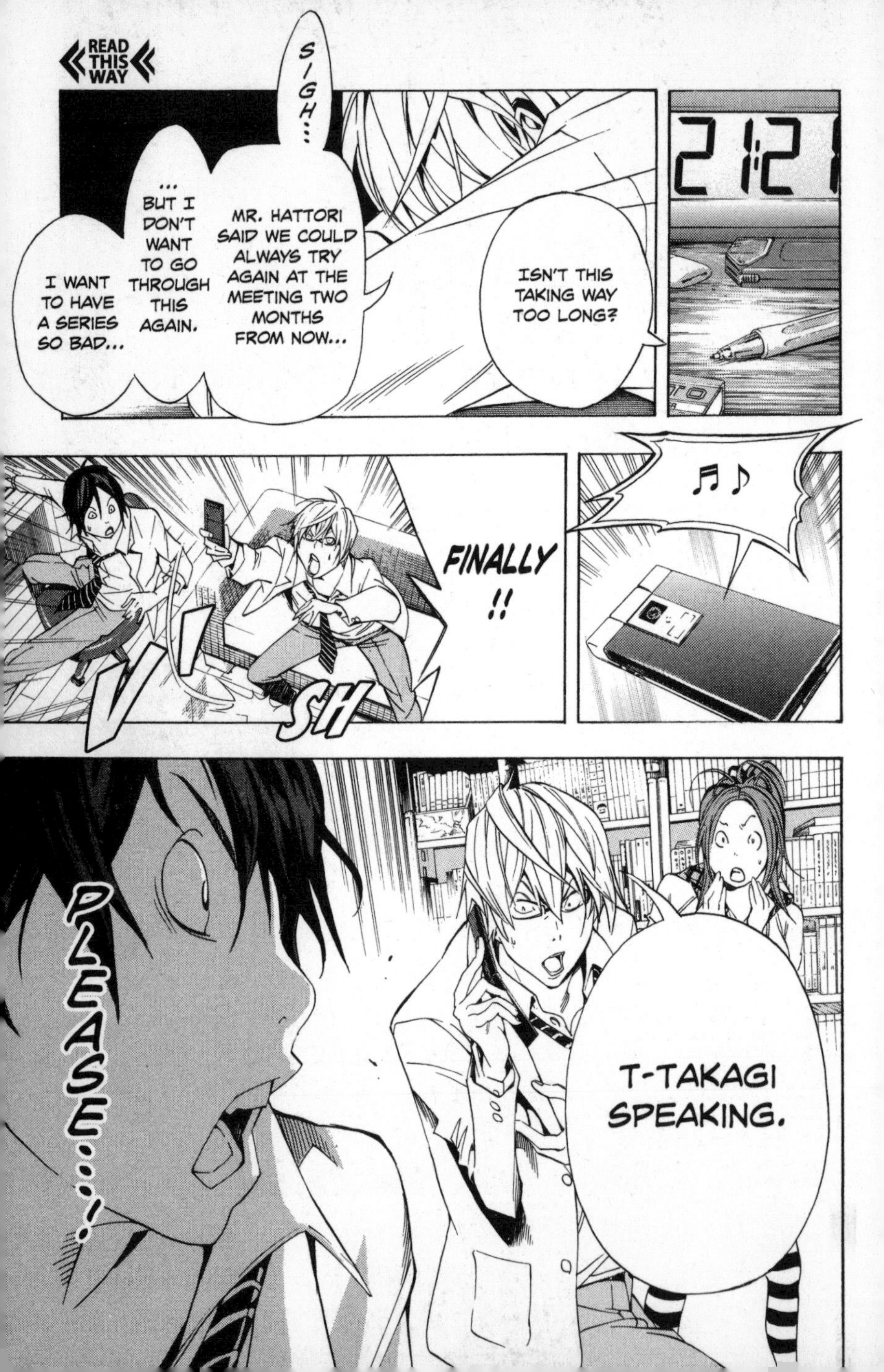
READ THIS WAY
21:21
ISN'T THIS TAKING WAY TOO LONG?
SIGH...
MR. HATTORI SAID WE COULD ALWAYS TRY AGAIN AT THE MEETING TWO MONTHS FROM NOW...
... BUT I DON'T WANT TO GO THROUGH THIS AGAIN.
I WANT TO HAVE A SERIES SO BAD...
♬♪
FINALLY!!
VSH
T-TAKAGI SPEAKING.
PLEASE...!

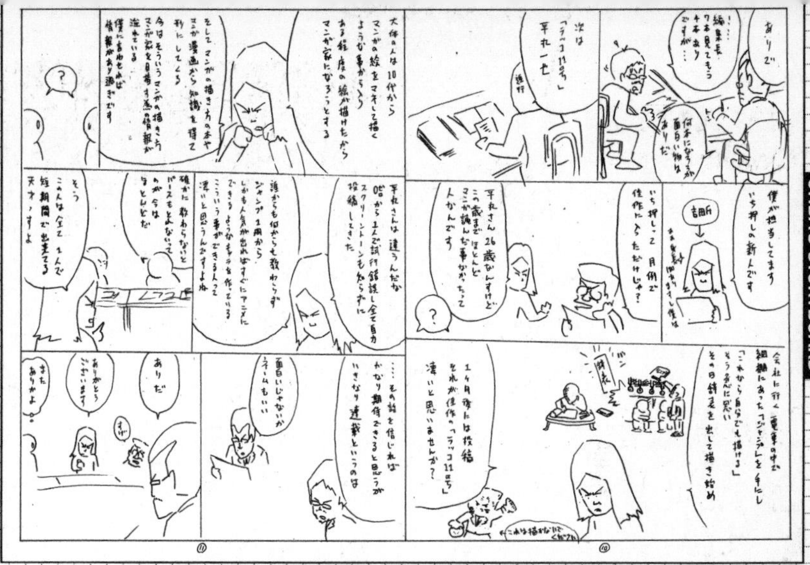
OHBA'S STORYBOARD
ありだ
編集長 7本見てもう4本ありですが……
何本になろうが 面白い物はありだ
次は「ラッコ11号」 平丸一也
僕が担当してます いち押しの新人です
吉田
いち押しって 月例で佳作に入っただけじゃ?
平丸さん 26歳なんですけど この歳まで ほとんどマンガ読んだ事なかったって人なんです
?
会社に行く電車の中で 網棚にあった「ジャンプ」を手にし これなら自分でも描けると思い その日辞表を出して描き始め
辞表
1ヶ月後には投稿 それが佳作の「ラッコ11号」
凄いと思いませんか?
10
大体の人は10代から マンガの絵をマネして描くような事から ある程度の絵が描けたから マンガ家になろうとする
そして マンガの描き方の本や 漫画から知識を得て 形にしてくる
今はそういうマンガの描き方 マンガ家を目指す為の情報が 溢れている
僕に言わせれば 情報があり過ぎです
?
平丸さんは違うんだな 0から1人で試行錯誤し全て自力 スクリーントーンも知らずに投稿してきた
誰からも何からも教わらず ジャンプ1冊から しかも人気が出ればすぐにアニメにできるようなものを作っている こういう事ができるんって 凄いと思うんですよね
確かに 教わらないとパースもとれないのが今はほとんどだ
そう こんな全て1人で 短期間で出来てる 天才ですよ
……その話を信じれば かなり期待できると思うが いきなり連載というのは
面白いじゃないか ネームもいい
ありだ
ありがとうございます
まじ
またありかよ。
11

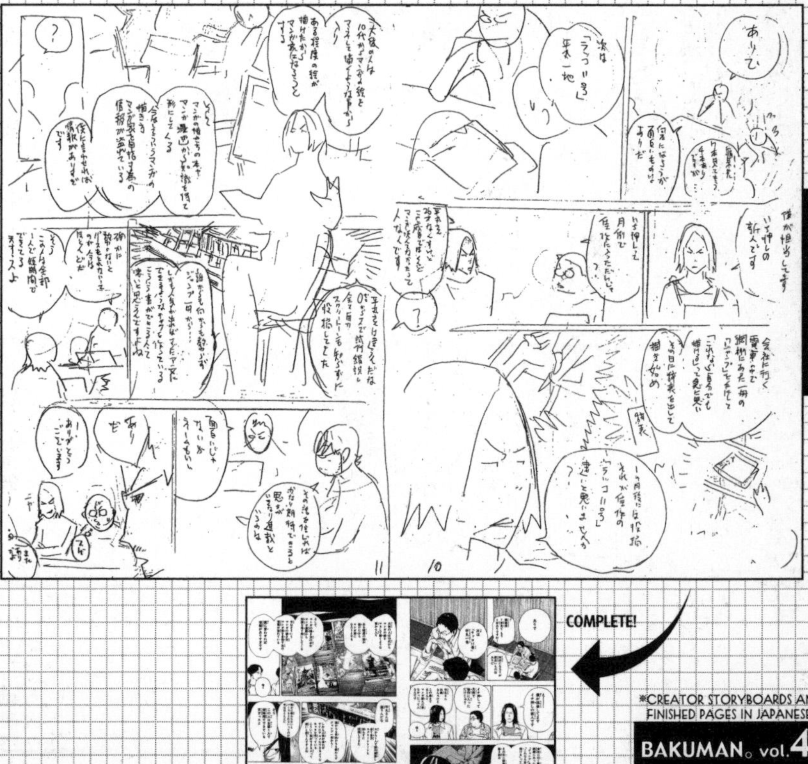
OBATA'S STORYBOARD
ありで
次は「ラッコ11号」 平丸一也
?
辞表
11
10

COMPLETE!

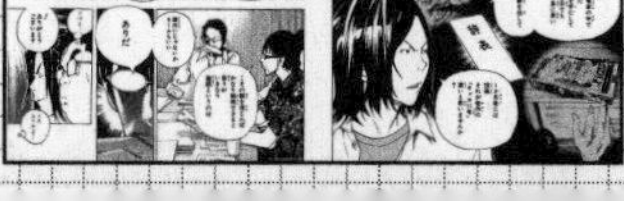

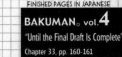

※CREATOR STORYBOARDS AND FINISHED PAGES IN JAPANESE

BAKUMAN。 vol.4

"Until the Final Draft Is Complete"

Chapter 33, pp. 160-161

CHAPTER 34 PURSUER AND PURSUED

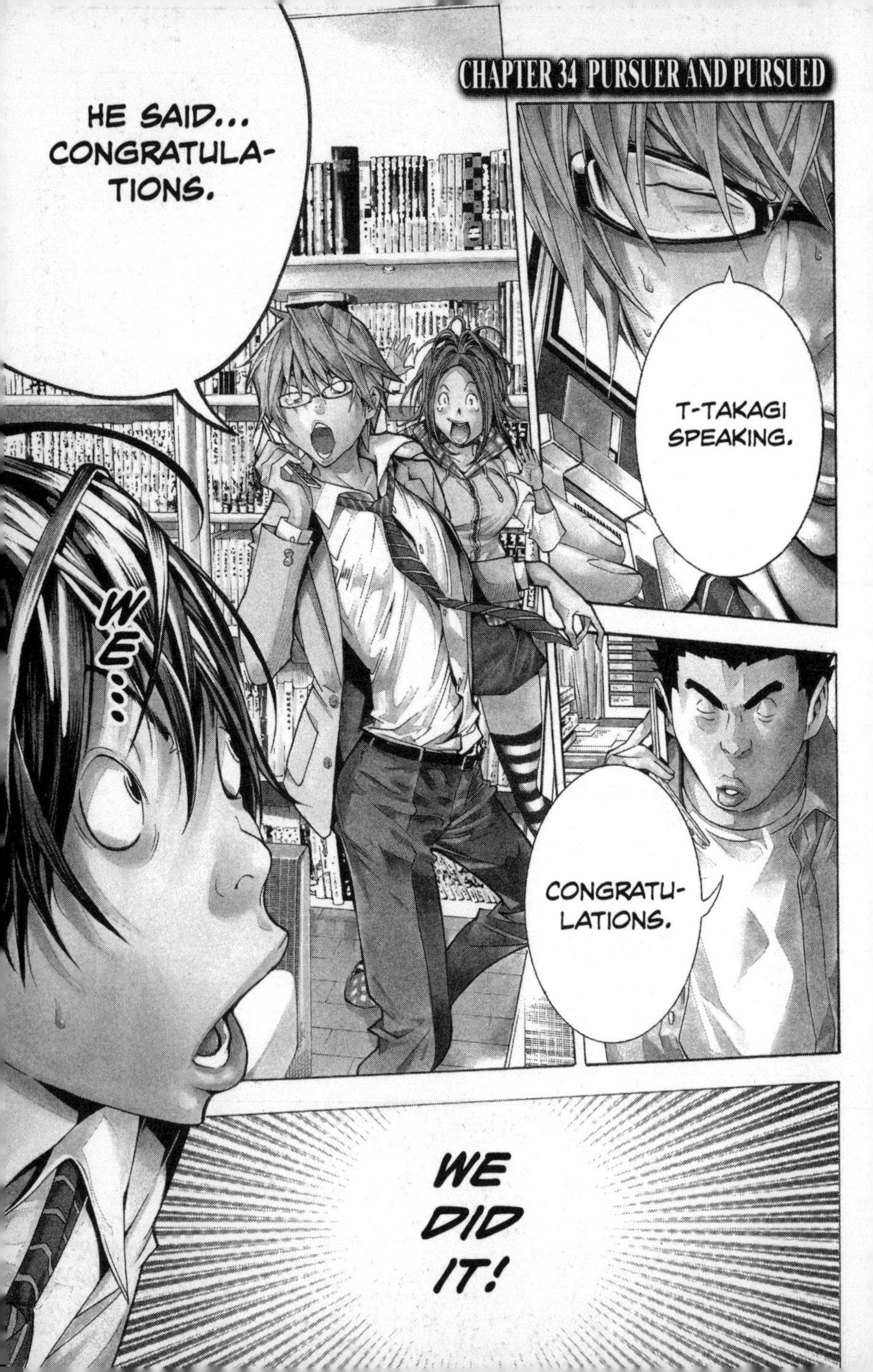
T-TAKAGI SPEAKING.
CONGRATU-LATIONS.
HE SAID... CONGRATULA-TIONS.
WE...
WE DID IT!

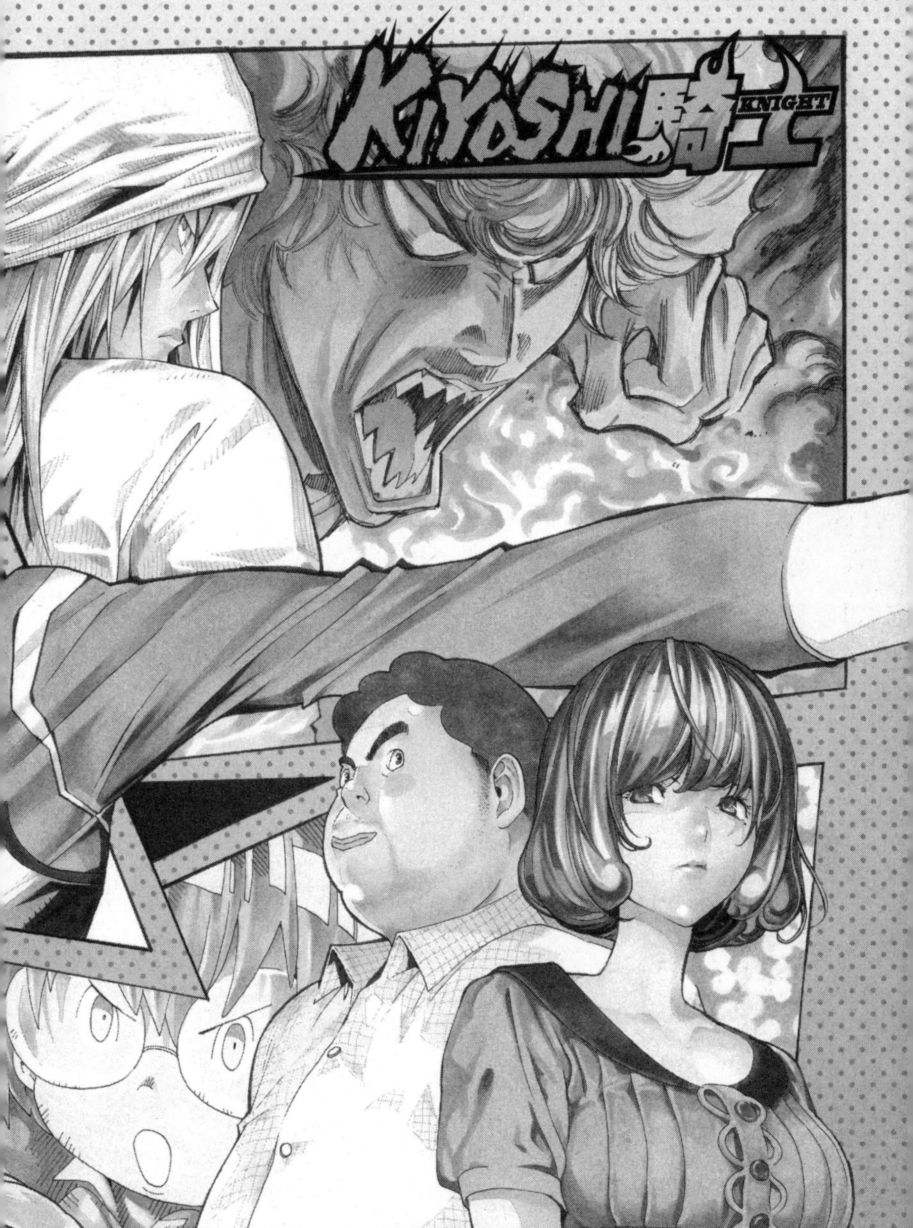
KIYOSHI 騎士
KNIGHT

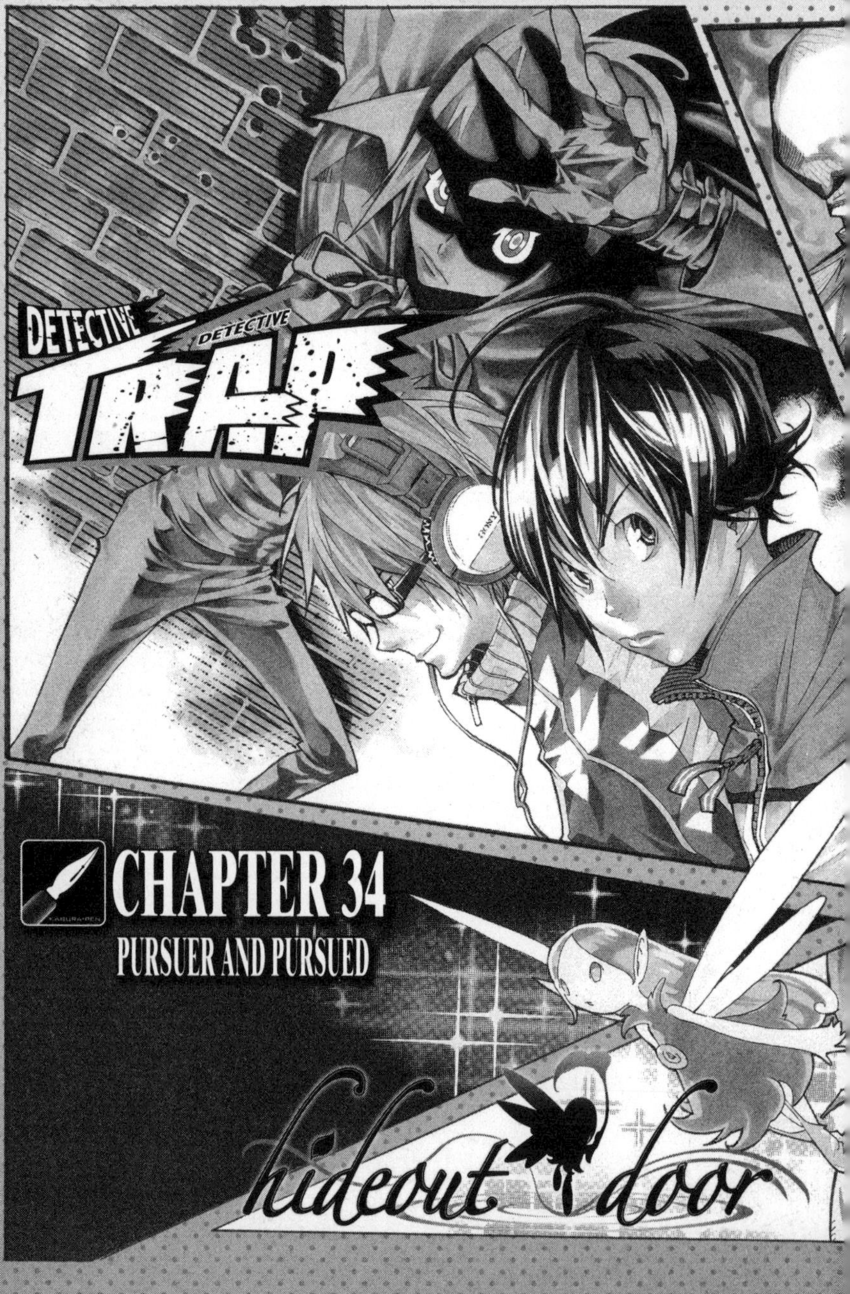
DETECTIVE
DETECTIVE
TRAP
CHAPTER 34
PURSUER AND PURSUED
hideout door

BAKUMAN。

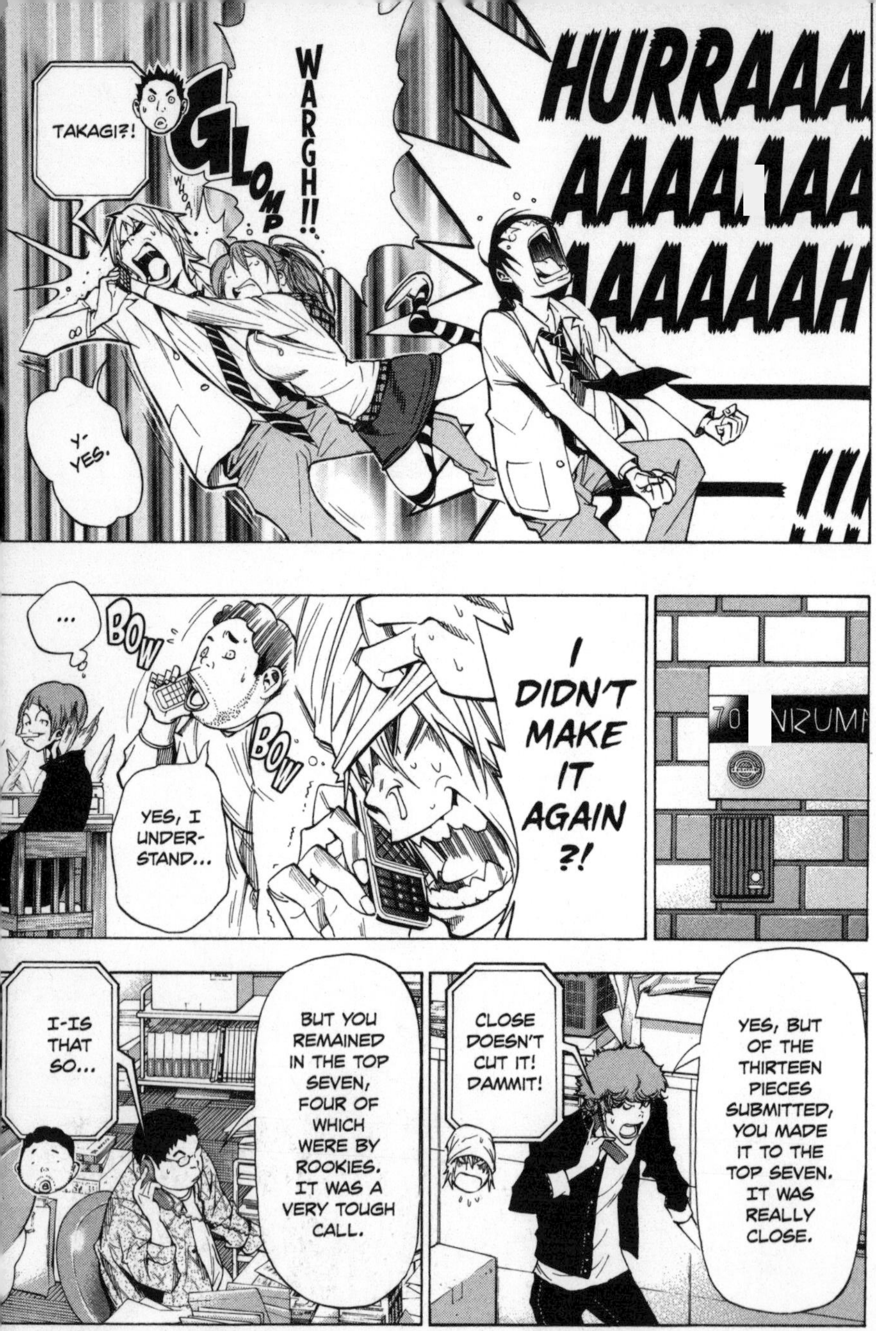
HURRAAA
AAAAAAA
AAAAAAH
!!
WARGH!!
GLOMP
TAKAGI?!
WHOA
Y-YES.
70 NIZUMA
I DIDN'T MAKE IT AGAIN?!
BOW
BOW
YES, I UNDERSTAND...
...
YES, BUT OF THE THIRTEEN PIECES SUBMITTED, YOU MADE IT TO THE TOP SEVEN. IT WAS REALLY CLOSE.
CLOSE DOESN'T CUT IT! DAMMIT!
BUT YOU REMAINED IN THE TOP SEVEN, FOUR OF WHICH WERE BY ROOKIES. IT WAS A VERY TOUGH CALL.
I-IS THAT SO...

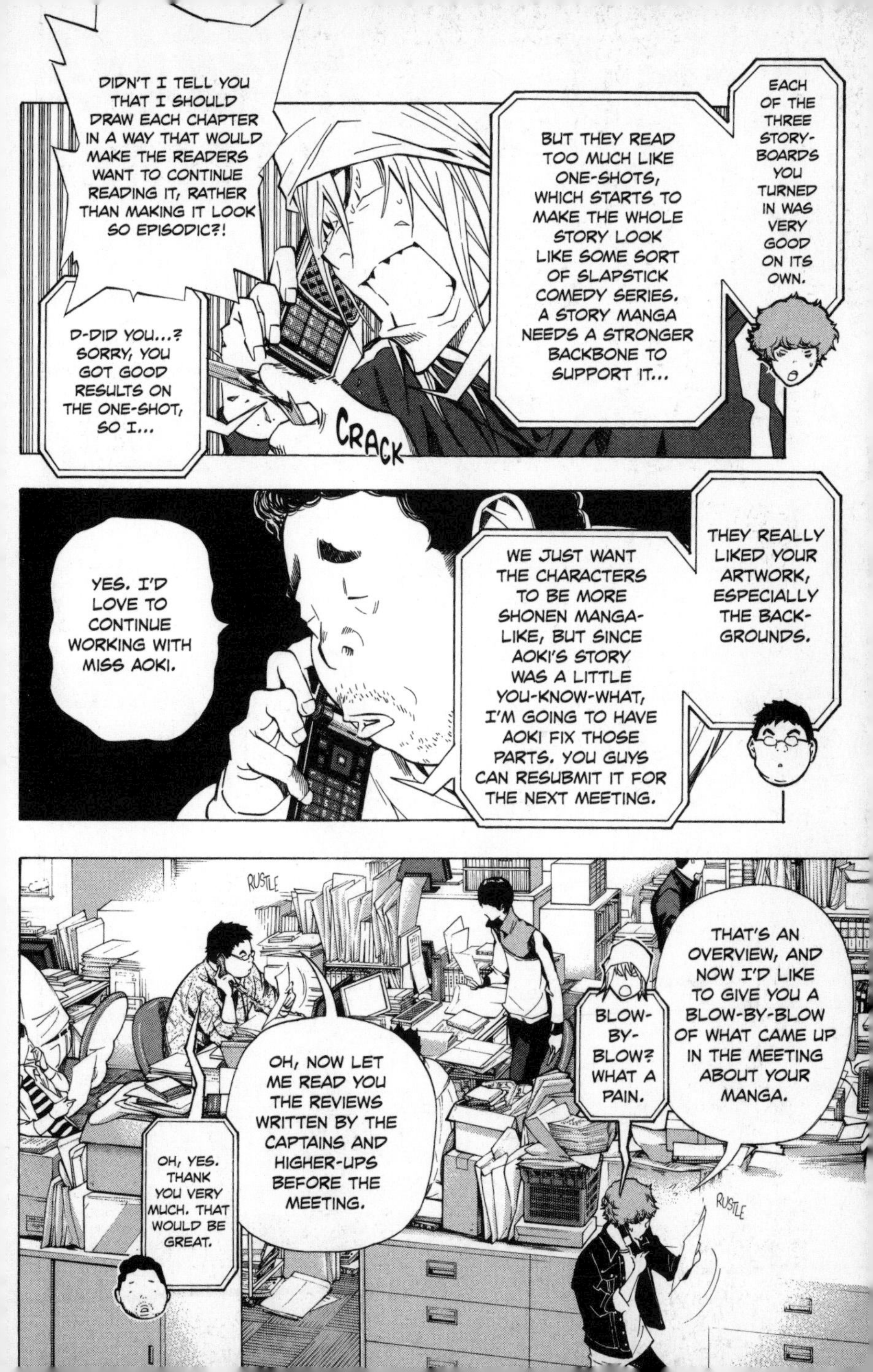
EACH OF THE THREE STORY-BOARDS YOU TURNED IN WAS VERY GOOD ON ITS OWN.
BUT THEY READ TOO MUCH LIKE ONE-SHOTS, WHICH STARTS TO MAKE THE WHOLE STORY LOOK LIKE SOME SORT OF SLAPSTICK COMEDY SERIES. A STORY MANGA NEEDS A STRONGER BACKBONE TO SUPPORT IT...
DIDN'T I TELL YOU THAT I SHOULD DRAW EACH CHAPTER IN A WAY THAT WOULD MAKE THE READERS WANT TO CONTINUE READING IT, RATHER THAN MAKING IT LOOK SO EPISODIC?!
D-DID YOU...? SORRY, YOU GOT GOOD RESULTS ON THE ONE-SHOT, SO I...
CRACK
THEY REALLY LIKED YOUR ARTWORK, ESPECIALLY THE BACK-GROUNDS.
WE JUST WANT THE CHARACTERS TO BE MORE SHONEN MANGA-LIKE, BUT SINCE AOKI'S STORY WAS A LITTLE YOU-KNOW-WHAT, I'M GOING TO HAVE AOKI FIX THOSE PARTS. YOU GUYS CAN RESUBMIT IT FOR THE NEXT MEETING.
YES. I'D LOVE TO CONTINUE WORKING WITH MISS AOKI.
THAT'S AN OVERVIEW, AND NOW I'D LIKE TO GIVE YOU A BLOW-BY-BLOW OF WHAT CAME UP IN THE MEETING ABOUT YOUR MANGA.
RUSTLE
BLOW-BY-BLOW? WHAT A PAIN.
RUSTLE
OH, NOW LET ME READ YOU THE REVIEWS WRITTEN BY THE CAPTAINS AND HIGHER-UPS BEFORE THE MEETING.
OH, YES. THANK YOU VERY MUCH. THAT WOULD BE GREAT.

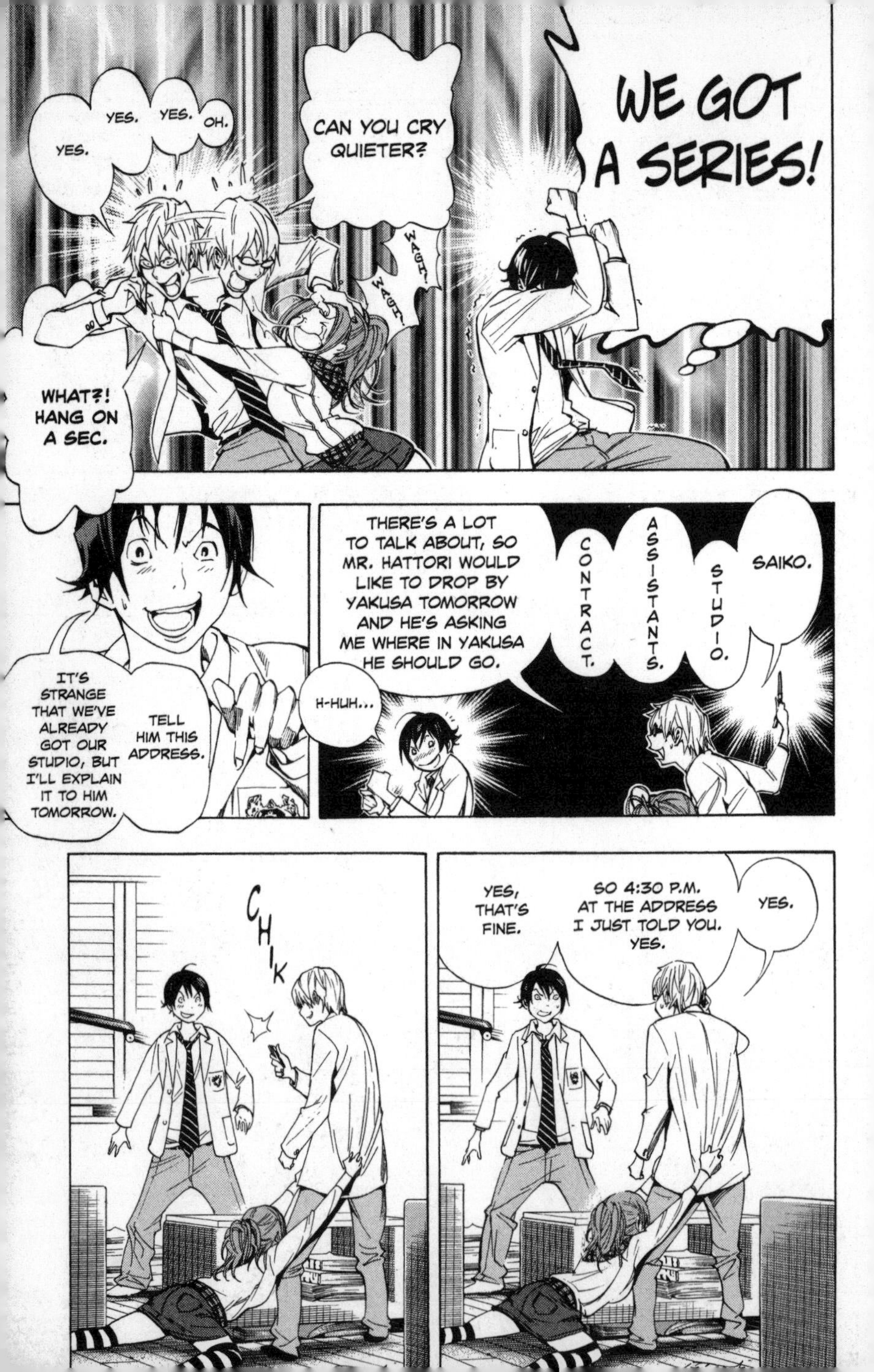
WE GOT A SERIES!
CAN YOU CRY QUIETER?
WAGH! WAGH!
YES. YES. OH. YES.
WHAT?! HANG ON A SEC.
SAIKO.
STUDIO.
ASSISTANTS.
CONTRACT.
THERE'S A LOT TO TALK ABOUT, SO MR. HATTORI WOULD LIKE TO DROP BY YAKUSA TOMORROW AND HE'S ASKING ME WHERE IN YAKUSA HE SHOULD GO.
H-HUH...
TELL HIM THIS ADDRESS.
IT'S STRANGE THAT WE'VE ALREADY GOT OUR STUDIO, BUT I'LL EXPLAIN IT TO HIM TOMORROW.
YES.
SO 4:30 P.M. AT THE ADDRESS I JUST TOLD YOU. YES.
YES, THAT'S FINE.
CHIK

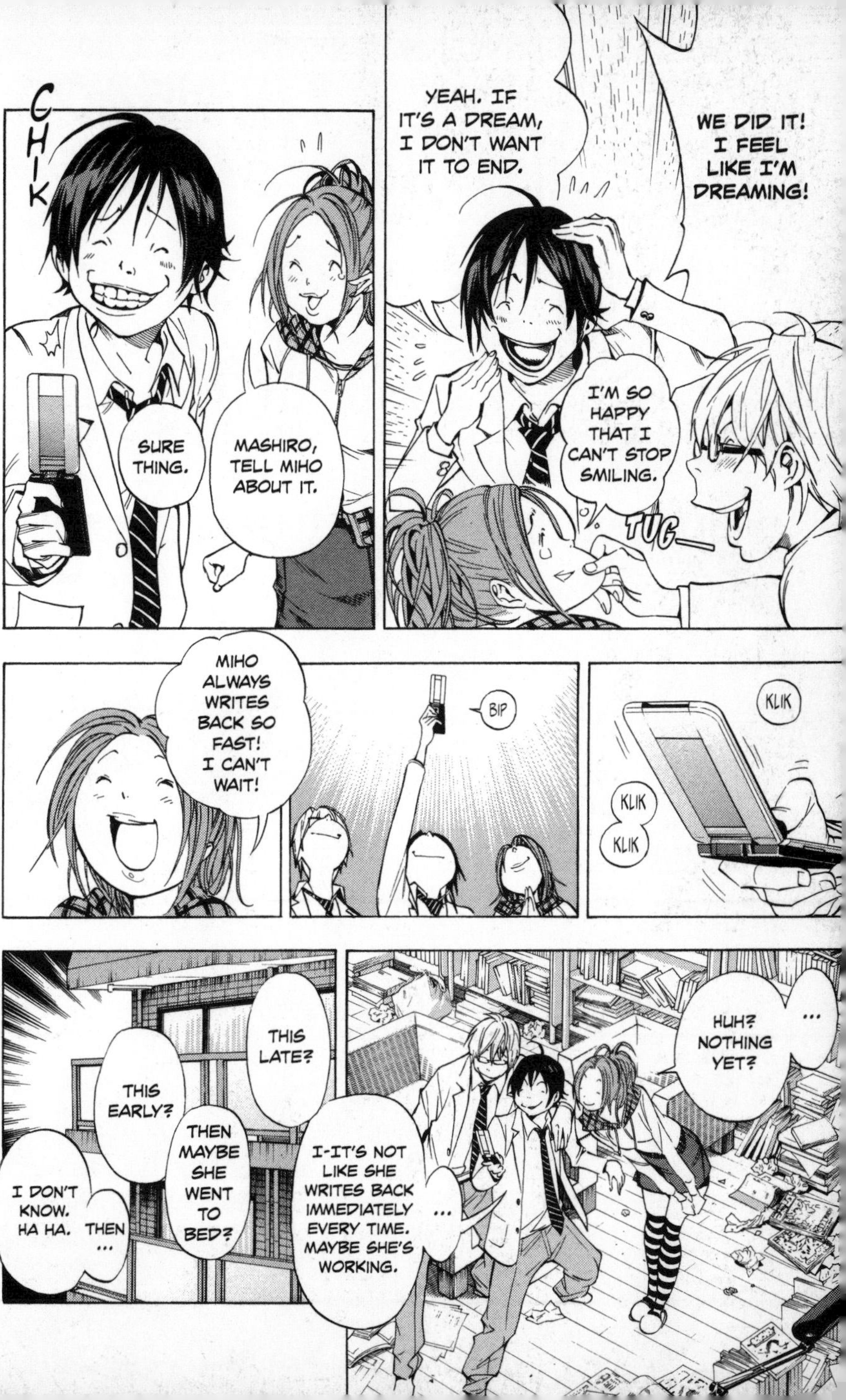
WE DID IT! I FEEL LIKE I'M DREAMING!
YEAH. IF IT'S A DREAM, I DON'T WANT IT TO END.
I'M SO HAPPY THAT I CAN'T STOP SMILING.
TUG—
CHIK
MASHIRO, TELL MIHO ABOUT IT.
SURE THING.
KLIK
KLIK
KLIK
BIP
MIHO ALWAYS WRITES BACK SO FAST! I CAN'T WAIT!
...
HUH? NOTHING YET?
...
I-IT'S NOT LIKE SHE WRITES BACK IMMEDIATELY EVERY TIME. MAYBE SHE'S WORKING.
THIS LATE?
THIS EARLY?
THEN MAYBE SHE WENT TO BED?
THEN ...
I DON'T KNOW. HA HA.

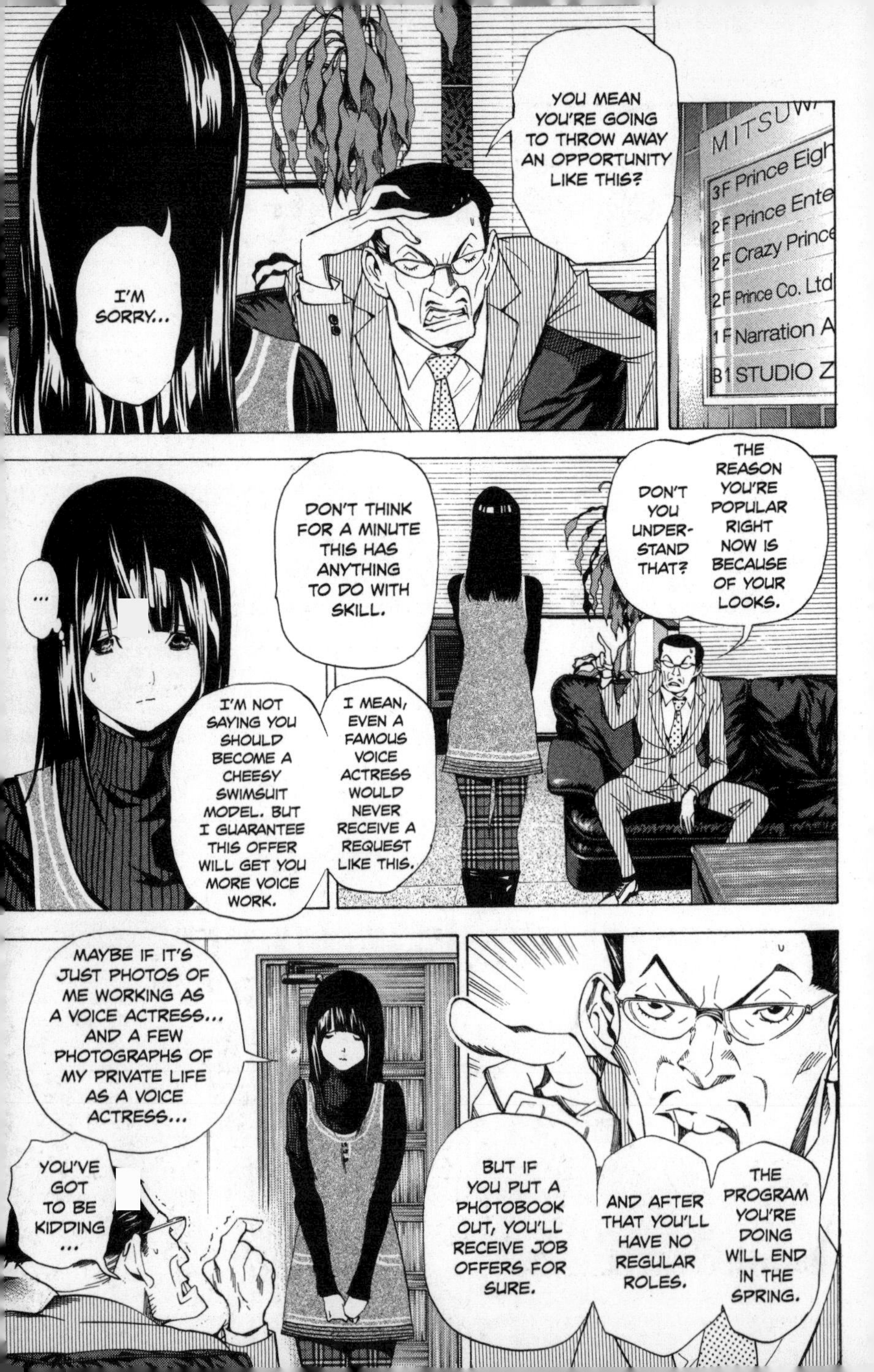
MITSUW
3F Prince Eigh
2F Prince Ente
2F Crazy Prince
2F Prince Co. Ltd
1F Narration A
B1 STUDIO Z
YOU MEAN YOU'RE GOING TO THROW AWAY AN OPPORTUNITY LIKE THIS?
I'M SORRY...
THE REASON YOU'RE POPULAR RIGHT NOW IS BECAUSE OF YOUR LOOKS.
DON'T YOU UNDERSTAND THAT?
DON'T THINK FOR A MINUTE THIS HAS ANYTHING TO DO WITH SKILL.
I MEAN, EVEN A FAMOUS VOICE ACTRESS WOULD NEVER RECEIVE A REQUEST LIKE THIS.
I'M NOT SAYING YOU SHOULD BECOME A CHEESY SWIMSUIT MODEL. BUT I GUARANTEE THIS OFFER WILL GET YOU MORE VOICE WORK.
...
THE PROGRAM YOU'RE DOING WILL END IN THE SPRING.
AND AFTER THAT YOU'LL HAVE NO REGULAR ROLES.
BUT IF YOU PUT A PHOTOBOOK OUT, YOU'LL RECEIVE JOB OFFERS FOR SURE.
MAYBE IF IT'S JUST PHOTOS OF ME WORKING AS A VOICE ACTRESS... AND A FEW PHOTOGRAPHS OF MY PRIVATE LIFE AS A VOICE ACTRESS...
YOU'VE GOT TO BE KIDDING...

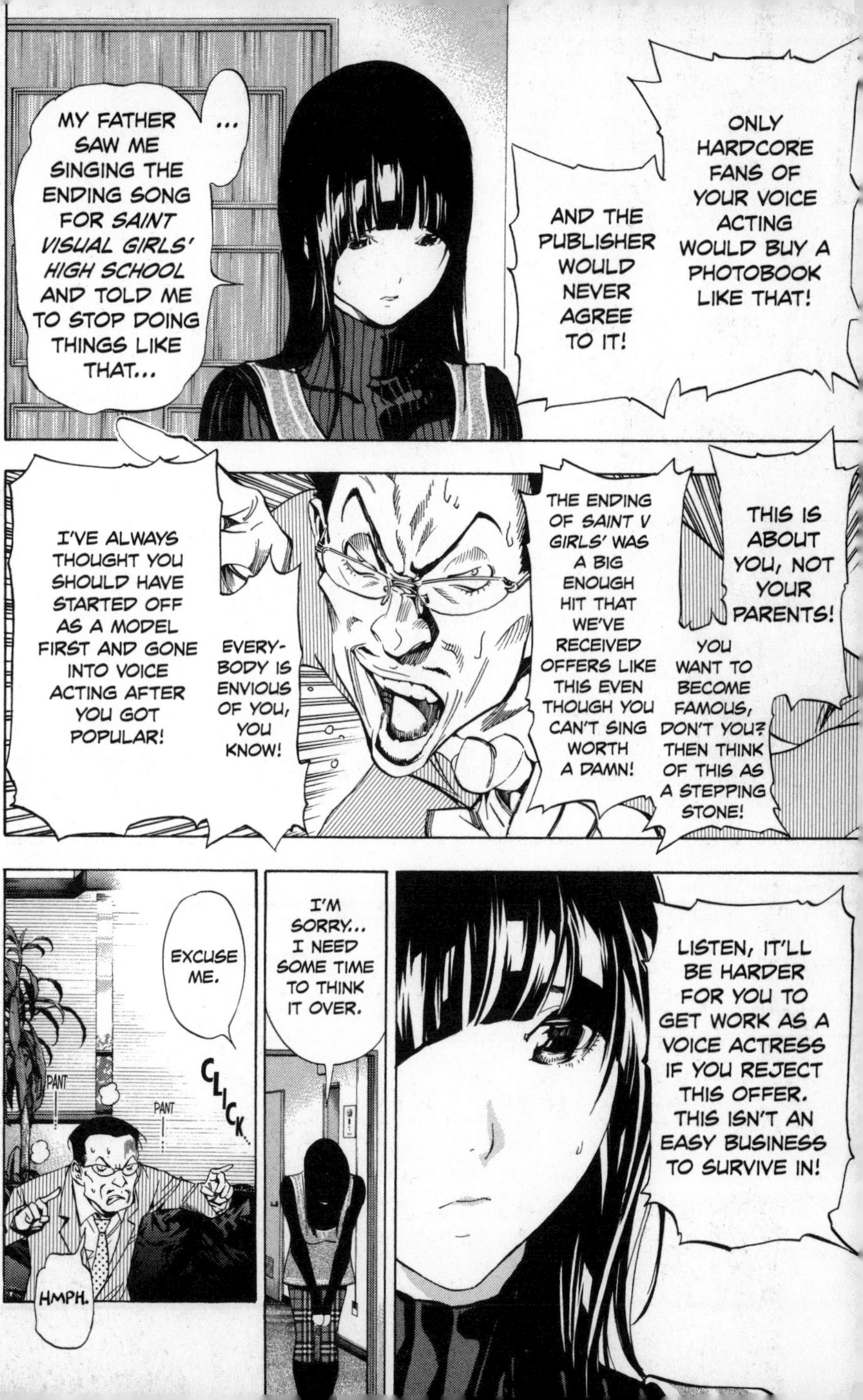
ONLY HARDCORE FANS OF YOUR VOICE ACTING WOULD BUY A PHOTOBOOK LIKE THAT!
AND THE PUBLISHER WOULD NEVER AGREE TO IT!
...
MY FATHER SAW ME SINGING THE ENDING SONG FOR *SAINT VISUAL GIRLS' HIGH SCHOOL* AND TOLD ME TO STOP DOING THINGS LIKE THAT...
THIS IS ABOUT YOU, NOT YOUR PARENTS!
YOU WANT TO BECOME FAMOUS, DON'T YOU? THEN THINK OF THIS AS A STEPPING STONE!
THE ENDING OF *SAINT V GIRLS'* WAS A BIG ENOUGH HIT THAT WE'VE RECEIVED OFFERS LIKE THIS EVEN THOUGH YOU CAN'T SING WORTH A DAMN!
EVERY-BODY IS ENVIOUS OF YOU, YOU KNOW!
I'VE ALWAYS THOUGHT YOU SHOULD HAVE STARTED OFF AS A MODEL FIRST AND GONE INTO VOICE ACTING AFTER YOU GOT POPULAR!
LISTEN, IT'LL BE HARDER FOR YOU TO GET WORK AS A VOICE ACTRESS IF YOU REJECT THIS OFFER. THIS ISN'T AN EASY BUSINESS TO SURVIVE IN!
I'M SORRY... I NEED SOME TIME TO THINK IT OVER.
EXCUSE ME.
CLICK...
PANT
PANT
HMPH.

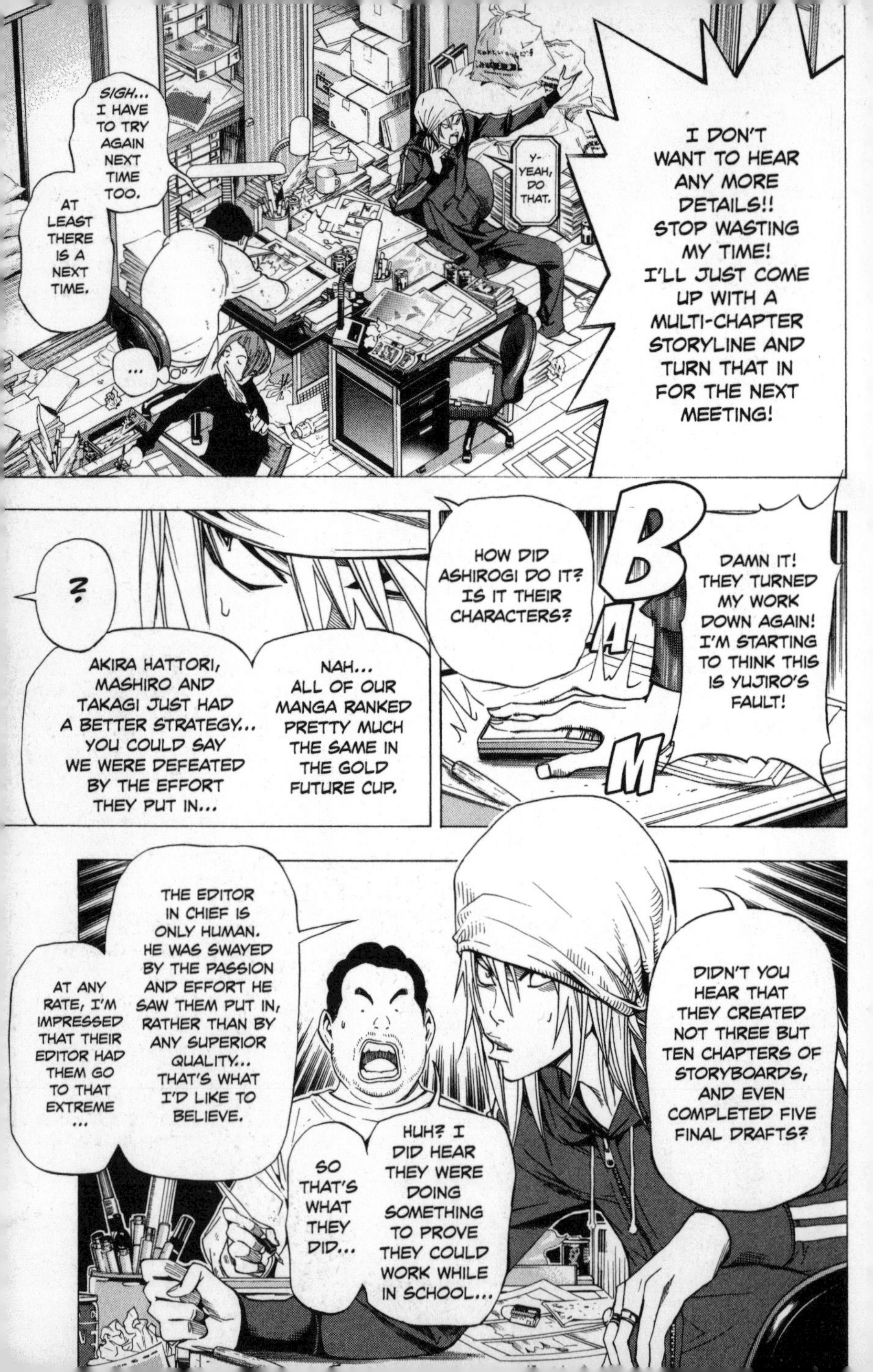
I DON'T WANT TO HEAR ANY MORE DETAILS!! STOP WASTING MY TIME! I'LL JUST COME UP WITH A MULTI-CHAPTER STORYLINE AND TURN THAT IN FOR THE NEXT MEETING!
Y-YEAH, DO THAT.
SIGH... I HAVE TO TRY AGAIN NEXT TIME TOO.
AT LEAST THERE IS A NEXT TIME.
...
DAMN IT! THEY TURNED MY WORK DOWN AGAIN! I'M STARTING TO THINK THIS IS YUJIRO'S FAULT!
BAM
HOW DID ASHIROGI DO IT? IS IT THEIR CHARACTERS?
?
NAH... ALL OF OUR MANGA RANKED PRETTY MUCH THE SAME IN THE GOLD FUTURE CUP.
AKIRA HATTORI, MASHIRO AND TAKAGI JUST HAD A BETTER STRATEGY... YOU COULD SAY WE WERE DEFEATED BY THE EFFORT THEY PUT IN...
DIDN'T YOU HEAR THAT THEY CREATED NOT THREE BUT TEN CHAPTERS OF STORYBOARDS, AND EVEN COMPLETED FIVE FINAL DRAFTS?
HUH? I DID HEAR THEY WERE DOING SOMETHING TO PROVE THEY COULD WORK WHILE IN SCHOOL...
SO THAT'S WHAT THEY DID...
THE EDITOR IN CHIEF IS ONLY HUMAN. HE WAS SWAYED BY THE PASSION AND EFFORT HE SAW THEM PUT IN, RATHER THAN BY ANY SUPERIOR QUALITY... THAT'S WHAT I'D LIKE TO BELIEVE.
AT ANY RATE, I'M IMPRESSED THAT THEIR EDITOR HAD THEM GO TO THAT EXTREME...

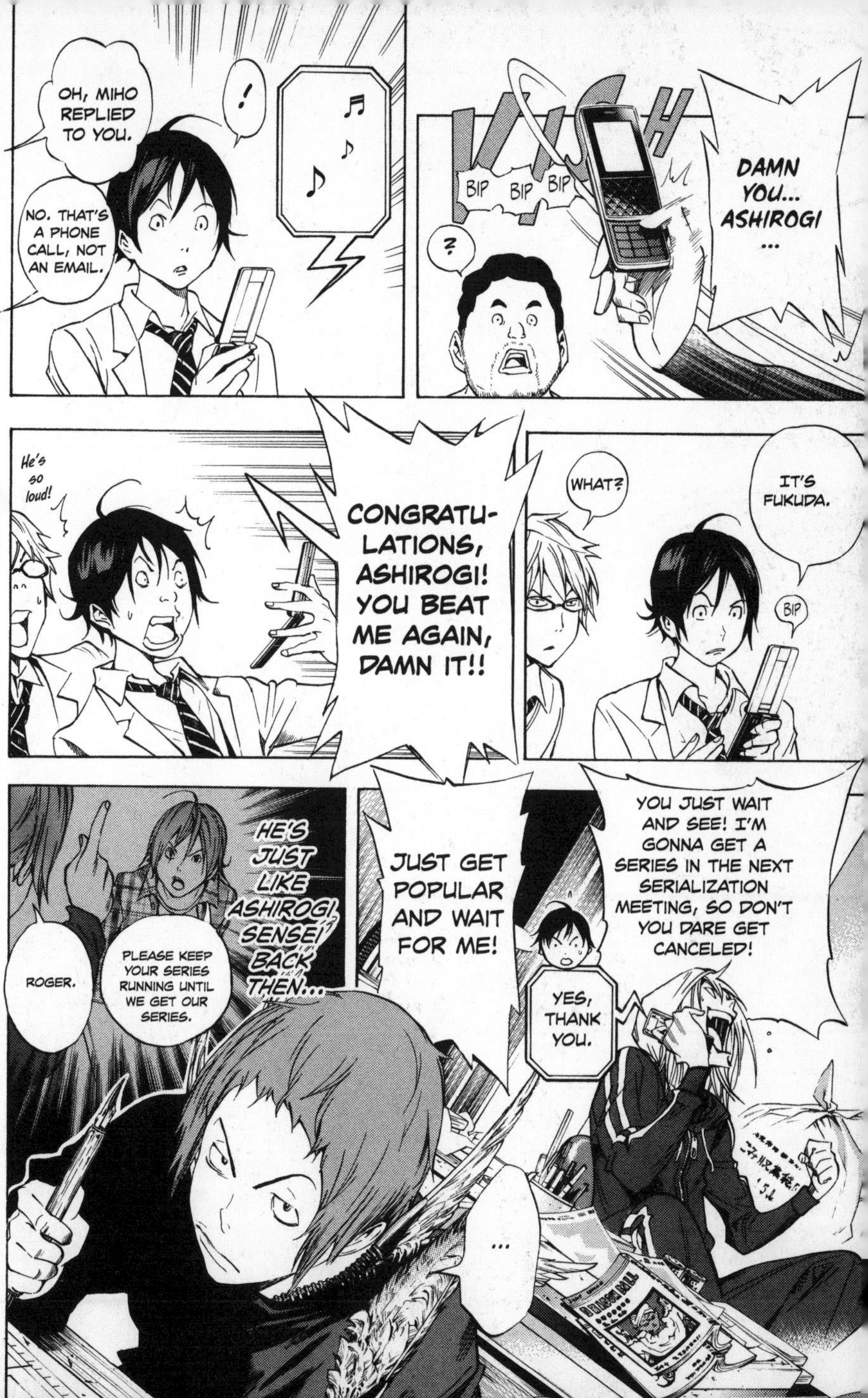
BIP BIP BIP
?
DAMN YOU... ASHIROGI ...
!
OH, MIHO REPLIED TO YOU.
NO. THAT'S A PHONE CALL, NOT AN EMAIL.
IT'S FUKUDA.
BIP
WHAT?
CONGRATULATIONS, ASHIROGI! YOU BEAT ME AGAIN, DAMN IT!!
He's so loud!
YOU JUST WAIT AND SEE! I'M GONNA GET A SERIES IN THE NEXT SERIALIZATION MEETING, SO DON'T YOU DARE GET CANCELED!
JUST GET POPULAR AND WAIT FOR ME!
YES, THANK YOU.
HE'S JUST LIKE ASHIROGI SENSEI BACK THEN...
PLEASE KEEP YOUR SERIES RUNNING UNTIL WE GET OUR SERIES.
ROGER.
...

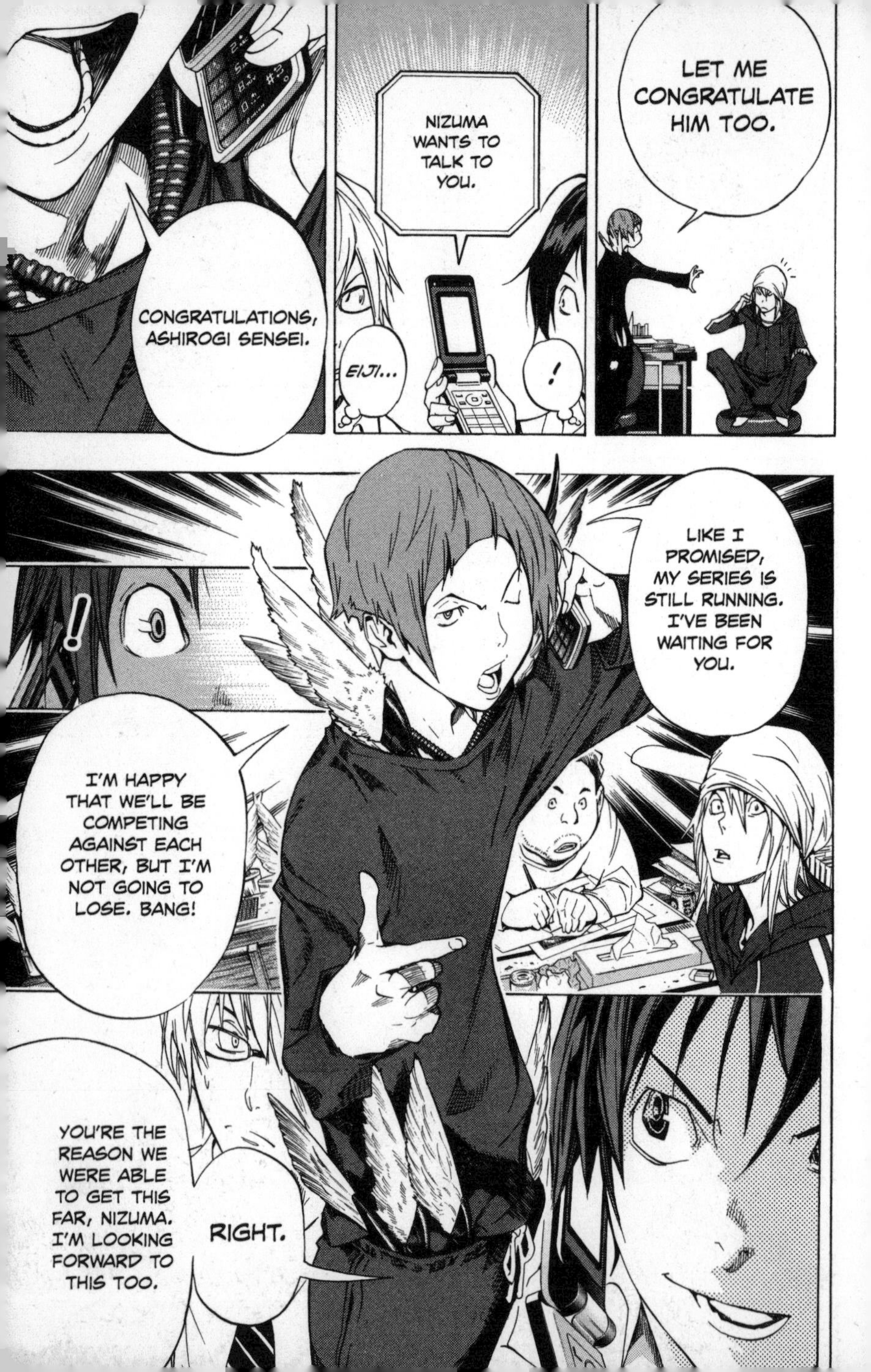
LET ME CONGRATULATE HIM TOO.
NIZUMA WANTS TO TALK TO YOU.
!
EIJI...
CONGRATULATIONS, ASHIROGI SENSEI.
LIKE I PROMISED, MY SERIES IS STILL RUNNING. I'VE BEEN WAITING FOR YOU.
!
I'M HAPPY THAT WE'LL BE COMPETING AGAINST EACH OTHER, BUT I'M NOT GOING TO LOSE. BANG!
RIGHT.
YOU'RE THE REASON WE WERE ABLE TO GET THIS FAR, NIZUMA. I'M LOOKING FORWARD TO THIS TOO.

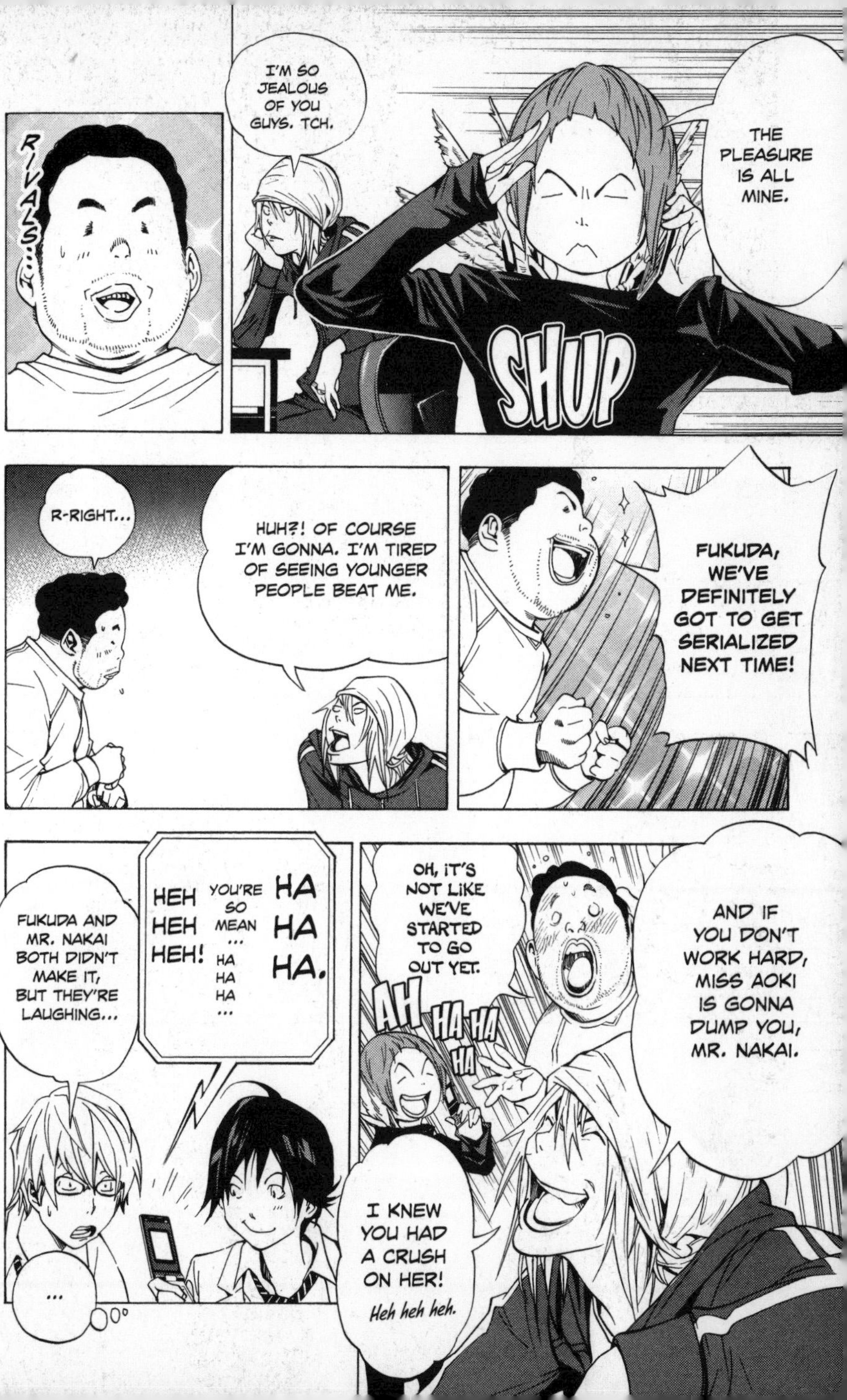
THE PLEASURE IS ALL MINE.
I'M SO JEALOUS OF YOU GUYS. TCH.
SHUP
RIVALS...
FUKUDA, WE'VE DEFINITELY GOT TO GET SERIALIZED NEXT TIME!
HUH?! OF COURSE I'M GONNA. I'M TIRED OF SEEING YOUNGER PEOPLE BEAT ME.
R-RIGHT...
AND IF YOU DON'T WORK HARD, MISS AOKI IS GONNA DUMP YOU, MR. NAKAI.
OH, IT'S NOT LIKE WE'VE STARTED TO GO OUT YET.
AH HA HA HA
I KNEW YOU HAD A CRUSH ON HER!
Heh heh heh.
HA HA HA.
YOU'RE SO MEAN... HA HA HA...
HEH HEH HEH!
FUKUDA AND MR. NAKAI BOTH DIDN'T MAKE IT, BUT THEY'RE LAUGHING...
...

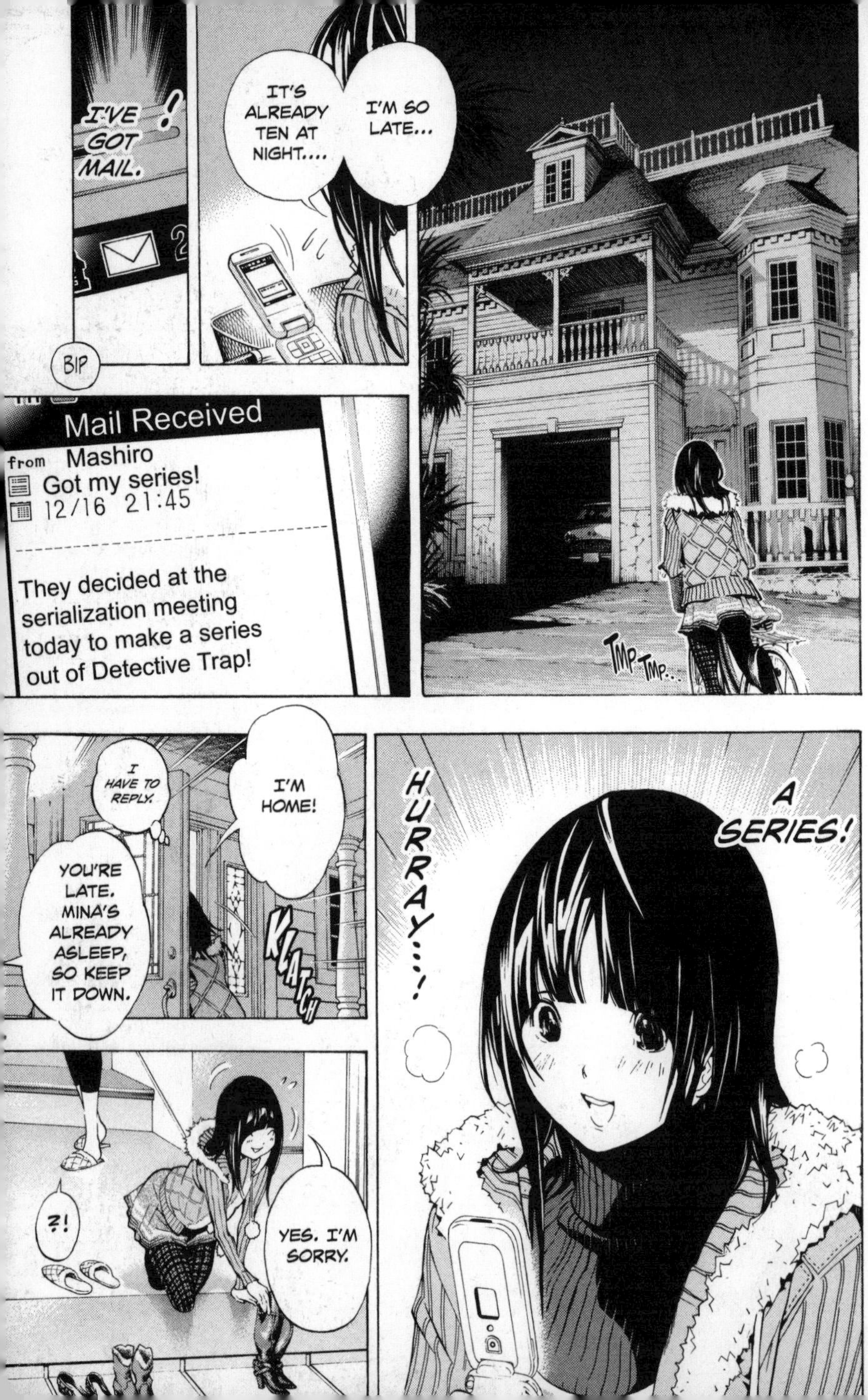
TMP TMP...
I'M SO LATE...
IT'S ALREADY TEN AT NIGHT....
I'VE GOT MAIL. !
BIP
Mail Received
from Mashiro
Got my series!
12/16 21:45
They decided at the serialization meeting today to make a series out of Detective Trap!
A SERIES!
HURRAY...!
I'M HOME!
KLATCH
I HAVE TO REPLY.
YOU'RE LATE. MINA'S ALREADY ASLEEP, SO KEEP IT DOWN.
YES. I'M SORRY.
?!

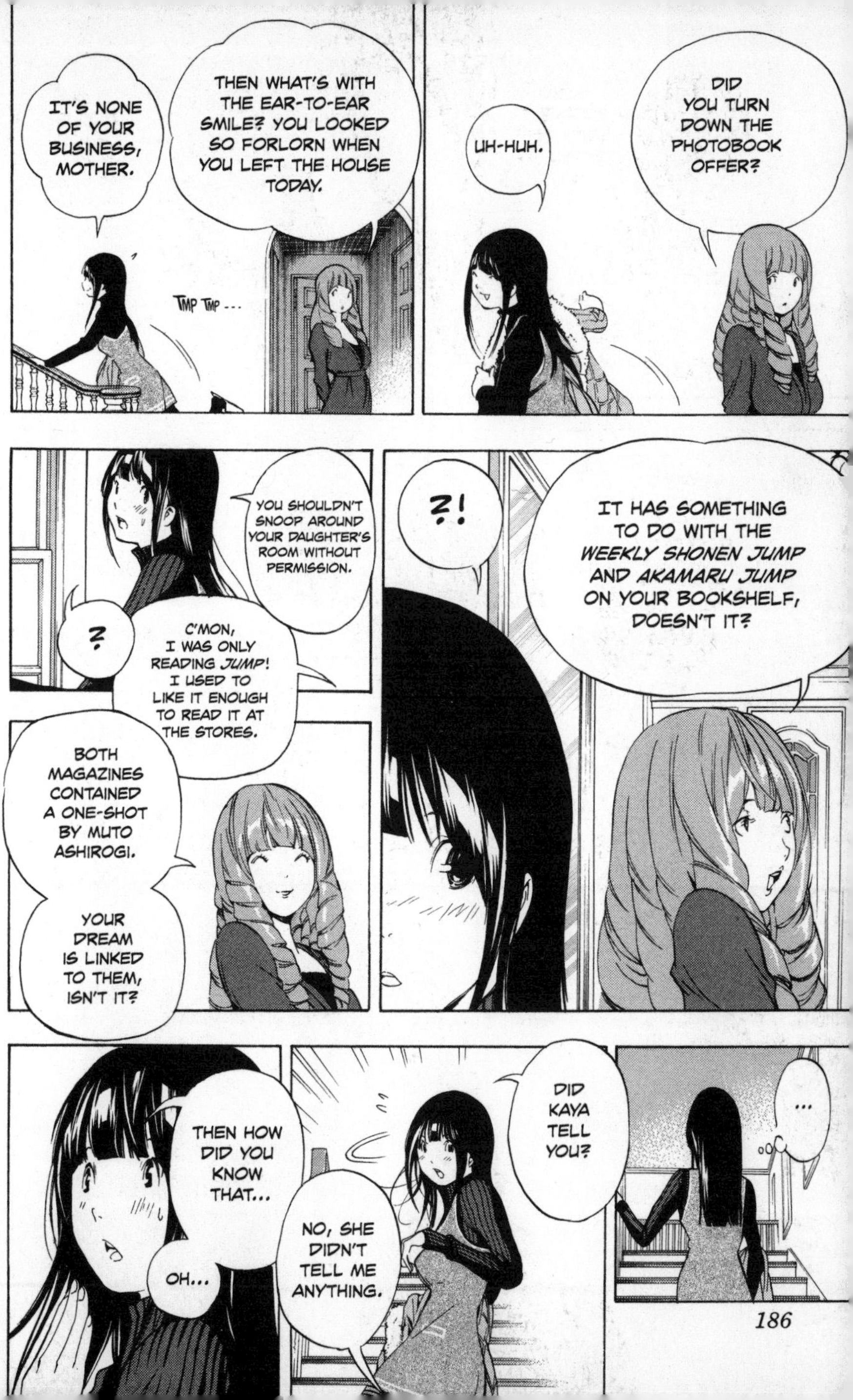
DID YOU TURN DOWN THE PHOTOBOOK OFFER?
UH-HUH.
THEN WHAT'S WITH THE EAR-TO-EAR SMILE? YOU LOOKED SO FORLORN WHEN YOU LEFT THE HOUSE TODAY.
IT'S NONE OF YOUR BUSINESS, MOTHER.
TMP TMP...
IT HAS SOMETHING TO DO WITH THE *WEEKLY SHONEN JUMP* AND *AKAMARU JUMP* ON YOUR BOOKSHELF, DOESN'T IT?
?!
YOU SHOULDN'T SNOOP AROUND YOUR DAUGHTER'S ROOM WITHOUT PERMISSION.
?
C'MON, I WAS ONLY READING *JUMP*! I USED TO LIKE IT ENOUGH TO READ IT AT THE STORES.
BOTH MAGAZINES CONTAINED A ONE-SHOT BY MUTO ASHIROGI.
YOUR DREAM IS LINKED TO THEM, ISN'T IT?
...
DID KAYA TELL YOU?
NO, SHE DIDN'T TELL ME ANYTHING.
THEN HOW DID YOU KNOW THAT...
OH...

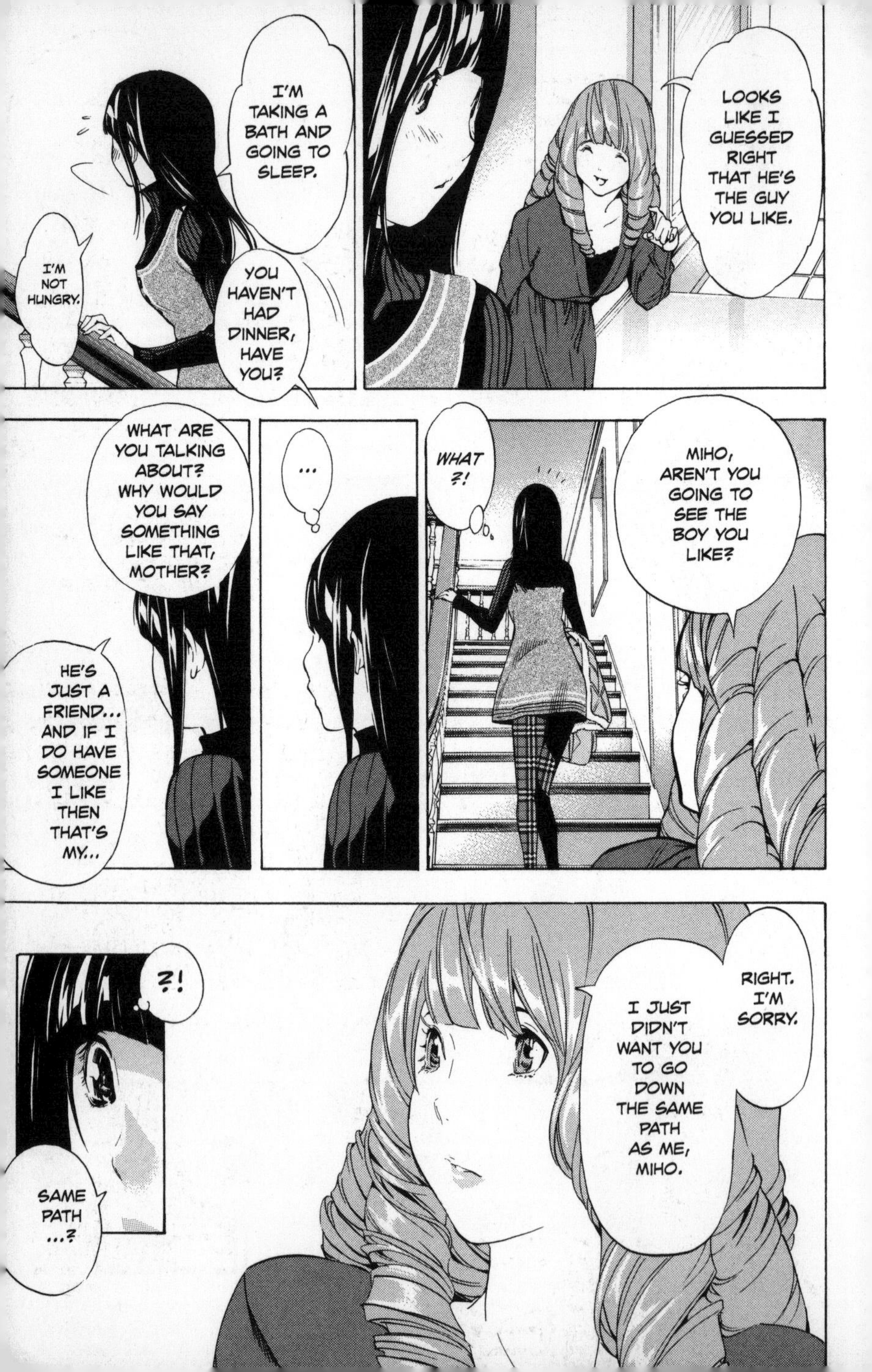
LOOKS LIKE I GUESSED RIGHT THAT HE'S THE GUY YOU LIKE.
I'M TAKING A BATH AND GOING TO SLEEP.
YOU HAVEN'T HAD DINNER, HAVE YOU?
I'M NOT HUNGRY.
MIHO, AREN'T YOU GOING TO SEE THE BOY YOU LIKE?
WHAT ?!
...
WHAT ARE YOU TALKING ABOUT? WHY WOULD YOU SAY SOMETHING LIKE THAT, MOTHER?
HE'S JUST A FRIEND... AND IF I DO HAVE SOMEONE I LIKE THEN THAT'S MY...
RIGHT. I'M SORRY.
I JUST DIDN'T WANT YOU TO GO DOWN THE SAME PATH AS ME, MIHO.
?!
SAME PATH ...?

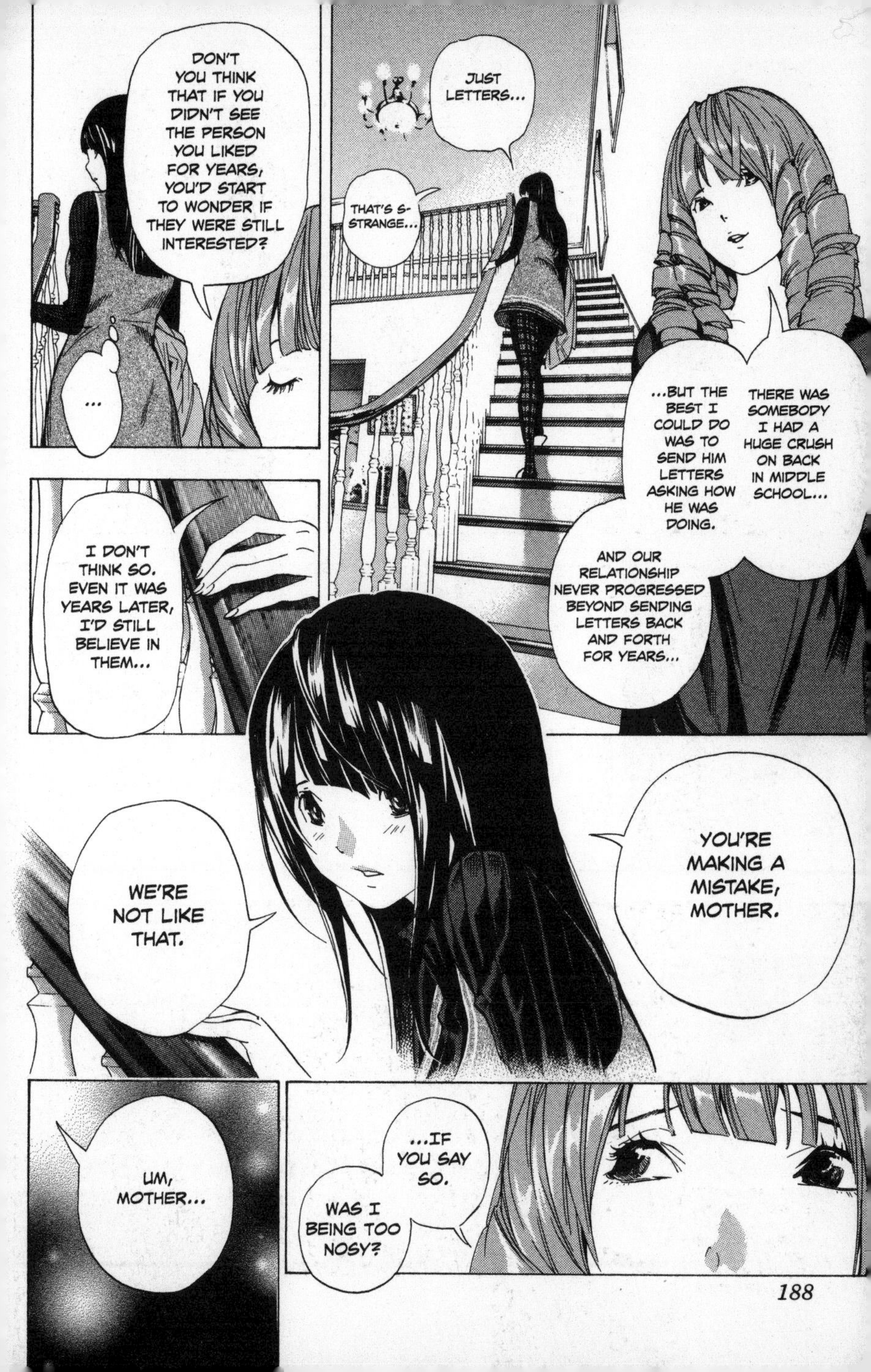
THERE WAS SOMEBODY I HAD A HUGE CRUSH ON BACK IN MIDDLE SCHOOL...
...BUT THE BEST I COULD DO WAS TO SEND HIM LETTERS ASKING HOW HE WAS DOING.
AND OUR RELATIONSHIP NEVER PROGRESSED BEYOND SENDING LETTERS BACK AND FORTH FOR YEARS...
JUST LETTERS...
THAT'S S-STRANGE...
DON'T YOU THINK THAT IF YOU DIDN'T SEE THE PERSON YOU LIKED FOR YEARS, YOU'D START TO WONDER IF THEY WERE STILL INTERESTED?
...
I DON'T THINK SO. EVEN IT WAS YEARS LATER, I'D STILL BELIEVE IN THEM...
YOU'RE MAKING A MISTAKE, MOTHER.
WE'RE NOT LIKE THAT.
...IF YOU SAY SO.
WAS I BEING TOO NOSY?
UM, MOTHER...

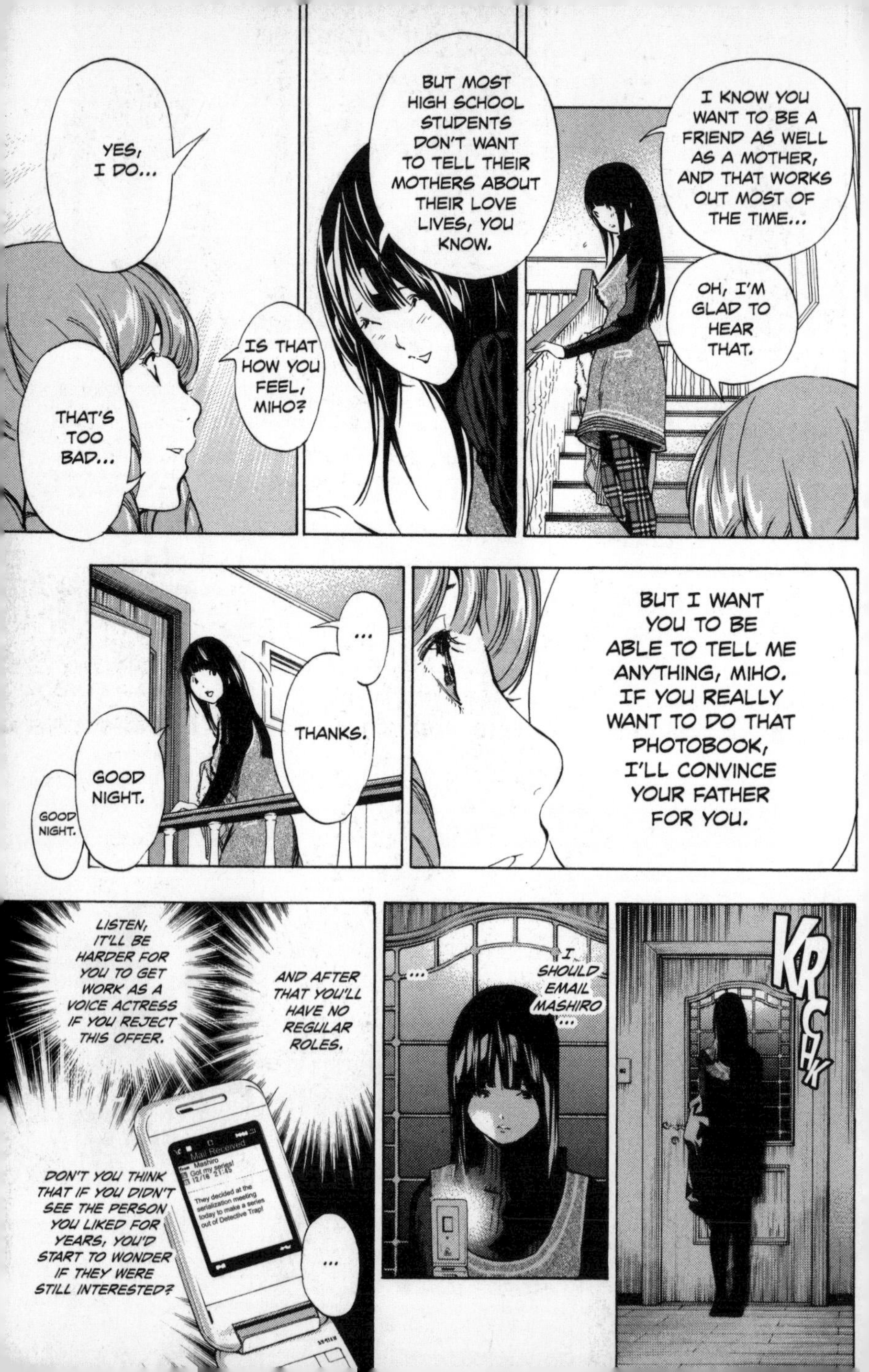
I KNOW YOU WANT TO BE A FRIEND AS WELL AS A MOTHER, AND THAT WORKS OUT MOST OF THE TIME...
OH, I'M GLAD TO HEAR THAT.
BUT MOST HIGH SCHOOL STUDENTS DON'T WANT TO TELL THEIR MOTHERS ABOUT THEIR LOVE LIVES, YOU KNOW.
IS THAT HOW YOU FEEL, MIHO?
YES, I DO...
THAT'S TOO BAD...
BUT I WANT YOU TO BE ABLE TO TELL ME ANYTHING, MIHO. IF YOU REALLY WANT TO DO THAT PHOTOBOOK, I'LL CONVINCE YOUR FATHER FOR YOU.
...
THANKS.
GOOD NIGHT.
GOOD NIGHT.
KRCHK
I SHOULD EMAIL MASHIRO...
...
LISTEN, IT'LL BE HARDER FOR YOU TO GET WORK AS A VOICE ACTRESS IF YOU REJECT THIS OFFER.
AND AFTER THAT YOU'LL HAVE NO REGULAR ROLES.
Mail Received
Mashiro
Got my series!
12/18 21:45
They decided at the serialization meeting today to make a series out of Detective Trap!
DON'T YOU THINK THAT IF YOU DIDN'T SEE THE PERSON YOU LIKED FOR YEARS, YOU'D START TO WONDER IF THEY WERE STILL INTERESTED?
...

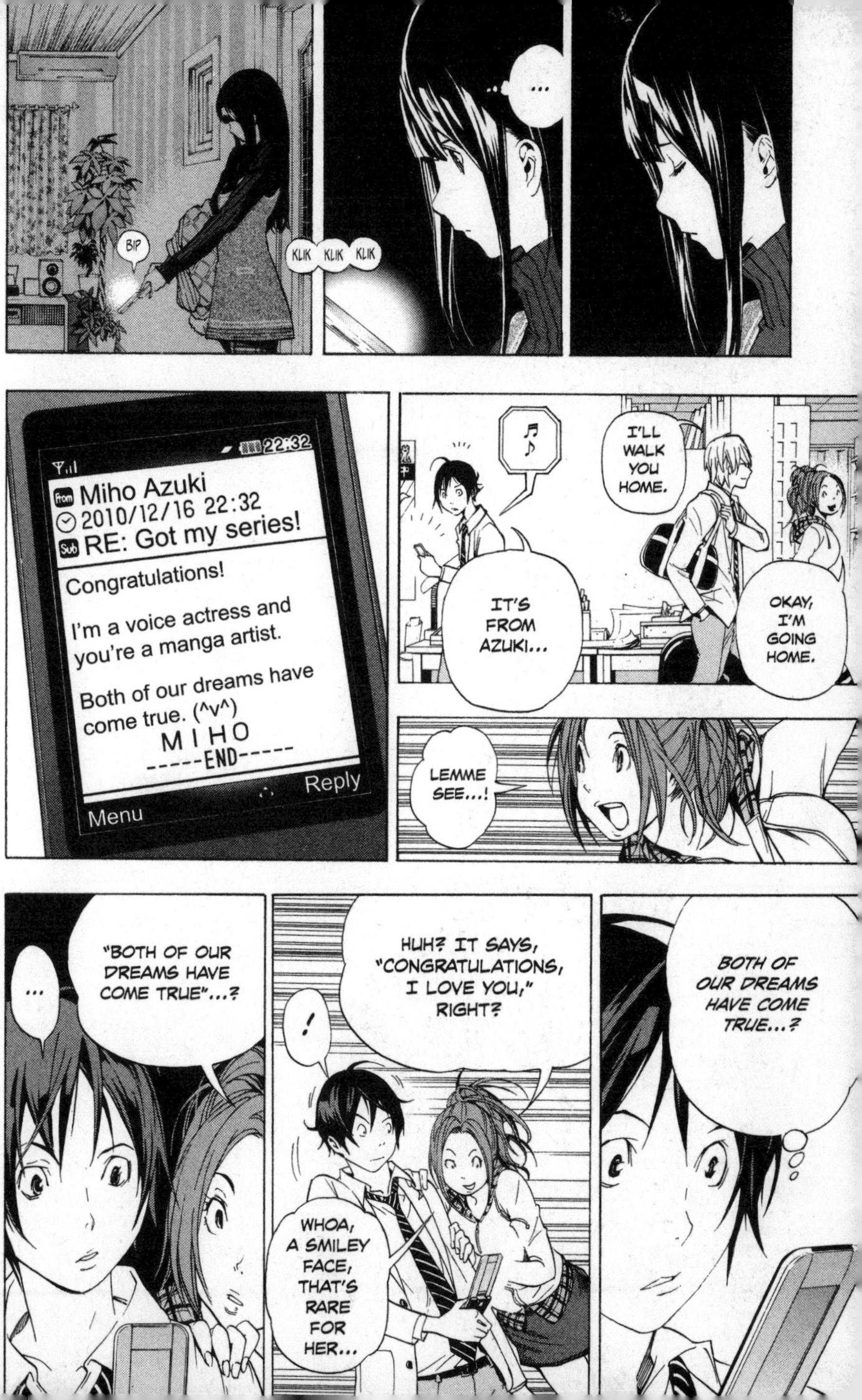
...
KLIK KLIK KLIK
BIP
I'LL WALK YOU HOME.
OKAY, I'M GOING HOME.
♪
IT'S FROM AZUKI...
LEMME SEE...!
Miho Azuki
2010/12/16 22:32
RE: Got my series!
Congratulations!
I'm a voice actress and you're a manga artist.
Both of our dreams have come true. (^v^)
MIHO
-----END-----
Menu
Reply
22:32
BOTH OF OUR DREAMS HAVE COME TRUE...?
HUH? IT SAYS, "CONGRATULATIONS, I LOVE YOU," RIGHT?
!
WHOA, A SMILEY FACE, THAT'S RARE FOR HER...
"BOTH OF OUR DREAMS HAVE COME TRUE"...?
...

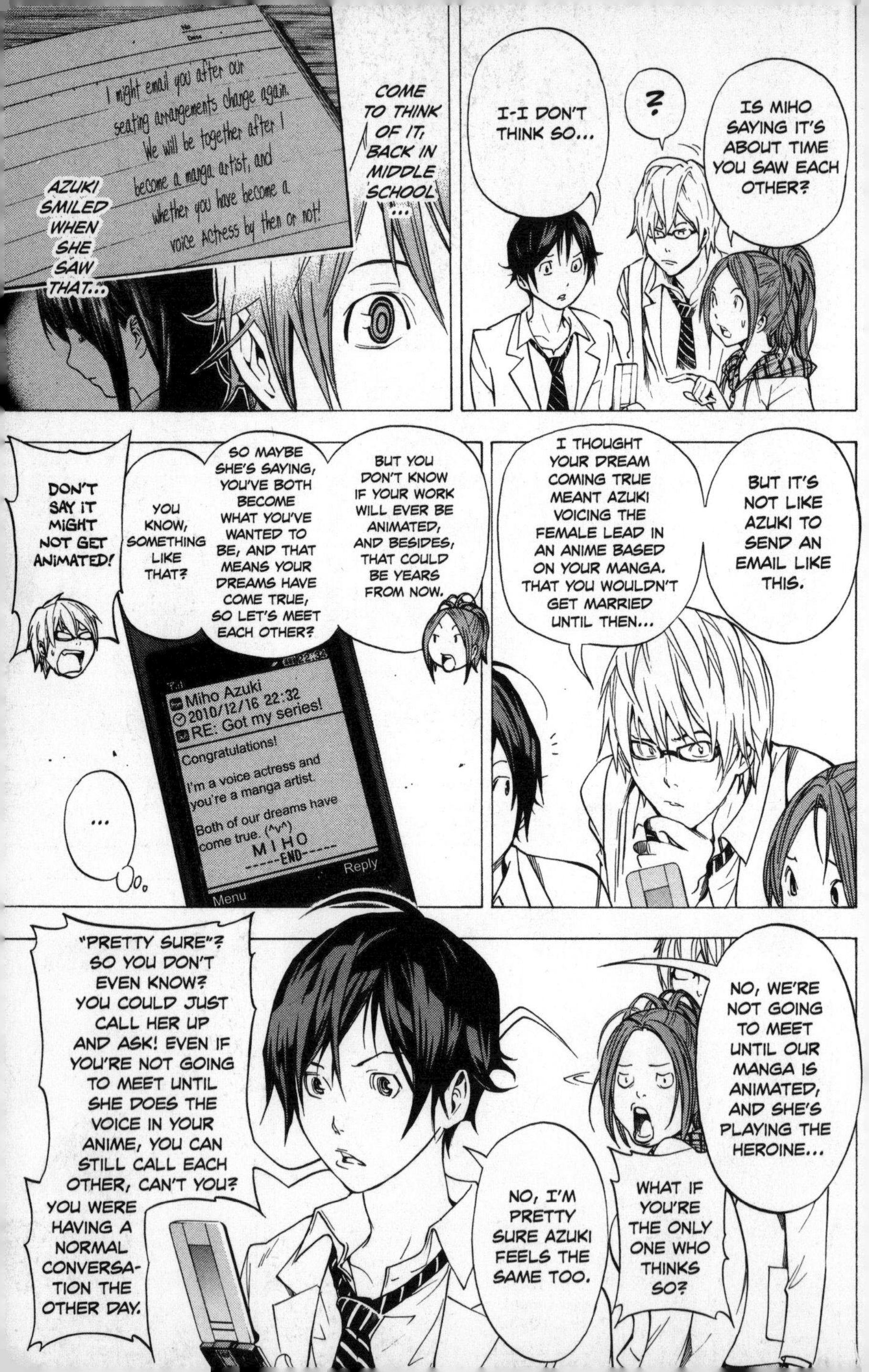
IS MIHO SAYING IT'S ABOUT TIME YOU SAW EACH OTHER?
?
I-I DON'T THINK SO...
COME TO THINK OF IT, BACK IN MIDDLE SCHOOL...
I might email you after our seating arrangements change again. We will be together after I become a manga artist, and whether you have become a voice Actress by then or not!
AZUKI SMILED WHEN SHE SAW THAT...
BUT IT'S NOT LIKE AZUKI TO SEND AN EMAIL LIKE THIS.
I THOUGHT YOUR DREAM COMING TRUE MEANT AZUKI VOICING THE FEMALE LEAD IN AN ANIME BASED ON YOUR MANGA. THAT YOU WOULDN'T GET MARRIED UNTIL THEN...
BUT YOU DON'T KNOW IF YOUR WORK WILL EVER BE ANIMATED, AND BESIDES, THAT COULD BE YEARS FROM NOW.
SO MAYBE SHE'S SAYING, YOU'VE BOTH BECOME WHAT YOU'VE WANTED TO BE, AND THAT MEANS YOUR DREAMS HAVE COME TRUE, SO LET'S MEET EACH OTHER?
YOU KNOW, SOMETHING LIKE THAT?
DON'T SAY IT MIGHT NOT GET ANIMATED!
Miho Azuki
2010/12/16 22:32
RE: Got my series!
Congratulations!
I'm a voice actress and you're a manga artist.
Both of our dreams have come true. (^v^)
MIHO
-----END-----
Reply
Menu
...
NO, WE'RE NOT GOING TO MEET UNTIL OUR MANGA IS ANIMATED, AND SHE'S PLAYING THE HEROINE...
WHAT IF YOU'RE THE ONLY ONE WHO THINKS SO?
NO, I'M PRETTY SURE AZUKI FEELS THE SAME TOO.
"PRETTY SURE"? SO YOU DON'T EVEN KNOW? YOU COULD JUST CALL HER UP AND ASK! EVEN IF YOU'RE NOT GOING TO MEET UNTIL SHE DOES THE VOICE IN YOUR ANIME, YOU CAN STILL CALL EACH OTHER, CAN'T YOU?
YOU WERE HAVING A NORMAL CONVERSA-TION THE OTHER DAY.

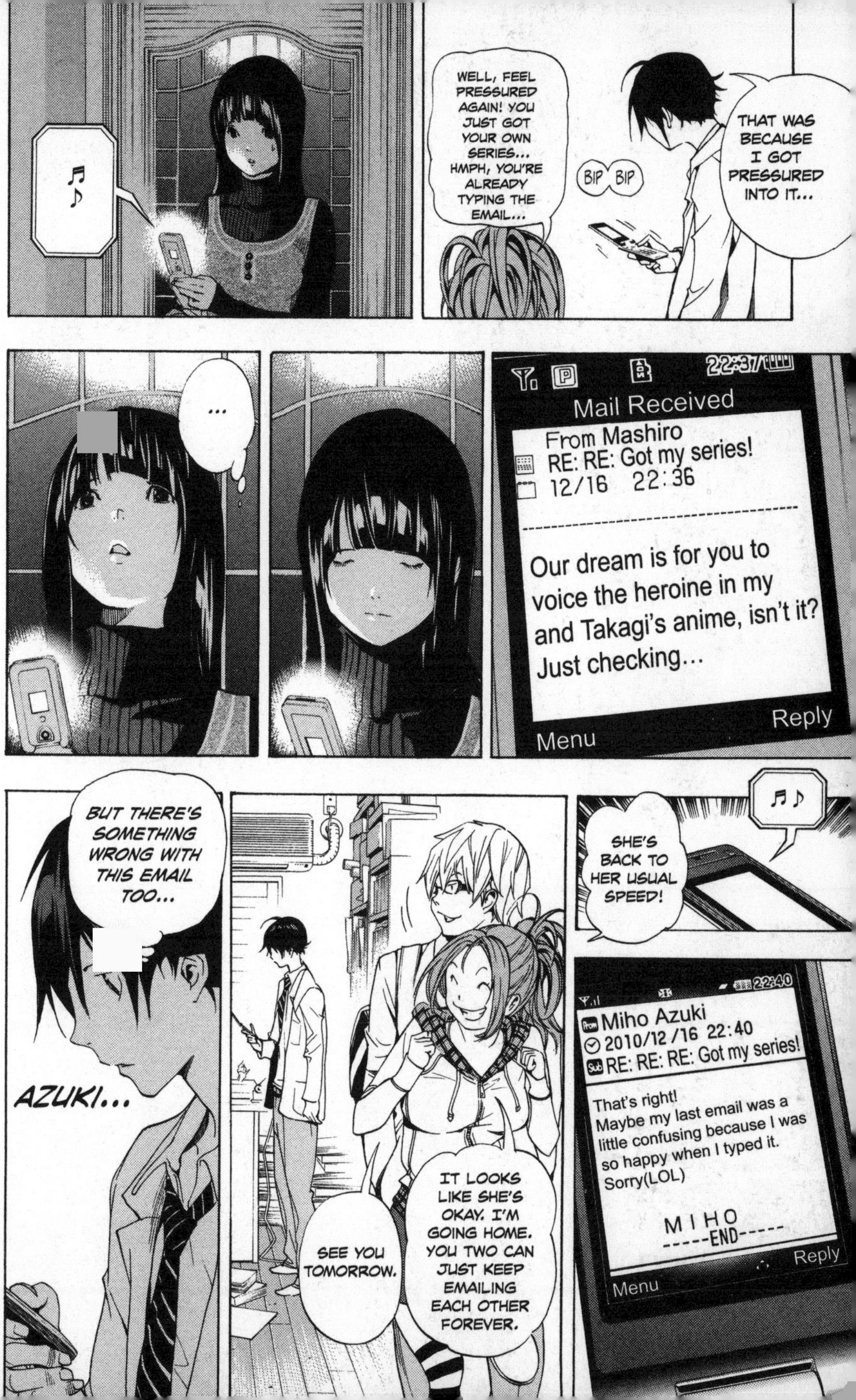
THAT WAS BECAUSE I GOT PRESSURED INTO IT...
BIP BIP
WELL, FEEL PRESSURED AGAIN! YOU JUST GOT YOUR OWN SERIES... HMPH, YOU'RE ALREADY TYPING THE EMAIL...
♬ ♪
22:37
Mail Received
From Mashiro
RE: RE: Got my series!
12/16 22:36
Our dream is for you to voice the heroine in my and Takagi's anime, isn't it? Just checking...
Reply
Menu
...
♬♪
SHE'S BACK TO HER USUAL SPEED!
22:40
Miho Azuki
2010/12/16 22:40
RE: RE: RE: Got my series!
That's right!
Maybe my last email was a little confusing because I was so happy when I typed it.
Sorry(LOL)
MIHO
-----END-----
Reply
Menu
IT LOOKS LIKE SHE'S OKAY. I'M GOING HOME. YOU TWO CAN JUST KEEP EMAILING EACH OTHER FOREVER.
SEE YOU TOMORROW.
BUT THERE'S SOMETHING WRONG WITH THIS EMAIL TOO...
AZUKI...

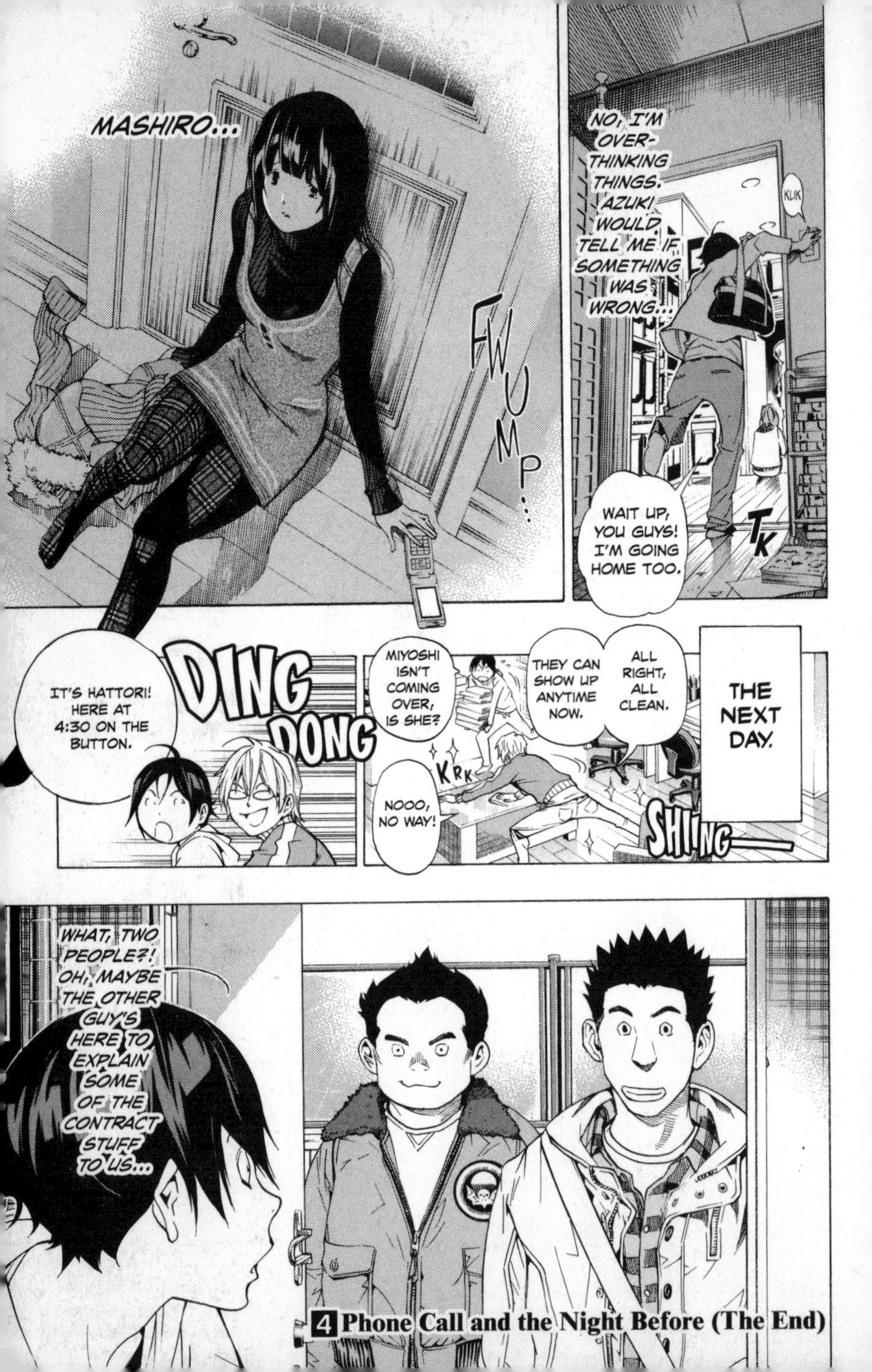
NO, I'M OVER-THINKING THINGS. AZUKI WOULD TELL ME IF SOMETHING WAS WRONG...
KLIK
WAIT UP, YOU GUYS! I'M GOING HOME TOO.
TK
MASHIRO...
FWUMP...
THE NEXT DAY.
SHIING—
ALL RIGHT, ALL CLEAN.
THEY CAN SHOW UP ANYTIME NOW.
MIYOSHI ISN'T COMING OVER, IS SHE?
KRK
NOOO, NO WAY!
DING DONG
IT'S HATTORI! HERE AT 4:30 ON THE BUTTON.
WHAT, TWO PEOPLE?! OH, MAYBE THE OTHER GUY'S HERE TO EXPLAIN SOME OF THE CONTRACT STUFF TO US...
4 Phone Call and the Night Before (The End)

OHBA'S STORYBOARD

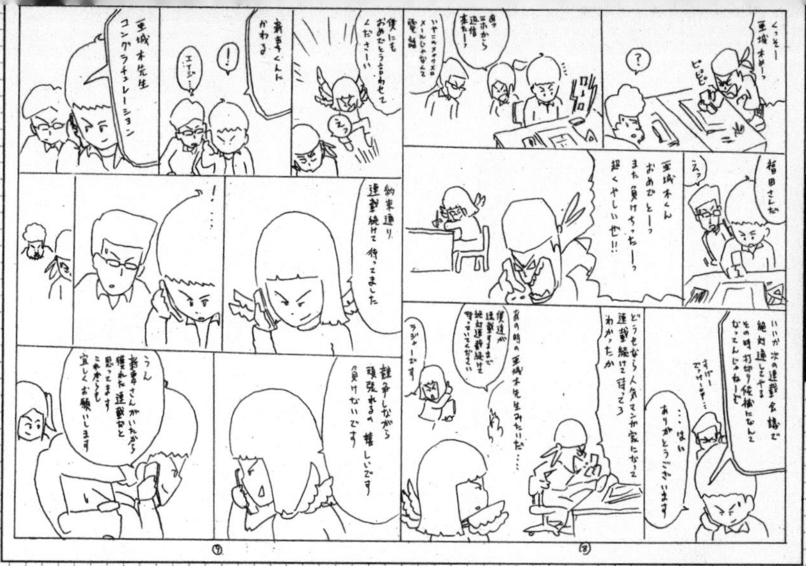

くっそー 亜城木めーっ
ピピピ
？
あっ ミホから 返信 来たー？
電話
福田さんだ
えっ
亜城木くん おめでとーっ また負けちったーっ 超くやしいぜ!!
いいか次の連載会議で 絶対通してやる その時打切り候補になんて なってんじゃねーぞ
すげー でっけー声…
…はい ありがとうございます
どうせなら人気マンガ家になって 連載続けて待ってろ わかったか
あの時の亜城木先生みたいだ…
僕達が連載するまで 絶対連載続けて 待っていてください
ラジャーです
僕にも おめでとう言わせて ください
えっ
新妻くんに かわる
！
エイジ…
亜城木先生 コングラチュレーション
約束通り 連載続けて 待ってました
！…
競争しながら 頑張れるの 嬉しいです 負けないです
うん 新妻さんがいたから 獲れた連載だと 思ってます これからも 宜しくお願いします

OBATA'S STORYBOARD

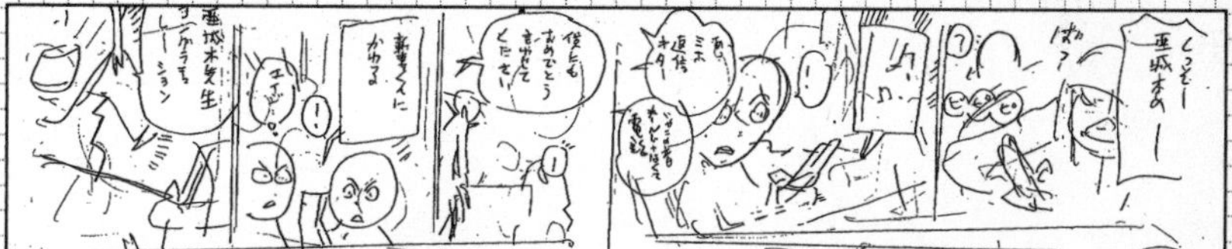

くっそー 亜城木めー
福田さんだ
えっ
亜城木くん おめでとーっ また負けちったー 超くやしいぜ!!

COMPLETE!

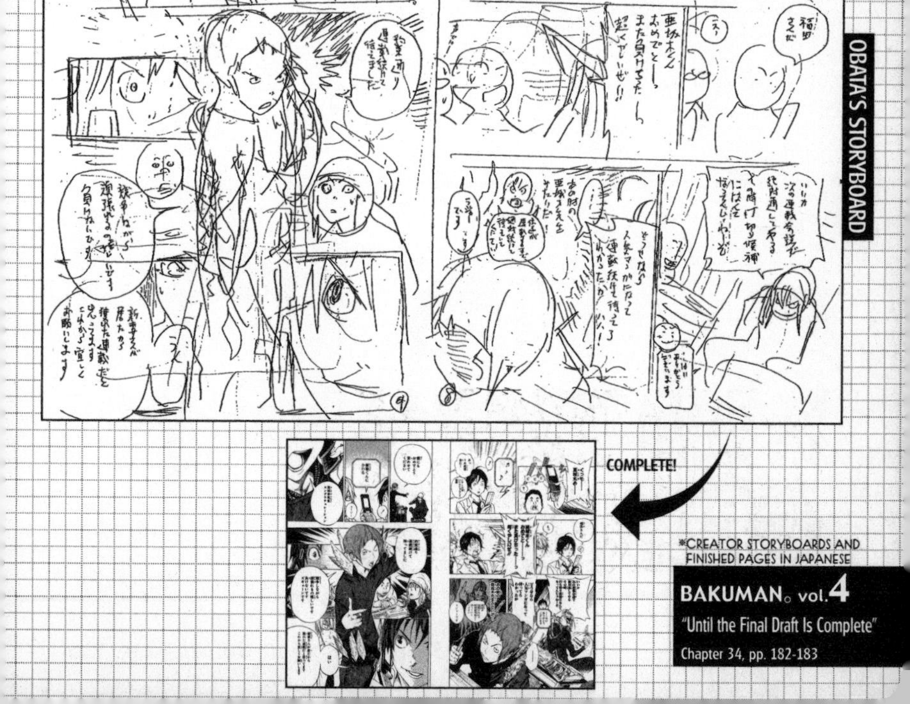

*CREATOR STORYBOARDS AND FINISHED PAGES IN JAPANESE

BAKUMAN。vol.4

"Until the Final Draft Is Complete"

Chapter 34, pp. 182-183

BAKUMAN。

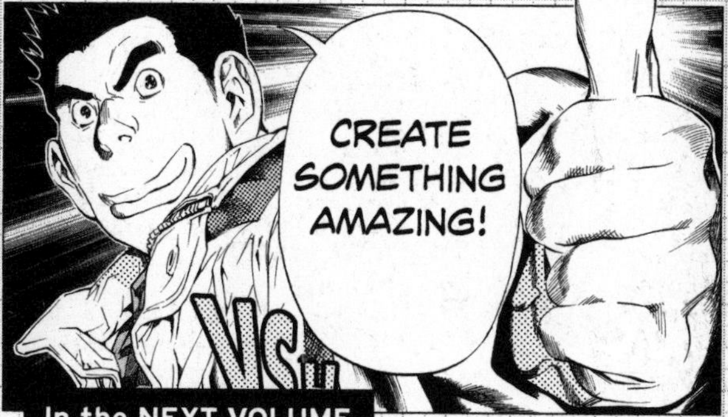
CREATE SOMETHING AMAZING!

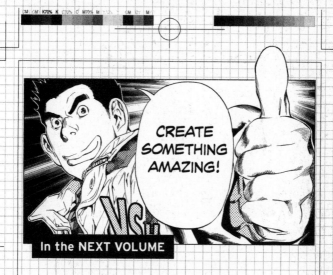

In the NEXT VOLUME

It's time for some huge changes as Moritaka and Akito finally get their own series in *Weekly Jump*. Can the team survive the pressure and workload? And will their rivals also be able to join them in the magazine?

Available June 2011!

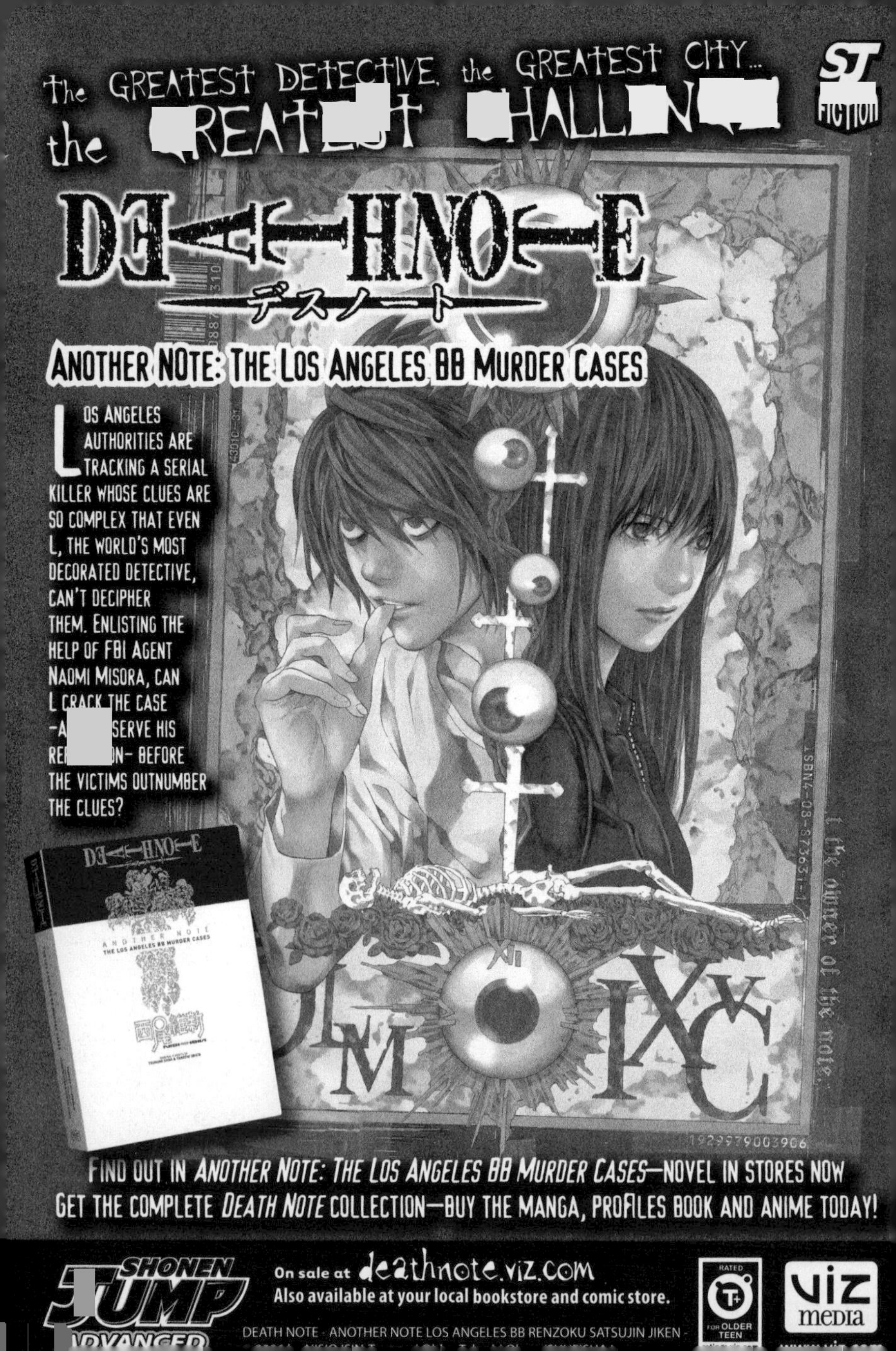

the GREATEST DETECTIVE, the GREATEST CITY...
the [illegible]REAT[illegible]T [illegible]HALL[illegible]N[illegible]
ST FICTION
DEATH NOTE
デスノート
ANOTHER NOTE: THE LOS ANGELES BB MURDER CASES
LOS ANGELES AUTHORITIES ARE TRACKING A SERIAL KILLER WHOSE CLUES ARE SO COMPLEX THAT EVEN L, THE WORLD'S MOST DECORATED DETECTIVE, CAN'T DECIPHER THEM. ENLISTING THE HELP OF FBI AGENT NAOMI MISORA, CAN L CRACK THE CASE -A[illegible]SERVE HIS RE[illegible]ON- BEFORE THE VICTIMS OUTNUMBER THE CLUES?
ANOTHER NOTE
THE LOS ANGELES BB MURDER CASES
FIND OUT IN ANOTHER NOTE: THE LOS ANGELES BB MURDER CASES—NOVEL IN STORES NOW
GET THE COMPLETE DEATH NOTE COLLECTION—BUY THE MANGA, PROFILES BOOK AND ANIME TODAY!
SHONEN JUMP ADVANCED
On sale at deathnote.viz.com
Also available at your local bookstore and comic store.
RATED T+ FOR OLDER TEEN
viz media
DEATH NOTE - ANOTHER NOTE LOS ANGELES BB RENZOKU SATSUJIN JIKEN -

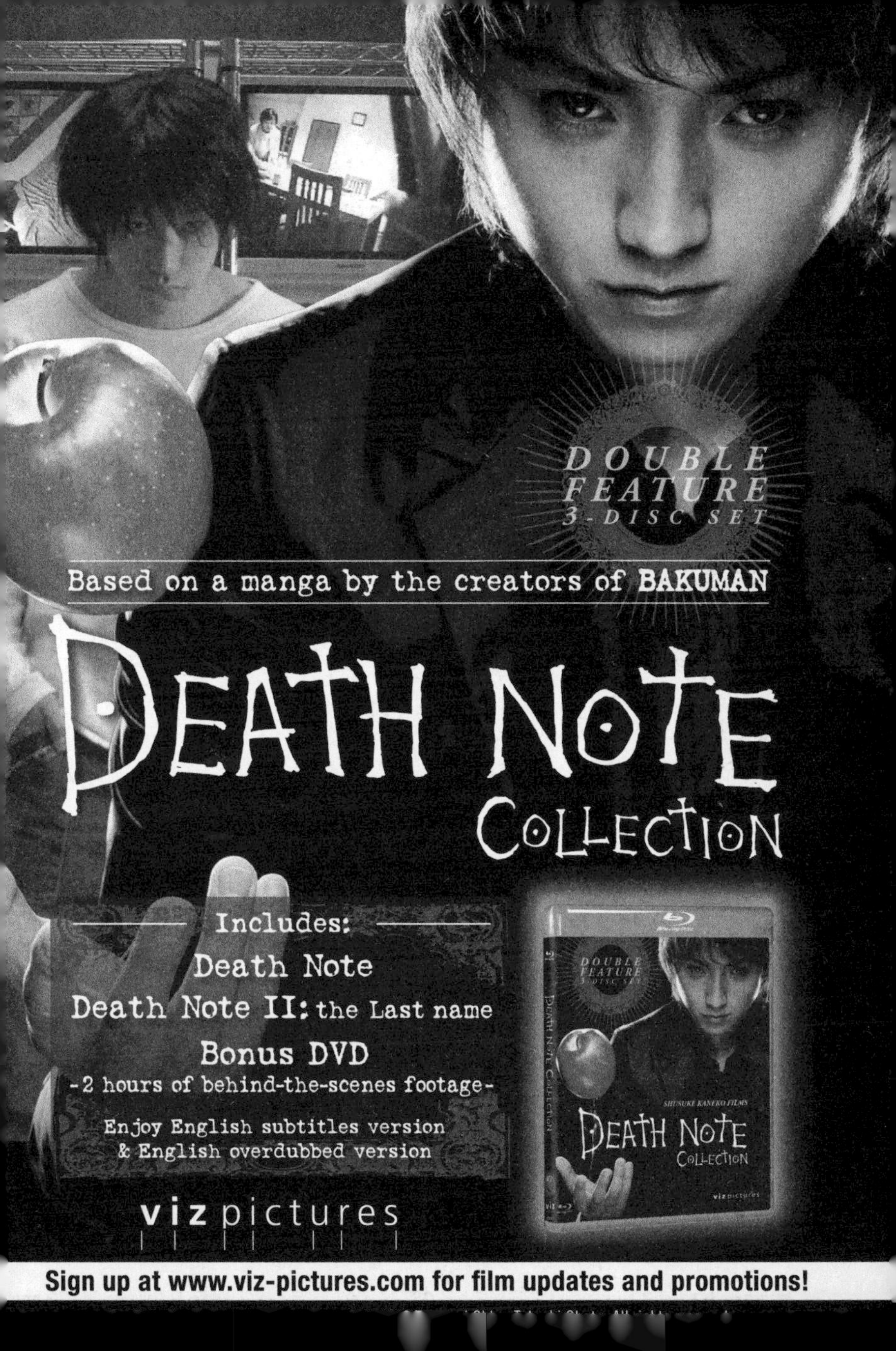
DOUBLE
FEATURE
3-DISC SET
Based on a manga by the creators of BAKUMAN
DEATH NOTE
COLLECTION
Includes:
Death Note
Death Note II: the Last name
Bonus DVD
-2 hours of behind-the-scenes footage-
Enjoy English subtitles version
& English overdubbed version
viz pictures
DOUBLE
FEATURE
3-DISC SET
DEATH NOTE
COLLECTION
Sign up at www.viz-pictures.com for film updates and promotions!

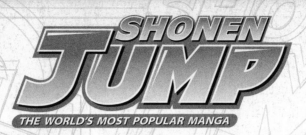
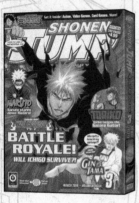 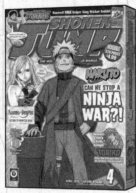 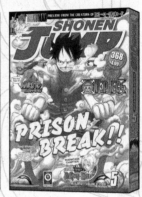